The

FIRST LADY OF FLEET STREET

The Life, Fortune
and Tragedy of
Rachel Beer

EILAT NEGEV
AND
YEHUDA KOREN

The Robson Press

This edition published in Great Britain in 2012 by
The Robson Press (an imprint of Biteback Publishing Ltd)
Westminster Tower
3 Albert Embankment
London SE1 7SP

First published in 2011 by JR Books.

ISBN 978-1-84954-399-6

10 9 8 7 6 5 4 3 2 1

A CIP catalogue record for this book is available from the British Library.

Set in Sabon and Centaur
Printed and bound in Great Britain by CPI Group (UK) Ltd, Croydon CR0 4YY

Contents

Prologue

*Late May 1903. Earl's Court, a two-story
stone mansion in Tunbridge Wells.*

A slight woman sits erect in her chair, nearly swallowed by her
weighty crepe mourning dress. Heavily framed mirrors, priceless
paintings, dim-gilt Chinese cabinets, and fresh lilies and orchids
adorn every inch of the spacious drawing room.

She is almost numb in the presence of the seventy-three-year-old
barrister sitting opposite her. Though he is a Master in Lunacy, summoned by the court to certify her mental state, Thomas H. Fisher is
not a physician, and has not been schooled in psychiatry. This woman's fate lies in his hands—if he signs a document certifying that she
is of "unsound mind," she will be stripped of many of her rights,
won't control the considerable inheritance due to her from her
wealthy husband, and will be consigned to the outside "government
of herself, her manors, messuages, lands, goods and chattels."

That he is there is not surprising. Three physicians have already
examined this woman and filed their reports, all at the request of her
own family. One of them, Dr. George Henry Savage, is a leading expert in the field of lunacy. Though in his book *On Soundness of Mind
and Insanity*, published that very year, Dr. Savage admitted that
"what is sane in one man is insane in the conduct of another, and

what may be sane at one period of our lives would be insane at another," his assessment of this woman allowed for no such ambiguity. He pronounced her of unsound mind after one short interview.

Still, she might have filed legal documents. She could have tried to refute the judgments on her sanity. She has not, and she will not. She sits passively, instead, sensing that these matters are a *fait accompli*—the verdict has already been reached, and the forces allied against her are too strong to be defeated.

ONE MIGHT ASSUME that Rachel Beer, the woman in question, was just another pampered English lady, either too proud or too ill-prepared by a life in which her every need was met by others to do anything but surrender meekly to outside judgments. In truth, she was anything but that stereotypical Victorian lady. She achieved a more stunning kind of success than can be measured in bank accounts or stock portfolios.

In the late nineteenth century, women were denied the vote and were not given equal access to education. It was actually believed that too much intellectual activity would cause them nervous breakdowns. It was at this time that Rachel Beer owned and edited the *Sunday Times* and, eventually, *The Observer.* She was the first and only woman to edit two national newspapers, over eighty years before another woman was to take the helm of a Fleet Street paper. When one considers that many of her women contemporaries hardly had access to a newspaper, her accomplishments are all the more remarkable.

The few women who managed to crack the leaded glass ceiling in journalism and in most other careers in Rachel Beer's time provoked extreme antagonism, and their assertiveness was perceived as a threat. Female journalists were often restricted to the so-called "Women's Sphere," reporting on the latest frocks, frills and society gossip. Politics were considered out of bounds for them, and they weren't welcome in the Press Gallery of the House of Commons. Though she was deprived of the tips and connections to which male journalists had ready access, Rachel Beer adamantly refused to limit herself to "feminine" topics. She fearlessly raised her voice on foreign and domestic matters throughout her time at both the *Sunday Times* and *The Observer.*

As an editor, Rachel Beer championed causes like the Public Amusements Bill, an innovative means of reducing crime and reforming morals through ratepayer-funded free educational and entertainment functions for the lower and middle classes. A working woman herself, she also stood for various women's causes. At the Women's International Congress, she made a memorable statement: "It was Victor Hugo who said that the nineteenth century is the woman's century. At the root of the whole question lies the demand for the right—no, not to vote—but to labour, and to receive adequate pay for work done." She even took on traditional male bastions, calling for the resignation of the commander-in-chief and the elimination of his wasteful and expensive position.

She and her husband, Frederick Beer, who inherited *The Observer* from his father, were leading London socialites—exhibitions, musical soirées, and theatre and opera performances were held at their opulent Mayfair mansion, and they were frequently featured in the society pages. Their collection of paintings was coveted by museums, and—as Rachel was a gifted pianist and composer—they also owned a wide array of the finest musical instruments. But though the Beers were fortunate enough to have been born into wealth, and didn't deny themselves luxuries, they clearly understood the obligations that came with that privilege. Their philanthropic efforts were impressive in their breadth and the level of their generosity.

Rachel was evidently a woman in love with life, the possessor of a vigorous and adventurous soul. Why, then, at forty-five, did she submit so passively to those questioning her sanity and her ability to care for herself? Why did she allow herself to be torn from her active life and her prestigious position in society?

In seeking answers to these questions, we must look not only at Rachel's astounding life and career but at the meteoric rise to riches of two prominent Jewish immigrant families. Rachel Beer (née

Sassoon) was the daughter of S. D. Sassoon, the grandson of the family's patriarch, Sheikh Sason ben Saleh. The Sassoons' ascent to power and wealth spread their considerable influence from Baghdad to Bombay and beyond, eventually leading them to prominence in London, the great commercial centre of the world. Her husband's family had its roots in the harsh Frankfurt ghetto. His father, Julius Beer, relocated to London and made his fortune through investing in the emerging technologies of the time—railroads and submarine telegraphy. When Rachel and Frederick married, they united the wealth and histories of their grand families.

Taken together, the couple's life history encompasses vaulting ambition, familial discord, tragic early death, overwhelming grief, the evolving role of women in society and in journalism, and the role of the press in social reformation. Theirs is a story of the painful decisions made by people in their struggle to reconcile career and family, love and duty, individual happiness and social welfare. So, though they lived in Victorian England, Rachel and Frederick's story transcends the particularities of that time and place.

The
FIRST LADY OF
FLEET STREET

CHAPTER ONE

Portraits and Personalities

In August 1893, the fashionable photographer Harry Bedford-Lemere spent several days at Rachel and Frederick Beer's mansion in Mayfair. Bedford-Lemere had made a name for himself photographing the opulent homes of the era. His work was commissioned by wealthy homeowners, architects, decorators and property agents, and it often appeared in society and lifestyle magazines. Through his still-existing photographs, it's possible to take a virtual tour of the Beers' home and to get a vivid sense of the life they shared together.

A water fountain gurgled in the marble-lined hall of 7 Chesterfield Gardens, and on a tall pedestal stood *La Guerre,* a statue created by the famous French sculptor Antoine Louis Barye. It was a small-scale reproduction of one of four figurative works carved in stone on the pavilion façades of the new Louvre in Paris. Frozen in bronze, a soldier sat on a crouched horse, about to unsheath his sword, as a young boy next to him raised a horn to his lips. Though impressive in its scale and execution, *La Guerre* hardly presented a pastoral image of welcome—instead, it created an undercurrent of unease. The Beers had eagerly acquired the statue just a few months earlier in Paris, shortly after it was cast and put on sale. Owning a piece by the most celebrated French sculptor of the Third Republic was both a statement of wealth and a projection of their sophisticated artistic taste.

Like the statue that graced their doorstep, the Beers' choice of architect was somewhat eccentric. The job went to the renowned C. J. Phipps, who had designed dozens of theatres all over Britain. Looking to the eighteenth century for inspiration, Phipps and Rachel cluttered the entertainment rooms of the house with mixed gilt French revival furniture in the Louis XVI style, colorful marbles, bronzes, crystal chandeliers, velvet drapes and Persian carpets. Heavy brocades and damasks upholstered the furniture and hung from the walls, nearly muting all sounds. Phipps's theatrical taste was clearly manifest in the house, and some of the rooms closely resembled stage settings. There was a "Moor-esque" smoking room for gentleman visitors, which suggested a harem with its draperies, poufs, hexagonal tables and hookahs.

All of Rachel and Frederick's possessions projected the image that they were widely travelled, interested in foreign affairs and world issues, and very fashionable. Their home, in all its extravagance, was the ultimate blending of Rachel's Eastern background, Frederick's adventures abroad and Victorian Englishness.

Rachel's nephew, the poet Siegfried Sassoon, spent many hours in his aunt's lavish home. He recalled sitting in the drawing room, where he and his family would wait for the chronically late Mrs. Beer. Siegfried and his brothers were dumbfounded not only by the splendour of their aunt and uncle's home, but also by the ceremonial rules by which the couple conducted their lives. Passing through the massive portico and the doors with their grille of gilded metalwork, they were "bowed to by the solemn but delighted butler." It must have felt very much like they were entering the domain of royalty, and they felt obliged to "converse in undertones."

Finally, Aunt Rachel would come bustling in, smelling of violets, fashionably dressed, with an enormous feathered hat on her head. Her ears would sparkle with sapphire earrings and her hands with diamond rings. Rather than hug or caress the boys, she would instead offer her cold, ivory cheek to each of them in turn. Responding to the beat of a gong, they would move into the dining room, which was reachable through a narrow passageway with mirrored walls and bamboo handrails down each side, suggesting a gently sloping bridge. Crowned with a metal-domed ceiling, the room was decorated in the oriental style, with blackened bamboo flooring, asymmetrical bamboo chairs, and objects from the Far East, including swords with ivory handles and a sentimental painting of two Japanese geishas.

Of all the unique decorative elements in Chesterfield Gardens, what young Siegfried remembered best was this mirrored passageway: "We always stopped to marvel at our multiplied and diminishing reflections, which couldn't be counted . . . 'I can see simply hundreds of myself!' my younger brother would exclaim. And I would outdo him with, 'I can see thousands and millions and trillions of myself, getting tinier and tinier all the time, like ancestors!' " he later wrote.

Rachel never tried to conceal her Eastern ancestry. The frequent costume balls she attended (and sometimes held) gave her a welcome opportunity to play up her exotic features by dressing as an oriental lady. These were also occasions to display a fraction of her treasure trove of diamonds, rubies and precious jewels. When she dressed in this style, she would wear several strings of pearls in various lengths, Indian-style, hanging nearly to her waist, a rope of pink coral crisscrossing her thighs, and several Indian gold and carved coral bracelets hugging her bare arms from the shoulder down.

Rachel loved this outfit and the image it projected so much that she displayed a photo of herself wearing it on the mantelpiece of her home. She also gave a copy to Theresa Sassoon, Siegfried's mother, who set it on her own mantelpiece next to a photo of Frederick Beer, his face adorned with a moustache and small whiskers, wearing a tweed tailcoat and a brown billycock, holding a stick, resting his foot on a rustic seat.

But while she was proud of her exotic roots, Rachel felt thoroughly English and wanted to be perceived as such. Having one's portrait painted by a leading artist was one way of acquiring an English provenance, and to this end, the Beers commissioned Henry Jones Thaddeus to paint separate portraits of each of them. Jones Thaddeus was well known in fashionable London circles and he charged exorbitant rates for his work. For her sittings, the thirty-one-year-old Rachel wore a dress of deep golden silk with a low décolletage—*le dernier cri*—and the newly fashionable high shoulder line. Her dark curly hair was worn "drawn simply back, revealing the ears, into a French pleat," and she chose to adorn herself with none of her exquisite jewels; instead, her only accessory was an ostrich feather fan on a tortoiseshell stick. The background chosen for the portrait was the verdant English countryside; it depicted this Bombay-born London dweller as if she were a member of the landed gentry.

Normally, portraitists tend to idealize their sitter's appearance, but the painting of Rachel reveals a lack of symmetry in her face. "It certainly shows a concern for veracity and 'likeness,' " said Dr. Brendan Rooney, Jones Thaddeus's biographer. Far more subjective, Siegfried Sassoon thought that the portrait reflected his aunt's "dark loveliness and the faintly smiling sweetness of her un-departed youth." After Rachel's death, her devoted nurse and personal assistant, Miss Ross, bought the painting. She later sold it to Siegfried, who hung it over the large fireplace in his library.

Bedford-Lemere was allowed unlimited access to the Beers' home. The photographer even placed his tripod in Rachel's bedroom and study, capturing its silk-covered walls and ceiling. The French secretaire, where Rachel did most of her writing, was positioned close to her dressing table, and both faced the huge Jones Thaddeus portrait of Frederick, which loomed over the fireplace. Over the course of years, the painting has disappeared, and its image lives on only in Bedford-Lemere's photograph.

For two people who were individually characterized as being shy and introverted, the Beers spent a great deal of time out in society and hosting events in their home. Much of Frederick's time was spent enjoying his favourite pastimes of racquets, golf and billiards, or in the pursuit of favourable connections. Often, these activities crossed paths. To keep in good physical condition, he enrolled at the Prince's Club, where he could not only enjoy the use of several indoor croquet courts and a tennis court, but also move among other illustrious members of the club, such as the Prince of Wales and the Duke of Cambridge. For political discourse, Frederick joined the Devonshire Club, which was Liberal, and for conversation concerning travel and foreign countries, he went to the St. James's Club, much favoured by diplomats. As a philanthropist, he supported the Newspaper Press Fund, and he was also a member of the Royal Institution, which was devoted to scientific education and research.

For her part, Rachel was active in various nurses' welfare charities and was a member of the Association of Women Pioneer Lecturers, which sent female speakers to address audiences throughout England, "instructing the people to become useful citizens, and also give the congenial employment to hundreds of highly educated women."

Society columnists, meanwhile, recorded Rachel's visits to concert halls and the theatre. *The Sporting Times* made note of "the oriental aristocratic features and magnificent diamond tiara of Mrs. Beer," and *The John Bull* complimented her "pale, blue satin, trimmed with handsome embroidered gauze, and pink roses at the rouche at the hem." Owning newspapers was the couple's entrée to London's most prestigious events, where they met "royalties, the aristocracy of birth and genius, 'the salt of the earth.'" They were also invited to the most notable weddings, including that of Henry Morton Stanley in Westminster Abbey. The Beers' gift to the African explorer was a silver reading glass.

The couple attained true social eminence, however, when they hosted the Prince of Wales, his sister Princess Helena, and her husband and two daughters at a special theatrical event held at their home. For three successive evenings at the end of February 1891, a procession of princes and princesses, dukes and duchesses, arrived at the Beers' residence for the sold-out, "long anticipated Tableaux Vivant." This upper-class amusement consisted of groups of costumed actors posing in various frozen compositions. The Beers went to great expense and trouble to perfect the show, and the famous Mrs. Bancroft, who had retired from acting six years earlier, agreed to direct and perform in the event. The show consisted of fourteen specially selected scenes with elaborate lighting effects, breathtaking costumes and props.

The cast of thirty actors and models, as well as musicians, singers and an army of stagehands, produced a spectacle worthy of commercial theatre. The classical scenes of beauty, romance and death, situated in royal courts, were inspired by well-known works of art. The merry French monarch Charles II sat on his throne surrounded by his many mistresses; one court beauty in pink satin and silver lace was sitting at his feet, "and another had a black and tan spaniel on her lap." Of the five Dene sisters, all of whom were famous models, three took part in the show. Dorothy, the model for Leighton's *Flaming June* and the inspiration for Shaw's Eliza Doolittle, was Queen Katharine of Aragon, in scenes from her divorce, trial and death. For what seemed like an eternity, the performers had to keep motionless with upturned eyes, "until the curtain went down after several encores," recalled Lady Glover, who played the role of Marie Antoinette and whose little daughter was an angel in a flowing white gown with wings.

None of Rachel's Jewish relatives attended the performances, and if they had, they would certainly have recoiled upon hearing Gounod's *Ave Maria* accompanying the next tableau: a group of nuns in the cloisters who "were all chosen for their good looks." When the lights were turned back on, "there was not a dissentient voice as to the brilliant success of the whole performance." The proceeds were given to the Royal School of Art Needlework and the Home of Rest for Nurses.

While Rachel was hosting, organising and attending these society functions at night, by day she was using her opinion pieces in the *Sunday Times* to promote many of the same causes the evening events supported—the arts, women's advancement and the plight of the indigent. In a sense, she led two public lives—one as an active member of high society and another as a socially conscious journalist. She managed to seamlessly merge these two selves; but sadly, she was unable to truly have it all.

CHAPTER TWO

Flight from Baghdad

Less than a *minyan*—the quorum of ten male Jewish adults required for public prayer—remains today in Iraq, the last remnants of one of the oldest Jewish communities in the world. Jews first arrived there when Nebuchadnezzar, the King of Babylon, exiled them from the Holy Land into the area more than 2,500 years ago. Prior to the founding of Israel in 1948, and just before reprisals against Jews in the Arab world accelerated, there were 130,000 Jews in all of Iraq. An estimated 120,000 of them fled the country between 1950 and 1951.

The first documented member of Rachel's family is Sheikh Sason ben Saleh, her great-grandfather, who was born in Baghdad in 1750. None of the sheikh's early ancestors are known to have held any official posts, though this search is complicated by the fact that neither Baghdadi Jews nor the Arabs they lived among had surnames; instead, a person was identified as the son or daughter of their father. It was only when the family settled into British-ruled India in the 1830s that they converted the first name of their progenitor, Sason, meaning "joy" in Hebrew, into a surname, modifying it to the presumably more genteel-sounding Sassoon.

For four decades, Sheikh Sason ben Saleh held a double post: Sarraf Bashi, the chief treasurer of the Baghdadi pasha, and Nasi, president of the local Jewish community. His main task was to collect taxes that were levied on the community, and he had the power to punish his subjects with fines or lashings, even when the law forbade such treatment.

Traditionally, the role of Nasi in Baghdad was filled by a descendant of King David, and in ancient times, when the Nasi rode about town dressed in a gown woven with threads of gold and silver, passersby would stop and proclaim, "Give honour, ye nations, to the seed of David." This explains the legend that the House of Sassoon sprang from the biblical king; however, that lineage cannot be verified. Nor can the claim that the Sassoons' ancestors were forced to flee the Holy Land in 586 B.C., following the destruction of the Temple in Jerusalem by the Babylonians. The story goes that fifty years later, when Jews were encouraged to return to the Holy Land, the Sassoons chose to stay in Mesopotamia.

A different historical trail also has the Sassoons leaving the Holy Land by force, but at a different time: according to this version, they were among the exiles when the rebuilt Temple was destroyed, again, in A.D. 70. Allegedly, they were taken into captivity in Rome, from where they migrated to Spain centuries later. In 1492, refusing to convert to Christianity, they were expelled with the rest of the Jews by the Catholic monarchs and were among those who continued eastward, landing in Turkey and eventually settling in Baghdad. In later years, when the family became anglicised, they designed a coat of arms, choosing a golden lion holding a scepter over a majestic blue background—the symbol of the Kingdom of David.

During Rachel's great-grandfather's reign as Nasi, in the late eighteenth century, ten thousand of the eighty thousand inhabitants of Baghdad were Jews. While they resided in their own quarter in the northwestern part of the city, it was not a ghetto, and they suffered no humiliating restrictions. At the time, the Jewish quarter of Baghdad existed as a community heavily influenced by its Arab neighbours: the Jews there spoke Arabic, used it in their religious services, and wrote Arab words and phrases in Hebrew characters. Their manner of dress was similar to that of their compatriots, and though they observed the Jewish dietary laws their cuisine was, nevertheless, Arabic. They were liberal minded, candid and very inquiring. "The fine race of Jews at this place strikes every traveller, but their chief object is gain, and to be fruitful, and to multiply," reported the Christian missionary Reverend Joseph Wolf, who visited the city in 1824.

If their chief desire was indeed to be fruitful and multiply, Baghdad was ideally suited to their needs. As the gateway to the vast market of India through Basra, a thriving commercial enterprise existed within the city. Prominent among the merchant princes was Sheikh Sason ben Saleh, who made his fortune in the bazaars through commerce, money changing and banking. The sheikh was able to improve his prospects by marrying well—at the age of twenty-six, he married Amam, the daughter of a reputable local family and the niece of a Nasi. Whether it was simply by dint of his own hard work or the result of his newly acquired family connections—most likely some combination of the two—the sheikh assumed the positions of Sarraf Bashi and Nasi just five years after his wedding. This began an impressive run of good political fortune for the Sassoons. Years later, they would hold titles, gain admittance to Queen Victoria's court, and belong to the intimate circle of the Prince of Wales.

SHEIKH SASON SURVIVED the rise and fall of eight pashas. The fact that he served under so many governors is an impressive feat, but it is also indicative of the turbulent political arena in which he operated. The court was wrought with intrigue and conspiracy, and mortal danger was never more than a few missteps away. But with the promise of great power and immense profits, these risks were well worth the taking. The sheikh was also eager to use his position to benefit his community—he saw himself as benefactor, patron and protector of his people against the greedy pashas and the hostility of the Muslims.

The biblical command to procreate—*pru urvu*—was of paramount importance in the Jewish faith, since producing male offspring would safeguard the future of the dynasty. As a result, men were allowed to take a second wife if their first one did not bear sons after

nine years of marriage. The sheikh and Amam were not able to produce a child within that time frame, but he chose not to take a second
wife. He was rewarded for his loyalty when, fourteen years into their
marriage, he and Amam were blessed with their first child, a boy. Six
more sons and one daughter would follow in swift succession.

Sheikh Sason and his family lived exceedingly well. In the early
nineteenth century, Baghdad had "a very rude appearance," and only
the houses of the rich were finely painted. By comparison, the sheikh's
mansion was an imposing brick-clad building; the one remaining
photo could not capture its enormity. Even so, what it does show—
carved wooden pillars and railings, capacious balconies, and arched
corridors that were nearly ten meters high—rivals the lavishness of
Rachel and Frederick Beer's mansion in Mayfair. The ground floor
was used for the sheikh's considerable business operations, while the
entire clan—parents, offspring and their families—lived on the floors
above. One of its main luxuries, coveted by others, was its natural
cooling system—brick caves were built into the house with pits containing water.

It was into this family that Rachel's grandfather, the sheikh's second son, David, was born in 1792. Family lore holds that he was the
brightest of all the children. From a young age, the sheikh guided
David through the labyrinthine world of commerce and banking, and
he showed a flair for finance. Though he had only religious schooling,
David was fluent in four languages: he prayed in Hebrew, conversed
with his neighbours in Arabic, spoke Turkish with the government
officials, and conducted international business in Persian. His linguis-
tic abilities saw him in good stead, since the family firm now imported and exported silk, cotton, sheepskins, horses, dates, pearls
and metalware from around the region.

A suitable bride was found for David in Hannah, the daughter of
Abdullah Joseph Faraj, a leading merchant and a prominent public
figure from Basra. At the time of their marriage, David was only fifteen and Hannah thirteen. The young couple had difficulty conceiv-
ing, and their first daughter wasn't born until after eight years of

marriage. They must have felt relieved when two years later a son (and heir) followed, then two other children—a boy and a girl. But all four young Sassoons were left motherless when Hannah died at the young age of thirty-two.

Traditionally, a widower was introduced to a new partner soon after the year of mourning was complete, often from within the deceased wife's family to avoid friction and to maintain continuity. At a time when boys became husbands at the age of fifteen and girls were married off between the ages of eight and twelve, preliminary talks of betrothal had already been conducted with other families for the sixteen-year-old Farha.

But Farha was the niece of David's deceased wife—a fact that sealed her fate. Her new husband was thirty-six, and she was merely four years older than his eldest daughter.

As the sheikh advanced in years, David served as his right hand not only in the family business but also in his public duties. The posts of treasurer and president of the Jewish community were regarded as semi-hereditary, and David had good reason to believe he would be taking over from his father. In 1817, though, a new pasha was appointed and the sheikh was overthrown from office—a rival merchant, Ezra Gabbai, bribed his way in and took over as Nasi.

Daud Pasha was a former slave, who was said to have learned his tyrannical and brutal methods of ruling from his past masters. His avarice was not sated by the heavy taxes he imposed on the Jewish community, so he invented malicious new methods of extortion in order to keep his coffers filled to his satisfaction. For those unfortunates who could not pay their taxes or meet the other monetary demands made of them, there was but one fate: they were whipped to their bones.

Indicative of his duplicity and cunning, Daud Pasha connived to establish his own independent kingdom and sever his connections with the Turkish Empire. To secure his position, he set about crushing all possible resistance, and, suspecting that David Sassoon was informing on him to the Sultan in Constantinople and agitating for his dismissal, Daud Pasha locked the younger Sassoon behind bars. Justifiably paranoid, the pasha feared that even those that he had promoted might turn against him, and as a result, he had Gabbai arrested as well. As much as the Sassoons might have rejoiced at their archenemy's ill fortune, David was horrified when Gabbai was strangled in his cell under the pasha's order. This act of senseless savagery did not bode well for his own future.

Daud Pasha had already refused an imperial demand to release David Sassoon; nevertheless, he agreed to meet with the man's father. It's unclear how the sheikh succeeded in having his son released—and at what price—but the pasha's condition was that the prisoner would be banished from his native city and sent to Basra, three hundred miles away. This southernmost port town in the Persian Gulf was still under his jurisdiction, so though David would be out of sight, he would not be out of reach.

Father and son knew they could not trust the fickle-minded pasha and that time was of the essence. They hurried to the anchorage on the bank of the Tigris River, and were frustrated to learn that the next sailboat to Basra would not be leaving until the following week. With no real alternative, they paid an exorbitant price to the captain of a cargo vessel, who agreed to set sail immediately, no questions asked. To ensure his safety, David had his servants rush home to retrieve the clothes and provisions he would need for his escape. He had no time to bid farewell to his wife and children.

David's father warned him not to tarry in Basra, but to leave at once for Bushire, in Persia, in defiance of Daud Pasha's decree. All of their precautions and their sense of imminent danger proved prescient. Even as David's boat was sailing down the Tigris, Daud Pasha renounced his previous decree and ordered the prisoner's return. An urgent messenger was sent by boat to arrest him, and a furious chase ensued. Upon arriving in Basra, David quickly chartered another vessel and sailed that very evening to Bushire, as far from the pasha's grasp as he could get under the circumstances.

The pasha's messenger found the captain of David's escape boat, who confirmed that his Jewish passenger was already gone. Returning empty-handed to Baghdad, the messenger paid for his failure with his life.

BUSHIRE WAS MORE than just a potential safe haven. The long tendrils of the East India Company had reached this fishing village and were in the process of transforming it into its centre of operations. Despite the company's influence, however, it was still "a miserable place," according to the traveller David d'Beth Hillel, who happened to pass through there at the time of David Sassoon's escape. Two hundred Jews resided in Bushire, many of them goldsmiths, and d'Beth Hillel received the impression that most of them were poor and ill-treated by their neighbours.

Obviously this was a rather small-scale playing field for someone with the skills David Sassoon possessed, but it was an ideal place to begin again. To his advantage, David had business experience and expertise, fluency in Persian, and a network of connections with local traders, many of whom had made use of the Sassoon countinghouse and credit facilities in Baghdad. Not knowing when or if his family would join him, or whether he would ever be able to return home, he started a modest export-import business.

It was his good fortune that just a year later, in 1829, his wife and four children were able to escape Baghdad; Daud Pasha was too preoccupied with his own troubles to harass them. Though he was eighty years old at the time, and the journey would be rough for him, Sheikh Sason chose to join them, leaving the rest of his children and grandchildren behind. Still hoping for a change of government, they had decided to remain in Baghdad.

In later years, succeeding generations of the Sassoons hushed up the story of the sheikh's removal from his post as the pasha's treasurer and rewrote their history to say that he had retired due to old age. No words were spoken about his son David's time in prison, and the flight from Baghdad was described as a business venture—David had taken the journey on his own initiative, primarily out of a desire to put an end to the unbearable extortion that marked life in Baghdad under Daud Pasha. Understandably, the mighty Sassoons were embarrassed to be associated with a dismissal and, worse yet, an imprisonment and an unlawful escape from the authorities, even though David had committed no crime. Only in 1942—by which time the Sassoon empire had shrunk considerably—did the family reveal the truth about David's imprisonment and his flight to Bushire; however, they still remained stubbornly silent about the ousting of the patriarch.

A few months after arriving in Bushire, Sheikh Sason passed away and was buried in exile. By that time, swords were being brandished in Baghdad. After Daud Pasha declared independence from the Ottoman Empire, a special envoy was sent from Istanbul, demanding his surrender. He replied by killing the messenger—evidently, the least enviable of jobs in that time and place—and the Ottoman army besieged the city. Even nature showed no mercy for the miserable Baghdadis: the Tigris flooded the streets, demolishing large parts of the city, and bubonic plague ran rampant among the flood victims. Within a month thirty thousand people had lost their lives, and the rest took flight. Daud Pasha lost most of his soldiers and, in the summer of 1831, the Sultan's army marched in and took Baghdad, bringing an end to the upheaval.

David Sassoon followed the news from afar. Though the end of the conflict offered great relief to Baghdad's Jews and he could now safely return to his hometown, which desperately needed people of his calibre to revive and restore it, he had already decided what his future held.

After spending so many years at the mercy of Muslim governors, David and many others viewed the British presence in the East as a kind of salvation, and were attracted by the limitless commercial prospects it created in international trade. David had traded with British-controlled Bombay while he was still in Baghdad, so he had some experience in dealing with British and Indian merchants. Now he was ready to take the next step and to make the move to Bombay.

David made a preliminary trip and was overwhelmed by the thriving city. He met with some associates and officials, and paid a visit to the small community of former Baghdadis who had settled there. Only a few of the thirty Jewish families had achieved the Indian dream and were flourishing personally and commercially, but David was not daunted. He made some business arrangements and found a house that could serve him as both an office and a home for his family.

For the second time in four years, David Sassoon took hold of his destiny. He was forty years old—an advanced age at a time when the average life expectancy did not extend much past thirty-five—but he refused to turn back or to settle for his and his family's present circumstances. The fact that his young wife was expecting their first child together only hastened his decision to replant his family and his business interests in new soil.

Starting out in Bombay, David's main resource was not inherited wealth but his business ingenuity. The high cost of the bribes that had eased his escape from Daud Pasha, and the division of the Sassoon property and funds among all of his siblings when he and his father left Baghdad, meant that David had only a modest amount of money to bring into this new venture. The timing of his move was fortunate, since a few months after his arrival the East India Company was weakened by a series of British government acts that deprived it of its trading monopoly, opening the gates for private entrepreneurs like David. Still, he was extremely cautious—he began by entering tried and tested markets, learning from his competitors' failures. He also made good use of the personal contacts he had in Persia and in Baghdad, where his brother-in-law, who had been in jail with him, was now president of the Jewish community.

Starting with a small countinghouse and warehouse, David was soon buying up wharfages. Eventually he began importing and exporting all manner of merchandise, including silver and gold, silks, gums and spices, cotton, wool and wheat. "Whatever moves over sea or land, feels the hand or bears the mark of Sassoon and Co.," noted one of their contemporaries. He also acted as a banker to small traders in need of funds, while buying and selling cargo for others on commission.

On July 19, 1832, shortly after the Sassoons settled in 9 Tamarind Lane, Farha gave birth to her first child, who was named Sassoon David (S.D.). Over the next twenty-three years, she'd mother nine more children—five boys and four girls. Altogether, there would be fourteen children in the Sassoon clan from David's two wives, and these children would be the foundation of the family business. Like the Rothschilds, their counterparts in Germany, the Sassoons' success was attributable to the loyalty, dedication and discipline enforced in their close-knit, patriarchal family. "He trained them to be chorus masters with himself as conductor," wrote Stanley Jackson, the biographer of the family. In contrast to traditional immigration patterns, David's brothers stayed on in Baghdad and did not follow him to his new business empire. They remained small traders, and he sent them regular handouts.

Wishing to give his children the opportunity to benefit from their family heritage, David sent his eldest son, Abdullah—later, Sir Albert Sassoon—to Baghdad to receive an education and to gain business experience. His other sons would follow. In general, the Sassoons continued to rely greatly on their heritage. They used the unique Baghdadi Judeo-Arabic dialect among themselves and in their business correspondence, maintaining it as a secret code against commercial espionage. In addition to their religious schooling in Baghdad, the children were taught mathematics, English and French by private tutors. One by one, as the boys reached the age of bar mitzvah, they were harnessed to the plow that was David Sassoon & Co.

As an indication of their international enterprises and cross-cultural horizons, the company's letterhead stationery was printed in three languages—English, Hebrew and Arabic. The Hebrew text is slightly different from the others—it reads, "David Sassoon and Friends," with an additional religious saying—"God keep them and save them"—beneath it. In fact, there were no friends, no partners or associates involved in the managing of the business at this point—just David Sassoon and his sons.

When the house in Bombay became too small for the growing family and expanding operations, the offices and the dwelling shifted to the much larger premises at 4 Forbes Street, near the port.

CHAPTER THREE

Opium and Further Expansion

Given the burgeoning international markets and the variety of goods that were being moved back and forth across the waters, David Sassoon could not be content in dealing with just the Turkish and Persian empires for long. A vast market of 400 million people was waiting just around the corner.

But the problem with trading with China was that while it offered foreign merchants tea and silk, the traditional mode of life there and the emperor's edicts made it impossible to sell the Chinese Western goods. Since barter was not an option, any imports from China had to be paid for in hard currency, like silver. What's more, the Chinese were extremely suspicious of outsiders—they felt superior to the foreigners, whom they described as foul-smelling barbarians, and nicknamed them "big noses" or "hairy ones." Foreign merchants could not operate directly inside of China, and they were at the mercy of the Chinese guilds that had a monopoly over foreign trade. The guild authorities set the volume of trade, dictated the prices and charged customs duties. The foreign merchants swallowed their pride, but it was much harder to swallow the negative trade balance.

Only one of the products that were processed in India could tip the scales. Opium. It was the sole painkilling and tranquilizing drug available at the time, and it was also used for reducing fever and for treating diarrhea, rheumatism and bronchitis. Though the Chinese emperor restricted the import of opium for any but therapeutic use, eager merchants and corrupt Chinese officials schemed to keep the flow of drugs for illicit use moving. Gradually the recreational use of opium spread across the country, and millions became addicted. In 1820, five thousand chests of opium were exported to China yearly; ten years later, that figure had risen to twenty thousand. Great care was taken to ensure that the drug was manufactured specifically to suit the tastes of the Chinese.

There is an eternal fascination with the idea of striking it rich instantly, and history is filled with stories of lucky souls who possessed "the Midas touch." One tale attributes David Sassoon's meteoric rise to riches to his habit of picking up his own mail at the post office. Waiting in line, the story goes, he noted that his chief competitor was receiving large amounts of mail from China. He made some hurried inquiries and learned about the new prospects of the opium trade. And the rest is history.

As is true of most legends, tales and myths, it is difficult to accept these details as literal truths. In a tightly hierarchal family business, it is highly unlikely that the patriarch would trouble himself to pick up the company's mail. More credit should be given to David's familiarity with current affairs and his economic status than to clandestine observations made at the post office. Most of the opium trade at the time was in the hands of Jardine, Matheson and Co., and their records show that David Sassoon was already shipping the drug to Canton in 1834, two years after his arrival in Bombay. It would be later, though, that it would make him his fortune.

The Chinese objected to the import of opium on more than just moral grounds. They demanded silver bullion in exchange for their tea and silk, but foreign merchants began to pay them in opium instead—a practice that destabilized the Chinese economy. The Chinese appealed to Queen Victoria to stop flooding China with the "source of evil." But opium was legal in Britain and, in the words of Hamilton Lindsay, a former officer of the East India Company in China, "the injury to health and morals inflicted by the use of gin in

England, surpasses those of opium in China." With this prevailing mind-set, it's no wonder that the demands of the Chinese fell on deaf ears. In return, the Chinese set twenty thousand chests of opium on fire and threatened to execute any foreign merchant caught in the trade.

Britain could not acquiesce to the Chinese threats, because they needed the immense profits they were earning from the sale of opium. The money covered much of the expense of the British governance of India, in addition to other imperial projects and colonial wars in the area, and it was also being invested in the production of cotton in India.

In June 1840, waving the flag of Free Trade, Britain launched a military operation known as the First Opium War. It ended two years later with the Treaty of Nanking, which forced the Chinese to open five ports for foreign trade and to pay $21 million in reparations for the opium they had destroyed. The Chinese refused to lift their ban on the sale and use of the narcotic; however, since the new ports were declared exterritorial, foreign merchants enjoyed immunity and could not be prosecuted for handling opium.

It was at this point that David Sassoon adroitly decided to scale up his operations. In 1843, David Sassoon & Co. opened its first international branches for all commerce, including opium, in Canton and Hong Kong. David entrusted them to his second son, Elias, who added a third base, in Shanghai, in 1845. With the opening of these new branches of the family business, each male in the House of Sassoon would be sent to serve time in China, like mandatory military service. Much of the success of these branches can be attributed to the Sassoons' group mentality—loyalty, trust and the ability to think alike.

The Sassoons became so well established in the opium trade that they began to operate their own small fleet of sailing vessels for the purpose of shipping the drug, one of which was the well-armed opium clipper *Henry Ellis*, named after the famed Irish explorer. In good weather, the journey from Calcutta to Canton and back took about three months; in bad weather, much longer. But the clippers were not just subject to the strong headwinds of the winter monsoons; they also had to weather the fierce Chinese pirates who swarmed the waters.

On April 19, 1850, David Sassoon and a few fellow merchants published a letter in *The Times*, thanking Her Majesty's navy "for the zeal, perseverance and courage" that the patrolling war ships had exhibited as they "so effectually destroyed the enemy's forces." One of these attacks was waged against sixty-four boats with three thousand pirates who were armed with over one thousand guns.

Great Britain's opium revenues, which amounted to several million pounds sterling a year, were reported in the House of Commons, and updates on the state of the opium trade were a standard item in the financial pages of its newspapers. In August 1851, there was concern over the soaring prices—from $210 per chest of Malawa opium, to $725. "The rise was quite unlooked for," remarked *The Times*, adding that the market was eagerly awaiting the arrival of one of the Sassoon family's ships, carrying 1,075 chests, which might suppress "the upward tendency of prices."

Nearly four million Chinese became habitual opium users following the Opium War, especially in the major cities. For example, 55 percent of all men in Shanghai were considered addicts. The Chinese newspaper *Nanhui xian zhi* (*Nanhui County Gazetteer*) reported in 1878 that "the amount of money spent on it exceeds that spent on rice." The flow of *yang yan*, "foreign smoke," gradually spread inland, and reached even the remotest villages. The "flower-smoke shops" had become notorious as dens "for secret adultery," complained the newspaper.

Given the hefty profits they were raking in, it was easy for officials in London to brush aside the moral issue. "A matter of race . . . as the Aryan races preferred alcoholic drinks, so the Turanian consumed opium," said George Campbell, Secretary of State for India, in a parliamentary debate. *The Thistle and the Jade*, a book celebrating 150 years of the Jardine, Matheson & Co. trading company, provides a mealymouthed Western *raison d'être* for the opium trade:

In India, it was the ordinary poor man's comfort and restor-
ative. Rajput camel drivers fortified themselves with it, as Calcutta rickshaw wallahs would do some day. If then the Chinese
took it too, why, what was the harm in that? Or if harm there
was, it was perhaps because instead of drinking it in a normal
decent, medicinal manner, they chose to smoke it.

In later years, the Sassoons would—understandably—try to down-
play their role in the opium trade, which had in actuality provided a
considerable increase in their fortune. Those who did refer to it were
quick to point out that "exporting it would have been considered no
different from exporting tea or coffee today."

The House of Sassoon had made a decided turn in the economic
and geographic direction of their business. It was as if the magnetic
lure of hard currency was urging them forward, onward to their next
destination.

CHAPTER FOUR

Their Dual Identity

David Sassoon was a great benefactor of his adoptive city, and he donated vast sums of money to public welfare in Bombay. Even so, he never considered himself an Indian Jew. Though he would never set foot in Baghdad again, he would always identify himself with his home country—and he made sure that the rest of his family held the same respect as he did for Baghdadi traditions.

The Sassoons were part of a very insular community. Of the quarter of a million citizens of Bombay in the 1830s, only 2,250 were Jews, and just 350 of them were from Baghdad. They did not mingle with other Jews; they established separate communities and observed their home traditions in their own synagogues. The Baghdadi rabbis continued to govern their spiritual lives, though it took two months for a question on religious matters to travel to Baghdad and back.

As Orthodox Jews, the Sassoons began each day with early prayers at the synagogue, and twice during the day all activity in their offices would be paused for communal prayers. Every Friday afternoon, business operations were shut down until Monday, and no work was done on Jewish holidays.

The patriarch still looked very much the part of a noble Baghdadi Jew, and he ensured that his sons also adhered to the Jewish-Baghdadi code of dress. His long, groomed, snowy beard and his oriental garments added much to his dignified aura, and Sir Richard Temple, the

Governor of Bombay, admired his "rich turban and flowing robes [that] made up a picture worth beholding." The Sassoons' way of dressing presented another barrier to their assimilation into life in Bombay, but it suited their small Orthodox community, which disapproved of Western dress. David d'Beth Hillel discovered this when he strolled through Bombay with a beard and English dress—he suffered much harassment from other Jews on suspicion that he was "proselytised to Christianity."

By adhering to their Baghdadi style of life, the Sassoons were a minority within a minority; they were outsiders among the Parsee, Hindu, Muslims and Mongols. Isolated as they were, they befriended India's British colonial rulers out of necessity, and gradually they became "imagined Britons," in the words of the author Dr. Chiara Betta. In addition to Jewish holidays, the Sassoons began to celebrate Queen Victoria's birthday and the year of her accession to the throne, and they proudly flew the Union Jack over all of their institutions.

David and his sons trod a very fine line between familial and racial insularity and their position as imagined Britons—with both efforts being rewarded. Combined with their Eastern background, the Sassoons' familiarity with British culture and customs helped to ensure their commercial success. Their comprehension of the British code of commerce and their ability to blend in with government officials gave them an edge over local competitors. Equally, while their European rivals found it difficult to accustom themselves to the oriental way of doing business, the Sassoons were in their element, making deals solely with a handshake.

David's cooperation with the British would eventually pay off in another way. For Eastern businessmen and merchants like the Sassoons, becoming a British subject was a passport to privilege. In September 1853, twenty years after settling in Bombay, David was issued a passport of British citizenship as a token of appreciation for promoting British interests in the region. His signature on the document— in Hebrew—misled researchers, who concluded that he was illiterate in English; an existing photo of David Sassoon, signed by him in both languages, suggests otherwise. Signing in Hebrew may have been his way of declaring that his newly acquired British citizenship had no bearing on his inner identity as a proud Orthodox Jew.

The patriarch was also appointed Justice of the Peace by the Government of India, "so that the settlements of petty differences among the Jews rest with him." The *London Illustrated News* commended the fact "that a beggar of his tribe is rarely or ever seen asking alms in the streets, as they know they have only to seek relief at the hands of Mr. Sassoon to find it." But the Sassoons extended their philanthropy to all castes and creeds, starting a European-style general hospital in Poona that remains in operation to this day, 150 years after it opened. In Bombay they set up a reformatory and industrial training centre for juvenile offenders, a mechanic's institute (today the David Sassoon Library) and an asylum for the relief of destitute invalids.

They also established a Jewish school that not only taught English, Hindustani, Arabic and Hebrew, but also geography, arithmetic, bookkeeping and European business management. Tuition was free. Opting for a modern curriculum did not imperil the traditional lifestyle; students at the Sassoon school were also taught ritual slaughtering so they could prepare kosher meat when they were sent to places without established Jewish communities. In keeping with the Sassoons' proud support of Bombay's British community, the pupils were taught the British National Anthem in Hebrew and English. The bilingual primer *Reshit Hallimud* ("First Reader"), which David Sassoon commissioned from the German-Jewish scholar Moritz Steinschneider, promised "to inspire the pupils in the pious respect for the early sources and the oldest customs of our faith and literature, with a regard for the land of our fathers, with patriotism and loyalty for the country and government to which they now belong." Almost all of the Sassoons' employees were Baghdadi Jews, the top graduates of this school. Stationed at the outposts of the Sassoon business empire, they could intuitively sense and execute the Bombay headquarters' strategy without waiting for the post, which took weeks to arrive.

The Sassoons could well afford their civic largesse. The patriarch's fabulous mansion, *Sans Souci* ("Carefree"), built in the mid-1850s in the elite Malabar Hill section of Bombay, could rival "some of the most noted ducal palaces in Italy." It was the scene of many legendary banquets, where its lavish gardens could accommodate as many as 1,400 guests. Today, the building houses the Masina Hospital, which is known for its Rehabilitation Centre for drug addicts. One of Sans Souci's exquisite crystal chandeliers and three of its cherubs can be seen today in the Bombay Opera House.

In order to keep up with the times and advance his family's interests, David took a bold step. He sent his fifteen-year-old son Abraham to study in London, rather than in Baghdad, where his other sons had been educated. Abraham was well prepared for the journey, as can be seen from the letter he sent his family upon his arrival in London, in late June 1855. In perfect English, he wrote:

> It is strange to say that I never felt so sick in my 50 days voyage while crossing oceans and seas, as I did while crossing the Straits of Dover. When I arrived at London, I took a cab for Guild Hall Coffee House and the next morning went to the place of my destination. I thus ended my trip by the Overland Route from Celestial Empire to Old England.

In the following months, Abraham's subsequent letters were copied and circulated within the family. They all savored his tales of London.

In planning his son's future, David made another carefully calculated decision. Though there was a large Sephardic Portuguese community in London, and Abraham could have studied with a Sephardic rabbi, David elected to have his son study under an Ashkenazi Jew from Germany. The instructor was Dr. Herman Adler, the son of the Chief Rabbi of Great Britain. Born in Hanover, Herman Adler received rabbinical education in Frankfurt and studied at the University of Leipzig and University College London.

Abraham began to study at the newly established Jewish public day school, "for the sons of our middle ranks," in Finsbury Square.

A year and a half later, he was prepared for entry into University College—an astonishing leap forward. "The classes which he is to attend are the English and Latin language and literature, mathematics, Natural Philosophy and probably Arabic," reported Dr. Adler back to Bombay. "I am also pleased to state that his moral and religious conduct is very satisfactory." This advancement was so exceptional that years later Sir Bartle Frere, the Governor of Bombay, publicly commended David Sassoon and encouraged other wealthy fathers to follow his example and send their sons "to learn not only what English gentlemen know, but what they feel and think."

But though Abraham was the first Sassoon to receive an English education and to spend time in London, he would not be the one to break ground for a London branch of the family business. That job would be left to Rachel Beer's father.

ALL OF DAVID Sassoon's sons were accustomed to following orders, and S.D. was no exception. Like most of his brothers, he was sent to Baghdad when he was a teenager to receive a Jewish education. All of the way from Bombay, his father supervised the matchmaking between S.D. and a suitable Baghdadi bride—Farha Reuben was a sixteen-year-old descended from the Shindookh family, who were highly regarded leaders of the community.

After the young couple wed in 1850, and before they had time to settle in Bombay and start a family, they were separated. S.D. was instructed to report to Shanghai for a tour of duty at the branch of the family business located there. For more than three years, his wife lived in Bombay with her in-laws, while S.D. returned home only sporadically for brief visits.

By the time Abraham sailed off to London to get his education, S.D. was back from China. Only then, after four years of marriage, could he and Farha finally start a family. They had their first son, Joseph, on December 31, 1855.

More of a scholar than a businessman, in 1855 S.D. added to his daily workload by establishing the biweekly paper *Doresh Tov*

Le'amo ("Bears good tidings for his people"), which he published and edited. Written in the Baghdadi Judeo-Arabic, the four-page paper, titled the *Hebrew Gazette* in English, brought shipping news from London and China each Friday. It also featured local news and police reports, Indian and Chinese commercial information, and, as S.D. himself described it, "much external affair as came to the knowledge of the editor through the medium of English newspapers . . . much space is devoted to current matters of interest, to the small settlement of Baghdad Arab speaking Jews who were not well versed in the English language." Now long extinct, it was the first Jewish paper in all of India to use Hebrew characters. The first two issues were handwritten on bluish paper by S.D. himself.

Most of the news in Sassoon's newspaper in 1857 had to do with the Indian Mutiny—the revolt of native Indian troops that had become a full-scale war, threatening the stability of British rule. The mutineers were cruelly dealt with:

> Two soldiers were blown from the cannon mouth. One was a Mohammedan Major Subedar, and the other, a Sepoy. Before they were blown up, their crimes were read out. The marine battalion were present to see and tremble. When they were blown up, they became a hundred pieces.

This harrowing report ended with an unlikely editorial comment—a Jewish expression of awe, *Rachmana Litslan* ("May the Merciful One save us from such fate"). A month after the mutiny began, the patriarch David Sassoon added his name to a letter addressed to the Governor of Bombay, stating "feelings of horror and indignation, at the accounts of the cowardly and savage atrocities perpetrated by the ruthless mutineers." He and the others expressed their unalterable loyalty and offered the governor their families' services "to be employed in any manner that your Lordship may consider most conducive." Lord Elphinstone welcomed the support but clearly understood the practical motives behind it. He wrote, "You justly feel that any attack upon the power and dominion of England is a blow aimed at your prosperity, at the developments of your trade."

Supporting the British government was soon to pay off for the Sassoons yet again. The instability generated by the mutiny shattered the value of government stocks, and merchants were in a panic to get rid of them. The House of Sassoon demonstrated both patriotism and bold business sense by buying the stocks in bulk at rock-bottom prices. Once the mutiny was crushed and the stocks soared again, they were counting their profits.

DAVID SASSOON MADE the decision to extend the family business to England in late 1857, thinking that by increasing the export of English goods to India and China he could also score additional points as a British patriot. His two eldest sons, Abdullah and Elias, were indispensable to the task of exploiting the booming Chinese market; as a result, the task of establishing the London branch fell to S.D., who was next in line.

Thrilled as he was, S.D.'s wife was expecting their second child, and his departure was postponed until after the birth. The decision to create a foothold in London would revolutionise not only his life but the lives of the entire Sassoon clan. Rachel Sassoon was born on April 7, 1858, and a week later S.D. left for the port of Calcutta. If he did well in London, he knew, the patriarch would allow his young family to join him.

In a rare photograph, taken on the eve of S.D.'s departure for London, the patriarch is seated on a majestic carved chair, his palms spread in a gesture of prayer. His elder sons, Abdullah and Elias, are dressed in identical flowing, long, white tunics over trousers, both resting a hand on their right hip, fingers spread. Only the departing S. D. Sassoon, tall and reed-thin, is conspicuous in his dark swallow-tail coat with a high-collar white shirt and a bow tie. A large skullcap covers his head. While all three are staring into the lens of the recently invented device known as the camera, S.D., all set up and ready to go, gazes dreamily toward the horizon.

CHAPTER FIVE

Gaining a Foothold

At the end of April 1858, the French entrepreneur and developer Ferdinand de Lesseps was in Constantinople, securing funding and political support for his ambitious plan to create a passage between the Red Sea and the Mediterranean. But a whole year would pass before he would swing a pickax and make the first dent in the trench that would eventually become the Suez Canal. With that short-cut to England unavailable to him, S. D. Sassoon had to make a long and exhausting overland desert crossing through Egypt, a journey during which his command of Arabic would prove immeasurably useful. By all accounts a keen traveller, he had already spent time in Iraq and China, and the unfamiliar scenery must have revived his sense of adventure and his inner Marco Polo.

A convoy awaited S.D. and his two menservants at the disembarking port of Suez. Each carriage was supported by only two wheels and drawn by two horses in front and two mules abreast, while the passengers sat three on each side. The group's plentiful luggage, meanwhile, was dispatched on a separate convoy of camels. Bone-weary and no doubt eager for their passage to London to conclude, they boarded a boat for the forty-eight-mile sail along the Nile to Alexandria. They would then endure fourteen more days on the *Sultan* steamship before entering English waters and docking at Southampton on May 25, 1858.

But it was more than just an enormous geographical distance that S.D. had to cross in relocating to London. While he knew everyone of any importance in Bombay's and Shanghai's business circles, he was a comparative alien in the financial Mecca of London. No longer able to rely on his seasoned father and dynamic brothers, he would have to forge his way single-handedly into the heart of the City. And he was also facing a cultural divide, with no Baghdadi community to cater to his religious and social needs. Even his younger brother Abraham had already returned to Bombay.

Foreign investors tend to trumpet their arrival by settling in the most illustrious quarters of their coveted new territory. S. D. Sassoon was no exception—he took an office right in the pulsing commercial centre of London, at 8 Leadenhall Street. Sharing the floor with ship and transport agents and fellow merchants who traded with India mitigated his loneliness. In choosing his home, too, he opted to place himself on the upper rung of the ladder, at the cost of being far from a Jewish neighbourhood. He obtained the crown lease for 17 Cumberland Terrace; its façade was one of the most breathtaking architectural panoramas in London. The white stucco terrace on the eastern edge of Regent's Park, designed by celebrated Regency architect John Nash, was originally intended for the courtiers of the Prince of Wales, whose palace Nash wished to build in the park. The palace plan was discarded, and the houses facing the park were leased instead to "the happy free-born sons of commerce of the wealthy commonalty of Britain." The front of Sassoon's new four-story residence was decorated with four enormous Ionic pillars, each crowned with a graceful neoclassical statue. It is still spectacular to this day.

JEWS IN ENGLAND had experienced much persecution in the twelfth century, and were subsequently expelled from the country in the late thirteenth century. Fortunately, their 350-year enforced absence had weakened public antipathy toward them. "English Protestantism possessed an active philo-Semitic strain," according to Professor Todd Endelman, an expert on the Jewish experience in Britain. Further, being an empire encompassing many races "precluded the development of xenophobic feelings." At the time S.D. arrived in London, though, Jews were still a tiny minority in the country—only 36,000 in a population of more than 17 million. Two-thirds of them lived in the metropolis—less than one percent of the 2.5 million Londoners. And though antipathy toward Jews had faded, it had not vanished. Jews had only been granted the right to engage in retail trade in the city in 1832, gaining the right to vote three years later. Just two months after S.D. Sassoon settled in London, Lionel de Rothschild was finally allowed to take the oath in Parliament, a major landmark in the thirty-year struggle for emancipation.

In Bombay the Sassoons had established their own synagogues to maintain their Baghdadi religious customs, but the handful of Iraqi immigrants who lived in London had no synagogue of their own. S.D. would have felt isolated among the Ashkenazim, who had a different type of liturgy, so he opted to become a member of the ancient Bevis-Marks Synagogue in the heart of London, within walking distance of his office. Though his Sephardic upbringing meant that he was more familiar with the liturgy of the Spanish and Portuguese congregants at Bevis-Marks, he still had to adjust to the specifics of their customs. In spite of this, the congregation's records show that S.D. devoted much time and money to its activities and held several of its highest offices.

The Victorians often felt "an almost perverse attraction toward the romantic and mysterious East," wrote historian Vivian D. Lipman. Consequently, these were good times for people like S.D., since the English ruling class was more willing to accept those with new money, especially those with "exotic" backgrounds. And while England's prime minister, Benjamin Disraeli, improved on his Eastern roots to imply the nobility of his birth, S.D. had a ready-made imprimatur, with princely origins in Iraq and India.

Work was not all-consuming for S.D.—he indulged his nonbusiness side by spending time at the Oriental Bookseller, whose large shop was conveniently located next door to him. The owners, James Madden & Co., were proud of their vast selection of travel books, and browsing the store's shelves, S.D. could nourish a lifelong passion. Though his health was not robust and he suffered from a dilated heart, he set out to organise a challenging three-month adventure cruise. The rough conditions would be doubly difficult because he would be observing Jewish dietary laws while travelling.

From the foot of the North Cape, S.D. wrote to his wife in India on Sunday, June 15, 1859. Though they conversed in Judeo-Arabic at home in Bombay, he preferred to write to her in his flamboyant English, in preparation for their coming reunion. Apparently, Farha was fluent enough to read his romantic, euphoric account of the trip. He addressed her with her anglicised name:

My Dear Flora,

. . . For the last fortnight I have had no night and could always read in my bed very conveniently. Last night I have climbed up the Cape with a guide and a travelling companion, reached the top half an hour before midnight, after nearly three hours hard walk, when lo! The ocean opened before our eyes, with the Sun gazing on us in his full glory. It's impossible to believe that the Sun at midnight can be seen so much above the horizon, as much as you would see him in Bombay two hours before sun set or about 2–3 PM . . .

I stopped fully one hour occupied in burning my coat with the Sun through a globe, making a large hole in less than five minutes, and having a hammer and chisel with me engraved my name and date on the block there. The sky round about the Sun is so clear, transparent and picturesque in its different colours of saffron, orange and blue that I only wish you were with me. However, I was not forgetful to drink (though in a tin glass) health to absent friends and three hearty churns to North Cape and the midnight sun. The journey I must confess was a very fatiguing one indeed, as I had to fast on night and day, but the idea of such romantic scenery and marvellous sights of the Polar region make you bear any thing.

I will try to be back in England as soon as possible, when I hope to find all your letters for which I am anxious. I hope you are taking care of Joseph and Rachel.

S.D. was fascinated by geographical explorations and surveys, and upon his return to London he joined the Hakluyt Society and contributed to the republication of primary accounts of others' voyages and travels. He also presided over a committee to finance an expedition to China and Abyssinia to locate the lost biblical tribes. Unfortunately, the man who was to take the voyage, Benjamin II, died in the midst of the preparations, so S.D. generously transferred a portion of his contributions to the man's wife and daughter.

In 1860, David Sassoon finally gave his blessing for Farha and little Joseph and Rachel to join S.D. in London. For reasons that are not entirely clear, they did not get there in time to celebrate the Jewish New Year with S.D.; instead, the trio celebrated it aboard the steamer *Ellora,* somewhere between Malta and Gibraltar. On Sunday, September 23, the family was finally reunited at the port of Southampton after twenty-eight months of separation. S.D. and Farha had lived apart for six of their ten years of marriage. Rachel was two and a half years old and she knew her father only from the photographs.

DESPITE EMANCIPATION, THE issues of Jewish loyalty and identity remained unresolved: were Jews merely the members of a religion, or were they also of a separate nation? The Earl of Derby, the Conservative leader in the House of Lords and, later, prime minister, summed up the prevailing attitude: "What the Jews were in Egypt, they are in England . . . though among us, they are not with us." No wonder British-born Jews and immigrants like the Sassoons had to demonstrate their Englishness at all times—in speech, dress, taste and opinion. To paraphrase the Jewish progressive scholar Moses Mendelssohn, grandfather of the famed composer, S.D. set out to be a Jew at home and an Englishman in public, and he raised his children accordingly. He and Farha wanted them "to adhere faithfully to the holy religion of our forefathers" and to their Baghdadi roots, while blending in with their British peers. In order to achieve the first part of this goal, the children were taught the family's traditional Judeo-Arabic dialect. And to help them integrate, S.D. and Farha gave two names each to the sons who were born after the move to England—one Hebrew and one English. Ezra, born nine months after his parents' reunion, was also called Alfred, and their youngest child, Meyer, was given the second name of Frederick. As an indication of how unsuccessful S.D. and Farha were in keeping the family's dual identity alive, neither son would end up using his Hebrew name. Even Farha would begin to go by the anglicised version of her name—Flora.

Emulating landed gentry, wealthy Jewish immigrants often bought country houses in England. Though S.D. Sassoon had no interest in any of the usual pursuits that went hand in hand with such a purchase—sports, horses, cricket or hunting—he decided to follow this trend nonetheless. In so doing, he risked the kind of sour welcome described by Anthony Trollope in his novel *The Last Chronicle of Barset*: "many of the county people had turned up their noses at them; sneering at the nouveaux riches, who had no roots, and came to honour and glory simply because of their wealth."

In June 1863, S.D. spotted an advertisement praising a fine old mansion called Ashley Park. The fifteenth-century estate in Walton-on-Thames was only a forty-minute journey from London by the South Western Railway, and boasted stabling for six or seven horses, carriage houses, beautiful lawns and flower gardens, some Scottish firs of very unusual size, "and extensive and most enjoyable pleasure grounds connected with the plantations and park." Legend has it that Oliver Cromwell stayed in Ashley Park during the trial of Charles I, and that Henry VIII presided over dancing in its magnificent banqueting hall. It was now owned by the twenty-eight-year-old Sir Henry Fletcher, the fourth baronet, a military man who felt the estate, which had been in his family for 135 years, was too large and expensive to keep. In October, with David Sassoon's blessing—and his money—S.D. paid Fletcher 48,500 guineas (£2.5 million today) for the property.

The red-brick gabled building, which had a one-hundred-foot-long gallery, came fully furnished, with a collection of curious old weapons such as halberds and crossbows. S.D. and Flora left everything in place, including a painting of Henry VIII hanging in the hall. Curiously, they also left the portraits of generations of Fletchers hanging throughout the house. Whether this was out of respect for Ashley Park's provenance or a remnant of their desire to be imagined Britons is difficult to say, but one must wonder what effect it had on their impressionable young children.

Ashley Park was an opulently appointed mansion. The main staircase was made of golden oak and was flanked by an open balustrade of a beautiful Renaissance pattern—scrolls of acanthus supported by figures of cherubs. The sitting room was "painted white and gold, with mantelpieces built in that indescribable style dear to Renaissance artists, like a broken pediment of a classic temple," admired Mrs. Mary Eliza Haweis, the high priestess of aesthetics of the time, who was a frequent contributor to the up-market home fashion magazine *The Lady's Realm*.

Flora Sassoon added an oriental touch with her choice of carpets, ornate silks and lacquered cabinets. And, though they saw fit to retain the portraits of the Fletchers, the Sassoons also chose to fill their home with portraits of their own family in their oriental attire. Mrs. Haweis thought that these were in "quaint contrast with the Renaissance and Queen Anne character of Ashley Park."

S.D. kept the house in Regent's Park to serve him during his weekdays at the office, and the entire family moved to London for the Jewish New Year and Passover to celebrate with their fellow Jews. Following his father's example, he planned to build a synagogue in the country home.

It was in this environment that Rachel and her siblings were raised. A precocious little girl from the start, Rachel had a healthy curiosity for the world around her. On family outings to the London Zoo, she recalled being "possessed of a desire for information concerning animals and their ways," but she complained that the signs on the animals' cages did not provide her with enough detailed information. Conscious of that shortcoming, and of their daughter's inquisitive nature, Flora and S.D. made a point of taking along an "encyclopedia perambulating with us on tram lines" on future visits to the zoo. The London Zoo remained Rachel's favourite escape, and even in later years, despite her busy schedule, she still found time to snatch a hasty hour among the animals. Ever the perfectionist, she once took the trouble to complain to the Secretary of the Zoological Gardens that she was "disappointed to find so poor and incomplete a show in the insect house."

CHAPTER SIX

Candidly and Constantly

Opening the London branch had expanded the House of Sassoons' financial horizons, providing them with access to the world's major money markets and allowing them entrance into the imperial business class. Their company continued to grow and they switched their focus to raw cotton.

The local growth in India was inferior to American cotton, so it formed just a fraction of the country's exports to England. The Lancashire spinning mills relied upon the superior crops from Alabama, which were the product of slave labour. But in April 1861, with the outbreak of the American Civil War, President Lincoln ordered a blockade of the southern ports, and Lancashire was starved of its raw material. Spinning mills and weaving sheds were closed and poverty skyrocketed by 300 percent. Unemployment numbers grew worse from week to week as one factory after another was shut down. The British market reluctantly cast its eyes toward the East, and the Sassoons immediately seized upon the opportunity. They had the money to invest, the connections with the plantations, and their own vast warehouses to rely upon. India was working full steam to supply Britain with raw cotton, which had become as dear as gold, and the Sassoons were well positioned to profit from it.

S.D. was quick to hire more staff, and he opened branches in Liverpool and Manchester, the heart of the distressed cotton district. He travelled there and back constantly to supervise operations, and to speed up business he made extensive use of the emerging invention of the telegraph machine. Soon the turnover from the trade in textiles was second only to opium for the Sassoons. It not only doubled their wealth, it also gained them the eternal gratitude of the Lancashire-born William Gladstone, who was then Chancellor of the Exchequer— a connection that would prove useful in the future.

Just as any other prosperous Jewish merchants would, the Sassoons felt obliged to donate a tithe of one-tenth of their income to charity (the *Ma'aser*), to assist their kinsmen in Bombay, Baghdad and Jerusalem. In England, too, S.D. donated several times to the Lancashire and Cheshire Operatives Relief Fund. Besides fulfilling his religious duty, donating to English charities was a way of meeting the right people and integrating into society, and he selected his beneficiaries carefully. He supported the Cancer Hospital in London, now the Royal Marsden, which was the first hospital in the world dedicated to the study and treatment of the disease. He also contributed to the Scottish Hospital, presided over by Prime Minister Palmerston; the Royal Caledonian Asylum in Holloway, a home for the children of Scottish servicemen who had been killed or disabled; and Mrs. Gladstone's convalescent home for orphans recovering from cholera. Mrs. Gladstone enjoyed the Sassoons' generosity several times over. With their impressive donation of one thousand pounds sterling, the old Newport Market slaughterhouse behind Leicester Square was cleansed and opened as a refuge for 150 adults and children. The family was promised that a building would be erected with the name of the patriarch, David Sassoon, permanently attached to it.

The sudden death of Prince Albert in December 1861 engulfed the nation in deep mourning, and S.D. was among the very first to donate to the Lord Mayor's fund for the erection of a colossal monument in London. At the request of his father, he also commissioned a statue of the prince to be placed in Bombay. The excessive fee paid by the Sassoons to sculptor Matthew Noble amounted to three thousand pounds; half of that sum could have purchased a lavish apartment on the Crescent at the time. Three years later, Noble still had only preliminary models to show the widowed Queen Victoria, who travelled to his studio herself to see them. Eventually, though, Noble did complete the work in 1869. The eight-foot-tall statue, which stood on an eleven-foot pedestal, dedicated by David Sassoon in English and Hebrew, can still be seen at the Bhau Daji Lad Museum, next to a bust of the patriarch himself.

S.D. heralded his family's Englishness by applying for a coat of arms, which was granted in December 1862. It was adorned with Jewish symbols: a palm tree for righteousness, a slit-open pomegranate for charity and prosperity, and a white dove hovering above, carrying an olive branch, the symbol of peace. The Latin motto they chose, *Candide et Constanter* ("Candidly and Constantly"), was repeated in Hebrew as well, with two words taken from a daily prayer— "Truth" and "Faith." S.D. affixed the massive coat of arms above one of the doors of Ashley Park.

The second of the Ten Commandments states, "Thou shall not make unto thee a graven image." Still, as orthodox as he undoubtedly was, David Sassoon in Bombay allowed himself to be photographed and sketched, and thus nothing hindered his son from approaching Mary Thornycroft to commission a sculpture of his wife and himself to decorate their mansion. Having sculpted Queen Victoria's children—and four full generations of the royal house—Mrs. Thornycroft was a renowned artist, much in demand. The hours the Sassoons spent in her studio helped them develop a relationship with the Thornycrofts, one that would be passed on to the next generation and eventually bring upheaval into both families' lives. The two marble busts of Flora and S. D. Sassoon were exhibited in the Royal Academy in 1864 but have not been traced since.

Anticipating the end of the Civil War and the return of cotton imports from the United States, the Sassoons escaped the ensuing price slump—and the collapse of the Bombay stock exchange—through the further expansion of their export of opium. They paid large advances to growers and dealers, "purchasing the crop before it was even planted," and in this way they saw off all of their major rivals, forcing them to withdraw from the trade. Soon, the Sassoons controlled a huge 70 percent of the Chinese opium market, and were able to set prices accordingly. Their activities were insured in London, and when they sued the Harris Insurance Company for a two-hundred-chest shipment that was lost, they introduced themselves at the Queen's Bench Division as "doing business largely in opium."

At that time in England, trading opium was still less damaging to one's reputation than profiting from the stock market. However, in later years, anti-Semites like Arnold Leese, a founding member of the Imperial Fascist League, blamed the Sassoons for "the Jewish rotting of China," which he claimed had escalated the Chinese dislike and distrust of Westerners into hatred. He accused the British government of protecting the Sassoon trade, "even to the extent of war."

S.D.'s daughter, Rachel Beer, was the editor of the *Sunday Times* when a Royal Commission weighed the pros and cons of the trade. Mrs. Beer found no moral fault with the export of opium; on the contrary, she thought that "great injury was done in India by the appointment of the Commission." She predicted that when the report was presented, "it will be found that the case of the anti-opiumists is shattered."

And indeed, after hearing 723 witnesses and filling 2,500 pages with its report, the commission concluded that opium production in India could continue. Though one can salute Mrs. Beer's finely tuned political senses, it's puzzling that a woman of deep social conscience who spent her life crusading against all kinds of injustice could ignore the devastation caused by the narcotic trade. Was she numbed by her allegiance to her family, whose representatives told the commission that "the Chinese who smoked or imbibed opium were better behaved, quieter and far more sensible, than those addicted to alcoholic drinks"?

Years later, Rachel's nephew, Siegfried Sassoon, expressed his fascination with his "jewelled merchant ancestors" and their "monstrous wealth," but he did not comment directly on the source of their bounty. It's hard to believe that the facts had escaped him. Was he embarrassed? He referred to his family's involvement in the opium trade obliquely in a text entitled "Jewish Gold," writing, "They made it in the East by dirty trading, millions and millions of coins."

With these additional profits from opium, David Sassoon & Co. expanded into the lucrative world of property. Foreseeing the expansion of Bombay and Shanghai, they bought up extensive land and buildings at rock-bottom prices. Their constructions transformed the skyline and architecture of Bombay. They built the city's first dock, which is still known as the Sassoon Dock.

With operations in Bombay running smoothly, the other Sassoon brothers took a break from business and started touring the world just as S.D. had done. In 1862, Reuben visited the Holy Land, while Abdullah came to London and was a guest at a banquet held by the Lord Mayor. He was in his element in society and, setting aside his Jewish Iraqi name, he began presenting himself as Albert. In late 1863, the two brothers embarked on a long tour together, starting with St. Petersburg, where they were received by Tsar Alexander II. During their tour, they were guests of honour of the philanthropist and banker Joseph Gunzburg, which began a long-lasting connection. In June 1864, they were back in London, enjoying a reception held by Prime Minister Lord Palmerston at his residence.

Meanwhile, their more introverted brother S.D. preferred to stay at home among his books and his collection of rare Hebrew manuscripts. In the little spare time he had, he studied and translated ancient manuscripts, wrote essays and served as a Fellow of the Society of Arts and of the Royal Society. He was also a council member of Jews' College and a Hebrew examiner for the Jews' Free School. He found in these activities a balance to his life as a wealthy entrepreneur.

In September 1864, the Sassoon brothers opened the firm's new and spacious London offices at 12 Leadenhall Street, an event that would mark a high point in the cooperative venture between David Sassoon's sons. But shortly after the new offices were up and running, their seventy-two-year-old father's health began to fail. On Saturday,

November 5, at three o'clock in the morning in his summer retreat in Poona, "he seemed to fall into gentle sleep, when he raised himself upon his couch, and called his eldest son, who was in England. He called for his son a second time, and sank upon his couch and died," reported the *Jewish Chronicle*.

As soon as Abdullah and Reuben returned home, they built their father a lavish mausoleum in the courtyard of his synagogue in Poona; though Ohel David (David's Tent) was more a reflection of their nouveau-riche extravagance than of their father's hardworking sensibility. In observance of the Victorian code of mourning, all of the firm's stationery was printed with a black border. Judging from the family archive, the Sassoons continued to use the stationery well after the customary first year. In 1859, before the cotton and opium booms that further enriched the Sassoons' coffers, the family fortune was reported to be over five million pounds. Abdullah/Albert and S.D., who were the eldest sons of David's two wives, were nominated as executors of his will. His first command was that they should continue to expand his charities. More importantly, he issued an edict stating that he expected his sons "to entertain brotherly affection for each other and on no account to allow any quarrel or dissention to arise amongst them, but to live in peace and harmony with each other, that they may enjoy together the bountiful wealth which the Almighty God has bestowed upon us."

It should come as no surprise that this order did not prevent a rift from developing within the family. Throughout his life, David Sassoon had given his sons the freedom to invest on their own and run parallel businesses as long as doing so created no conflict of interest or competition for the main company. He welcomed and applauded their ability to accumulate independent fortunes. At his death, his eldest son, Abdullah/Albert, became the head of the firm. Elias, the second in line, refused to accept this arrangement, and the ensuing friction and dispute resulted in Elias forming the rival firm E. D. Sassoon & Co. This initial fracture was just a preview of what was to come.

S.D. was undeniably successful, but he seemed temperamentally unsuited to his profession. He also lacked the vigorous good health required for his hectic life and multiple responsibilities; throughout their marriage, Flora Sassoon was concerned about S.D.'s health and about the increasing pressures that bore down on him. As his business reputation grew, he took on additional roles as the director of several companies unconnected with the Sassoon firm, including the Banks of Hindustan, China and Japan. Flora was relieved when, in April 1867, S.D.'s younger brother Reuben moved permanently to London, ready to share the burden. He was accompanied by their widowed mother, as well as his pregnant wife.

Though more of the Sassoons were leaving India, the family remained a vital and active presence there. Sir Bartle Frere, the Governor of Bombay, suggested that the city commemorate the patriarch, David Sassoon, with a statue. Generous donations poured in from around the globe, the donors including everyone from the Rothschilds to the grateful Lancashire mill workers. Even Mr. Gladstone contributed five pounds. S.D. was to play an active role in seeing the project come to fruition, and this deceptively simple task may have taken a greater toll on him than all of his other responsibilities.

The Sassoons commissioned Thomas Woolner, an acclaimed British sculptor, to create the memorial. Woolner carved the statue from white marble, working from a photograph of David Sassoon that had been taken just a few weeks before his death. Woolner depicted a man stricken in years, tall and well proportioned, "and of slenderness that tells more of intellectual energy than physical strength," wrote *The Spectator*. "The expression is very animated, and one reads in it a disposition self-reliant, cheerful and benevolent." *The Illustrated London News* was more critical of the piece; Woolner failed to display the expected artistic "drapery" of David Sassoon's cassock— "the folds about the arms are in particular ugly, and ill-understood. In the back view the poverty, even meanness, of the treatment, is very apparent."

. . .

ON SATURDAY, JUNE 22, 1867, the family celebrated Ezra/Alfred's sixth birthday in Ashley Park. S.D. waited for the first three stars to appear, marking the end of the Sabbath, so that he could return to the city. He stayed the night at 17 Cumberland Terrace, since he had a business meeting in the morning in the nearby Langham Hotel. The meeting over, he waited agitatedly for a cab to take him to Woolner's studio to inspect his father's memorial statue. Suddenly, struck by a sharp pain shooting through his chest, S.D. collapsed in the hotel foyer, never to get up again.

It was not an exceptionally hot day, as some biographers erroneously concluded—in fact, the temperature was around 13 degrees Celsius, and the regal-looking hotel boasted of its superior "system of perfect ventilation from above." The death certificate indicates that S.D. had been living with a dilated heart for many years. In the previous two and a half years, he had also suffered from emphysema, caused by heavy smoking.

The following month, S.D. would have celebrated his thirty-fifth birthday.

CHAPTER SEVEN

Fatherless

The mortuary hall in the Spanish-Portuguese cemetery on Mile End Road could not contain the multitude of mourners who gathered for S.D.'s funeral. The women squeezed in on one side, while the men surrounded the coffin. After the ritual cut was made to the lapels of S.D.'s closest family members, six men shouldered his coffin and the procession moved solemnly into the cemetery. The community custom forbade women from accompanying the deceased to his grave, so S.D.'s mother, his wife Flora, nine-year-old Rachel and the rest of the women watched the procession move toward row 111 of the cemetery. All they could see was a black wall of backs, and all they could hear were mumbled prayers.

S.D.'s father had been put to rest in a magnificent mausoleum in Poona, but the customs in London were more austere. All were buried alike, in simple shrouds, in identical plain pine boxes, under uniform, horizontally laid tombstones. A writer was commissioned to phrase S. D. Sassoon's epitaph in Hebrew and English, in which he was eulogized as lord and magnate, *Doresh Tov Le'amo* (one who "bears good tidings for his people"), evoking the title of the newspaper S.D. had published and edited back in Bombay.

FLORA AND HER children did not return to Ashley Park after the funeral. They stayed instead in their London home, receiving business associates and synagogue friends who came to pay their respects. Flora bought the burial plot next to her husband, making a clear statement that she did not intend to remarry and would not be returning to India.

Reuben Sassoon notified the London financial community by circular that, owing to the death of his brother, the business of S. D. Sassoon and Co. "must be closed and liquidated" and that he was establishing a new firm "under the style of David Sassoon and Co." It was clear to Flora that neither she nor her children would be part of it. Whatever her husband had achieved in this life had seemingly been erased.

S. D. Sassoon had been just thirty-three years old when he wrote his will in the year following his father's death. As executors he named his wife, his confidential clerk Edward Perugini, and his brothers Elias and Solomon, both of whom were scholars like himself and not bon vivants like Albert and Reuben. The will instructed them to invest his money in Indian government stocks and bonds—apparently, S.D.'s familiarity with the Indian world of commerce made him trust it more than other financial venues like the British stock market. He had donated generously to various non-Jewish charities throughout his life, but in his will he named only Jewish ones in London, Bombay, Baghdad and Jerusalem.

This clear expression of his allegiance to his faith was manifested in much stronger and more direct terms in another part of S.D.'s will. He wrote: "I enjoin upon all my children that they adhere faithfully to the Holy Religion of our Forefathers, and it is my trust and hope that they will make it their aim through life to intermarry amongst my own family." He intended for them to not only choose Jewish spouses, but to choose them from Baghdadi families related to the Sassoons. S.D.'s demands may seem harsh, but the purity of the family was of paramount importance to him. Nevertheless, none of his children would honour his wish.

The next item in the will caused much controversy. S.D. bequeathed Ashley Park—houses, cottages, gardens, lawns and pleasure grounds—to his eldest son, Joseph. In so doing, he was following the biblical custom of primogeniture, whereby inheritance was passed down to the firstborn male child. There was precedence for this within the Sassoon family—following the patriarch's death, Abdullah/Albert had moved into the palatial Sans Souci without any protest from his brothers. Similarly, when the patriarch gave the money to purchase Ashley Park to S.D.—the firstborn from his second wife—none of the brothers objected. Though S.D. ordered his sons to accept the provisions of the will as final and conclusive, the division and distribution of the estate would become a source of friction. Years later, when Joseph got married, his mother would be forced to vacate the mansion. And, anxious to gain their share of Ashley Park, his brothers Alfred and Frederick would contest the will, dragging Joseph to court.

In what seems a more directly punitive move, S.D. also made the edict that Flora would lose her guardianship over her children if she were ever to remarry. If she did, her brothers-in-law would assume legal responsibility for the young Sassoons. Furthermore, as long as Flora remained a widow she would enjoy a generous annuity of £1,000.

Coming of age, Alfred and Frederick were to receive a lump sum of £2,500 each, and a fund of £10,000 was secured for Rachel, "for her sole and separate and unalienable use and benefit free from the control or engagement of any husband." In many ways, the absence of Rachel's father strengthened her independence and freedom. Fathers in wealthy Victorian and Jewish families were dominant authority figures, and it's unlikely that S.D. would have allowed Rachel to pursue any work outside of the home. He would no doubt also have ensured that she was married by the age of eighteen, to an eligible Baghdadi-Jewish suitor.

AT THE END of the traditional week of mourning, Flora Sassoon returned to Ashley Park with her four children—Joseph (aged twelve), Rachel (nine), Alfred (six) and Frederick (five). Every autumn, in the month of the High Holy Days, they continued to make the move to their London house—first at 17 Cumberland Place, and later, 6 Grosvenor Crescent—to celebrate with their London relatives. They would also return to London in the spring to celebrate Passover. This was, in part, a practical move, since in accordance with Jewish custom every crumb of bread had to be removed from the house in preparation for the festival. It was a momentous task for the Sassoons' small team of servants to execute in the huge Ashley Park mansion, but a much more manageable one in their London home. Flora and Rachel would come first to supervise the work, and the boys would join them some days later.

Religion remained an important part of the family's life and the children's upbringing. For some years, S.D. had planned to build a synagogue in Ashley Park, but he died before the foundation stone was laid. In any case, it would have been impossible to gather the quorum of ten Jewish men required for a public prayer in their small town, Walton-on-Thames. The family adhered to the dietary laws and observed the Sabbath, and a visiting rabbi came regularly to teach the children Hebrew and religion. Joseph's bar mitzvah was celebrated in the Bevis-Marks synagogue in London in grand style, and Flora held a special fete for two hundred children of the Jewish Spanish and Portuguese community. "Grace was said by one of the pupils, and was followed by varied entertainment of music, singing and legerdemain," reported The Jewish Chronicle, appreciative of "the sympathy displayed by the wealthier section of the community toward our poor."

A tutor in residence, Arthur Read, who had studied at Queen's College, Oxford, gave private lessons to the children and prepared Joseph for the entry exams at his alma mater. As all three boys went on to study at Oxford and Rachel went on to become the editor of two national Sunday newspapers, the home instruction can be counted a success.

Visiting Ashley Park to see how his nephews and niece were getting on, Flora's brother-in-law Reuben was pleased with their religious and educational progress, but he thought they were being pampered. An extravagantly furnished billiards room was at their disposal, and in many ways the entire place was a kind of elaborate playhouse. The young Sassoons enjoyed exploring the rooms that fanned out in every direction, "passages here, closet there, steps up, steps down." They were mesmerized by a mysterious hollow passage that led to a monumental shield, behind which some unknown ancestor of the previous owners was said to be buried.

Yet it was not Reuben who had been given responsibility for the children in his brother's will. And since Elias Sassoon had broken away from the family, Solomon was in Bombay, and the clerk Perugini had left the company, this left Flora as the sole executor of her husband's wishes for his progeny. S.D. had not left any indication in his will that he wanted his sons to pursue careers in business, nor had he asked his brothers to incorporate them into the company when they came of age. He had left their choice of profession entirely to them and clearly did not expect them to follow in his footsteps. Flora shared a similar desire for her children, and with the untimely death of her husband she finally felt free to openly express her disdain for commerce. Detaching her children from the family business and their moneymaking, upper-crust relatives would allow this branch of the Sassoons to explore new avenues. It would give them more freedom, but it would also mean that they would live to see their fortune dwindle. "Your heritage in worldly goods may not be great, but there is a more worldly heritage than goods," wrote David Sassoon, Flora's eldest grandson, in his unpublished memoirs. His sons were amused by one arch comment that was made about the clan: "I know what is wrong with the world; there are not enough people like the Sassoons in it."

Flora's separation of herself and her young family from the financial and social world of the Sassoons was a gradual rather than immediate withdrawal. A short letter survives from the extensive correspondence between Ashley Park and the family in Bombay; written a year after S.D.'s death, it reveals the young Sassoons were still in close touch with their relatives. The black-margined sheets of paper show the calligraphic handwriting of S.D.'s thirteen-year-old son Joseph, who wished to impress his uncle with his fluency in Judeo-Arabic. Ten-year-old Rachel was less familiar with the Hebrew letters, and she added on in English, "Will dear Uncle Solomon accept a few kisses from his affectionate niece?" signing it Rachaluna, her Judeo-Iraqi pet name.

With a career in business not an imperative, Flora allowed her children to enjoy many leisure activities that previous generations of Sassoons had not had the opportunity to pursue. Befitting her wealthy upbringing, Rachel played the piano from childhood. One of her earliest public performances took place in the local parish, as part of the musical program to celebrate the rehanging of the church bells. Rachel was talented, but—being an introvert—she was ill at ease on stage, and she found composition more to her liking. In late 1881, when she was just twenty-three, her piano sonata in B flat major was published by Chappell of Bond Street, and it received a most favourable review in the *Neuen Zeitschrift für Musik,* the *New Journal of Music,* founded by Robert Schumann in Leipzig. The atmosphere of the work was contemplative and elegiac, and the reviewer complimented Rachel's healthy sense of humour in the last movement. At a time when so many compositions displayed technical skill, not raw talent, Rachel's was counted as one of the few maiden works to justify encouragement and support.

Soon after publication, this piano sonata was performed in a grand morning concert at St. James's Hall on May 23, 1882. Rachel Sassoon was the only amateur in a program that showcased Bach, Mendelssohn, Brahms and Wagner. By that time, she had also composed several works for the cello and violin, and a week later, at the Marlborough Rooms in London, the Czech musical family Brousil played Schumann's quintet, Mendelssohn's quartet, and the twenty-four-year-old Rachel's gavotte and tarantella for the cello. In December, her trio for piano, violin and cello was applauded as a remarkable work, melodious and fluent. Upon the publication of the trio, she was praised by *The Musical Standard,* the reviewer noting that her "score displays elegant writing and refined scholarship, whilst the work for the three instruments is well 'laid-out' for effect."

Rachel's brother Alfred, who was also musically inclined, took up the violin. The doting Flora promised her son a Stradivarius and, according to family lore, bought him not one, but two of the precious instruments, much to the dismay of Reuben, who was quick to report her extravagance to the family in Bombay. Years later, Siegfried Sassoon was impressed by the gypsy-like wildness of his father Alfred's violin playing. He was convinced that he had picked it up from his teacher, Pablo de Sarasate, the famous Spanish violinist and composer.

Rachel and Alfred were close siblings—they would frequently play duets together and they shared a mutual love for painting. Their efforts were framed and displayed around the house, hung side by side with the treasured works of art the family had acquired. The siblings had a quality of "frustrated gaiety and desultory charm" that appealed to Siegfried Sassoon, who later wrote:

> Both of them had a passion for jewels, and their moods were as though one looked into a diamond and saw its clearness change to the blue darkness of a sapphire. There was a sort of voluptuous aroma around them, which was entirely different from my mother's family, like the difference between healthy, outdoor flowers and the exquisite fragrance of a hothouse full of exotic blossoms.

In spite of her musical talents and artistic promise, Rachel was not given the opportunity to attend the Royal Academy of Music in London to hone her skills. In affluent families like hers, playing an instrument or holding a brush were merely respectable pastimes for a young woman, not potential careers, so she had to make do with the tutelage of a home music teacher, reinforced by hours of laborious practice. Nevertheless, with Ashley Park run firmly by her mother, assisted by a team of efficient servants, Rachel often found herself forcibly idle at home.

One task that Rachel was able to contribute to—and, indeed, was expected to—was her mother's philanthropic activities. In July 1872, the wife and daughters of Prime Minister William Gladstone were the guests of honour at Ashley Park, at a garden party thrown by Flora in support of Mrs. Gladstone's Newport Market Refuge charity. The acquaintance between the two families had begun some ten years earlier, when the Sassoons had shared financial and political interests with the Gladstones. Flora still supported Mrs. Gladstone's charities, and on this occasion she invited more than a hundred children from the Refuge to her home, paying for a special train from London and private carriages from the station to her mansion. The children enjoyed dinner and tea on the lawn, and the entertainment ended with a dance in the picture gallery to the sound of the Coldstream Guards band.

Taking part in her mother's charitable endeavors, however, could offer only a small respite from Rachel's dissatisfaction with her assigned role as a stay-at-home daughter, and she longed for more freedom. The writer Beatrix Potter, Rachel's contemporary, found herself in a very similar position and was deeply depressed by her lot. At one point, Potter made a will, concluding it with "the position of an unmarried daughter at home is an unhappy one even for a strong woman: it is an impossible one for a weak one." And, as a strong-minded woman not content with this lot in life, Rachel was looking for an escape route.

FOR AMBITIOUS ENGLISH Jews of the time, the way to achieve social acceptance was by succeeding in the ruthless London business world, not by graduating with honours from the academic institutions of Oxford and Cambridge. Only a dozen Jews, all male, attended either university during the 1870s. Choosing what seemed to them to be the lesser of two evils, however, Rachel's brothers broke the mold, and all of them attended the University of Oxford—Joseph was the first to receive his MA from Christ Church, while his younger brothers, Alfred and Frederick, left Ashley Park in October 1879 for Exeter College.

Though women—Jewish or otherwise—could study at Lady Margaret Hall or Somerville at Oxford, Girton or Newnham at Cambridge, and in London could attend University College, Bedford or Birkbeck, many parents feared that higher education would jeopardize their daughters' chances of obtaining suitable spouses and would turn them into argumentative wives. Physicians warned that intellectual activity was bad for women, capable of causing not just mental collapse, but sterility. On top of that, for Jewish parents, sending a daughter to Oxbridge, the stronghold of Christianity, was unthinkable. In the face of such obstacles, it is no wonder Rachel had to stay at home, leaving the pioneering efforts to others.

The first to accept the risks were exceptional mavericks. Phoebe Sarah Marks, later known as Hertha Ayrton, was probably the first Jewish woman to matriculate at university. Against incredible odds—her father was deceased and her mother made a modest living as a seamstress—she read mathematics at Girton, beginning in 1876. Perhaps it is telling that she considered herself to be agnostic, though she continued to be identified as Jewish. She successfully fought her way through the ranks, going on to become a renowned scientist in the field of the electric arc.

Much later, as editor of the *Sunday Times,* Rachel made her feelings on women's education known. In 1899 she published an interview with Ayrton, noting that now, in the laboratories of University College, "girl and boy students work shoulder to shoulder." "You will discover," the interview revealed, "that there are experts among these girls, and that the men students are the first to recognise their prowess." But though the prospects for higher education for women had improved considerably since her teens, not every university granted their female students the right to earn degrees, and Rachel called for equality:

> Years ago, it was conceded that women might reside, might
> read, might attend lectures, might go in for the examinations,
> and might . . . do exceedingly well therein, even occasionally to
> the overshadowing to the rightful heirs of university distinc-
> tions. But not yet may women win the mystic letters that should
> tell the world of their achievements. It is impossible to justify
> this incongruity. . . . Only the possession of degrees will be of
> use to a woman in her life's struggle. Must it be said that that is
> the reason why a male university has refused them?

She spoke out against a proposal that in order for a woman to be
granted a BA from Oxford, she should achieve honours in at least one
of the examinations. Men were not obliged to meet that same requirement. Why "should a woman be treated more harshly than a
man," while a "dunderhead male" could scrape in with a pass and
even continue on toward an MA, something that women were not
permitted to do under any circumstance, she argued. Firmly of the
opinion that a separate, female-only university would be fatal to the
interests of women, Rachel demanded that colleges be opened to both
sexes under the same terms.

PERHAPS IT WAS this burgeoning division in the lives of Flora and
S.D.'s sons and daughter that led to a striking group photo from the
mid-1870s that appears to portray the Sassoons of Ashley Park as
individuals on not especially intimate terms with one another. In the
picture, they gaze in opposite directions, each occupying his or her
own space. Rachel, then the age of a debutante, sits upright in the
far left corner, her slender figure in a fashionable ensemble of a
buttoned-up velvet jacket and overskirt. Her hands are clasped together in a muff of the same delicate white fur that trims her jacket
and hat. Head bowed down, she seems uncomfortable and lost in
thought. "She always seemed to be absolutely the most shy and silent
woman I had ever met," remembered politician and writer Justin
McCarthy. "She appeared to carry modest reserve to its extreme

verge and to shrink away as far as the manners of the drawing room would possibly admit, from any kind of general notice."

Although she was a hothouse flower, shy and demure in company, the power of her pen would allow Rachel to express her strong convictions with bold, incisive words.

CHAPTER EIGHT

A Court Jew

The marriage of Rachel Sassoon and Frederick Beer was a union of the East and the West in flourishing Victorian London. It was also the merging of the descendants of two grand families—Rachel and Frederick were each heir to an illustrious dynasty and a great fortune. The paths their ancestors had trodden were very different, but though they lived worlds apart, the Beer zur Kanne family in Frankfurt and the Sassoons in Baghdad were cut from the same cloth—members of a detached minority, they served as their sovereigns' Jewish treasurers. High-ranking court posts placed these families in positions of leadership in their communities. They were allowed to operate within the court, but could never be a part of it. Always at the mercy of their masters, they were subjected to the envy and opposition of their own people. They also had to contend with the fear and distrust that others felt toward Jews, especially in Frankfurt.

A huge image painted on the gates of the southern entrance bridge to Frankfurt depicted a monstrous sow surrounded by much smaller human figures. One of them was sitting backwards on the animal's back, holding up its tail to allow another to lick the pig's excrement. The others huddled underneath and suckled the sow's teats. Identifiable by their rounded and pointed hats, the figures were clearly intended to represent Jews. This reprehensible mural was impossible to miss upon entering the city, and Johann Wolfgang von Goethe, though a Gentile himself, was appalled that such a medieval anti-Jewish motif had been painted and maintained by the municipality of his birthplace. It was still displayed in broad daylight as late as 1800.

Though many great fortunes had their humble beginnings in Frankfurt's ghetto—including that of the Rothschilds, as well as the Beers—centuries of hounding and discrimination had left the majority of the Jews who lived there struggling to eke out an existence. The ghetto was built in the fifteenth century to segregate the town's twenty Jewish families. Three hundred years later, three thousand people were still living on that same narrow strip of land—just 330 meters long and 3 meters wide. The ghetto population was restricted to five hundred families, and only six new residents were allowed to join each year; nonetheless, two hundred houses covered every available square inch. Rising up five and six stories in height, they blotted out the sunlight, and tightly packed together as they were, the risk of fire was great and ever present. Homes that were originally built for one family now housed two or three, and every few years the residents would swap rooms, so that each family would have the chance to live in the most tolerable part of the building. All of the back windows facing the city were blocked from the outside by wooden planks so that the Jewish inhabitants would not be able to "spy" on their Christian neighbours.

Directions were not needed to reach the Frankfurt ghetto; the stench was the only compass required, as one traveller wrote at the time. Other contemporary accounts vied in their sickening depictions of the ghetto as the worst slum on earth—sewage ran freely and thousands of people in rags teemed through the single street, it was said, while in the hallways and staircases of the houses they congregated like "maggots wriggling in cheese." The wording of these accounts bears a vitriolic anti-Semitic tone, but it's true, regardless, that the *Judengasse* (Jews' lane) was a horrendously oppressive place to live. Ludwig Börne (Löb Baruch before converting to Christianity) characterized it as a "long dark prison into which the highly celebrated light of the eighteenth century has not been able to penetrate." He was clearly moved by the poignant situation of the ghetto's inhabitants, and in describing the horrific sight of small children creeping about in the filth of the ghetto, Börne, who had become a well-known satirist, set aside his sharp arrows: "If one were to consider play in childhood as the model for the reality of life, then the cradle of these children must be the grave of every encouragement."

Jews could only leave the ghetto and enter town for business, never for pleasure, and even then no more than two were allowed to walk side by side through the streets of Frankfurt. Coffeehouses, inns and public parks were forbidden territory altogether. The official reason was that the streets were too narrow for the use of people of both religions, and besides, since Jews were allegedly addicted to smoking tobacco, their smell might upset the Christians' sensitive nostrils.

Other restrictions were even crueler. To prevent Jews from defending themselves against assault, they were forbidden from carrying walking sticks. And at the cry *"Jud mach mores"* ("Jew, pay your dues"), they had to doff their hats, step aside and bow, even when the order came from a small boy and was directed at an elderly Jew. If they did not respond quickly enough, they could expect rocks to be thrown at them. Sundays and Christian holidays were curfew days and they were locked all day in the ghetto. There would be echoes of these prohibitions two centuries later when the Nazis rose to power.

This deeply rooted anti-Semitism in a flourishing financial centre was exacerbated by the fear of competition and led to the enforcement of harsh commercial regulations against Jews, including heavy taxes and restricted freedom of trade and movement. Each visit to Frankfurt was heavily taxed, and Jews were forbidden from selling most raw products, including wool, yarn, linen and hides.

Frederick Beer's ancestors were one of the lucky handful of Frankfurt's Jewish families who were able to break free from the vicious cycle of poverty, enjoying relative prosperity and grandeur. The surnames of German Jews were often derived from some aspect of their residence—the Rothschild clan, for example, took their name from their ancestral home, which bore a red shield—and the Beer zur

Kanne family were prosperous innkeepers whose surname was originated from the sign of a jug (*kanne*) that hung outside their inn. Tracing their ancestors back to the sixteenth century, the Beer zur Kannes' family tree had borne ripe fruit—several rabbis, but mainly great merchants and moneylenders, who were either the richest Jews in Frankfurt or close to it. The taxes the princes and dukes collected from their subjects were not sufficient to finance their military adventures, ambitious projects and, above all, their extravagant lifestyles; with the need for a never-ending cash flow the *Hofjuden,* the court Jews, served them well. In this environment, the family attained their commanding status well before both the House of Rothschild and the House of Sassoon rose to eminence—by the eighteenth century, the Beer zur Kanne men had been the renowned court financiers of several nobles for almost two centuries.

At the close of the Thirty Years' War in 1648, there were more than three hundred principalities in Germany and nearly each of them had its own court Jew. To hold this post, one needed personal capital, usually from trade or money-changing, knowledge of the international money markets, and an ability to raise funds through good financial credit. Court Jews also had to demonstrate dexterity in diplomacy and politics, and, as described by historian Selma Stern in her book *The Court Jew,* they needed to possess "a remarkable degree of industriousness and restlessness, a great interest in speculation and action, a strong desire for success, a lust for money and profit." Royals preferred Jews for this post, since they believed that these wealthy but powerless subordinates could be trustworthy and loyal, free of dynastic and sectarian commitments in any court intrigues.

When a prince or duke looked to expand his territory, his court Jew was the one to acquire the weapons and munitions for his soldiers. When a royal personage wanted to pamper his wife and mistresses, his court Jew was the one to obtain the diamonds and pearls. Court Jews also served as couriers, crossing precarious routes to deliver sacks of gold coins. In order to comply with their masters' caprices, they relied upon their family links and trusted networks of

co-religionists all over Europe, using these connections to their full
advantage.

But they were much more than the financiers of wars and luxuries;
they were entrepreneurs whose loans stimulated the state economy
and provided its most lucrative source of revenue. They performed
similar duties to those of a Chancellor of the Exchequer in our times.
In addition, they were put to use as secret agents and spies, and many
of them acted as consuls and diplomatic couriers in political councils,
armistice negotiations and military operations.

Court Jews were constantly at risk—if a deal fell through, they
were compelled to dig deep into their own pockets to cover the losses,
and some of the missions they were sent on were extremely dangerous. It was possible to end up bankrupt—or worse, dead—but with
these dangers came the opportunity for hefty rewards through interest and commissions. And, in return for their services, court Jews also
received special economic sanctions and some exemptions from
anti-Jewish decrees.

In many towns, though not in Frankfurt, where even the richest
and most privileged were forced to live in the ghetto, court Jews could
acquire or build themselves magnificent mansions in the most coveted
spots. Their fellow Jews envied them for this luxury and for the special amenities they alone could afford, like personal water pumps and
lavatories.

Court Jews were quick to drop the traditional Jewish attire that
had not changed since the early Middle Ages, instead adopting the
up-to-the-minute styles of their masters. In the late seventeenth and
early eighteenth centuries, the men's chaste long, dark cloaks were
replaced with brightly colored, short clothes in the French and Spanish fashion, and like the lords and nobles of the day, they also wore
full-bottomed wigs. Their wives wore multihued garments of rich,
heavy silks and velvet with puffed white sleeves and long trains, and
adorned themselves with gold and silver jewelery, precious pearls and
diamonds.

In many ways, the Beer zur Kannes led charmed lives, but they were still grounded in the reality of their ghettoized existence. No matter if they travelled for hours, days or weeks, spent time in the most lavish of palaces, homes or inns, they always had to return to the filth and impoverishment of the ghetto. It was impossible to reconcile these contrasting worlds, and they lived in a kind of schizophrenic state.

Though they felt at home in their masters' palaces, the court Jews remained pious and endeavored to leave the world of the court behind them when they entered the synagogue. Having a regular audience with princes and dukes, they were able to act as *shtadlans*— advocates for their community in times of distress—and, in this capacity, they believed that they were God's elect, angels of deliverance, princes of Israel; something that the rabbis, opposing the reign of Mammon, resented but were powerless to fight.

In the eighteenth century, anti-Semitic writings exaggerated the figure of the court Jew beyond proportion. Fearing Jewish domination, they accused court Jews of exploiting their employers' permanent financial shortages and their taste for luxury. The court Jew was turned into the epitome of a pushy parvenu, a parasite who lived off others' labour, cleverly mastering their appearances and customs to penetrate the corridors of power and secretly run state affairs. The most vitriolic personification of this stereotype was the Jew Suss, who was the protagonist of both Hauff's novella from 1827 and of Feuchtwanger's novel of the same name, which the Nazis later made into a propaganda film. The books and film were all inspired by the life and gruesome end of Joseph Suss Oppenheimer, the court Jew of Württemberg, who was executed in a human-size bird cage and left to rot in the market square.

Five generations before the birth of Frederick Beer, Beer Löb Isaak zur Kanne made his fortune dealing in goods, jewels, loans and money exchange. In the early 18th century, he and his brother Moses were by far the richest Jews in Frankfurt, worth half a million guilders. Courting danger and letting nothing stand in the way of his success, Beer zur Kanne was perfectly suited to the life of a court Jew. He served several dukes during his life and maintained an extravagant existence, employing several servants, including a cook, a housekeeper, a children's nurse, a manservant, a resident tutor and a few maids.

No matter how many domestic staff he could afford to employ, however, he was not immune to the sad fact that the overcrowding and poor sanitation in the ghetto caused high mortality rates—58 percent higher than among the non-Jewish Frankfurters—and he had the misfortune to lose his wife Zartel and several of their children. Other rich families in the ghetto also experienced deaths; Mayer Amschel Rothschild himself lost nine of his nineteen children. Following Zartel's death, Beer zur Kanne married her sister Sorle, but the couple did not have any children together.

Beer zur Kanne was the leader of the Jewish community in Frankfurt, a role he had finagled "through clever tactics, and perhaps even more, through his sharp wit and his family name," according to Selma Stern. The community maintained its own hospitals, schools and synagogues, and he ruled them all; no marriage was conducted without his authorization, for example. Beer zur Kanne exerted a Machiavellian reign of terror in the Frankfurt ghetto—"His word was law and nobody dared oppose him," records Stern—and he desperately clung to the post that had brought him such influence and profit.

In 1749, however, the four Kulp brothers—one of them the court Jew to the emperor in Vienna—challenged Beer Löb Isaak zur Kanne's autocratic rule. He was accused of trampling every law—refusing to hold new elections, handling the community finances single-handedly without allowing anyone to inspect the records, and embezzling 200,000 guilders. The community was divided by the bitter feud that ensued, which was fought not only with words but with fists and weapons. After several riots, which were suppressed by the city militia, the ghetto was put under military occupation to prevent more violence. At the community's expense, guards were stationed in front of Beer Löb Isaak zur Kanne's residence, while both sides spread false accusations and even went so far as to inform on each other to the emperor.

The turmoil lasted several years and estranged many families for decades. Much to Beer zur Kanne's dismay, he had to submit his files to the emperor's inspectors, but to his relief, they found only minor irregularities. In revenge, he had one of the Kulp brothers arrested and caused him grave financial losses, but his efforts to cling to power had lost Beer zur Kanne much of his financial and political clout. Though he was reelected, his authority was greatly compromised. Not forgiving the damage he had inflicted on the community, the chief rabbi then banned him. When Beer zur Kanne died in 1764, he was refused burial in the local Jewish cemetery and was laid to rest in the nearby Griesheim.

With the death of the patriarch, the family lost its position of leadership in the community, but Beer zur Kanne's youngest son, Löb Beer Isaak, soon restored the family to prominence. As the court Jew to five rulers, he amassed a great fortune; records show that he acquired shares in several crude-metal mines and speculated in jewels. But his activities were brought to an abrupt halt when his mental health suffered a serious decline and he had to be placed under the care of a trustee. He died in 1785, less than a year later, leaving behind a wife, Hawele, and two sons, and a fortune of 163,500 guilders.

To keep their titles and multiply their wealth, court Jews often married their relatives or the offspring of other court Jews; for that reason Löb's son Isaak was betrothed to Jachet Speyer, the daughter of a renowned banker and court Jew. An intelligent young man, Isaak became a banker and served as the agent to several dukes, becoming one of the richest Jews in Frankfurt. He was to be the last court Jew in the family, and—for many years—its last tycoon. It was fifty years after his death, and in London, that his great-grandson, Julius Beer, would exceed his ancestor's accumulation of wealth and status. He owed much to his forebears.

. . .

THE JEWS OF Frankfurt had difficulty trusting outsiders, even when they came offering a helping hand. In October 1792, Napoleon's soldiers took over the city, bringing the promise of *Liberté, Fraternité, Equalité* to the Judengasse; surprisingly, they were met with cries of "Down with the French!" Centuries of oppression had not dimmed the ghetto residents' loyalty and affection for their native city. The French retreated but returned four years later, shelling the town heavily; nearly 140 of the ghetto houses were reduced to ashes, and 1,800 Jews were left homeless. Most of the opulent Beer zur Kanne family houses, including the fifteenth-century inn that had given the dynasty its name, were burned down. The crippling damage was the first step toward liberation, however—though most preferred to settle near their former territory, for the first time the restrictions of the ghetto were lifted and refugees were allowed to seek shelter anywhere in town. But emancipation lasted only two years, ending with Napoleon's defeat in Leipzig in 1813. At that point, the medieval restrictions were re-implemented.

After decades of gaining and losing rights, in 1824 Frankfurt's Jews were finally recognised as equal citizens, though they still could not be elected to public offices. Some restrictions remained in trade and commerce, however, and only in 1864 did they finally gain full equality.

The road to emancipation was through general education, so claimed the Jewish Reform Movement, whose roots were in the French Revolution. Already, at the turn of the century, rich families like the Beer zur Kannes engaged private tutors for their children. These instructors taught the children German, French, geography, natural history and philosophy. An attempt to establish a high school with a secular curriculum in addition to the religious one encountered fierce opposition from the orthodoxy, who were hostile to any reform. Ignoring these hostilities, the reformers continued to press for change and progress.

In 1803, as he was passing a street corner in the town of Marburg, on the banks of the river Lahn, Mayer Amschel Rothschild was drawn to the melody of a Hebrew song. As he got closer, he noticed a boy busking. Rothschild was so impressed with the young boy's singing that, rather than tossing a few coins in his upturned hat, he decided to take the orphan to Frankfurt and entrust him to his chief clerk, Sigismund Geisenheimer. The boy became the first pupil of the Philantropin, a school "for poor children of the Jewish nation," which Rothschild established and financed. Samson Heine, father of the famous poet Heinrich Heine, was one of the school's benefactors. Within a short time, it went from being an industrial school dedicated to training deprived children for blue-collar labour, to a full-tuition school for children of the Jewish middle class, preparing them for the world of commerce. The pupils were taught the Torah as well as modern philosophy, science, electricity, chemistry and physics, with German becoming the language of study and prayer. There were non-Jewish teachers on the staff, and also non-Jewish students.

By its fiftieth anniversary, the Philantropin had 420 boys and 200 girls in attendance. Its teachers helped usher in the modern Jewish era, leading the reforms in Judaism. The orthodoxy labeled the reformists "criminals" for undermining their ancient religion; for their part, the reformists argued that by offering an alternative for those who would otherwise stray from the "medieval and petrified" customs, they were saving the community. By the end of the nineteenth century, two-thirds of the Frankfurt Jewish community belonged to the Reform Movement.

As a result of the bitter disputes the Beer zur Kanne family had been involved in, some of their descendants decided to shorten their name to the simpler Beer—this was an animal name, from the German *Bär* (bear), which had various spellings and was common among European Jews. Despite the improved status of Jews and the abolishment of commercial restrictions against them, the later generations of the family failed to repeat their ancestors' financial and political achievements, and were mainly local traders and paymasters.

Löb Joachim Beer, grandson of Löb Beer Isaak, was born in 1804,

and his parents separated when he was five years old, a rare occur-
rence at that time. His cousin Sophia suffered a similar fate; she was
left alone with her mother from the time she was nine. In their early
twenties, the two were betrothed, but their path to matrimony was
strewn with hurdles. Before they married, Löb Joachim wanted to
gain the necessary qualifications to become an English teacher, but
the records show that he failed the examination in 1828. He and Sophia had to wait five more years for him to pass the exams and take
the Jewish civic oath as a teacher.

Insanity plagued the unfortunate Beer family; Sophia's absent father, Abraham, was admitted to the municipal lunatic asylum and his
brother was designated his guardian. Abraham died within three
months. His epitaph in the community memorial book sums up
fifty-five years of torment: "Blessed be his memory, who suffered
great agony for many years." Desperately poor, Abraham left more
debts than capital, and to protect themselves from further losses, his
wife and daughter refused the inheritance, which was later auctioned.

In 1834, when Löb Joachim had finally passed his teaching exams,
he began working at the Philantropin. That same year, he and Sophia
applied for a marriage license, but now they faced the toughest of all
obstacles—the marriage quota. Only twelve Jewish couples were allowed to marry each year, since the Frankfurt city council wished to
curb the growth of the Jewish community, and, by rule, a man could
not even apply to marry before the age of twenty-five. Fortunately,
Löb met this initial qualification, since by that time he was already
twenty-nine.

At this major milestone in Löb's life, while he was waiting to see
whether he and his bride would be allowed to marry that year, he
submitted a request to the city council—he wanted to change his
name from Löb to the more Germanized Leopold. Happily, the request was approved, and the couple was also granted a license to
marry. The wedding took place on July 8, 1834, after which Sophia
joined Leopold at his father's house. But the salary of a full-time

English teacher at the Philantropin was not enough to support them all, so Leopold also gave private lessons in German, English, French, history and geography.

Leopold and Sophia's first son, Arnold, was born on March 15, 1835, and their second, Julius, on September 30, 1836. Even though they had moved away from orthodoxy, Reform Jews like Leopold Beer still circumcised their newborn sons, and as each boy approached his thirteenth birthday he was taught to recite his Torah portion in Hebrew for his bar mitzvah ceremony.

Both boys attended the Philantropin, but despite their educational training and religious upbringing, Arnold and Julius were the first in the long history of their family dynasty to deny any outward signs of their Jewishness—they did not cover their heads with skullcaps, they abandoned the dietary laws, and they chose not to observe the Sabbath. Unlike the Sassoons, who cherished the Promised Land and saw it as their spiritual centre, the Beers, as members of the Reform Movement, regarded the land of their birth as their only fatherland.

When Arnold, and then Julius, turned fourteen, Leopold made the decision to enroll them in a non-Jewish high school, the Frankfurt Municipal Gymnasium, in order to widen their academic prospects. According to the laws that were in effect at that time, Jews could attend universities but not teach in them; similarly, they could study law but not practice it. Although Arnold was a gifted writer and was drawn to the theatre, he chose to pursue medicine, a profession that Jews were actually permitted to practice. He studied at the University of Wurzburg, then in Vienna, and in Berlin he became the assistant of the celebrated Professor Rudolph Virchow, the pioneer of social medicine, anthropology and pathology, who was the first person to diagnose leukemia.

Julius was more commercially inclined than his brother and went into business instead of attending university. He could easily have thrived in the Frankfurt banking scene—in a city of only sixty thousand inhabitants there were nearly three hundred banks, many of them belonging to Jewish families, and the city stock exchange, teeming with activity, was one of the first places where Jews had established equal footing with Gentiles. But, instead, Julius Beer boldly chose to try his luck in England.

Frankfurt had always been the European centre for the distribution of English goods, and residents there generally admired all things British. By the 1830s, at least fifteen Jewish firms in the city were importing English textiles, and some had their own agents in Britain. Jewish Frankfurt was also bustling with news of the success of the London branch of the Rothschilds' bank. The city was "the Bank for the whole world," said Nathan Mayer Rothschild, who was sent to England in 1798. The first Rothschild had gone over to London without knowing a word of English and had succeeded. Julius had the advantage of a good command of the language and, at least in that respect, could expect a much smoother start.

CHAPTER NINE

A German in London

Though he certainly wished to become one of the titans of the financial world, Julius Beer did not opt for London just for its economic prospects. Much had changed for Jews in Germany since the days of Beer Löb Isaak zur Kanne—they had gained civil rights, reformed their religion and customs, and now had the opportunity to obtain a complete German education. But though they felt German, they remained culturally and socially isolated within their own country. Like other ambitious young Jews, Julius did not want to remain a pariah in his hostile homeland. England was perceived as welcoming and friendly to foreigners, and he could not but envy the freedom his co-religionists enjoyed there.

At that time, Germans were the largest immigrant group in England: 28,644, according to the census of 1861. However, Heinrich Dorgeel, author of *The German Colony in London* (1881), estimated that the figure was considerably higher. Most of the Jews who fled Germany, generally poor and uneducated, headed for the United States. The several thousand who immigrated to Britain were of a different stock—most, like Julius, were secularly educated members of the middle class who had capital and commercial experience. With their broader cultural outlook, they were better equipped to make their way into the ranks of the British middle class.

Julius would discover, though, that while freedom was on offer in

London, success was not guaranteed. He did not cross the Channel to take just any job for the sake of survival; he had set his sights much higher. But this ambitious young man did not have a commanding patriarch like Mayer Amschel Rothschild or David Sassoon to send him abroad, well provided, to open a branch of the family business. The Beer family wealth had almost vanished, and Julius's father was certainly no Croesus. All Julius had was his education and the desire to emulate and surpass the past glory of his ancestors, the court bankers. He kept his eyes fixed on their dazzling careers as the model that he would follow.

Julius arrived in London as soon as he finished high school, and he was only eighteen when he rented an office in Angel's Court, one minute's walk from the London Stock Exchange. Most of the other offices in his building were occupied by fellow stockbrokers. Distant relatives, the Frankfurt banking firm Speyer-Ellissen, gave him the foothold he needed in the financial world. Fast-rising American railway companies depended on foreign investments to finance the laying of more and more track, and they turned to the Frankfurt Stock Exchange to attract investors. The Speyer-Ellissen bank, which specialised in American securities, provided Julius with some stocks and bonds to sell in London.

But the young Beer appears to have started off on the wrong foot; in March 1855, soon after his arrival, he advertised in *The Times* that two New York and Erie Railway convertible bonds, worth one thousand dollars each, had either been stolen from him or lost. He warned all persons to be cautious against "receiving or negotiating the same, and any information respecting will be thankfully received." It's unclear whether the bonds—numbers 1165 and 1835—were ever retrieved; in any case, this early mishap did little to impair Julius's reputation, and bankers continued to require his services.

Though he had no family in London, Julius was not alone in the city—two of his friends, Louis Floersheim and Louis Schott, had settled there as well. In Frankfurt, the Floersheims specialised in English haberdashery and hardware, while the Schotts dealt in English tulle and lace. Together, the three young men would become business partners in various successful enterprises. And, in addition to cooperating professionally, they would remain close friends, sharing triumphs and tragedies as the years passed.

In the early 1860s, after residing in London for the minimum required period of four years, Floersheim and Schott applied for naturalization, stating that for their social and mercantile position they were "desirous to become citizens of the adopted country," which they had found receptive to their boundless energy and zeal for enterprise. For whatever reason, Julius Beer did not apply with them. He may have been unqualified on account of the frequent and lengthy business trips he had begun to take, which caused him to be absent from the country for longer than the maximum permitted period. But even in later years, when he spent all of his time in England building his business empire and raising his family, Julius never applied for British citizenship, though he would certainly have been granted it. Unlike S. D. Sassoon, who already in India was almost an Englishman and in London was a loyal subject with the aura of a raja, Julius Beer considered himself a German living in Britain, not British.

Indeed, as relieved as he was to have escaped the restrictions of his homeland, Julius did not sever his ties to all things German; he remained much attached to the cultural and social habits of his home country. Like many of his fellow expatriates, he joined German-speaking clubs and institutions, and in the summer of 1866, he followed with great concern the news from the battlefields of the Austro-Prussian War, which ended with a Prussian victory that exacted a heavy toll of dead and wounded. He was one of the two principal donors to the charity for "the Wounded Soldiers of the German and Bohemian Battlefields," the money for which was collected from German immigrants in England and sent back to Berlin.

Julius suffered no hostility as a result of these activities. He was fortunate to have arrived during a period of goodwill toward Germany, which had never been at war with Britain. Queen Victoria sprang from the German House of Hanover, and Her Majesty's children had a German father; "thus the reigning family [was] more German than English." Meanwhile, the influx of German-speaking Jews sparked the imagination of many English writers. Victorian novelists like Anthony Trollope and George Eliot—followed later by twentieth-century writers like Somerset Maugham, Agatha Christie, Rebecca West and Angus Wilson—depicted Jewish protagonists from Frankfurt, mostly financiers, or mentioned Frankfurt in their writing. Trollope's greedy Jewish hero of the novel *Nina Balatka* married his Christian lover, dreaming of a life where his people "did not live immured in a Jews' quarter, like lepers, separate and alone in some loathed corner of a city otherwise clean." Frankfurt's morbid ghetto stood in sharp contrast to the fairy-tale ascent to prosperity of German Jews in Britain, fascinating contemporary authors.

TAKING A NATIVE-BORN spouse is a well-known step to achieving smooth integration into a new society. Julius's friend Louis Floersheim was thirty-five years old when he married the twenty-year-old daughter of a late lieutenant colonel of the Royal Artillery; it was quite uncommon for a girl of the British officer class to marry a foreigner. Taking a non-Jewish, British bride would have been out of the question for a Sassoon man of the same generation, but like his friend Floersheim, Julius Beer suffered from no such constraints.

Julius's bride was burdened with the weight of not one, but two unusual biblical first names—Thyrza Keren-Happuch. In the Old Testament, Thyrza was the assertive daughter of Zelophehad, and Keren-Happuch was the beautiful offspring of Job, but although hers were Hebrew names, Julius's bride was not a Jew. His mother, Sophia, who was steadfastly Jewish and still living in Frankfurt, tolerated her son's marriage to Thyrza, and chose not to cut ties with him, despite the fact that he was the first member of his family to marry out of the faith. While still in Frankfurt, Julius had shied away from orthodoxy, and his move to England had accelerated the process of his secularisation; religion, Jewish or otherwise, had become meaningless to him. Though he stopped short of the baptismal font, he never set foot in a synagogue again, and when the couple's first son was born, on July 8, 1858, Julius took yet another step away from his heritage. He did not select from the reservoir of the Beers' traditional names, such as Isaak or Löb, but named his son Frederick Arthur.

Like her namesake, Byron's Thyrza, the heroine of his 1811 elegy who remains unidentified to this day, Julius Beer's wife is an enigma. There is almost no existing documentation of her life. According to the 1871 census, she was born in 1836 in Plymouth, Devonshire; however, her birth was not registered, an omission that is frustrating but not unusual, since only in 1874 did it become compulsory for English parents to register the births of their children. Yet another vital document missing from Thyrza's records is the registry of her marriage to Julius. Registration of marriage had been mandatory since 1837, so the lack of a certificate may indicate that the two married abroad; however, the certificate does not exist in the municipality files in Frankfurt either. Indeed, there are no records there at all about Julius Beer's life after he left for England.

In his writings, Siegfried Sassoon reflects on rumours he heard about Thyrza when he was a young boy. His mother, Theresa, who had never met her and was relying entirely on hearsay, told Siegfried that his poor uncle Frederick had a "bad heredity." "None of us had any notion what a heredity was. Apparently, it was something to do with his mother having been an opera singer," wrote Siegfried. Some of Siegfried Sassoon's biographers go so far as to suggest that Thyrza Beer led a life of scandalous promiscuity, cuckolding her husband and bearing him an illegitimate son—Frederick—whom she infected with syphilis.

No medical record has been found to confirm the rumour that Thyrza was syphilitic or that Frederick Beer ever suffered from that disease. The portrayal of Thyrza as an opera singer is equally undocumented. And Julius Beer's love and loyalty for his son are all too evident from his will, in which he left his entire fortune to Frederick, casting severe doubt on any claims that he was illegitimate.

. . .

WHILE THE SPEYER-ELLISSENS helped Julius gain his first financial foothold in London, the Erlanger family was his springboard to wealth. Raphael von Erlanger had worked for the House of Rothschild in Frankfurt, but he left to establish his own bank, initiating what would be a long rivalry between the two institutions. Raphael's son Emile, who was Julius Beer's senior by four years, joined the Erlanger bank as an associate at the age of seventeen. A visionary financier, he travelled to Egypt in 1854 with the entrepreneur Ferdinand de Lesseps, who was then mapping the route for the Suez Canal. Four years later, he was sent to France to establish the Paris branch of the family bank—Erlanger et Cie—which was involved in railroad and government bonds, becoming friendly with the French emperor, Louis Napoleon, while he was there. It would be on another continent— and amid another conflict—that, with a little help from Emile, Julius Beer's career would be established.

A YEAR INTO the brutal American Civil War, the Confederacy was in dire need of funds for purchasing war supplies from Europe. Expecting the South to triumph, Emile Erlanger proposed a huge loan. At that time, Julius Beer was dividing his time between London and Paris, and Erlanger sent him as part of a delegation to Richmond, Virginia, to finalize the details of the contract.

In late November 1862, Beer and two French associates disembarked in New York and took the train to Washington. From there, as described by the historian Ella Lonn in *Foreigners in the Confederacy,* "They secured a pass to Richmond without difficulty, for they were not recognised as representatives of the famous banking house." The proposed loan was much larger than the Confederacy could ever pay back, and Judah P. Benjamin, the Secretary of State for the Confederacy, complained that "the terms were so onerous that we could not assent to them." To help grease the deal, Beer offered Edward Carrington Elmore, the treasurer for the Confederacy, a job with Erlanger et Cie at three times his salary. Elmore declined the thinly disguised bribe.

After a laborious period of haggling, during which the amount of the loan was reduced from five million pounds to three, the Confederacy accepted the conditions, trusting that Erlanger's open door to Louis Napoleon would help them garner some much-needed political recognition. In addition, the purchase of the bonds by the European financial community—the Confederacy hoped—would serve as an incentive for European governments to support the South. Judah P. Benjamin secretly signed the contract on January 28, 1863, along with the three visitors from France. Beer and his colleagues kept a low profile throughout their long stay in America, and an announcement of the deal was made only once they were safely back in Paris.

At the beginning of March, Erlanger and Beer travelled to London to arrange and supervise the distribution of the bonds. On each note was the picture of an allegorical Southern woman, holding the Confederate flag while leaning on cotton bales and watching a ship on the far horizon. Symbolically, she was waiting for the blockade to end and the export of cotton to resume. In addition to earning the bearer 7 percent interest, a bond of £500 was equivalent to 20,000 pounds of cotton, which was redeemable upon request. The bonds were issued in Liverpool, Paris, Amsterdam and Frankfurt, but it was in London that the heaviest buying took place. Several of the leading Tories and noblemen purchased the cotton bonds, hoping for the speedy collapse of the United States. Others, who were sure of the South's victory, simply saw the bonds as an opportunity to acquire marketable cotton at bargain rates.

Ironically, the American Civil War and the cotton crisis placed S. D. Sassoon and Julius Beer on opposite sides of the fence. The Sassoons supported the North, while Beer was on the side of the South. Either way, both men ended up pocketing hefty profits—the Sassoons from the export of Indian cotton, and Julius from his commission from the Erlangers. The deal gave the Rothschilds an opportunity to denigrate Erlanger for supporting slaveholders, pointing out that he had converted to Christianity, but Erlanger received a massive £400,000 for the transaction, out of which Julius Beer was rewarded generously. The bondholders did not fare quite as well—with the defeat of the South the bonds were not honoured and were worth no more than the paper they were printed on.

CHAPTER TEN

A Girdle Round the Earth

With the American Civil War over, Julius could settle permanently in London. On December 30, 1866, Ada Louisa Sophia Beer was born, adding greatly to Julius's happiness. He had good
reason to believe his fortune would keep snowballing—he soon bank-
rolled part of the £200,000 capital needed for the construction of the
North Wales Birkenhead and Liverpool Railway, and he became the
main proprietor of the Hayling Railways in southern England. He
was also involved in the first Spanish tramway to be built in Madrid.
In February 1868, at the age of thirty-one, he opened his own banking firm, Beer & Co.

Julius did not turn his back on those who had helped him get this
far—his associates were his old friends Floersheim and Schott, and
the bank acted in London on behalf of the Erlangers in Paris and in
Frankfurt. The two businesses collaborated on various ambitious
ventures in transportation and telegraphy, and they established the
Public Works Construction Company, which built and maintained
railways, tramways, canals, waterworks, mining operations, gas-
works and telegraph lines around the globe. Creating a passenger
route from Brazil to Bolivia via the Madeira and Mamore rivers
was one of their grandiose projects. It involved digging canals and
constructing railways around falls and rapids, and setting up steam
navigation on the rivers. The project ran into physical and financial

difficulties and a heavy loss of lives, but by then Julius Beer was no longer involved. After taking his 10 percent commission for the loan of $500,000 he had arranged, he left the project.

Having conquered the Americas, Julius decided it was time to set his sights elsewhere on the globe. Lord Redesdale, an expert on Japanese affairs, found himself besieged by "many gentlemen with names absolutely unknown to me—many of them German" upon his resignation from the Foreign Office and return to London. These investors were anxious to make Redesdale's acquaintance, and "one gentleman, Mr. Julius Beer, ran [him] to earth in [his] club." The Japanese government wished to build the first railway between Shimbashi and Yokohama and was seeking investors in London; Julius was naturally intrigued. After cornering the diplomat, he bombarded him with questions: "Was it safe to lend Japan money? Was she solvent?" "Well," Lord Redesdale recalled, "I was able to reassure my cross-examiner upon that point." Using the information he gathered from Lord Redesdale, Julius and Emile agreed to grant Japan a one-million-pound loan, at an astounding rate of 12 percent interest.

Having learned the lesson that retired diplomats could be a useful source of inside information and connections, Julius began pursuing such individuals ardently. Sir Henry Lytton Bulwer, the former British ambassador to Constantinople, could not sustain his expensive lifestyle on his salary and allowances alone, and he was willing to cooperate with Julius in speculative deals. "The Turkish Government have voted for the points that we were obliged to insist upon," Beer informed Bulwer, thanking him for his "valuable advice." Julius was quick to express his sympathy when a great fire broke out in Constantinople in June 1870, consuming three thousand homes and taking the lives of nine hundred people, and was a major donor to the relief fund.

A seasoned traveller, Julius took a keen interest in the comforts of travelling—for personal as well as business reasons. Until 1873 there were no sleeping cars in the British railway network, and businessmen complained that they were always arriving at their destinations very late in the evening or early in the morning, having slept only a few hours, "and were barely awake for their appointments." Julius Beer was one of the financiers who imported six luxurious Pullman sleeping cars from Detroit for the Midland Railway Company. A guest of honour in the demonstration drive from London to Bedford, he and the other dignitaries who were present took pleasure in the Utrecht velvet, walnut, ebony and gold decorations, and the chairs "capable of being rotated on a pivot and of being inclined backwards at any angle."

The idea of owning a hotel chain also greatly appealed to the traveller in Julius, a frequent visitor to Paris, the Cote d'Azur and the Swiss Alps. He bought shares in the London & Paris Hotel Company, which proposed to run luxury hotels in the two capitals, en route, and in other select locations. The hotels would combine "the solid comforts of English life with the elegance and variety of French living," and they would offer the traveller a fixed tariff of charges, payable in either pounds or francs. The association ended badly—in court—but Julius's claim against the company was decided in his favour.

WITH THE GREAT success of Germans in general and Jews in particular—they formed a fifth of all the great City firms and half of the members of the London Stock Exchange—resentment inevitably began to develop. There was much anger toward those "Hebrew millionaires and plodding Germans who are the incarnation of the art of making money." Prince Edward, the Prince of Wales, supported his extravagant lifestyle with funding from German-born bankers as well as money from the Sassoons, and he was ridiculed for his strong German-Jewish accent—"I wonder where he got it?" pondered a contemporary aristocrat, only to answer, "Perhaps from his creditors."

Rising nouveaux riches who invested in ambitious railway projects, like Julius Beer, were provoking envy and suspicion, and this attitude was reflected in the literature of the time. One of Anthony

Trollope's protagonists, Augustus Melmotte (*The Way We Live Now*), was a railway baron—a swindler and imposter who floated shares of a proposed railway from Salt Lake City to Vera Cruz. Though Melmotte's ethnicity wasn't identified, the author hinted that he was a foreigner and a Jew, who was married to a woman from Frankfurt but "had declared of himself that he had been born in England and that he was an Englishman." In *That Boy of Norcott,* meanwhile, author Charles Lever complained that Europe had fallen into the hands of a few unofficial dynasties like the Nathanheimers—a loosely veiled reference to Nathan Rothschild—who "controlled the fate of nations with a word." Some novels cast a cloud of doubt over the immigrants' loyalty: "they speak English with hardly a trace of foreign accent, and they assimilate and turn themselves into perfect and complete Englishmen—still they are 'alien corn.'" Many held the opinion that, wherever he is, a German Jew will always remain a German.

Julius seemed to take no note of these growing biases; he had his eyes fixed firmly on the horizon, on the next great technological advancement. Endless miles of land were still waiting to be covered with railway tracks, but when Samuel Morse first tested his eponymous communication system in 1838, and the message of "a patient waiter is no loser" crossed three miles, human interaction was transformed forever.

Messages were able to cross great distances with the electrical impulses generated by the machine—first overland and then, in 1851, across the seabed, through a submarine cable from Calais to Dover. The discovery of gutta-percha, the latex of a tree that grew in South Asia, led to the invention of insulated copper cables that could be laid on ocean beds, immune to corrosion, and soon messages could be passed from continent to continent. Julius was eager to ride the wave of this new technological marvel.

Like the Speyer-Ellissens and Erlanger before him, John Pender would become a lifelong mentor, innovator and business partner for Julius Beer. Funded by money brought into their marriage by his second wife, Manchester cotton merchant Pender became one of the first telegraph entrepreneurs. His Anglo-American Telegraph Company laid the first transatlantic cables on the bottom of the Atlantic, two thousand miles between Valentia Island on the southwest coast of Ireland and Trinity Bay in Newfoundland. Julius became a director in many of the telegraph companies that were chaired by Pender, joining the ranks of other famous entrepreneurs such as Baron Julius de Reuters, the American financier Cyrus W. Field, Captain James Anderson and William Siemens. The Sassoons also joined the telegraph craze, which remained highly speculative. Some who invested in the new technology died in poverty or lost more than they gained, but Julius Beer grew from strength to strength.

The lesson that Britain had learned from the Indian Mutiny was that a direct, instantaneous link to all its colonies was crucial for the safety of the empire. Britain ruled submarine telegraphy—it had the upper hand in the manufacturing of cables; it had wealthy entrepreneurs with the capital to invest in the manufacture and installation of these cables; and it had a vast community of customers who would prosper from global communications. The investors also benefited from the common belief that, to prevent political friction, the construction and operation of international telegraphy should be left to private companies, not governments.

Sir Charles Bright, the renowned electrical engineer, counted Julius Beer as one of the commercial pioneers of ocean telegraphy, "prominent in the financing of these important schemes," and his American counterpart Cyrus Field complimented Beer for being "always ready to furnish means for the legitimate extension of submarine telegraphy." With Beer's money and directorship, cables were laid from Malta to Alexandria, from Singapore to China and Japan, and from Portugal to Brazil. To limit the risk, different companies were founded for partial legs of the way and were later amalgamated under one umbrella. The Eastern Telegraph Company was the world's largest, with John Pender as chairman and Julius Beer and Emile Erlanger as directors. Willoughby Smith, the electrical engineer who developed the insulated submarine cable, said that Julius Beer seldom appeared outside the boardroom, and, paraphrasing Alexander Pope, he wrote that "in fact his work was seemingly done by stealth, and no doubt he would have blushed to find it fame."

From a hesitant start in 1852, with just 30 miles of underwater cables, by 1886 130,000 miles of cables crisscrossed the globe, the gift of Mother Science. "How marvellous she is—this Electra!—this new Angel of Messenger of the Human Race!" wrote *The Daily Telegraph,* breaking into poetry in its praise of the new era and its wondrous form of communication. "Are we not, as Aladdin was, holding a magic lamp lightened by an invisible fire, rubbing a ring which we use without comprehending its might?"

In the pre-telegraph era, it took three weeks for a letter to cross the Atlantic and back. Now a person could send a message to the United States and get a reply within the hour. Messages were transmitted at seventeen words per minute, and, because the number of messages had increased twentyfold, the cost was reduced from 20 pounds sterling per message, to four shillings per word. Newspapers, relying on the receipt of news from abroad, were among the major beneficiaries of the new technology.

The inauguration of direct telegraphic communications from Falmouth to Bombay, a major project in which Julius was involved, was celebrated at John Pender's mansion in June 1870. The display of "scientific mockery against human limits" began when the Prince of Wales sent a cable of congratulation to Lord Mayo, the Viceroy of India, receiving an answer in four minutes. His Royal Highness then dropped in electrically upon His Majesty of Portugal, the Khedive of Egypt, and the American president Ulysses S. Grant. During the party, he touched all four corners of the earth with the "metallic whisper" of the telegraph machine. All present felt "the little planet strangely compact and small," or in the words of *The Observer,* "London spans the ocean, and puts a girdle round the earth." The exchange of greetings was printed out by an electrical siphon recorder, the precursor of the modern inkjet printer, in its maiden appearance in England. Then "the Spirit of the Wire was allowed to sleep—only to enter this day into the service of humanity, a willing, wonderful, beautiful and beneficial slave."

This was a pivotal moment in the life of the Victorians—"We are, in truth, on the threshold of new times, when time itself, as we have hitherto understood it, is telegraphed out of existence," wrote *The Daily Telegraph*. The new invention was perceived as the magic wand that could be used to settle international disputes by arbitration instead of the sword. "The cable nipped the evil of misunderstanding leading to war in the bud," rejoiced John Pender. Other advantages were clearly evident—to the financial markets, to the press and even "Mrs. Jones [who] may know for a shilling that Jones is going to bring a friend to dinner." But by the end of the century, a sense of disillusionment would creep in as well—the rapidity of communicating through telegraphy could sometimes undermine sober thinking.

JULIUS BEER WAS enjoying the fruits of his hard labour; in September 1868, he moved into 23 Park Crescent, on the opulent southeast side of Regent's Park. The house had been designed by the famous John Nash, and one of the previous tenants was Joseph Bonaparte, the eldest brother of Napoleon and the ex-king of Naples and Spain. Located just half a mile from the Sassoons, the Beers' mansion was stucco-faced, with a wine cellar in the basement and a substantial attic. It had a glass roof, and the windows of the first-floor living room opened onto a promenade balcony, making it airy and bright. The Beer family bedrooms were on the second floor, in a chain of rooms, each one opening onto the next. Folding oak doors led to the spacious billiards room. And to top off the extravagant effect, the entrance hall was paved with mosaic tiles, arranged in a classical pattern. The £350 annual rent also included a double coach house and a five-stall stable situated in the mews behind the house.

A year after taking up residency there, Julius and Thyrza had both their children baptised in the Holy Trinity Church on Marylebone Road. It took place on December 30, Ada's third birthday, when

Frederick was eleven. The late christening indicates that Julius was in no hurry and that religion and ceremonies did not matter overly much to him, but choosing the Anglican creed was one more step away from his ancestors' faith and the final move toward making England their home, affirming the children's integration.

Just over a decade after he left Frankfurt, Julius Beer could proudly stand in line with his ancestors. Like them he was a "court financier," though not of dukes and princes but of governments. The financial scope of his ancestors had been limited to their localities; Julius had outdone them with his world-embracing enterprises.

But it was his next undertaking, though it would not prove profitable, that would save him from obscurity.

CHAPTER ELEVEN

170 Strand

Money was a powerful tool for breaking down the barriers of the class system, but achieving those ends was easier for S. D. Sassoon than it was for Julius Beer. Regardless of the fact that they traded in opium, the Sassoons were esteemed international merchants; Julius Beer's past was in the Frankfurt ghetto, and in London he was a nouveau riche who had made his money in the stock exchange. As a result, all that he accomplished carried the opprobrium of speculation. But while the Sassoons cared deeply about being accepted members of British society—receiving (and issuing) desirable invitations and appearing in society columns in newspapers—Julius was indifferent to how he was perceived. He made choices based on profitability, not appearances, and he would never attain the level of respectability and acceptance that was enjoyed by the Sassoons. Even so, he was to make one particular business move that would boost his reputation.

At the beginning of 1870, *The Observer* and the plant where it was printed were bought by a "group of gentlemen interested in finance," for a bargain price of £3,500. The most notable member of the group was the thirty-four-year-old Julius Beer, who would soon become the newspaper's sole proprietor. For the next three decades, the oldest Sunday newspaper would remain in his family.

• • •

UNTIL THE LATTER half of the eighteenth century, there were no Sunday newspapers in England. The 1677 Sunday Observance Act forbade all labour on the Lord's Day, exempting only works of charity or of necessity. No products except for milk were sold, and even that could only be sold before nine o'clock in the morning and after four in the afternoon. In 1698, William III added a further exception to Charles II's act: mackerel too could be sold before and after divine service.

These government-imposed strictures were not the only reason that there were no Sunday newspapers—the seven-day newspaper was never a tradition in England as it was in France and the United States. The few attempts to print Sunday editions of the dailies had all failed; "So we have our extensive and peculiar Sunday press," quipped Alfred P. Wadsworth, economic historian and editor of *The Manchester Guardian.*

The first Sunday newspaper in England, the *British Gazette and Sunday Monitor,* was a family affair, launched on March 26, 1780, by Mrs. Elizabeth Johnson, who had a printing business in Ludgate Hill. The only debt she paid to the holy day of worship was a twelve-line religious instruction column on the front page, and the four pages of four columns each were designed for those who had neither the money nor the leisure time for a daily paper. It caught on immediately. After ten years, Mrs. Johnson could boast of a circulation of 4,000 copies, at a time when the average sale of a London morning newspaper was 1,500 copies per day.

Smelling a profit, other entrepreneurs followed suit; one of them was W. S. Bourne. Expecting to reap "a rapid fortune," he borrowed one hundred pounds sterling and launched *The Observer* on December 4, 1791, anticipating that Christmas advertisements and sales would help him turn an immediate profit. In line with the paper's name, its logo of an all-seeing eye symbolised its self-imposed duty to observe society and politics. A looped ribbon bore the words "Sunday Advertiser." Seven months later, the ancient emblem was adorned with the Latin motto *Nunquam Dormio* ("Never Sleeping") flanked by the classical goddesses of Justice and Liberty. In November 1793, the eye was dropped altogether.

Bourne, who had worked for the post office in London, had some literary ability but no business skills. To attract the maximum possible readership, he traded in sensational gossip and crime stories, paying special attention to rapes, abductions, rick fires (fires in stacks of hay or straw) and stagecoach accidents. Content of this sort seemed a rather puzzling choice for a paper that vowed to "conduce to the happiness of society." Bourne soon found himself up to his eyes in debt, and his brother, who was the head of the family stagecoach business in Limerick, came to his rescue by covering his losses. By the end of the eighteenth century, the newspaper's circulation climbed to 6,000, with most of the copies sold within the confines of London, though a special Monday edition was also printed for the countryside. With businesses closed on Sunday, the proprietors used "horn boys"—lads wearing caps with the name of the paper emblazoned on them—to sell their wares "by the aid of shrill voice and trumpets—to the disturbance of the whole neighbourhood."

All of this was a thorn in the side of Lord Belgrave, who drafted the Sunday Newspaper Suppression Bill that was debated in the House of Commons in May 1799. The success of The Observer, he said, was a weapon of infidels "to deter Christians from a decent observance of the Lord's Day." He called for the enforcement of the still-existing Sunday Observance Act and an increase in the penalty for violations from five shillings to forty. He also demanded that any violation would lead to confiscation of the copies in the street, and that vendors would be brought before a magistrate who would have the power to confine them for up to fourteen days.

The bill was opposed by the Irish playwright and MP Richard Brinsley Sheridan, who argued that "there was an exception in favour of selling mackerel on the Lord's Day; but might not the people think stale news as bad as stale mackerel?" William Windham, the Secretary of War, objected to the comparison since "readers of Sunday weekly papers seldom expected fresh news in them; besides, news were not necessary to a man's well-being as food was." The bill was voted down but the selling of Sunday newspapers still remained an offense. Today, out of the nine Sundays available at the time, only *The Observer* survives, making it the oldest extant Sunday newspaper in England. Its seniority and colorful history lent it an appeal that proprietors could not resist, and though it has been passed from hand to hand like a baton in a relay race, it has never ceased to run to this day.

THE PRESS MAGNATE William Innell Clement bought *The Observer* in 1814, just over half a century before the Beers would take the helm, and—with his editor and manager, Lewis Doxat—turned it into an influential publication. They increased the editorial staff and paid their writers handsomely, engaging the very best theatrical and literary critics of the day; they also enlarged the format, used better-quality paper and introduced other important innovations. Clement and Doxat were the pioneers of pictorial journalism, using copperplate engravings to illustrate reports of crimes and royal events. In February 1820, the police exposed a plot to assassinate the entire cabinet and overthrow the government; *The Observer*'s illustrations reconstructed the subsequent raid on Cato Street. The paper also took a stand on the issue of freedom of the press when it published reports from the court proceedings before all of the eleven defendants in that same case were sentenced. Clement "demurred to the bottling up of news until it had become stale," making himself liable to a fine of five hundred pounds, but the fine was never enforced.

Most of the paper's columns were printed on Friday night, and the rest were wrapped up as late as four or five o'clock on Sunday morning. Occasionally a private train was hired to deliver crime reporters from assignments in the countryside so that they could meet their tight deadlines. The paper's chief reporter, Vincent Dowling, was provided with a special boat to rush him back from France after he was granted an exclusive with the exiled Queen Caroline, whose husband, King George IV, had attempted to divorce her.

In February 1821, a new and fierce rival emerged—*The New Observer*. This competitor not only traded on *The Observer*'s title, but it also adopted as its own the emblem of the all-seeing human eye. In October 1822, it was renamed the *Sunday Times*. Seven decades later, both papers would be owned and edited by the Beer family, though they would ostensibly maintain the long-running competition between the two.

On average, each issue of *The Observer* would sell about 15,000 copies at the time, while a successful daily sold a maximum of 3,000 copies. War, state funerals, first-degree murder, and large and important public pageants or ceremonies were a sure recipe to boost any newspaper's sales. And indeed *The Observer* had record sales—of 61,500 copies—in July 1821, when it reported on the coronation of George IV, including four illustrations. The issue was sold at double the regular price. The paper went on to adopt a new masthead—the lion and the unicorn fighting for the crown—and enraged its competitors by stating that it was "patronised by her majesty and all the royal family." The Royal Arms remained *The Observer*'s masthead until 1989.

These were good times for journalism. Following the French Revolution, which had shaken the old established order in Europe, a middle class had evolved, and newspapers provided this group with access to information that had previously been denied them; information that only the aristocracy had routinely enjoyed and exploited. Gradually, as they "gained corresponding influence and power, they turned to the press to keep themselves informed," writes *The Observer* historian Professor Alfred Gollin. Not only the merchants and manufacturers but also their clerks and servants were hungry for news.

The government recognised the influence the newspapers had over public opinion and sought to suppress them by levying heavy stamp duties on every copy. Newspapers became dear and, at the price of seven pence, which equaled a labourer's daily wage or the price of a pound of meat, many could not afford them. One solution people developed was to pool their money on Sunday to buy a shared copy. Only on their day of rest did they have the time to read a newspaper, and those who could not read could "listen to one being read out loud in alley houses and barber shops." But while one arm of the government, the Treasury, tried to milk newspapers for all they were worth, another arm, the Home Office, actually poured money into them. Since newspapers held such sway over the masses, it stood to reason that they could be powerful tools as well as dangerous enemies. From 1816 to 1840, *The Observer* accepted "monies from the government in return for supporting their points of view."

With the death of Clement in 1852 and the retirement of his editor and manager Lewis Doxat five years later, *The Observer* lost circulation and diminished in importance. The next editor was Joseph Snowe, Doxat's assistant, whose unpopular support of the North during the American Civil War caused a further decline in readership. He was replaced by *his* assistant, Mr. M'Dermont, but the newcomer was not able to reverse the downward trend. Sales now did not exceed 3,000 copies a week. What followed, of course, was a drop in advertising revenue. It's no wonder, then, that the Clement family was inclined to get rid of the paper—though the abolition of the duty on newspapers in 1861 allowed for a drop in price and an increase in circulation, *The Observer* had become more of a burden than a boon.

Twenty years earlier, *The Observer* had been valued at more than twenty thousand pounds, but Julius Beer and his associates bought it for a mere fraction of that. In May 1870, Julius offered the editorship to his friend Edward Dicey. The entrepreneur and the journalist had struck up a relationship some years before; Dicey, who had studied at Heidelberg, was an expert on foreign affairs and a widely travelled correspondent, and Julius had consulted with him on some of his overseas investments. Though they differed on the issue of the American Civil War—Julius's interests lay with the South, while Dicey supported the North—they were both critical of Gladstone's foreign policy.

Dicey had recently resigned from *The Daily News* after only four months as editor, following fierce disagreements with the owner. *The Observer*'s circulation was much smaller, but he accepted Beer's offer outright and filled the office of editor for the next nineteen years. He would constantly remind his staff that *The Observer* was not a weekly paper, but a daily one that just happened to come out on only one day in the week, bringing the latest news of Saturday.

Julius Beer did not buy *The Observer* as "a rich-man's toy," nor did he set out to become a press magnate. He declined to join the press circles and took little interest in their professional and social activities; his new title of newspaper proprietor was not meant to open doors into the higher echelons of Victorian society. He was also very well aware that the annual proceeds from the paper fell short of any one of his many business ventures. But as one of his contemporaries, Thomas Hay Sweet Escott, the editor of *The Fortnightly Review*, said, Beer was "a man of much intellectual subtlety and keen interest in foreign affairs." Escott also went on to praise his colleague Dicey for making *The Observer* "a well-informed critic of the less-known diplomatic movements." The newspaper was a passion for Julius—it spoke to his fascination with the world around him.

Ever practical, Julius also intended for the newspaper to help with his world-embracing enterprises—to be a platform for promoting favourable foreign policies. A typical example was when *The Observer* called for the annexation of Egypt to the British Empire; Beer and Dicey clearly had their own interests in mind in supporting this move, as both were investors with Credit Foncier Egyptien. "The great Julius Beer," the London *World* wrote of him in September 1879, "who cannot only make the Egyptian market dance to his tune, but who keeps a newspaper and a very able editor to aid him in doing it."

AS A SPONSOR of railway and telegraphy enterprises, Julius was well aware of their revolutionary potential for the press. Before the advent of submarine cable, news travelled by steamers that sailed on alternate Wednesdays from New York and Boston and made the passage to England in some ten days, arriving late on Saturday or early on Sunday, "and thus the most stirring news of the gigantic conflict between North and South, was communicated in the first instance to the British public in the morning issues of *The Observer* or in its special editions." The telegraph increased the reach of the press—now news from the United States or any other part of the world could be transmitted almost instantly, giving international news an immediacy that it had previously lacked. The world was becoming smaller.

In the pre-telegraph days, an editor could go to bed with a clear conscience, confident that the last post was in and "nothing could happen to mar the ingenious speculations which he had contributed to his journal for the next morning," recalled George Washburn Smalley, the *New York Tribune* correspondent to London at the time. But now that telegrams were coming in all day long, an urgent, game-changing dispatch might arrive after the editorial had gone to press and the editor to bed—one that would turn his editorial into nonsense.

BEER AND DICEY focused on continental news—in particular, the enmity between France and Germany. In a special noon edition on September 4, 1870, *The Observer* was the first to announce the capture of the Emperor Napoleon III and the capitulation of Sedan. As Bismarck's army was closing in on Paris, Dicey, sensing the unfolding drama, decided to send an eminent writer there who could convey the human tragedy. He offered the war correspondent assignment to his friend, the librettist W. S. Gilbert, who left immediately for Paris.

Fittingly, Gilbert's dispatches, sent by post, read more like letters to a friend than a journalistic account. On the train from Calais to Paris, Gilbert shared a compartment with four "very noisy Frenchmen of the small bourgeois type," who kept him awake all night— "They felt some curiosity to know what business could take an Englishman to Paris in such a time." The French did not believe him to be a journalist, and pointed at the luggage tag that carried his full name, William Schwenck Gilbert. To abate their suspicions that he might be a Prussian spy, he handed them one of his newly minted visiting cards. As Gilbert himself wrote:

> But, as it turned out, this step was particularly unfortunate, for one of them, who spoke a little English, remarked, *"Mais, 'Observer,' Monsieur, sela veut dire 'Espion,' n'est ce pas?"* I was forced to admit that the word might be so translated, but I explained that it happened to be the name of the newspaper I represented, and corroborated this statement by producing a copy of your last week's impression. This evidence, coupled with the argument that a professional Prussian spy would scarcely advertise his calling on his visiting cards, appeared to reassure them, and we parted at Paris on very friendly terms. However, you will not be surprised to hear that I decline to publish the name of your newspaper on my visiting cards during my present stay in Paris.

On Sunday, September 11, 1870, Dicey published three successive unedited reports by Gilbert. With the Prussian army less than forty miles away from the City of Light, Gilbert felt sorry for the Parisians, who seemed completely unprepared for the invasion—"The French are crouching like criminals in a condemned cell, waiting for reprieve, or for the confirmation of their doom." He went on to describe how some desperate Parisians were prepared to commit mass suicide, rather than see their city occupied:

> It is said that the catacombs are stored with thousands of barrels of petroleum, which will be exploded if the Prussians enter Paris. The cellars of the Hotel de Ville are filled with gunpowder— the Louvre is also undermined, and arrangements have been made by which petroleum is to be forced by hydraulic pressure

through the gas mains of the city. The wells are to be poisoned, the bakers have been supplied with strychnine, with which they are to charge their bread *à discretion*.

After ten days in the besieged city, Dicey telegraphed Gilbert an urgent message—to hurry home. Under Prussian occupation, his war correspondent would hardly be able to dispatch new reports anyhow. Dicey's handling of the coverage of the Franco-German War earned the paper unprecedented sales.

Dicey realised that the newspaper "stood in sore need of reorganisation," and to upgrade his cadre of writers he approached his friend, the composer Arthur Sullivan, and offered him the post of music critic. He told Sullivan that "the public might appreciate a more independent tone of musical criticism, than was then in vogue." Sullivan's first assignment was at the gala of Fabio Campana's new opera *Esmeralda*, in Covent Garden:

The whole work sounds like caricature of a modern Italian opera, in which the mannerism and absurd conventionalisms of this popular school are exaggerated to a degree nothing short of ludicrous . . . and from beginning to end, there is not one bar of melody, or passage of harmony which betrays original thoughts, either in conception or treatment.

Dicey was surprised by Sullivan's harsh judgment, which "formed a marked contrast to the wishy-washy eulogistic notices which appeared in most of our contemporaries," but, nevertheless, he sent the review to press. Though it was unsigned, as was customary at the time, Sullivan's style was unmistakable. Within a few days, both proprietor and editor were threatened that if they continued publishing such reviews, advertisements for musical performances would be canceled. Dicey was faced with a dilemma, and as he wrote in his *Recollections of Arthur Sullivan*:

I had to consider other people's interests, as well as my own, and I came at once to the conclusion that—to put the matter plainly—the game was not worth the candle. It was, as I held, no part of my duty as an editor to elevate the tone of musical criticism, and I entertained grave doubts as to whether there was a sufficient public interested in musical notices to increase our circulation to such an extent as would have compensated us for the money lost accruing from the withdrawal of operatic and concert advertisements.

He had no alternative but to discharge Sullivan. Much to his relief, the composer assured him that he had already been questioning whether it was prudent for him to criticise in print members of his own profession. It was probably the one and only review that Sullivan ever wrote for the press. Thankfully, the incident did nothing to mar Dicey's lifelong friendship with the operatic duo Gilbert and Sullivan.

The Observer not only needed a new music critic, but a new drama one as well. One Saturday night, exhausted after submitting his theatre review to the *Weekly Dispatch,* the drama critic Clement Scott went to the Arundel Club to get some supper, smoke a pipe and enjoy a chat. It was two o'clock in the morning when Dicey rushed in and approached his table: "I'm so glad I found you," he said. "I'm in a bit of difficulty, and I think you can help me out of it if you will." He told Scott that his drama critic had failed to turn up at the theatre, and there was not one word about the important new play; would he come down to the office, late as it was, and write just a few lines? "You can be back at the club in half an hour," Dicey assured him.

"I saw my opportunity and grabbed it," remembered Scott. Instead of a few lines, he submitted a column and a half at lightning speed; the following morning he was offered the post of drama critic, "one of the plums of the profession." For two years, he wrote reviews for *The Observer,* "and another on the same subject and in a different style for the *Daily Dispatch* on Monday morning." In addition to the double bill, Scott also wrote for *The Daily Telegraph*, for Julius enjoyed a close friendship and business partnership with the paper's proprietor, Lionel (Levy) Lawson, and also employed Lawson's other star writers, George Augustus Sala and Frank Lawley. When the burden of his threefold commitment became too heavy, Scott bowed out, recommending Ernest Bendall as his successor.

Beer and Dicey were of a completely different calibre from their predecessors. Much effort was put into stressing their independent point of view and overcoming the former image, formed under Clement, of *The Observer* as a mouthpiece for the government; still, it was a hard image to shed. On May 30, 1871, after ten weeks of unsuccessful workers' uprising, Karl Marx read his fifty-page manifesto "The Civil War in France" to the General Council of the International in London. He celebrated the Paris proletariat "as the glorious harbingers of the new society," and the press went into a frenzy—the German was depicted as a ruffian and a threat to British and world stability. Of all the newspapers that attacked him, Marx was especially agitated that "the government paper—*The Observer*—is threatening me with prosecution—let them dare! I laugh at these scoundrels!"

The pair made a good team. Julius monitored the newspaper from his business office in the City, trusting Dicey completely and giving him a free hand. *The Observer* journalist John St. Loe Strachey, later the editor of the *Spectator* for thirty-eight years, reconstructed the atmosphere at 170 Strand: "There was a sort of easy-going, old-fashioned, early-Victorian air about *The Observer* Office of those days which was very pleasant. Nobody appeared to be in a hurry, and one was given almost complete freedom as to the way in which to treat one's subject."

They all appreciated Dicey's shrewd, brief hints—gems such as "never write for the mere sake of writing." "Another of his characteristic maxims was, 'If you are not sure, leave it out,'" recalled Ernest Bendall. His staff considered him to be "the most helpful editor whom any beginner ever had, and the most considerate in his light but firm control of a more mature contributor. Essentially a man of the world, and more worlds than one, he was always to be relied upon for a detached, level-headed view."

Subscribers in the countryside needed to visit the railway station to pick up their copy of *The Observer,* which was sent early Sunday morning by the first train leaving London. Readers in Paris could buy it on Sunday afternoon in a kiosk in the Boulevard des Capuchins. In times of war, *The Observer* published a second edition in the early afternoon, to include "important intelligence being received from abroad."

Orange-colored contents bills accompanied every special issue to prevent vendors from selling a regular edition of the paper under the pretense that it was a special one. It is believed that the record sale was on Sunday, November 26, 1871, when a special update was issued on the grave illness of the Prince of Wales. At 11:25 that morning, Sandringham doctors issued an encouraging medical bulletin, and by 2:30 p.m., *The Observer*'s street vendors already cried out that His Royal Highness "has passed upon the whole a quiet night."

In spite of a long history of antagonism toward *The Observer,* the *Quarterly Review* credited Beer and Dicey for producing the best Sunday newspaper, "an admirably conducted newspaper of the highest character . . . the tone of its articles is dignified and sensible. The principles are those of moderate Liberalism, and the editor has the wisdom to refrain from those coarse imputations, evil motives, and dishonest purpose to his opponents." But though *The Observer* was gaining prestige, the same could not be said of profits. Transforming the paper into a high-class political journal cost Julius in circulation, and while in the early days of the newspaper it sold more copies than any daily, by the time Dicey had put his changes into full effect they were selling a trifling few thousand, compared to the tens of thousands a daily could manage.

Elsewhere, though, everything that Julius touched seemed to turn to gold. His telegraph cables and railway tracks were stretching out to embrace the globe, and he had joined other capitalists and leading

European bankers to found the London Banking Association. "The excitement of the city was the very breath of his nostrils," marvelled one of his contemporaries. Beer's ability to make a fortune while other men were only thinking about it was credited to "all the genius of his race for finance."

CHAPTER TWELVE

Five Funerals

Savoring his success, Julius Beer had more time to pursue personal enjoyments and spend time with his family. Just like S. D. Sassoon, he joined the Royal Geographical Society, which promoted expeditions to uncharted lands; not merely a pleasurable pastime for Julius, it also opened up new business opportunities. And as a member of the Royal Botanic Society, he enjoyed weekend strolls with Thyrza and their children in the experimental garden in Regent's Park. The beautiful grounds were right next to their home, and they revelled in the palm houses and the water lily house.

But overhanging the family's bliss was a dark shadow cast by little Ada's delicate health. For long periods of time, Ada had to be kept isolated from the outside world, her only companion Nellie Ganz, the daughter of a German-born neighbour. But as her early years passed, Julius and Thyrza began to take hope—in the second half of the nineteenth century, child mortality rates were at their highest from birth up until the age of five, and children were thought to be out of the danger zone after they were ten.

When his father died in Frankfurt in May 1873, Julius promptly invited his mother to come over to England. Whatever reservations Sophia Beer may have had about her son marrying out of the faith and having his two children baptised, she settled willingly enough into 11 Devonshire Place, the house Julius rented for her, which was close to his own.

The winter of 1874 was a remarkably severe one, and a day after Christmas, just before her eighth birthday, Ada's fever soared, her throat became sore and swollen, and a red rash erupted all over her body. Her doctor pronounced a terrible diagnosis—scarlet fever. This most infectious and dreaded disease was, according to Dr. Charles West, the pioneer of British pediatrics, "so deadly, that medicine is unable to stay its course even for a moment, and then it destroys life in a few days, sometimes even in a few hours." The chances of recovery were so poor and the disease so widespread that three out of five children who were infected would die, and even those who survived were seriously impaired. That year the virulent epidemic swept through England, and countless children fell ill. Good nutrition and strict hygiene provided some protection from this atrocious disease, but even so, well-to-do children who were infected died from it as often as the most deprived did.

Ada had been struck with the more virulent form of the disease— anginose scarlet fever. There was almost nothing that the doctor and nurses could do besides making her rest and fighting to keep her temperature down to prevent convulsions. On Tuesday, January 5, 1875, after eleven days of agony, she succumbed to the illness; one of the last victims of the year's epidemic, which claimed twenty-six thousand young lives. The highest death rate was in London, and especially in Marylebone, the Beers' neighbourhood.

The grief-stricken Julius decided to have his daughter buried in the most fashionable necropolis for people of his social standing, the western section of Highgate Cemetery. The funeral took place on the following Saturday, and Ada Louisa Sophia was put to rest in the Terrace Catacombs, which were above and behind the Lebanon Circle. The eighty-yard-long gallery had 840 individual recesses from floor to ceiling, lining both sides of the building. Ada's lead coffin was placed in recess number thirteen, shut behind a small glass pane.

Julius was not content with the common vaults, however, and assisted by the managers of the cemetery, he looked for a finer resting place for his beloved daughter. Among other showpiece sites, he was brought to the spectacular Egyptian Avenue. Guarded by a pair of obelisks, the monumental gateway resembled a large Pharaonic arch. On either side stood a pair of columns decorated with closed lotus buds. The gateway led into a "Valley of the Kings"—a row of stone chambers, eight on each side, locked with heavy metal doors. The unique feature of the chambers was that the entrance was at ground level, thus avoiding the eeriness of having to descend into a cellar. Impressed by what he had seen, Julius paid £137 for family vault number four.

On December 23, 1875, Ada's casket was removed from the Terrace Catacombs and placed on one of the brick shelves of the family vault, which had room for twelve coffins. "Over the years, the dead have slept in undisturbed and gloomy splendour, awaiting the next turn of the key in the rusting lock, the shaft of light that will briefly penetrate the darkness, and the arrival of yet another member of the family, to take his or her ordained place on the shelves," wrote the cemetery historian Felix Barker. For the bereaved, a vault gave a sense of continuity, some consolation in the thought that it was a place of family reunion.

But still Julius was not content. On his numerous visits to the cemetery, he continued to look for a place and a monument that could reflect the depths of his sorrow. He spotted a plot of ground on a splendid peak, just above the Lebanon Circle, not far from Egyptian Avenue and an aged cedar tree. Upon purchasing it for £800 in July 1876, he approached the office of Sir George Scott, who had recently completed the Albert Memorial; the renowned veteran architect was suffering from ill health and his sons had taken on his work. John Oldrid Scott designed for Julius a Portland stone and marble mausoleum, which to this day is probably the largest private memorial in London. Fifty feet high, with a pyramidal roof that was carved to appear tiled, the dome was lit through patterned stained-glass windows and topped with a cross. The interior of the mausoleum was fashioned in quattrocento style; the blue and gold mosaics were brought from Italy and laid by Giulio Salviati, who had also worked on the Albert Memorial. The floor was a black and white marble inlay with incised floral decorations, and the iron gates were made by Messrs. Farmer and Brindley. The bill for the entire work amounted to £5,000—the price of a luxurious London house at the time.

Sir Nikolaus Pevsner, the renowned historian of art and architecture, praised the mausoleum as "the only strikingly spectacular monument" in the entire cemetery. Writing in 1951, he went on to describe the pyramidal roof as "à la Halicarnassus," which led to the belief that Julius Beer had set out to imitate one of the Seven Wonders of the World—King Mausolus's tomb in Asia Minor, located in what, today, is the city of Bodrum in Turkey. The fourth-century B.C. monument, which stood 140 feet tall, was reduced to ruins by an earthquake and the Crusaders. It was graphically reconstructed on paper 150 years later based on short historical descriptions. However, when *The Builder,* the leading architectural journal of Victorian England, described the Beer mausoleum based on information supplied by the architect, it did not refer to any sort of Halicarnassian influence.

In *The Builder*'s sketch of the mausoleum, taken from the architect's files, the cornice above the doorway carries the inscription "Mausoleum of the Family of Jules Beer." In the actual building, it was eventually shortened to "Mausoleum of Julius Beer." Julius thought of adding a motto in Latin, but changed his mind at the last moment.

As much as the builders were urged to finish the work in time for the third anniversary of Ada's death, they were a month late. Family and friends gathered again on February 20, 1878, when Ada's coffin was removed once more and taken to her final resting place in a sarcophagus in the lower part of the back of the mausoleum, concealed from the public eye.

But the work was not yet complete in Julius's eyes, and another artist was summoned—Henry Hugh Armstead. He too had worked on the Albert Memorial, making eighty-four life-sized figures in marble for the podium of the Prince Consort's memorial, as well as four bronze statues. Armstead sketched several scenes of a woman and a little girl for the statue Julius had commissioned. In one of them, the mother, her reddish hair collected behind her head, clasps her hands in prayer, as if she is waiting beside her sick child's bed. In another version, the kneeling mother embraces her daughter, one hand resting on the child's shoulder, the other wrapped around her waist; this time the child is the one immersed in prayer. The design Armstead and the Beers ultimately chose shows an angel embracing the praying little girl. Her eyes are closed and her head reclined. Armstead named his work "memorial to an only daughter." The carving took much longer than was estimated, and it was only in 1880 that the marble relief was moved into an arch-shaped niche in the mausoleum.

Julius was free to erect this enormous and extravagant monument to his daughter because the cemetery had no planning regulations. The mausoleum became a source of admiration, envy and emulation. A year later, when Henry Enderby Eaton died, his father, the first Baron Cheylesmore, erected a memorial—though smaller and more restrained—just a few yards away from the Beers' burial site.

The Victorians believed that cemeteries were places "wherein a few hours may be profitably spent." On weekends, men put on their tall hats, women donned their crinoline dresses, and they went strolling down the wide, winding paths of Highgate Cemetery. The landscaped garden rose in terraces and, as the contemporary writer Edward Slack rejoiced, "the air was beautifully clear, the sun shone brightly, birds carolled and the sky was like that of Italy." Visitors admired the variety of flowers, majestic trees and shrubbery surrounding the monumental marble structures. The graveyard sculptures presented an outdoor museum, and encountering celebrity names and reading the poignant epitaphs became a rather macabre sort of entertainment. Once visitors climbed up to the Terrace, they were treated to a panoramic view of London, with the dome of St. Paul's and the snaking Thames in the horizon; though the vista was somewhat blocked by the soaring Beer mausoleum.

After Ada's death, Julius became the main benefactor of a charity for the orphans of the German community in London, and of the East London Hospital for Children. He bequeathed a lifetime annuity of fifty pounds to his daughter's sickbed companion, little Nellie Ganz.

The loss of Ada took a heavy toll on the Beer family. Though the lease for 23 Park Crescent was in force until 1889, Julius and Thyrza felt unable to face life in the house where their daughter had died. They moved just around the corner, to Portland Place, the widest street in London, whose houses were designed by leading neoclassical architects Robert and James Adam in the late eighteenth century, and had undergone further transformation by John Nash. The magnificent number 27 was much larger and more opulent than its neighbours, and it had retained more original details than any other house in the street, such as the interior decorations based on the painted wall murals that Robert Adam had documented in Pompeii.

An ardent collector of art, Julius amassed an array of masterpieces, the most precious being Millais's *The Carpenter's Shop (Christ in the House of His Parents),* which he bought just after Ada's death. This controversial painting was first exhibited in 1850 at the Royal Academy. Upon its unveiling, Charles Dickens was shocked by Millais's realism, which made the Holy Family look wretched and monstrous: Mary with a distended throat, "so horrible in her ugliness," Joseph with dirty toenails, Saint Anne with swollen hands, and Jesus as a "hideous, wry-necked, blubbering red-headed boy." Dickens warned future viewers to prepare themselves "for the lowest depth of what is mean, odious, repulsive and revolting." At Queen Victoria's request, the painting was brought to Windsor Castle for her inspection. *Blackwood's Magazine* had "great difficulty in believing a report that this unpleasing and atrociously affected picture has found a purchaser at a high price."

Julius apparently did not share the common public opinion of the painting. He saw something else when he looked at it—the devoted family of a wounded child, whose kneeling mother waits upon him with loving sympathy while his father holds his hand and tenderly inspects the injury. This reverence for the image of parental love in the face of adversity can also be seen in the cycle of seven watercolor paintings inspired by Shakespeare's *A Winter's Tale* that Julius commissioned from the Frankfurt painter Leopold Bode. The miraculous reunion of the parents with their lost daughter Perdita—whom they had believed to be dead—was a consolation for the grieving Julius and Thyrza. "We hope the London public may be permitted to gain a glance at them before they are finally settled in their place," wrote *The Academy* of the paintings.

THOUGH THE MAUSOLEUM took much of his time and energy, Julius continued to expand his business. He moved *The Observer* to new and extensive premises in 396 The Strand, and installed fast rotary printing machines, which enabled the staff to go to press at four-thirty a.m., later than any other Sunday paper. However, those upgrades had no effect on circulation figures, which remained around 3,000 copies, compared to 250,000 of *The Daily Telegraph* and 60,000 of *The Times*.

In May 1878, Julius purchased and revived *The Electrician,* a weekly journal of theoretical and applied electricity and chemical physics. He entrusted the editorship to Charles Biggs, who was grateful that Julius "never sought to influence the free opinion and conclusions of those whom he had placed at the helm of one of his smallest literary ventures." *The Electrician* gave detailed accounts of the latest inventions and discoveries in electricity and telegraphy, enabling entrepreneurs like Julius himself to keep their fingers on the pulse of the advances in technology. The advertisements in the journal reflected the Victorians' fascination with gadgets and technology—there were ads for a "telephone-alarm," "the best battery for intense currents," "electric burglar detectors" and "the sphinx patent key-ring and puzzle."

In late August of that year, just before Frederick was about to start university, Julius took him on a walking tour of the Swiss Alps. They were joined by Julius's brother, Dr. Arnold Beer, John Pender, and a friend of Frederick's. The intimate outing was to become an international incident, reported at large by major British, Swiss and American newspapers.

In Julius Beer's account of the story, his party of five arrived in the late afternoon at the Rigi Kulm Hotel, not far from the town of Davos, intending to watch the sunrise from the summit of the mountain. Frederick asked for four or five bedrooms and was told that there were only two rooms available, with five beds between them. Julius stepped in and asked for at least one additional bedroom. He had only uttered half a dozen words in German when he "was interrupted by the landlord, who shouted out, 'Get away with you; be off,' and added a number of offensive epithets." Arnold tried to intervene, but the hotelier jumped from his seat, struck Julius on the face, seized his walking stick and broke it in two. At that moment, "a gang of luggage porters, who were standing about the hall, made a most brutal attack upon the rest of the party." One of the porters grabbed Frederick's head under his left arm and hammered away at his face with his right fist.

Bleeding, half stunned, and with injuries on their heads and elsewhere, the tourists retreated to the next village. Julius telegraphed a letter of complaint to *The Times*, and the hotel skirmish became a news event as more reports arrived from the Alps. One group of British tourists expressed their indignation in a letter to *The Times*, after hearing of the event from "the two senior members of the party, one a German gentleman long resident in London [Julius Beer], the other a member of the House of Commons [John Pender]."

Julius and the hotelier filed complaints against each other at the police station; the hotelier countered Julius's claims, saying that Julius had been the aggressor. He went on to say that Mr. Beer had held a fist in his face and shouted, "We are newspaper editors and members of parliament, and we will teach you. We will put you into the newspapers." Frederick had punched him in the chest, exclaiming, "I will kill you." Then Arnold had drawn a revolver, and "Julius Beer struck me with the white metalled handle of his stick on the head, across the nose, and on my right hand."

The truth of the competing stories was never resolved. While the society journal *The World* painted Beer's group as the villains of the tale, ridiculing Julius ("the Portland Place pet") and John Pender ("Cable Jack") as a pair who "are ready to make a match to fight any two men of their age and weight," *The Saturday Review* was more favourable toward the tourists. The latter publication claimed the event would go down as "famous in the annals of hotel-keeping," and it advised tourists to Switzerland to take precautions against short-tempered landlords by adding knuckle-dusters (brass knuckles) or perhaps revolvers to the essential travel gear of thick boots, glycerin and an ash Alpenstock. Beer's account is supported by the American writer Mark Twain, who also climbed the Rigi Mountain that very August, and stayed in the hotel. He complained that "the crusty portier and the crusty clerks gave us the surly reception."

Upon the father and son's return, the family nest was emptied when Frederick left for Magdalene College, Cambridge, to study mathematics and classics. Dr. Arnold Beer, Julius's older brother, extended his visits to London, making their mother's house his permanent address. For a time, Dr. Beer had been conducting parallel careers, as a physician specialising in syphilis and a playwright. Eventually, he chose the stage, and began travelling frequently between London and Paris. All of his six plays were classical tragedies that failed to provide him with a livelihood. Never married, he was generously supported by Julius, who put forty thousand pounds sterling for him in a trust.

IN JANUARY 1880, just after the fifth anniversary of Ada's death, Julius, who had been "out of health for some months," took time off from his numerous business ventures. He travelled alone to his favourite resort of Menton, on the French Riviera, where he rented a villa, intending to enjoy the warm weather until the summer. On Saturday, February 28, he went for a drive with his London friends, the banker James Matthews and his unmarried daughter Victoria, who was Julius's age. At dinner that night, he seemed in good health; the next day he was seized with a sudden—fatal—attack of apoplexy. It is unclear whether it was his brain or heart that failed him. He was forty-three years old.

Since Julius's daughter Ada had been baptised, there were no obstacles to burying her in the consecrated ground at Highgate. But Julius's case was different. No evidence was found that he had ever converted to Christianity, in his daughter's lifetime or afterward, and the archive of Highgate Cemetery holds no record that Julius ever presented a certificate of his baptism. But since the cemetery was a private commercial enterprise, and a hefty profit was involved, it appears that no embarrassing questions were asked. His body was transported to London, and on March 8, 1880, he was laid to rest in the sarcophagus next to his beloved daughter.

His death came as a shock, since, although he had gone to France to recuperate, "no immediate anxiety was entertained by his friends," as *The Observer* reported. In his obituary, Edward Dicey lauded Julius's great vigour of intellect and the clarity of his judgment, adding that "of the numerous enterprises in which Mr. Beer took a prominent part, there was none in which he felt a keener personal interest than in the prosperity and influence of *The Observer*." The Mercantile Bank of the River Plate lamented the death of their associate, "whose untiring energy and resources were repeatedly of great value to the bank, and whose counsel were always to the greatest advantage."

According to the *Dictionary of Business Biography*, a minimal estate of £100,000 was the criterion for the deceased to be recognised as a prominent Victorian entrepreneur. Julius Beer left four times as much. Unlike S. D. Sassoon, who endowed his family with a spiritual legacy and made moral demands on their future conduct, Julius was much more liberal in his bequests and he did not set any conditions for his family to meet; his only stated wish was that they take good care of the mausoleum. If he ever had any doubts as to his wife's fidelity or his son's legitimacy, his will, written three months before his death, certainly does not provide any indication of them.

Frederick was the main beneficiary of his father's estate. Like S.D., Julius did not expect his son to continue his projects, which had been tailored to his own interests and abilities. Frederick received an annuity of £1,000 and inherited Julius's railway and telegraph stocks and shares, but he was not awarded an executive role in any of his father's businesses. The luxurious hotel Julius owned in Richmond—Castle Hotel—was sold, but Frederick decided to keep *The Observer* and *The Electrician,* including the buildings that housed the two operations.

Julius made sure that his family would be able to maintain the luxurious lifestyle to which they were accustomed. His wife, Thyrza, received an annuity of £3,000 and was allowed the first choice of any objects she desired from their mansion, as well as "all the hair jewels and personal ornaments and property which belonged to our dear daughter Ada, and [her] photographs and pictures and busts of her." Sophia, Julius's mother, was given the leasehold of her London residence, an annuity of £2,000 and her choice from the remaining items. His brother, Arnold Beer, received a lifetime annuity of £1,000 and any books he desired from Julius's rich library. And to each of his ten closest friends, among them Louis Floersheim and Louis Schott, Julius bequeathed £50 to purchase some mementos from his house. He was also very generous with his employees, granting each of them a year or two of salary.

The remainder of Julius Beer's estate was to be invested in stocks and securities and kept in a trust for Frederick, the income from which was to be paid to him and his future wife and children. None of Julius's relatives in Germany were mentioned in the will, nor were any members of his wife's family in England.

Dr. Arnold Beer was disconsolate over the sudden loss of his beloved, only brother. He returned to Paris, and on July 13, 1880, he died in his room at the Grand Hotel on the Boulevard des Capucines. The cause of his death was pneumonia. Just four months after Julius's death, the dwindling family members once again walked up the hill leading to the Beer mausoleum.

That month Thyrza and Frederick vacated 27 Portland Place, which was auctioned off along with the stables and sold for £12,550. Mother and son remained in the classy Regent's Park area, moving to 9 Cambridge Gate.

Five months later, on Christmas Day, Sophia Beer, Frederick's grandmother, suffered a heart attack and passed away at the age of seventy-one. Her daughter-in-law and grandson honoured her final wish to be transported back to Frankfurt and buried next to her husband in the Jewish cemetery there.

Just six weeks had passed since this latest loss when, on February 10, 1881, Thyrza Beer died at age forty-three. Apoplexy caused by cerebral congestion was the cause of death. She was the fourth member of her family to be laid to rest in the Beer mausoleum.

CHAPTER THIRTEEN

The Marriage Market

Meanwhile, after forty years in India, the Sassoon family had shifted their centre of operations to England. In 1872, five years after S.D.'s death, his brother Abdullah Sassoon was knighted for his services to the empire, becoming Sir Albert. He relocated to London, where he joined his brothers Reuben and Arthur, who had already made the move. His wife Hannah, who was pious and retiring, chose not to join him. Only one brother, Solomon, would remain in charge of the firm in Bombay.

The London Sassoons did not display the energy or discipline necessary to maintain the stranglehold they once held over certain markets and enterprises. They were no longer fingers clenched together into a fist as they had been during their father's life; instead, they indulged in parties, gambling and horse racing, and spent little time in their offices. Their lax work habits did not seem to negatively affect their admittance into London society, however—quite the contrary. While in India they were merely accepted by the European community, they were courted by the high and mighty in England. "These nabobs, with their spicy flavour of the orient, were accepted with amused, if sometimes, malicious, tolerance by Society (no opprobrium attached to their profitable sideline in opium trade)," wrote Anthony Allfrey in *Edward VII and His Jewish Court*. Albert's and Reuben's sumptuous mansions were said to be among the most desirable London addresses, and they acquired additional country estates and houses in Brighton, where they lavishly entertained the rich and famous.

Edward, the Prince of Wales, undoubtedly their most prestigious guest, allowed them to support his extravagant and expensive tastes. Prince Edward relied upon Reuben's advice for investing in the stock exchange, and Reuben was the "Keeper of" the prince's "Privy Purse for Turf purposes." As members of the prince's close inner circle, the Sassoons stayed at Sandringham and Windsor Castle. Reuben accompanied the prince on his continental tours, and the two of them were often seen walking arm in arm. They did so with such frequency that eyebrows were raised when the prince was seen without his Jewish companion.

As much as they had ingratiated themselves with the English, the Sassoons still maintained their Eastern identity. They continued to use Judeo-Arabic in their family correspondence, addressing each other by their Iraqi names. The brothers remained observant Jews, and Reuben even built his own private synagogue in his London house, but they were no longer leaders of the Jewish community, as they had been in India.

For her part, Flora Sassoon disapproved of her brothers-in-law's lifestyle, and she and her children maintained their distance. While Albert, Reuben and Arthur continually sought amusements, on the rare occasions that Flora held parties at Ashley Park, they were fundraising events for the various charities she supported.

OVER THE YEARS, Rachel had grown into a strong and independent woman, and she and the equally self-possessed Flora began to clash over her future. For a young woman of Rachel's background, there was but one possible vocation—marriage. Though she was well provided for by her late father, matrimony was seen as the desired goal for her; spinsterhood would be a failure. Flora had married at the age of sixteen, but at twenty-three Rachel was still in no hurry, and at this point there were no favourable suitors in sight. Creative and erudite, she refused to settle for the sheltered but unchallenging existence of a society matron. She was determined to lead a purposeful life.

In January 1881, Rachel and her mother attended the ultimate Jewish society wedding—the marriage of Leopold, son of Lionel de Rothschild, the first Jewish member of Parliament, to Marie de Perugia. The bride's sister was Arthur Sassoon's wife. The couple's families were both so influential that the wedding marked the first time that the Prince of Wales ever attended a synagogue, where the ceremony took place. The prince also gave a toast to the young couple during the wedding breakfast, which was held at 2 Albert Gate, the home of Rachel's uncle Arthur. The event received full press coverage, and it was reported in *The Illustrated London News* that "the bride-cake weighed 180 lbs, and was adorned with orange blossoms and maidenhair ferns." Flora Sassoon was usually quite reserved about wealth and royalty, and she was quoted as calling the Rothschilds the "hairy-heeled ones"—someone of low breeding aspiring to belong to the nobility—but she no doubt wished a similar match for her daughter and an equally elaborate celebration.

Rachel's personal views on womanhood and marriage can be inferred from the columns she later wrote in the *Sunday Times*. She identified deeply with Dr. Sophia Kovaleskaya, a Russian mathematician who personified the "clever daughter"; women like Dr. Kovaleskaya believed they had duties of greater importance than matrimony and motherhood. The popular opinion of these women was that they did not want to marry, and most men did not view them as good prospective wives, turning instead to "the herd of geese who are driven yearly to the market, and who go cackling to meet their fate . . . the ones with 'good heads' are set apart to lead celibate lives, while those who are 'hard of understanding' are brought in the marriage market."

The modern concept of wifehood was, in Rachel's opinion, an impossible ideal that few women could realise. She wrote:

Few among women can be lover, mother, gourmet, saint, brilliant conversationalist, a good housekeeper, mistress, companion, and nurse all at the same time. Men expect too much. When polygamy was in vogue, a man risked his domestic happiness in compartments. If one partner of his fortunes proved a failure, he could try a second, third, or even twentieth spouse. But there was trouble by the heart even in those days. Nowadays, the only chance of repairing initial error is death or divorce. Perhaps, after all, the patriarchs did not have the best of it, for English wives have made England what it is, and their substitutes have yet to be discovered.

One of Rachel's male readers wrote to her, criticising "much of the young 'Modern Woman'—to say nothing of the elderly girl"—whose sole aim was to enter into a wealthy marriage at any cost. Spinsters were willing to work like galley slaves to achieve this goal and even to "change their religion at a moment's notice," he complained. A debate ensued when this letter was published, and Rachel singled out a response from an elderly spinster, who claimed that women had little option but to marry, since they did not have the education to obtain independent positions. The matrimonial system would only be perfected if women were the ones to choose their partners, the reader concluded. Rachel remarked sarcastically that with the giddy and inconsistent nature of men, they would continue flitting from flower to flower even after being chosen and secured.

When it came to the notion of marriage as a form of economic or social advancement, Rachel sided with Edith Lanchester. This daughter of an affluent architect held an honours degree in science from London University and was a member of the Social Democratic Federation. Edith fell in love with fellow activist James Sullivan, a railway clerk from a working-class family. The twenty-four-year-old Edith declared that she intended to move in with her lover and live in "a free union," since marriage destroyed women's independence. Her father blamed her decisions on her "over education" and was quick to summon a mental health specialist to examine her. After only thirty minutes with his patient, Dr. George Fielding Blandford declared her insane. His duty was to certify whether a person was contemplating suicide; he reached his verdict on Edith's health because he believed she was unable to see that her decision would mean utter ruin and social suicide.

Dr. Blandford left his report with Edith's family, and, as she prepared to leave for work, her father and three brothers pinned her arms to her sides with a rope and dragged her toward a blinds-down carriage, which took her to a private lunatic asylum. Under the pressure of colleagues and the press, Edith was reexamined three days later by the Commissioner in Lunacy, who found her perfectly sane, though somewhat foolish.

Upon Miss Lanchester's release in November 1895, Rachel wrote in her *Sunday Times* editorial that she personally found the woman's views of marriage interesting and important, but that the vast majority of the British "are not advanced thinkers, and are accustomed to resent any opinions which are more than five per cent ahead of their own." Rachel used this example in an impassioned article calling for the reform of the marriage laws. But what troubled her even more about Miss Lanchester's story was the lunacy doctor's abuse of power:

Miss Lanchester's stunned sense of propriety will have served a good end, if society learns that respectable mad doctors will not be allowed to imprison those from whom they differ in opinion. Reverse the case and see how it looks. Suppose a fine, young middle class man of twenty-four, announces to his parents and the world that, actuated by the noblest of motives, he rejects the idea of marriage, but is about to set up housekeeping with a girl of the artisan ranks. Would any doctor in England certify to his lunacy and pop him under lock and key with his hands tied? And yet, many well-to-do young men of twenty-four take the very same course Miss Lanchester proposes to take without any more serious stigma resting upon them than the reputation of gallantry.

Growing up without a father meant that Rachel was not subjected to the customary matchmaking efforts. Her mother was at a loss, fearing that her only daughter would be left on the shelf. To draw attention to Rachel and enhance her prospects, Flora commissioned a portrait from Archibald Stuart Wortley, a pupil of Sir John Everett Millais. In May 1882, *Miss Rachel Sassoon* was exhibited at the Grosvenor Gallery, which was fast becoming the rival of the Royal Academy, with other exhibitors including Millais, Whistler, Leighton, Burne-Jones and Holman Hunt. The twenty-four-year-old Rachel was dressed in dark green velvet, with "sweet oriental eyes and oriental skin, relieved against a many-colored medieval wallpaper," reported the *Sunday Times*.

Encouraged by this triumph, Flora decided to invite the family's old artistic acquaintances the Thornycrofts to Ashley Park so that she might arrange a further venture in the same vein. The two families had remained in contact in the twenty years since Mary Thornycroft had made busts of S.D. and Flora. Theresa Thornycroft, who was twenty-eight and still unmarried, accompanied her parents on the visit. She took a liking to Rachel, but was intimidated by the great dark eyes of Flora; when they turned upon her she felt "like a bottle of Batty's Nabob Pickles." The guests were invited for a weekend boating excursion, but Theresa asked to be excused.

Arrangements were made for Hamo Thornycroft, the most accomplished artist among his siblings, to sculpt the still-single Rachel for what amounted to a second Victorian upper-class personal advertisement. In November 1882, he began working on the statue. Most of the sittings took place in his London studio between January and February, and Rachel came as often as twice a week. He was working "fearfully hard" on the statue, sometimes until two in the morning. Rachel had decided to wear a modern silk sack-back dress that hugged her wasp-thin waist and featured a square, low-cut neckline that brought out her swanlike neck. Her wavy hair was arranged in a chignon, revealing her clear features and wide eyes. A snake-shaped bracelet wrapped itself around the top of her right arm and another clasped her left wrist. She was seated on a round piano stool, and she held the score of Beethoven's sonatas open on her knees to reflect her dedication to music. The statue was scaled to half her size.

During the long sessions in his studio, Hamo began to feel that Rachel was romantically interested in him, as he told his daughter Elfrida years later. To further that impression, he was invited to an exotic ball at Ashley Park, "which as it took place in the hothouse atmosphere, he could never stand: it 'put him off altogether.'" But it wasn't just the intensity of the Sassoons' home that made him unresponsive to Rachel—for many months he had been enchanted by another. Agatha Cox was just fourteen years old when they first met, and Hamo, twenty-eight at the time, confessed that he had "lost [his] heart to her entirely." Thomas Hardy thought that Agatha was the most beautiful woman in England, "on whom I thought when I wrote *Tess of the d'Urbervilles*." Her youth, beauty and decided views were too strong a force for Rachel to compete against.

Wary of the agnostic and radical Agatha, the Thornycrofts tried to distract their son's "mind in favour of someone of their own choosing," wrote his daughter, Elfrida Manning. "A rumour was spread that he was already 'bespoken'—although the identity of the lady in question was left unclear. One candidate was the beautiful Rachel Sassoon." Agatha was not unaware of Rachel's presence, and "could not forbear asking if music was 'a strong point' with Miss Sassoon? And her verdict on the statue when she saw it was that it was 'graceful, but her face is not pleasing.'"

On April 2, 1883, Hamo Thornycroft wrote in his diary, "Finished Sassoon statuette in clay"; a week later Rachel invited her mother and some relatives to the unveiling of the work. She began the day with Mary Gladstone, the prime minister's daughter, who—at thirty-five years old—was also unmarried and was described as being "late in finding herself." The two of them did a studios round in Holland Park, stopping at the homes of George Frederic Watts and Frederick Leighton, and taking tea with Edward Burne-Jones and his wife in his new garden studio.

Thornycroft's studio was overrun by people, "mostly ladies, many of them friends of the Sassoons, Semite types," he later reported to Agatha Cox. "These chattering swells, the old ladies, preferred to look at the works of art with thick veils down, I suppose out of extreme sense of propriety, out of fear or the wrath of jealousy of Aphrodite, whose statue a visitor may expect of course to see in a studio." He was pleased that Flora Sassoon "was most excited with pleasure at seeing her daughter's statue so much admired by her friends."

The plaster model of Rachel's statue, named *A Sonata of Beethoven,* was ready in time for the opening of the social season—the prime time of the teeming marriage market. The first major event of the season was the May exhibition at the Royal Academy, where Rachel's statue was unveiled. *The Observer* gave the piece a favourable review, saying, "He proves in his graceful statuette of Miss Sassoon how invaluable are the higher qualities of style even in a work of pure realism." The *Athenaeum* was more contentious: its critic found the head too big and the neck too long for a statuette. A year later, the statue, this time in white marble, was exhibited in the Grosvenor Gallery. After several decades with the Sassoon family, it changed hands, and was last auctioned by Sotheby's in London in April 2002, for £3,346.

As a means of distracting Hamo's attentions from his beloved, and as a lure for attracting suitors for Rachel, the artwork can only be described as a failure. In June 1883, Hamo and Agatha announced their engagement. One romantic liaison between a Thornycroft and a Sassoon had not come to fruition but, meanwhile, another was secretly budding.

WHEN THEY FIRST met, Theresa Thornycroft was eleven and Alfred Sassoon was a mere three-year-old child. Because of the age gap, it was decidedly not love at first sight, but twenty years later the eight-year age difference presented no barrier.

Alfred was a pampered son—despite having two of his own Stradivarius violins and the best teachers money could buy, he was too indolent to pursue a musical career, or any career, for that matter. After two years at Exeter College, Oxford, he stopped attending, choosing instead to embark on a Grand Tour of the Continent. When he reached Paris, he settled there, splashing his money around and courting no lesser figure than the actress Sarah Bernhardt, who was many years his senior. Returning home to England, he planned to continue living idly on his dead father's fortune.

It was while accompanying his sister Rachel to the Thornycrofts for a sitting at Hamo's studio that Alfred once again saw Theresa. Like all her siblings, she was an artist, and it was art that drew them together; Alfred soon enrolled at the Royal Academy to study sculpture. The fact that Theresa was a devout Christian who held ardent High Church beliefs seemed to Alfred a trifling matter, since he had distanced himself from Judaism by this time. As a be self-centred young man, the apple of his mother's eye and very accustomed to getting his own way, he did not foresee the inevitable turmoil such a match would cause.

In the first decades of the nineteenth century, conversion and intermarriage among wealthy Ashkenazi Jews was increasing. In 1839, Hannah, the daughter of Nathan Mayer Rothschild, who founded the English branch of the dynasty, wished to marry British politician Henry Fitzroy. Her mother adamantly objected, and if Hannah's father had been alive it is doubtful whether she would have even broached the subject. Her dowry was withheld and all of her relatives except for one brother chose not to attend the wedding ceremony; nevertheless, Hannah's mother escorted her to the church—though in an unadorned, plain carriage—and dropped her off in front of it. Over the years, two more Rothschild daughters married out of the faith. *The Jewish Chronicle* lamented, "If the flame seized on the cedars, how will fare the hyssop on the wall?" criticising the leniency of the Rothschilds, who put up with the transgressions of their children. The only open act of condemnation from within the family was the male relatives' absence from these marriage ceremonies. Being admonished in such a manner did not stop a fourth Rothschild, another Hannah, from marrying the fifth Earl of Rosebery.

Apostasy had been quite common among wealthy Sephardic Jews, but that was less than a century earlier. Not anymore. Wary of their families' response, Alfred and Theresa secretly married on January 30, 1884, in St. Mary Abbot's Church, Kensington, without representatives from either of their families. While the Thornycrofts eventually rejoiced in the marriage and accepted their Jewish son-in-law, Flora Sassoon could not contain her rage.

Theirs was the first wedding in her household, the seventh among the grandchildren of the patriarch David Sassoon; all but her son had found a Jewish spouse. Choosing to marry a Gentile was the ultimate desecration of S.D.'s will—he had expressly asked his children to marry their cousins, nieces or in-laws. Marrying outside the clan was undesirable; marrying outside the faith was intolerable, a blemish on the entire House of Sassoon. Flora perceived Alfred's act as insolent rebellion, a slap in the face, and in the eyes of her judgmental brothers-in-law it was a starkly obvious sign of her maternal failure.

Alfred's marriage was a test of Flora's familial authority, and she feared it would set a bad example for her other children. She had to establish some kind of deterrent, and she chose to punish her son fiercely. Her options were limited—Alfred was already twenty-two, and she could not withhold his father's inheritance. Her only weapon was to express her indignation vehemently and visibly, which was no less than what her family and her community expected of her.

Family lore has it that Flora rushed to the synagogue, cursing her son and all of his future offspring, then sat the ritual period of seven days of mourning for her "dead" son. But though this story has been passed through the generations, it is very doubtful that Flora stood in the synagogue and cursed Alfred for all to hear. She may have felt such bitterness in her heart, but she was probably too private and too proud to air her family's business so publicly. The likely source of the rumour is Theresa Sassoon, who had strong reasons to resent her mother-in-law.

Nevertheless, Flora Sassoon's rage was a force to behold. She forbade her other children from having any contact with Alfred. Her eldest son, Joseph, was timid and under her thumb; he dared not disobey her. But having been attracted to a Thornycroft herself, Rachel could understand why Alfred felt that religion was no obstacle. What's more, Rachel and Alfred were close siblings, and she and Theresa were already bosom friends. She was the only Sassoon who refused to sever her ties with the newlyweds. This first act of openly defying her mother would be a source of strength for her in the future.

Now all eyes turned to the twenty-eight-year-old Joseph. After earning his MA, he had returned to Ashley Park, spending much of his time in his father's library. An intellectual, he was an active member of the New Shakespeare Society, which set out to popularize the playwright by promoting readings and study groups, pointing out that "there are few better ways of spending three hours of a winter evening indoors or a summer afternoon on the grass." His uncles, Albert and Reuben, could not risk another scandal, and they acted preemptively, quickly finding Joseph a pious Jewish bride from a wealthy—though not Baghdadi—family.

The Sassoon brothers had first met Baron Horace de Gunzburg twenty years earlier, when his daughter Louise was just a toddler. Gunzburg had received his title for his services as a court Jew, and he owned his own banking house and shipping company in Russia, along with sugar refineries and gold mines. He was also the head of the Jewish community of St. Petersburg. The Sassoons reunited with the baron and his now ravishing daughter in May 1883, in Moscow, at the coronation of Tsar Alexander III, which was probably when they were inspired to make the match.

Nine months after his brother defied his late father's edict, the compliant Joseph travelled to St. Petersburg to meet his future bride and marry her. There was concern on both sides when he failed to arrive at the Gunzburgs' home at the appointed time, but he was eventually tracked down in Berlin. Joseph's unplanned detour always puzzled the family—did he get cold feet at the last minute? If so, he must have collected himself, because the wedding went forward as planned, conducted by the Chief Rabbi of St. Petersburg. Joseph's nuptials balanced the troubling news of the birth and Christian baptism of Michael, Alfred's first son.

While the senior Sassoons played matchmaker for Rachel's elder brother, no prearranged marriage was forced upon her. Sons in magnate families were responsible for preserving and multiplying the family wealth; less pressure was put on daughters, since they were not involved in the family business and were seldom heirs to large fortunes. It was also less critical for the daughters to find Jewish mates, since according to Jewish law their children would still be Jewish. In most cases of intermarriage in wealthy Victorian Jewish families, the partner marrying outside the faith was a woman.

Rachel had a horde of suitors but, enlightened and strong-minded, she rejected them all, always suspecting that they wanted her for her wealth. She was determined not to marry just for the sake of it; she would wed only if she found the right partner—one who wouldn't take away her independence.

It became clear to Flora and Rachel that they would have to leave Ashley Park to the newlyweds, Joseph and Louise. Flora chose to relocate to Brighton, where her mother-in-law and two of her husband's brothers had already bought houses. She also vacated her London house in Grosvenor Street. A bickering widow and her spinster daughter treading on each other's toes was a recipe for disaster, and Rachel decided that her only viable option for parting from her mother and doing something more worthwhile than waiting around for a husband was to become a nurse. She had, by then, abandoned her dream of making a career in music, and for a long time she had been contemplating rolling up her sleeves and doing more than the checkbook philan-thropy that was her uncles' style. In 1884 she took advantage of the timing of her mother's move to Brighton to pursue her plans.

Doing charitable work would not damage Rachel's chances in the marriage market, so her family did not object to her choice. Nursing, too, was seen as a perfectly respectable pastime for young women of class, owing in no small part to the work of "The Lady with the Lamp." "Before the days of Florence Nightingale, nursing, strange to say, was at its lowest ebb," Rachel later wrote. "It was left to a class of women of whom Dickens drew some lurid pictures which were singularly true to nature. 'We always engage them without any char-acter'; a well known doctor wrote, 'as no respectable person would undertake so disagreeable an office.'" Florence Nightingale, who rose to fame in the 1860s, was the one who showed that there was "nothing derogatory in nursing, but on the contrary, that it was one of the noblest works in which women could engage." Many ladies of wealth and culture answered Nightingale's call and trained as nurses. Hospital matron Miss Isla Stewart was proud that a housemaid was seated next to a baronet's daughter, "and all the gradations of rank between these two may be found at the same table."

Just a few months after Rachel began working as a nurse at the Brompton Hospital for Consumption and Diseases of the Chest, an-other sculptor, Signor Forcardi, was commissioned to commemorate the new phase in her life by making a terra-cotta bust of her in her official hospital costume; apparently, Mrs. Sassoon had not yet given up on her daughter's marriage prospects. Reporting on the statue in its column "Court and Fashion," *The European Mail* described Ra-chel as "a young lady of fortune."

On October 29, 1884, Mary Gladstone, the prime minister's daughter, wrote in her diary: "Visited Rachel Sassoon in the Con-sumptive Hospital." At the time, Rachel was living at Mills Thomas Lodging House at 59 Sloane Street, walking distance from the hospi-tal. Tuberculosis, the Great White Plague, had claimed the life of one in every five of the hospital's patients. The disease was incurable, and Brompton tended to over ten thousand patients a year.

Rachel had found her niche in the hospital. "No object could be more merciful or philanthropic than this—to nurse the sick and suffering back to life and health," she wrote. "In the treatment of the sick, as much depends upon the nurse as on the doctor—sometimes more." It was a draining and perilous enterprise, but her position at Brompton gave her the chance to effect palpable improvements there—a heady experience for a young woman who had only just escaped her family. Rachel did not fear confronting her superiors, despite her status as a mere junior nurse. She was horrified to see that the infected patients' "sputum, instead of being burnt, was poured into the lavatory waste-pipe, causing the probable dissemination of noxious germs and indescribably bad smells in the early morning, many of the windows having been closed at night." Her criticisms reached attentive ears, and the regulations were changed. Rachel's career of championing good causes had begun.

In later years, as a journalist, Rachel would explore issues of public health and the status of nurses. She was indignant that the "sisters of mercy" were treated in a fashion "no better than white slavery," and were "exploited by private institutions, which made a profit out of their labour and paid miserably." Rachel was extremely proud of the two years she spent at the hospital and always included them in her curriculum vitae, emphasising that it was an unpaid job.

IN THE SUMMER of 1885, Baron Horace Gunzburg and several of his sons travelled from St. Petersburg to pay a visit to their new in-laws. In a group photo taken at Ashley Park, Flora sits stiffly, looking away from the camera with a reserved smile, while Rachel, clothed in a light white dress, seems troubled and gloomy. Though she was still part of the Sassoon clan at the time, she already appears far removed from her family.

One of the last Sassoon gatherings Rachel took part in was her grandmother's funeral, on January 16, 1887. Farha Sassoon was seventy-five years of age, and for the previous twenty years she had been living in England. Upon her death, her sons wished to acquire a family plot in the Spanish and Portuguese Cemetery in Mile End. They had thought of burying Farha next to her eldest son, S.D., but since he had died so many years ago the nearest vacant plot was twenty-seven rows away. In the austere custom of the London Sephardic community, no mausoleum was allowed to be built on the plot—no works of art, decorated fences or marble arches; just a plain strip of land to accommodate a score of unified, flat headstones for the Sassoons, identical for all members of the community. Quite a contrast to the Beer family's mausoleum.

CHAPTER FOURTEEN

A Newspaper Heir

In just under a year, Frederick Beer, aged twenty-two, had been bereaved of his entire family—his parents, grandmother and uncle. He had no kin left in England and he had never been in touch with the few distant relatives who remained in Germany. An air of perpetual gloom was added to his natural timidity; he must have been terrified for his own health, since all of his dear ones had died so abruptly in their early forties. Floersheim and Schott, his father's German friends, stepped in to fill the void left by his family. Edward Dicey, the editor of *The Observer* and Frederick's most senior employee, also became a devoted father figure.

Frederick was now an immensely rich man, the sole beneficiary of the entire family wealth and, most likely, the youngest newspaper proprietor in all of England. He kept the eight servants the family had employed at 9 Cambridge Gate, and two of his university mates moved in with him; though, in the aftermath of so many deaths, he gave up his studies at Cambridge. Dicey, who had long been an advocate of exploring and experiencing the world, advised Frederick that it might do him good to get away from England for a while. Plenty of sun and a dry climate were a remedy for all sorts of ills and miseries, and, besides which, travelling would expand Frederick's acquaintance with foreign and political affairs. Being a frequent visitor to

Egypt—in fact, he was a director in the Ottoman Bank there—Dicey encouraged him to go to Cairo and to continue southward to Khartoum.

In December 1881, both Frederick and Dicey were absent from London, leaving the entire workload for *The Observer* to the assistant editor and manager, Brockwell Dalton. Accompanied by his friend Arthur Sullivan, Dicey returned home in late April 1882. Clearly bitten by the travel bug, the young Beer would remain abroad until the spring of 1884.

Much as his father had done, Frederick granted Dicey full autonomy over *The Observer*. The paper had begun to attract "world-wide attention and respect" in recent years, and it continued to evolve under Dicey's leadership. He was a Liberal turned Unionist and *The Observer* followed his political transformation, publishing arguments in favour of an Anglo-German understanding and in opposition of Home Rule in Ireland.

Dicey invited Henry Lucy, the much admired journalist and humorist, to write a parliamentary column. Already writing for nine London dailies, Lucy demanded, and got, "full freedom of judgment and perfect liberty of speech." His column, "Cross Bench," which ran for twenty-nine years, became one of *The Observer*'s trademarks.

With a full head of silver hair and a luxuriant upturned moustache, Lucy was quite a remarkable character. At a time when journalists were free to divide their loyalty, he was also writing "Pictures in Parliament" for *The Daily News* and "Essence of Parliament" for *Punch*—ensuring that each column was distinct in style and treatment. His secretary would arrive at ten-thirty in the morning and he would dictate his articles for *The Observer, The Daily News* and *Punch*, with the occasional magazine article thrown in. They would also attend to his considerable private correspondence. By lunchtime "a pretty fair day's work was completed."

Years later, Lucy was dining with the Beers when Rachel, who was under pressure to compose a lengthy weekly editorial column for the *Sunday Times*, asked him how he managed if he happened to be taken ill on Friday morning, the time set apart for writing the "Cross Bench" article. Lucy was taken aback by her question, before answering that he "had never sent empty away the printer's boy awaiting at noon on Friday for *Observer*'s copy."

While Lucy's take on matters of government added to the paper's credibility, his column didn't necessarily increase its financial prospects. Crime and punishment boosted newspaper sales but, in keeping with Dicey's trademark restraint, *The Observer* was far less sensational in its treatment of these subjects than other newspapers were. Dicey generally took the higher road, and one lurid incident in particular demonstrates his firm approach.

Kate Webster was a domestic servant of thirty, who pushed her mistress down the stairs during an argument. She then strangled her, dismembered the corpse and boiled her up, disposing of the remains in the Thames. For two weeks, Webster lived in the house where the murder took place, assuming her mistress's identity. She was only caught when she attempted to sell the victim's property. Six days of dramatic trial resulted in a death sentence.

The press was excluded from the execution, though it didn't stop them from giving lengthy and vivid descriptions of the hanging. In his weekly column, entitled "The First Topics of the Day," Dicey protested against the press's exclusion: "All sensational reports of executions are to be deprecated, and every effort made to discourage them; but every leading newspaper should have the distinct right of sending his reporter to lay clearly before the public a simple and impartial account of the proceedings." The press was needed, he argued, to verify that the sentence had been carried out as humanely and carefully as possible, and to ensure that justice had not been frustrated by a mock execution. The presence of the press would prevent rumours that the criminal had bribed his or her way out of punishment. "Anything like sensational accounts ought to be kept in check, all that concerns the public is to know that the criminal has been duly executed," concluded Dicey.

The Observer did not shy away from the always contentious issue of capital punishment. In one notable article, Dicey took on electro-cution, which had recently been introduced in the United States as a way of executing convicted criminals. He questioned whether criminals should be "politely bowed out of the world by a man of science, armed with an electric battery" instead of being given an undignified exit through hanging. On the other hand, he wondered why in England—unlike most other countries—the condemned were not allowed to walk to the gallows with a pipe or cigar in their mouths. Dicey speculated, "Who can tell how much the strain on the nerves in the agonizing minutes that precede death may be lessened by a few whiffs of tobacco? And even the British Anti-Tobacco Association would hardly have the heart to take the pipe out of the hands of the condemned criminal at the foot of the gallows."

Sometimes, though, a scoop was just too good to be missed, and even Dicey would stoop to including all of the salacious details. On every Saturday at about midnight, after the editorial proofs had been revised, Dicey would dine at the nearby Garrick or Fielding Club in case any important news came in before the paper went to press. On May 6, 1882, he was just about to leave the office when the subeditor came into his room in great excitement, handing him a telegram that had just arrived from their correspondent in Dublin: "On examination, it was found that Mr. Burke had received several stabs near one region of the heart, and his throat had been cut almost completely across," it read.

These words described what came to be known as the Phoenix Park Murders. The victims were Lord Cavendish, Chief Secretary for Ireland (who had just been sworn in that day), and Mr. Thomas Burke, the Under Secretary. Dicey's main concern was to guard the grisly details of the political murder from competing newspapers; he alerted his staff that they would be going to press later than usual, so that their rivals wouldn't be able to copy their news. It was only then that he sent messengers to the government offices and to the houses of the ministers in town, "to learn if any confirmation had been received of this astounding intelligence." Waiting for an official response, he wrote a short editorial.

On Sunday *The Observer* was indeed late in reaching the streets, but when it arrived it was the only newspaper to give a full account of the gruesome crime. Dicey's rivals were green with envy. Years later John Hollingshead, a journalist and theatre manager, tried to claim that he had been the one to break the news of the murders to Dicey, well before midnight, while Dicey was playing whist at his club. According to Hollingshead, the editor was unimpressed, continuing to shuffle his cards. Dicey dismissed Hollingshead's claim, and *The Observer*'s scoop has gone down in the history of British journalism.

ALL OF THIS time, Frederick Beer had been detached from life in England, completely immersed in his exploration of foreign lands. His lengthy tour ended in March 1884, just before Khartoum was besieged by Sudanese tribes. Frederick managed to make it back to London in time to avoid the worst of the conflict. He would eventually write about the experience.

Back home, Louis Schott, his father's old friend and associate, offered him the lease for his Mayfair house at 14 Stratton Street, which had recently been refurbished with gas pipes and hot and cold water taps. The cul-de-sac was one of the choicest locations in London, and the houses overlooked the Duke of Devonshire's splendid garden.

Frederick could easily afford to live in such a desirable area. When he reached the age of twenty-six, he was given by the trustees of his father's estate forty thousand pounds, a part of the inheritance. What he was not given was an occupation or vocation. He seemed to have neither the inclination nor the business talent to follow in his father's footsteps, but *The Observer* gave him an identity. Owning a newspaper, he was more than just a rich heir; he was a man who stood high in society and was welcomed by dignitaries. Despite his proprietary interest in *The Observer*, Frederick's return did not infringe on Dicey's authority as editor.

Frederick was a generous employer with a laissez-faire attitude toward management. He pampered his staff with annual dinners, at which excellent banquets were served at the luxurious Markwell's Hotel in Brighton. "The speeches were brief and to the point, and the interval between them were pleasantly filled up with excellent songs." All seventy-two members of *The Observer* staff and guests returned to London in a special saloon carriage.

In time, Frederick turned more of his attention to his journalistic enterprises. Throughout the summer of 1886, he and Edward Dicey were putting the final touches to their newest brainchild—realising that most readers had neither the time nor the inclination for a prolonged study of the morning paper, they had devised a short-format daily. It was designed to meet "the special requirement of railway travellers and others who wish to learn at a glance what is going on in every department of news." *The Journal* was to be published at *The Observer* premises and produced by its staff. Unencumbered by editorials, lengthy parliamentary debates or exhaustive reports of public meetings, all the news of the day was to be arranged "as to convey its gist and purport in a comparatively narrow space accompanied by short comments and notes."

It was an innovation in journalism, and they launched the first issue on Monday, November 1, 1886. On each side of the masthead were charts of the day's weather, including information on wind direction. The notice to the readers—and press colleagues—reassured everyone that the object was not to compete with existing dailies, but to answer the need for a concise and clear form of news. *The Journal* was a forerunner of the free dailies that are nowadays distributed to commuters. Most of the items were just a hundred words long, based on the Reuters telegrams that were piling up at *The Observer*'s offices anyway. The only exception was the juicy adultery details from Lady Colin Campbell's divorce suit, which ran up to a thousand words daily.

The Journal promised its readers that advertisements would not encroach upon the four full pages of news and would, instead, be printed on extra pages. But it appears that the idea of headline reading was premature—despite the low price, just one penny, and the ideal launching time, the holiday season, *The Journal* failed to attract enough readers and did not bring in any advertisers, not even personal ads. The issue of Monday, December 20, 1886, carried no indication that it would be the last one, but apparently Beer and Dicey decided to pull the plug that day, after only seven weeks in print.

A few months later, Frederick sold his shares of the Star and Garter Hotel in Richmond, another luxurious establishment he had inherited from his father. Executed in the Italian Romanesque style, this palatial hotel was a meeting point for the Bank of England's directors and the City syndicates and it was boasted that one thousand guests could dine there at the same time. The young, rich heir could easily afford to give up the connections with the likes of the Star and Garter's guests that could have paid handsome dividends.

CHAPTER FIFTEEN

Rien sans Peine

The circumstances that led to Rachel Sassoon and Frederick Beer meeting are unclear, but they were evidently well suited from the start. Both of them had been born with the proverbial silver spoon in their mouths, though Frederick's total fortune of £400,000 surpassed Rachel's legacy fortyfold. They were almost thirty, free from paternal scrutiny, and had just completed an active phase in their lives—he, travelling, and she, nursing. Regarding herself as a pioneer woman, Rachel felt as if she was on an equal footing with Frederick, and she expected to have a free hand in their relationship, to be the queen of her own world. They shared a mutual appreciation of art, a tendency toward introversion and a gentle disposition.

They were also, it seems, very much in love.

For Rachel, living in London on her own, it was easier to conceal the budding romance from her mother, who was at a safe distance in Brighton. Her wariness was understandable—the birth of Alfred's two sons had not softened Flora's heart, and Rachel knew that her choice of a spouse would be no better received than her brother's. Ultimately, though, she was willing to pay the price of being banished forever from the family circle. With no such family ties to contend with, Frederick prepared a prenuptial agreement in anticipation of the marriage, witnessed by his solicitor and Edward Dicey, in which Rachel was promised a generous annuity of £1,100.

Rachel's wedding marked the second occasion on which a Sassoon was married in a church, but she went one step further than her brother. On Wednesday morning, August 3, 1887, the day before their wedding, the couple entered the Holy Trinity Church in Chelsea, accompanied by a handful of supportive friends. "Dost thou renounce Satan and all his works and all his pomps and vanities?" the priest asked. Water was sprinkled, a white garment was laid on Rachel's shoulder, and she became the first Sassoon to be baptised an Anglican.

Rachel was not obliged to convert in order to marry Frederick, and she knew she would never be forgiven for defying her father's command and her mother's wishes, but she was a free spirit, not a dutiful daughter. She saw baptism as an act of convenience: it would make life easier for any future children, and it would mean that she and Frederick would not be parted in death, but could be interred together in the Beer mausoleum in Highgate. Despite her conversion to her husband's faith, she remained uncommitted to any religion. Indeed, she was rather critical of organised religion—she publicly denounced the Christian passion for conversion and criticised the Society for Promoting Christianity among the Jews, which spent its entire annual budget of £42,266 to baptise six Jews, five of them children. Rachel viewed the expenditure of vast sums on missionaries as a present-day replacement for "the methods of the Dark Ages, when men would slay, burn, maim and ruin their fellow creatures." She also cynically remarked, "The conversion of Jews is a more expensive occupation than either yachting or the turf."

Rachel and Frederick returned to the church for their wedding the day following her baptism. In the registry, she deducted six years from her age. No one from her family was present, not even her brother Alfred and her beloved sister-in-law Theresa, who gave birth to the couple's third son on that day. Rachel's closest friend in attendance was Helen Thornycroft, and her guests of honour were the Gladstones, headed by William and Catherine. William, who was in between premierships, sat at the head of the table at the wedding breakfast, and Siegfried Sassoon was told that the Grand Old Man chewed every mouthful eighty times. As a child, he wondered whether Gladstone "did so while consuming his slice of Auntie Rachel's wedding cake." The groom was escorted by his father's friends Schott and Floersheim, and the ever-present Edward Dicey.

Flora Sassoon's humiliation at her daughter's union was magnified by the fact that her brother-in-law Albert had, at that time, secured a superb match for his only son, Edward. He was to be married to Aline, daughter of Baron Gustave de Rothschild. The 1,200 guests at their wedding represented the crème de la crème of society, and the Prince of Wales and the Shah of Persia, neither of whom could attend the wedding in France, sent presents to the new couple. The streets of Paris had not witnessed such a procession of carriages since the wedding of Napoleon III in 1853.

As she expected, Rachel became the ostracised daughter. Her cousin's wedding, which took place just two months after her own, was the first event on the Sassoon calendar from which she was excluded. Soon afterward, her youngest brother, Frederick, was diagnosed with tuberculosis, and she was not allowed to nurse him or even visit him. He died eighteen months later in 1889, aged twenty-seven, and was laid to rest in the family plot in London. Rachel was not permitted to pay her respects.

In later years, she published in the *Sunday Times* "A Modern Royal Love Story," a piece concerning Duchess Pauline of Württemberg, daughter of Prince Eugen and his wife Mathilde, which read like a coded message to her mother. It told the tale of a member of the Württemberg royal family who "was right in following the dictates of her heart, in opposition to the advice of all her relations." Duchess Pauline's life bore a striking similarity to the details of Rachel's own. Pauline was Rachel's senior by four years; as a child, "she always wished to know the reach of everything," and she developed into a charming little girl, "a clever conversationalist with a great thirst for knowledge." As a young adult, Pauline "had a great wish to learn nursing, and she took a great interest in reading about the healing of diseases." When she was twenty-one years of age, her father fell ill and she nursed him until his death.

At her father's bedside, she met Dr. Melchior Willim—here the article swooned, its purple prose slipping into the realm of the romance novel—"and one day they awoke to the fact that they loved each other, and that life alone was impossible." The duchess laid the matter before her mother and family, "having fully made up her mind that, whatever they might say, she would marry the man of her choice." Like Flora Sassoon, Pauline's mother was "very angry at what she termed her daughter's foolishness . . . she was treated with severity—in fact, everything was done to persuade her to give up her lover, but with no avail." Pauline resigned her title of duchess, renounced all her rights, and in 1880 she "married the man she loved." She made an excellent doctor's wife, "ministering to the wants of the poor, sick and suffering" and fighting for women's rights. Seventeen years into the marriage, Pauline declared that her life was full of happiness and she "never had any reason to regret her choice." This last statement was certainly true of Rachel and Frederick.

The young couple had a passionate interest in both the visual and performing arts. Together they frequented auction houses and toured artists' homes, acquiring a large number of paintings. They readily lent their masterpieces to museums and galleries, and further supported the world of art by donating to the Artists' General Benevolent Institution. Rachel believed that "artists were more liable than almost any other class of men to intense mental suffering and anxiety when misfortune came upon them."

Assessing the Beers' inventory today, Martin Beisly, senior director of nineteenth-century European art at Christie's auction house, judges it to be a very good quality collection, with an evident continental, if somewhat sentimental, taste. The French paintings in the collection—major works of Corot and Courbet—were more impressive than the English ones, and female artists were also well represented, among them Rosa Bonheur and Laura Alma Tadema. They also owned the voluptuous painting of the Bacchanals by Peter Paul

Rubens, as well as two more priceless masterpieces by the renowned Flemish master. Though both Frederick and Rachel had strayed from Judaism, they owned a portrait of a rabbi by an unidentified artist, and David Roberts's painting *Jerusalem*. Beisly, who has encountered Jewish themes in the art collections of many Jews who had abandoned their faith, sees it as "a sort of feeling that one should make some gesture toward the Old Faith."

A definite jewel in their crown was *Orpheus and Eurydice* by G. F. Watts. The well-known Greek myth tells of the musician Orpheus, in Watts's incarnation naked but for a lion's skin around his waist. He gained Pluto's permission to reclaim his wife Eurydice from the underworld, on the condition that he would not set eyes on her until they were above ground. But he could not resist, and the painting depicts Orpheus clutching his lifeless, almost naked beloved as she falls backwards into the abyss, her mane of hair billowing about her. It was one of eight versions that Watts created on this theme and probably the largest. Frederick and Rachel adored this sensual painting and hung it over their mantelpiece, in the most central and eye-catching position in their home.

To celebrate their union and solidify their status among the elite, the couple designed a family crest. Their choice is puzzling, yet also revealing. They decided on a pelican in an act of self-sacrifice and maternal devotion, the large bird tearing its breast open with its long curved bill and feeding its starving brood with its own blood. Early Christians used this particular symbol as a reminder of Christ and his sacrifice, but it also had a striking resonance in the faith of the couple's forefathers. Although Rachel's parents were Orthodox Jews and Frederick's family originally practiced Judaism, neither of them appears to have known that the pelican is a bad omen in Judaism, a symbol of grief, desolation and ruin. That they chose an explicitly Christian emblem in the first place shows how detached they were from their roots. Their choice is also telling in another sense—it reflects their desire for children.

The pelican piercing her own breast had been a popular choice for family crests since the sixteenth century, but the Beers' motto, *Rien sans Peine,* was unique. Though a cliché—loosely translated it means "No pain, no gain," "Nothing without suffering," or "Nothing gained without trouble"—the words were rarely used as a part of a coat of arms. The motto was Frederick and Rachel's statement of their intention not to rest on their laurels, despite being wealthy heirs, and to a degree they both made good on that promise. (In reality, the motto would have been more fitting for Julius Beer, Frederick's father, and his laborious rise to fortune.) They used the crest widely, and had it printed at the head of their stationery, embroidered on their linen and tablecloths, and embossed on the gilt buttons of their servants' waistcoats.

Even the couple's black French poodle, Zulu, proudly displayed the family crest. After shaving a large patch on the dog's back, the premier London dog clipper, Mr. W. R. Brown of Regent Street, used his battery of machine clippers, razors and scissors of every shape and size to clip into Zulu's fur the pelican's upright wings, hovering over four open-beaked nestlings. It is difficult to imagine the intricacy of the work, especially when it came to adding in the motto *Rien sans Peine;* "Probably a hint to the poodle to remain passive in the clipper's hand," joked *The Strand Magazine* when it covered Brown's work in 1896. Zulu was driven in a carriage to Mr. Brown once a month so that the crest could be renewed, and the price for the complex pattern was equivalent to two weeks' salary for a copying clerk in the city or for a general labourer.

Some biographers use the poodle's unusual haircut to demonstrate that Rachel and Frederick had lost touch with reality—in terms of their extravagant lifestyle, their eccentricity and their desire to establish themselves as fully English. In context, the decision to have their prized pet emblazoned with their family crest is not as outrageous as it may seem at first glance. The Beers were far from the only couple to seek Mr. Brown's services; in addition to crests and monograms, wealthy dog owners in England would express their patriotism by ordering shamrocks or thistles for their pets. This special type of dog grooming was particularly popular among sports aficionados; one dog's coat was clipped to show the image of a boxer (of the human sort) throwing a knockout punch, while another was decorated with a scene from Derby Day, complete with horse, course, crowd and the name of the winner. At that time, Mr. Brown had his hands full with work. His and his wife's average output was three dogs a day. Some of the more intricate lace patterns took two sittings to complete.

SINCE THE SASSOONS had ostracised Rachel for marrying Frederick, her family could not fill the void left after the loss of his own. Fortunately for Frederick, his wife had close connections within the upper reaches of London society, and these friends served as a substitute family for the newlyweds.

Following their marriage, the young Beers and the Gladstones kept in close touch, and Rachel and Frederick marked their first wedding anniversary at the Gladstone estate at Hawarden, North Wales. It was almost exclusively a family gathering, including Gladstone's children and their spouses. Gladstone refrained from talking politics in the presence of the ladies, and discussed at length the question of "whether it would be better to make young men good athletes or good walkers." He voted for the walkers, and Frederick, who had experienced mountaineering in the Swiss Alps, could not but admire the seventy-nine-year-old statesman, who was known for his arduous walks. Three years later, the families also holidayed together in the newly opened Hotel Metropole in Brighton.

The Gladstones had watched Rachel grow up, and now that she was an adult and had married into more money, Catherine Gladstone was ready to link her with one of her many charities. Following in the footsteps of her mother, who had for many years supported Mrs. Gladstone's Newport Market Refuge, Rachel became involved with St. Mary's Training Home for Young Servants, at Notting Hill. "To prevent young girls from drifting into a life of shame and misery," the house offered lodging and training to fourteen girls aged twelve to sixteen. For a year, they were taught housekeeping, sewing and some laundry work and cooking—enough to qualify them as kitchen maids. Four beds were reserved for the graduates in case they were between jobs, but they were only allowed to stay if they kept themselves respectable.

Mrs. Gladstone found in Rachel a generous and dedicated benefactress, and the acquaintance with the prime minister's wife was no small gain for the ambitious young hostess, who seemed intent on weaving her own social network. In 1898, when Mrs. Gladstone retired from the presidency of St. Mary's, she nominated her daughter-in-law and Rachel as her replacements. "It is doubly delightful to think of you taking my place," she wrote affectionately to Rachel. "And I do feel so grateful, looking back, that it has pleased God to give you a happy, useful life."

The Country Gentleman was quick to predict that Rachel Beer was "a lady who is to blossom as a political hostess." In a manner of speaking, the magazine was prescient in its remarks; what it didn't anticipate, and what Rachel herself did not reveal publicly until after she had been married for some time, was just how involved in political matters she wished to be. Making the move from philanthropy to journalism and activism may seem natural, but during her era the women who wrote for newspapers were almost always confined to domestic topics. Later, as editor and owner of the *Sunday Times,* while Rachel was not averse to writing on these subjects, she hardly limited herself to such material. She wished to move beyond the domestic sphere and influence the public agenda.

RACHEL BEER'S JOURNEY to becoming the editor of not one but two major national newspapers was a gradual one, but it undoubtedly reflects her temperament—her great perseverance and strong-mindedness.

Fleet Street gossip at *The Observer* had it that the proprietor's wife was poking her nose into her husband's business. And it was true that Rachel was brimming with ideas for the paper, most of them stemming from her desire for social change. She suggested to Edward

Dicey an article on Garden Cities, and the seasoned editor summarily brushed it off—if industrialists would profit from moving their factories from town centres to more open districts and less expensive suburbs, they would already have done so. Mrs. Beer didn't relent—why, she wondered, was it that a new idea needed to be adopted and carried out before it could be recommended to the public?

At the end of March 1889, Edward Dicey and Frederick Beer came to a gentlemen's agreement to cease their collaboration; *The Observer* was to publish the retiring editor's letter, announcing that after nineteen years his connection with the paper was now at an end. "Feelings of mutual regard and esteem which have characterized our long and close relations are not affected in any way"—his departure, he stated, had been decided on by both himself and the newspaper's proprietors. By all accounts, Frederick was the sole proprietor of *The Observer*, so the plural term hints at Rachel's meddling in the affair. The newspaper continued publishing Dicey's views on current affairs for many more years, though mostly as very lengthy "letters to the editor."

Frederick hired Henry Duff Traill as Dicey's successor. Traill, the "most polished of newspaper literateurs," had contributed to *The Observer* in the past, though he had never edited a newspaper before—his last senior post was as the chief political editorial writer for *The Daily Telegraph*. A likeable person, he was hailed as the only editor in town who "could edit and laugh at the same time." He encouraged his journalists to add witty, humorous touches to their work, but even with that added note of levity he still maintained Dicey's high standards. He was loved by the entire staff. "He was no feminist," though, and the clash with Rachel, who held advanced views on women's emancipation, was only a matter of time.

In late April 1891, nearly four years into her marriage, Mrs. Beer sailed into Traill's office, and being a woman "who liked to exercise authority . . . raised objections to the line he was taking on some public question." Traill, according to the writer Francis Gribble, "pointed out to her—quite politely, I am sure, for he was always polite to everybody—that Mr. Beer has appointed him to be the editor of *The Observer*. And she, in reply, protested that he was insulting her."

Foreseeing the inevitable, Traill was quick to submit his resignation, and the incident became the talk of Fleet Street:

> They tell us that some changes are in store for *The Observer*
> A so-called Unionist affair, chock-full-of Tory fervour
> The Traill that was so clear
> It seems will disappear
> And in place of him, the owner Mr. Beer, will henceforth edit—
> His name suggests that he would fill the 'tiser with more credit.

Fun magazine, where these lines appeared, was somewhat inaccurate in its prediction—Traill was replaced not by Mr. Beer but by Clement Kinloch-Cooke, the experienced editor of *The Pall Mall Gazette* and of *The English Illustrated Magazine*. Outraged by the mistreatment of Traill, the staff of *The Observer* showed outright hostility toward their new boss, who in turn behaved like "a boisterous bull calf in a crockery shop, scattering the personnel in all directions, without thereby securing fixity of tenure."

During his first week at *The Observer*, the bumbling Kinloch-Cooke collided with none other than the formidable George Bernard Shaw. The playwright had been commissioned to review the new exhibition at the Royal Academy. When the article was published, Shaw was livid:

> Cooke is such an unspeakable greenhorn, that when he got my article—which I need hardly say was a very good one—he could not make head or tail of it. So instead of sending to me, he helplessly handed it to his "proprietor," who preceded [sic.] to mutilate it, interpolate scraps of insufferable private view small talk, break it into paragraphs in the wrong places, scissor it with obvious little puffs of his private friends, and generally, reduce

its commercial value (not to speak of its artistic value) about
1800%.

Shaw's "First Notice" in *The Observer* was not followed by a second
one—"I burned my boats and left the galleries forever," he later
wrote.

Fourteen years later, Shaw returned to this incident again, this
time accusing not Frederick, but his wife, whom he referred to as "a
Jewish lady who had an interest in the paper." He claimed that she
was the one who had padded his article out "to an extraordinary
length by interpolations praising the works of the Jewish lady's acquaintances." Shaw never forgot the insult, and again, at ninety-one
years old, when he was assembling his assorted reviews for publication, he accused Rachel (though not by name) of planting in his article "eulogies of painters of no account, who had invited her to tea."

Kinloch-Cooke would soon discover that he was not alone in the
editor's room. Rachel "descended on *The Observer* in the guise of
contributor. Soon followed the role of assistant editor," wrote journalist Bernard Falk, many years later. As the owner's wife, she com-
manded respect, but the dynamic Rachel wanted more. She wanted to
be obeyed. Falk claimed that Mrs. Beer called the shots, though she
left the drudgery of the newspaper's day-to-day details in Kinloch-
Cooke's hands.

RACHEL HAD NEVER intended to be just a society hostess, limiting
herself to charity work. While her brothers lived comfortably on their
father's inheritance, she was the only one of S.D.'s children to pursue
a profession and a business. Her husband's involvement in journalism
doubtless influenced her choice of vocation, and it provided her with
the perfect platform for expressing her opinions.

Frederick had never taken an active role in running *The Observer*,
which allowed his wife to test the waters and gain some experience in
writing and editing. But the confusion and antagonism her involvement created had already led to the resignation of two popular

editors. For her, editing *The Observer* full-time was not an option, since it would place her in the undesirable position of being her husband's employee. Replacing him and becoming proprietor-editor of *The Observer* was equally unthinkable, since it would rob Frederick of his position. In any case, Rachel found *The Observer*'s sobriety and dignity "a trifle ponderous" for her taste, and it was impossible to change its tone without alienating its long-established readership.

It became clear that if Rachel intended to thrive in journalism she would need a newspaper of her own, one that reflected her wide-ranging interests in politics and economics, foreign affairs and the colonies, women's rights, music and art, welfare and education, fashion and society. Though she had enough of a fortune to launch a new paper, she preferred to buy an established one, and she chose to wait for the right opportunity.

Her decision to make journalism a full-time career encouraged her husband to follow suit, and to put the new Beer family motto—*Rien sans Peine*—into action. In April 1893, *The Observer* announced that "Mr. Frederick Beer, the owner, would take a more active part in the editorial department than he had done hitherto." By a stroke of fortune, the *Sunday Times* was soon offered for sale, and the Beers decided to purchase it with the intent that Rachel would be in charge. It had dual appeal—it was a veteran newspaper of general interest, and one whose long history of constant upheavals made it an excellent platform for change.

CHAPTER SIXTEEN

A Newspaper of Her Own

Though an indefatigable impresario, dramatist and librettist, Augustus Harris had come to find owning the *Sunday Times* too much of a burden. Fleet Street was not shaken by the news of his abdication, since it was well known that the paper "changed its owners almost as often as King Solomon changed his wives." Word reached the editor, Arthur à Beckett, who was annoyed that the sale had been conducted over his head. He was desperate to learn the buyers' identity but Harris refused to divulge the information. His attempts to discover whose employ he would soon be under proving futile, Beckett turned to the occult—a mystic who claimed to have the power of automatic writing scribbled that the new proprietor was "Beer," and added the word "*Observer.*" For some strange reason, the words were nonsensical to Arthur à Beckett.

INSTABILITY HAD BEEN part and parcel of the *Sunday Times* since its inception in 1821. Politicians, publishers and impresarios had all taken turns at the helm, hoping that the paper would help them promote their personal interests. Some of the owners didn't think much of professional editors, taking that role upon themselves, and for thirteen years, from 1864 onward, the paper had no editor at all. When the results and profits were not satisfactory, each owner swiftly disposed of it.

The paper's founder, Henry White, was a strong opponent of the government. At the collapse of his Sunday paper *The Independent Whig*, he came back on the scene with *The New Observer*, complete with the stolen emblem of the all-seeing eye, which he included in an attempt to get a free ride on *The Observer*'s long-standing reputation. After just two months, in April 1821, White renamed his paper *The Independent Observer*, keeping the eye emblem. Still not pleased with the sales, and hoping that a change in name would result in a change of fortune, he relaunched the paper as the *Sunday Times* on October 20, 1822. Clearly this was not enough—just three months later the impatient White sold his brainchild to a group led by the lawyer and MP Daniel Whittle Harvey.

The Observer remained a source of rival inspiration, and the *Sunday Times* was quick to adopt their competitor's use of drawings "to supplement verbal records of remarkable events." However, it could not compete with *The Observer*'s late closing time. The first edition of the *Sunday Times* "catered specially for agriculturists and sporting men," and was printed on Friday night, in order to make the early trains on Saturday mornings. A second edition was printed on Saturday afternoon, in time for the Sunday morning postal delivery, and a third on Saturday night.

The newspaper was met with mixed reviews. "An excellent paper for families, the greatest care being always taken to exclude anything which could bring blush to the cheek of female modesty," commented James Grant, the editor of *The Morning Advertiser*. In *The Monthly Review of Literature* in 1837, a contemporary critic dismissed the compliment and accused the paper of containing too high a dose of crime stories, to satisfy "the prurient curiosity of middle-aged virgins and elderly gentlewomen, who are understood to be its staunchest supporters."

By 1838 the competition seemed to be won—circulation had exceeded more than twelve thousand copies, compared with *The Observer*'s more modest three thousand copies. When Whittle Harvey sold the paper to the book publisher A. J. Valpy, he received a record price of fifteen thousand pounds.

The successful serialization of Dickens's and Thackeray's novels in monthlies and booklets prompted the *Sunday Times* to become the first newspaper to publish entire novels side by side with news and commentary. "In these stirring times men scarcely find leisure for the perusal of volumes," the newspaper informed its readers and critics. As a first offering, they printed William Harrison Ainsworth's *Old St. Paul's,* for which they generously paid one thousand pounds in 1841. The then popular author's historical romance was set during the Great Plague and the Great Fire, and was published in fifty-two weekly instalments. Nine more novels followed and circulation soared to twenty thousand copies.

In the late 1850s, the *Sunday Times* restricted its sensational news coverage and retreated into semi-literary journalism, increasing its respectability. The next owner, E. T. Smith, a wine merchant turned impresario, expanded the newspaper's coverage of theatre, racing and boxing, and increased its entertainment and book reviews. Soon it became the most influential publication on the arts, known especially for its writing on the theatre. The paper employed the best critics of the day, including Clement Scott and Joseph Knight.

Come 1887, Colonel George FitzGeorge, the illegitimate son of the Duke of Cambridge, was the man at the publication's helm, until he was obliged to comply with the wish of Her Majesty the Queen, who wanted him to give up letters and live cleanly like a gentleman. He sold the *Sunday Times* to Miss Alice Cornwell, better known as Princess Midas.

Alice was born in Essex, the daughter of a railway guard. The Cornwells emigrated to Australia when Alice was a child, where Mr. Cornwell became a gold prospector, but Alice soon returned to England to study at the Royal Academy of Music in London, winning several gold medals and composing numerous pieces for the pianoforte during her time there. Upon the death of her mother, she was obliged to return to Australia, where in a dramatic change of direction she studied geology and mining and struck gold in the Midas mine in Sulky Gully, Ballarat. A shrewd businesswoman, she was credited as "working with all the skill of the male miner."

Returning again to London in late 1887, Alice bought the *Sunday Times* both to publicize her upcoming mining ventures and as a gift to her fiancé, journalist Phil Robinson. Some elderly ladies were rather shocked at Alice's decision to own a Sunday newspaper, until she put their minds at rest and explained to them that nearly all of the work was done on Saturdays. "One of the ladies thereupon determined to take the paper but not to read it until Monday," Princess Midas told the magazine *Woman's Day*. She scoffed at her predecessors for doing "only a scissors and paste affair, with hardly any original news."

With Robinson as editor, the couple declared war on their old rival *The Observer*, pledging "to knock the sleepy and expensive [newspaper] on the head." They dropped the price to one penny and reduced the amount of arts coverage. But gold beckoned Miss Cornwell back to Australia, and Robinson, a rather reluctant editor, soon joined her there after a few months on the job. Veteran *Sunday Times* journalist Joseph Hatton took over, but he left not long after they did. Though the husband and wife duo eventually returned to London, they seemed to have lost interest in the paper.

Hermann Klein, the then music critic for the *Sunday Times*, tipped off Augustus Harris in 1891, informing him that the newspaper was, once again, available for purchase. Harris, the manager of the Drury Lane Theatre, jumped at the opportunity. He had recently collaborated on some of the dramas he produced and had been roundly ridiculed by the *World* as a man "who could not write anything." Harris was suing the newspaper for libel and wanted to prove it wrong. For that reason, recalled James Glover, his master of music at Drury Lane, he "immediately became the proprietor of the *Sunday Times*, and proceeded to write a column of notes every week on anything and everything, headed 'Here, There and Everywhere,' and signed it, 'The Knight Errant.'" Harris planned to present the manuscripts of his articles in court in order to prove his case.

Klein was the intermediary in the purchase, and the grateful Harris offered him the editorship. Klein turned down the offer, so Arthur à Beckett, the assistant editor of *Punch,* was appointed instead. Beckett chose to keep his position at *Punch,* working both jobs; it was no wonder, therefore, that he did "faulty work" at the *Sunday Times.* "With such a double burden, even his irrepressible energy could guarantee neither accuracy nor originality," wrote A.J.A. Morris in the *Oxford Dictionary of National Biography.*

Harris held on to the paper for three years; then, on July 2, 1894, it was sold to the Beers. Frederick became the registered proprietor but immediately handed over the newspaper to his wife. For Rachel the step was a precarious one, primarily because of her gender. It was only very recently, in the mid-nineteenth century, that publishers had begun to discover women as a distinct readership, let alone accept them as editors. In the 1890s, the success of women's magazines and journals had convinced proprietors to include "sections and regular columns written by and for women" in general newspapers. The Society of Women Journalists was founded in 1893, with over 200 members out of a total number of 660 lady journalists in Britain.

Journalism had become an increasingly attractive profession for women, offering better pay and more freedom to "a woman moderately intelligent, having the ordinary high school education" than other professions. To become a teacher, a young woman needed an expensive college education and prolonged training. And after all of that, her earnings would still be less than that of a journalist, who the popular guide of the time *Press Work for Women* declared "has had no training at all, and in many successful instances has no mental qualifications which in any other occupation would be estimated at a high rate." The disadvantages of the profession were the constant strain it put on the nerves and the inherent instability—the many who remained freelancers had no steady income and found it hard to make a living. What's more, newspaper and magazine editors often took advantage of women's eagerness and balked at paying them for their work, on the grounds that it was sufficient gratification for them to see themselves in print.

The so-called "New Woman" who emerged at the end of the nineteenth century challenged existing gender norms. As a result, she provoked antagonism—her assertiveness seen as a threat. Though the National Association of Journalists admitted women, they considered them a menace, and did what they could to safeguard male spaces against female ambitions. The Press Gallery of the House of Commons was out of bounds for women, and editors preferred men "for the 'rough and tumble' work of outside reporting"—a complaint of journalist Mary Billington in 1896. Female journalists were typically restricted to the "Women's Sphere," reporting on "frocks and frills, with laces and chiffons and the other mysteries of Dame Fashion." They also covered social functions and celebrities, and discussed philanthropy and topics like labour and nursing.

Though she complained of restrictions in England, Mary Billington for one seems not to have envied her American counterparts their lot, instead writing proudly:

> English lady journalists have not so far descended to any of the vulgar sensationalism and semi-detective business which has discredited the American reportresses . . . Happily, our editorial methods and our own instincts as gentlewomen do not lead us to try being barmaids or going out with costermongers on a bank holiday for the purpose of "getting copy."

To increase their credibility, though, "English Lady Journalists" often resorted to the deception of using male pseudonyms when reporting "hard news," while men who wrote on women's subjects hid behind female ones. Female editors were employed only in ladies' and home journals, and even then they were a rarity. In an era in which women were not allowed to vote, it's no wonder that the editorship of general newspapers was barred to them, since most editors were active members of political parties.

In her novel *Sowing the Wind,* published in 1867, Elizabeth Lynn Linton created a strong-minded woman-journalist:

> . . . that's what we women want so much—that varied knowledge got by men—the knowledge you pick up among each other at clubs, and lectures, and in studios and places. You have much different friends—one is an artist, another an engineer, another a chemist, and so on; and if you have brains you can keep yourself informed of the last things in art, science and politics. But those of us who have any brains—and they are precious few! get no help from one another, except about babies or fashions.

Few women broke out of the female ghetto and made their way permanently into other sections of the newspaper, but for those who did, in making this transition, family ties were invaluable. Upon the death of George Morland Crawford, *The Daily News*'s correspondent in Paris, he was replaced by his widow, Emily, who had collaborated with him in the past. Similarly, Jessie Couvreur became the Brussels correspondent for *The Times,* taking over from her late husband.

RACHEL BEER DID not have the university education that most male editors did. She was also deprived of the tips and networking contacts that were there for the taking in London's all-male clubs. Rachel entered the race at a disadvantage, but she was determined to compete with her male rivals and win on their terms.

Rachel was wise enough not to leap into her new role before she was fully equipped to handle it; she intended to return to the first tradition of the paper and to serve simultaneously as its editor and its owner. To prepare herself for that challenge, she consulted with several leading newspaper editors and drew much inspiration from William T. Stead, the legendary former editor of *The Pall Mall Gazette* and founder of *The Monthly Review of Reviews,* who had introduced the genre of the interview to the British press. Stead believed in "Government by Journalism"—he argued that newspapers were a substitute for the House of Commons, since the politicians who served in the House hailed from the upper classes and were not able to understand the common man's needs. He believed that the power of politicians should reside, instead, with those nearest to the people, and that only the press "is at once the eye and the ear and the tongue of the people," especially of outcasts and the disinherited. "There is no such democratic debating-place as the columns of the press," he wrote, "the great court in which all grievances are heard, and all abuses brought to light."

Stead was well known for his relentless campaigns to effect change in the government. His reports on the wretched conditions in London's slums led to a Royal Commission that recommended low-cost, improved housing for the poor, and his sensational investigation into child prostitution resulted in an increase in the official age of consent from thirteen to sixteen. Stead's approach went hand in hand with Rachel's charity activities for the young and the sick, her disapproval of MPs' idleness, and her sympathy for the hardships of the working poor. Her credo was that a responsible paper's first duty was to chronicle news "and interpret its significance by the light of the Ten Commandments."

After becoming the legal owner of the *Sunday Times,* Rachel still left the daily running of the newspaper to the bewildered Arthur à Beckett, and did not call at the office. She used this time to analyze the contents of the paper, judging them against her exacting standards and brainstorming how she could counter weaknesses with new columns and features. She intended to use her paper to express her principles and to influence public opinion in what she "believed to be the right direction."

In an interview she granted to the writer Arnold Bennett, then editor of *Woman* magazine, she declared, "I am an Imperialist, but I want to be an Imperialist peacefully." And her words to Mary Billington were that she felt rather strongly about the need for a Sunday paper "taking somewhat wider and more imperial views, and especially on colonial and Indian matters, which deserved a fuller recognition."

It's not surprising that Rachel, with her roots in Baghdad and India, and her husband's ancestry in Germany, had such a world-embracing point of view. She compared nations to people, calling England "corpulent and middle-aged," and she firmly believed that, like people, nations would inevitably decline if they were cut off from external activities and resources. With the firm conviction that no nation could or should live in isolation, Rachel set out "to make the English public interested in what happens outside its borders . . . foreign affairs should not be a matter on which an Englishman can safely be ignorant."

Accordingly, she chose for her editorials the heading "The World's Work" and the motto "What should they know of England, who only England know?" An ardent admirer of Rudyard Kipling, she borrowed these words from his poem "The English Flag," written in 1891. Rachel considered her role an act of patriotism "to combat the notion that England was only an island, and to emphasise the fact that its influence was world-wide."

John Augustus Sala, one of the most popular and prominent English journalists and columnists of his time, was asked to continue writing his column "Echoes of the Week," which had for many years been the pride of the *Sunday Times*. To the "Yesterday in Paris" column, which chronicled the latest from the City of Light, Rachel added one named "Cousin Jonathan's Doings," which brought intriguing news from America. She also launched a weekly column called "In the Witness Box," where politicians, social activists, artists, female pioneers and people who had made the headlines were interviewed by "the *Sunday Times* cross-examiner." Occasionally that cross-examiner was Mrs. Beer herself, for Stead had revealed to her the trick of the interview trade: "Profess to know more than the person from whom you are wishing to obtain information, so that he may not be unwilling to tell you what he knows, being under the impression that you know it already, and more."

At the dawn of Mrs. Beer's reign, a journalist was sent to interview her for *The Sketch*. He expected to find her at 7 Chesterfield

Gardens, but the footman directed him to Fleet Street. The new flame-red sign of the *Sunday Times* had just been hung on the building. The reporter was surprised by the bare walls and the uncarpeted floor. "I suppose you will import some of the brightness and luxury of May-fair into your special sanctum here?" he inquired.

"Not until the paper has earned them for itself," Mrs. Beer was quick to respond.

"Isn't the idea of all the business involved in editing just a little appalling!" he asked patronisingly.

In no time, Mrs. Beer overwhelmed him with her clear and coher-ent plans for her paper, her resolve to cater for all classes of readers, and to borrow hints from every journalistic success, foreign as well as English. "We should, I think, try to stimulate the imagination of our readers, by giving them a wide range of news. A Sunday paper should, I think, be judicial, not controversial. We want to rest on Sunday, not fight; to cultivate a benevolent rather than a pugnacious spirit. Don't you think so?"

"Shall you cater especially for your lady readers? Women will ex-pect attention from an editor of their own sex."

Mrs. Beer was not to be beguiled into any promises to give femi-nine affairs more than their share of attention hitherto given them in the paper. She stressed that she would be an editor first and a woman afterwards.

Enchanted by Mrs. Beer's intellect, wit and sense of humour, the reporter concluded that her paper was in no immediate danger of becoming the mouthpiece of that "monster of the moment," as the New Woman was called. "In the hands of its lady editor, the *Sunday Times* will be no mere new toy of a pretty woman, but a power to be wielded with wisdom and discretion." He was convinced, too, "that the woman editor is resolved to be no mere figurehead, but the real captain of the craft."

CHAPTER SEVENTEEN

46 Fleet Street

Like many editors of her time, Rachel Beer chose to do much of her work from home—so she installed a telephone connection with the Fleet Street office and the Beers converted a room on the third floor of 7 Chesterfield Gardens into an office to enable her to work effectively.

Rachel's worktable was strewn with all manner of reference books, the floor was piled high with magazines, and the book-lined walls almost hid the doors. There were comfortable couches on which she could rest when the demands of her work became too much, and an open piano allowed Rachel to indulge in what was still one of the greatest pleasures in her life—music. "As the bright sun streams in, it is hard to realise that Hyde Park is not a hundred yards away, and that the woman who works there, might, if she chose, leave all responsibility on one side and join the crowd whose sole aim is to be amused," remarked Arnold Bennett, who interviewed Rachel in her home office for *Woman* magazine.

Dictating articles to a secretary was a convenient status symbol, but Rachel chose not to have one. She also opted to write with a fountain pen rather than a typewriter. She had been advised that agitation, emotion and restlessness could all be subdued by the deliberate action of moving one's hand calmly and gently across paper, producing "a paradise of equanimity," and that typewriters deprived their users of this remedy for the nerves. It came with a cost, however—her fingers were like blotting-paper and seemed to be perpetually stained with ink, the result of writing nearly three thousand words on different subjects for her column each week. Her handwriting was quite wild and erratic, and her nephew Siegfried Sassoon often wondered how the printers succeeded in deciphering it. It was the most illegible hieroglyphics he had ever seen; "When she wrote to us, we used to have a family council to make out what her letter meant."

Rachel's first editorial appeared on September 30, 1894. Without further ado, she plunged straight in—discussing weighty affairs from the start. Knowledgeable, articulate and witty, Rachel wrote with vigour and conviction, as if her columns had been appearing continuously for years on end. She began with the Sino-Japanese war over control of Korea, touched upon the state of British colonies around the globe—Australia, South Africa and the West Indies—and then focused in on Russia. "On Tuesday," she wrote, "a shiver was sent through the nerves of Europe by the news that the Tsar was ill . . . his appearance certainly gives colour to the belief that he suffers from kidney disease. For many years he has been in the habit of consuming vast potations of Kwass—a sort of mead"; no doubt it was the keen eye of a nurse that guided her pen. Tsar Alexander III was gloomy and depressed, Rachel noted, except when "listening to the conversation of his sprightly mother-in-law." She chanced a joke—"He is probably the only man in Europe who finds rest and refreshment in the chidings of his wife's mother"—then cynically remarked that for the tsar death from natural causes would be fortunate—his father had been murdered and his grandfather committed suicide.

When the tsar did indeed die three weeks later, Rachel was aghast at the graphic clinical descriptions with which the press recorded his demise. The next time a potentate was stricken with disease, she hoped, the press would stick to the sick man's temperature, and all other details would be withheld from the breakfast tables—"they are incompatible with appetite, and are unnecessary for the stimulation of sympathy. Indeed our sorrow may increase as the tendency to nausea is removed."

On the home front, Rachel expressed her disappointment in the current roster of politicians, who were lacking in charisma. She complimented instead her champion and family friend Mr. Gladstone, whose "marvellous capacity in this respect made him the political conscience of a million homes." The last item in her first editorial addressed a domestic issue of a different note. The Painters' Trade Union was protesting against Baroness Burdett-Coutts, Rachel's former neighbour in Stratton Street. Instead of employing professional house painters, the wealthiest woman in England had decided to entrust the work to her stablemen. Unlike other newspapers, Rachel sided with the union and the professionals, who "were languishing for want of a job."

Next to her editorial, Rachel announced in the society column "Our Fixture List" the forthcoming marriage of her uncle Frederick David Sassoon and Jeanette Raphael, a family celebration from which she would sadly be excluded.

AWARE OF HER readers' interest in horse racing, Rachel also added training reports to her paper, even though it meant considerable expense. The success of these reports forced other Sunday papers to follow her example. "Letters to the editor" sent to 46 Fleet Street were from now on addressed to "Madam," and readers began to feel comfortable conversing with Rachel on subjects that had once been reserved for men. With Frederick's consent, the chief subeditor of *The Observer,* Charles Lincoln Freeston, was transferred to assist Rachel at the *Sunday Times,* but Freeston survived only a few months under her leadership.

During the week, a parade of subeditors, reporters and newspaper messengers would call at Chesterfield Gardens. And on Saturdays, Rachel would be driven down to Fleet Street, her drafted editorials in hand. In her office, she would pore over the latest news, and when something caught her attention she would straightaway add comments about it to her editorial.

On one such instance, she was handed a report that affected her deeply, brought by her correspondent from the Westminster coroner's court. In the last round of a boxing match, well on his way to winning the £80 prize, twenty-three-year-old Walter James Croot received two blows from his American opponent. He fell on the back of his head and was taken to an upper room in the Sporting Club, where he died in the morning, never regaining consciousness. His opponent was accused of manslaughter, but it was deemed an accident by the jury. Rachel was appalled that the commercial interests of the sport took priority over the safety of the people who participated in it; she called for a change in the rules that permitted such incidents to be essentially considered a part of the game. But she failed, and the ruling still stands today.

Rachel felt strongly that the press could be used as a power for good; W. T. Stead, whom she regarded as the "apostle of the press, and the father, as it were, of modern journalism," exposed the naked truth and bitterly advised her to find out which way the wind was blowing, and trumpet it. She recalled their conversation years later:

> "My dear child," Mr. Stead said, "the whole matter is contained in a nutshell, if you will only listen for two minutes—even for less time—you will know the whole of the inner workings of journalism . . . In order to establish for a newspaper a position to impress its readers with a sense of your influence, it is needful before all things to find out what people are about to do, and then recommend them to do it. By such means is the public impressed with your sagacity and power, and so you may gain a real influence which may or may never be exercised."

Stead's disillusionment was apparent, and his comments reveal the seamy side of the profession, in which politicians and the press scratched each other's backs and scoops were offered in return for promised press support. Rachel disapproved. She called upon the press to desert "the comfortable and harmless position of the fly on the wheel, which would be thought to move the machine" and take part in the steering. She believed that an independent newspaper like her own, which held "views that might not be generally held" and advocated "policies that are not likely to come off within any time in which the interest of the reader might be sustained," could attract readers as long as it made sure that it obtained the very best news, as well as "the best financial and sporting information."

In keeping with this philosophy, she criticised her colleagues whose cheers or jeers were predetermined by their political affiliations. The curious public has no more opportunity to learn the facts than the inhabitants of outer space, she complained; her own paper would be free from party prejudices and "its political views [would be] based wholly upon national considerations." Standing outside the strictures of party, Rachel and her journalists would watch MPs' squabbles "as an entomologist observes the contest of rival tribes of ants."

Rachel's independent approach was supported by the externally imposed isolation she faced as a female editor. Much of a male editor's day was generally spent conferring with men in power and creating pacts with them, but Rachel's gender prevented her from ready access to these figures. An admiral would not inform her about the ill-prepared state of the navy, and politicians would refrain from whispering to her about party intrigues. Even Prime Minister William Gladstone refused to talk politics with Rachel, in spite of their long friendship.

Disenchanted with the posturing of politicians, Rachel didn't hold back from condemning their loose tongues and the slanderous words they threw at each other. In Rachel's view, if an inhabitant of Mars were to visit England during the general elections and were to form his opinion of the candidates from what their opponents said of them, he would get the impression that they were all habitual drunkards, heartless libertines and known swindlers. Compared to Parliament, "Sodom and Gomorrah would have contained a virtuous population. Contrasted with the average MP, Nero himself was an enlightened philanthropist." When the election was over, she noted that the losers attributed their defeat to anything but their own incapacity.

Once they were elected, Rachel was certain that the clubs, restaurants and theatres would be full of the victors every night. They would pose as victims of hard work, "whose exhausted systems require a vacation six times the length given to the working journalists, and twelve times that of the city clerk." The crux of the matter was, she wrote, as follows:

> Wealthy peers may have all the virtues of saints and all the abilities of senior wranglers, but if they do not know where the shoe pinches the masses, it is idle to pretend that they can deal effectively with the misery and wants of our millions of workers.

Much to Rachel's disdain, Lord Rosebery and his government did not have a single wage earner among his ministers.

Though not a party member or sympathiser, despite her privileged position Rachel's ideas nonetheless gave off a faint whiff of socialism. Criticising the government's revenue policies, she called for taxing "the right classes—those who could best afford it," and suggested taxes on many of the luxury items that she and Frederick enjoyed themselves, including pianos, top hats, billiard balls, playing cards, cats, bicycles and servants. And though she lived on the fortune made on the Stock Exchange by her late father-in-law, she warned that the Stock Exchange had "developed a secret power that has already proved injurious to the community and may easily become a danger to the State," and called for a public overhaul of its management. "There is too much consideration for profits of members of the Stock Exchange, and far too little for the welfare of the investing public," she wrote, going on to say that speculation in electric lighting companies had "postponed for a decade the development of that method of illumination."

Rachel was an ardent supporter of the working class's struggle for better pay and improved working conditions. She advised the trade unions to cooperate and prevent competition between the sexes, since "women accept the same class of work that is done by men at about a third of the men's pay, and thus gradually drive their husbands, fathers and brothers out of employment." No issue in labour relations escaped her attention. She campaigned against the absurdly high payments made to retired officials and the misery of the aged poor ("a menace to our civilisation"), advocating pensions for workers aged sixty years of age and older. The latter act finally passed in Parliament in 1908, but pensions were granted only to those aged seventy and older. Rachel also concerned herself with smaller matters, from the dearth of cheap but respectable eating houses for City clerks, to how a leading London firm of drapers forced all of their employees—including the humble messenger—to buy tall stovepipe hats at their own expense.

She distinguished between the unemployable—those who were unable or unwilling to adjust to the fast pace of progress ("the wastrels which the potter throws out; they can neither be turned into a cup nor a jug")—and workmen who were willing and able to work but unable to find jobs. She pressed for a state unemployment insurance program to be implemented for the latter; unfortunately, it would take another fifteen years, until 1911, for the first unemployment insurance legislation to pass in Parliament.

Wasteful and misplaced public spending was also a focus for Rachel. Upon reading the reports of the Committee of Public Accounts for 1893–94, she remarked that though it was "not as interesting as a blood curdler from the pen of Rudyard Kipling," some passages were nevertheless "enough to cause a cold perspiration to bedew the forehead of the average income tax payer." The military expenditure of England—a nation surrounded only by water—was out of all proportion; it was a full five times greater than the amount spent by

Germany, a country hemmed in by both France and Russia. Rachel dismissed as "mere claptrap" the argument that the subject of army finance was so obscure and complicated that none but trained military experts were equipped to discuss it. Arguing that the army was not being managed on sound business principles, she called for a profound reduction in costs and a marked increase in efficiency.

ONE INCIDENT IN particular clearly illustrates both Rachel's unique political views and her tenacity. In 1890 a Royal Commission led by Lord Hartington had recommended the abolishment of the office of commander-in-chief, but the government failed to act. Soon after starting as the *Sunday Times*'s editor, Rachel seconded this recommendation, and declared that in the interests of the country the seventy-seven-year-old Duke of Cambridge should retire from his post. She found the duke, who had been commander-in-chief for almost forty years, a man of "low intellectual calibre," who opposed improvements to the conduct of modern warfare. "It is simply appalling to think what might have happened if serious work had arisen for the British army during recent years," she declared. Her personal campaign—"one crying in the wilderness"—called for his resignation and the abolishment of the office; it would mean a net saving of two million pounds per annum for the government.

Despite the pressure he was under to resign, the Duke of Cambridge clung to his post. Sources in the Horse Guards leaked the information that he would retire only in 1897, after completing a full sixty years in uniform. But in November 1895, under the accumulating pressure of the press and public opinion, he finally gave in, retiring earlier than planned. Still unrelenting, Mrs. Beer advised the duke that now that he was free from military command he should use his leisure hours to attend to his other post as ranger of Hyde Park, which had become so dangerous that crossing it "at safety at certain hours, it is necessary for ladies to obtain an escort." She encouraged his successor, Lord Wolseley, whose authority in the role was now greatly modified, to take notice of the obesity of the majors and colonels of the Volunteer Regiments, "the backbone in the defence of this country." Many of them, Rachel wittily observed, were "of too full habit to be efficient in the field. To be 40 inches round the waist is incompatible with military fire and efficiency." In 1904 the post of commander-in-chief was finally abolished.

Not one to rest on her laurels, Rachel soon turned her attention elsewhere, tackling yet another controversial issue. On September 8, 1895, she earmarked a new target—"As the *Sunday Times* has been instrumental in securing the retirement of the Duke of Cambridge by sheer perseverance and repetition of its demands, this journal has determined to keep a warm corner for the special benefits of the Post Office Department." Ever the imperialist, she advocated a flat fee for letters sent within England and all over the rest of the empire, arguing that "cheap communication is the life and soul of trade, and is the raw material of diffused wealth."

The new stamp, the Imperial Penny Postage, would cost the government just seventy thousand pounds a year, a fraction of the vast sums that were squandered by incompetent officials each year on erecting palatial post offices. She hunted down the officials who objected to the plan and published their inflated salaries. Rachel, who was fond of quoting Kipling, asserted: "They do not know England. They are the veriest type of Kipling's 'poor little street bred people.' The two words most often on their lips are 'can't' and 'shan't.'" It took the Imperial Penny Postage three more years to be inaugurated, on Christmas Day, 1898.

MRS. BEER'S NEXT brainchild was the Public Amusements Bill—a bill that she believed would lead to the moral reformation of the poor and, ultimately, a reduction in crime. She invested time and money in the creation and promotion of this bill, engaging lawyers and experts to help her make her case. As she argued:

Fourteen million pounds sterling now spent on crime and pauperism is largely the result, not directly of drink, but of the ugliness and monotony of life that lead to the formation of drinking and gambling habits. . . . Moral reform of the individual will come through free access to dancing music and concerts, theatre, sports like cricket and football, and any games excluding those involving the use of cards or dice. Personal redemption through art would enter into "the veins of the nation's life."

To sway her readers' sympathies and persuade them to support free public amusements subsidised by their taxes, Rachel asked them to imagine what it would be like to live in one confined room with their families, as many less fortunate people did. "Add to eating, sleeping and illness, the necessary washing of clothes and the cleansing of persons," she wrote, "—No wonder that the suffocating, hard-toiling family-head, cannot resist the magnetism of the gin-palace. . . . To shut a public house on such a man is a mere piece of class tyranny, unless a fresh and purified house for the public is open for him and his like." To Rachel the solution was clear—councils should provide airy, warm and cheerful halls where men might go in the evenings with their wives and children, where wholesome refreshments might be obtained at a low cost.

Rachel sent her proposal to members of Parliament, clergymen, newspaper editors and county councillors, and she took the trouble of personally meeting with key decision makers. She was disappointed to discover that projects such as hers had better prospects if they emanated from political leaders, or even their secretaries or minor adjuncts. Without an official stamp of approval, the interest of her eminent listeners waned, and "the conversation was abruptly changed to 'when are you going to give another party, or why do you not go oftener to the Opera?'" Although in her mind she was not simply a Mayfair lady, it was going to take some time and a firm commitment to convince others of that truth.

Another hurdle was the potential cost of the project. The Marquess of Salisbury, who was soon to become prime minister, wrote to

Rachel to say that a bill such as her Sunday Amusements proposal would not pass in Parliament since the burden of rates was already heavy.

Undaunted, Rachel tried to stir public opinion in her favour. She sent her correspondents to interview leading artists, hoping to rally their support. But Sarah Bernhardt objected to state-aided theatre, and George Bernard Shaw's assessment was that "there are many people who don't use theatres, who even look upon them as the gates of Hell, and they will ask, why the rates they pay are to be used for providing amusements of which they disapprove. Bread would be a good thing to communise, because everybody used it." On the whole, her idea of social reform through entertainment was rejected as too utopian.

After the failure of the Public Amusements Bill, Rachel channeled her disappointment into supporting other, already existing, free Sunday activities. She thought there was nothing drearier than a Sunday in London to a man who was neither a churchgoer nor member of a club; as she put it, "there are other windows to the soul besides churches and chapels." She commended the London County Council for its open-air concerts and applauded Parliament's decision to open national museums and art galleries in London on Sunday afternoons from two in the afternoon until dusk. However, the latter experiment failed—the museums, galleries and libraries remained deserted, and were eventually re-shut on Sundays. Music was the only Sunday recreation that actually attracted audiences. Rachel wrote, "It will, of course, take time to form popular taste in music in London, nor can we reasonably hope that the butcher boy will just yet desert his beloved comic songs for the peerless joys of Chopin and Beethoven. But we are clearly on the high-road to a condition of things representing an improvement in popular taste."

Despite the fact that Sunday hours failed to draw crowds, the tenacious Rachel was not ready to give up entirely—she just took a slightly different tack. She began calling for the opening of all museums and the principal public art collections in rotation at least one

Saturday a month until midnight, "with bands and refreshments, that would be of the nature of an educational *conversazione* for the people, at merely nominal entrance fee, or entirely free of charge." She also proposed that excursions to the countryside be combined with the orthodox keeping of the Lord's Day. In the age of swift and inexpensive locomotion, people could easily benefit from travelling and spending time in the fresh air, which would be conducive to peaceful and harmonious thoughts. In the evenings, after relaxing in the charms of Nature and before returning home, "the jaded inhabitants of towns" could walk into one of the local churches and pray there "more efficiently."

When *Punch* published a mock serenade to celebrate what made the English what they are, along with the monarchy, the legal system, cricket fields and farms, they included Sunday:

> . . . for Sunday, the one day out of seven
> Designed to draw our English thoughts from earthly things to
> Heaven;
> The day on which no Lawson nor Harmsworth may appear,
> The day kept strictly sacred to Church and Mrs. Beer;
> On which with good and pious things our moral thanks we
> drench . . .

Of all the Sunday newspapers at the time, the most popular was *Lloyd's Weekly News,* which was the first to sell a million copies, followed by the *Reynolds's News* (350,000), and *The Sunday Chronicle* (175,000). The *Sunday Times* sold a fraction—just a few thousand—and Rachel was flattered that it was nevertheless shortlisted as "one of the causes of the predominance of the Anglo-Saxon."

CHAPTER EIGHTEEN

A New Woman

A few months after Rachel assumed her role as editor of the *Sunday Times*, the Society of Women Journalists held its winter session. Miss March Phillipps was to discuss the topic "Women as Editors," but "having reflected that one swallow does not make a summer," she changed her focus to "Women in Journalism." Mrs. Beer's case demonstrated that women did not lack "sufficient resource, critical faculty, and discrimination to take command of a paper for general readers," but she was still the only exception to the rule.

Rachel strongly advocated women's right to vote, though she was not a member of the suffrage movement. The movement's opponents held that women had no right to the vote since they were discharged of the citizenship duties that fell upon men, such as jury service and participating in the defense of the country. In 1899, when four American states gave women the vote, Rachel called upon England to emulate Colorado, which recognised women's right and duty to sit on juries and to enlist in the army. "Whether a corps of Amazons will speedily be formed as the upshot of this new law remains to be seen. . . . When the first female regiment is enrolled, the last logical stronghold of the anti-female suffrage will fall before it," she predicted.

America was a laboratory for producing precedents, according to

Rachel. Giving women the ballot had revolutionised elections in Colorado. "The candidates for congress used to be nominated in the saloons," civil rights activist Susan B. Anthony told the *Sunday Times* when she came to London in July 1899. "They had only got to suit the men who assembled there. But now, neither Democrats nor Republicans can afford to please just saloon men. Candidates who please other than saloon frequenters must be chosen, and thus the women's vote affects the balance of power, and elevates society." The American guest was optimistic about the future of the suffrage movement in England; in the early 1880s, only the most liberal of the Liberals endorsed their work, but by the late 1890s, "the Suffrage movement are quite the fashion, and all hands are stretched out to us."

Even more than the vote, Rachel believed in professional equality. As was common elsewhere in Europe, English women could study law, but they could not appear in court; to Rachel this was a travesty. To gain support for her cause, Rachel published the plight of the Belgian lawyer Mademoiselle Marie Popelin, whose opponents at the Belgian corporation of lawyers argued that a woman was a "frivolous creature, given to gossiping, her mind set on dress and hairdressing," and was thus not fit to wear the cap and gown. On Mademoiselle Popelin's visit to London, the *Sunday Times* was quick to secure an interview. "Do you think many women would have entrusted their affairs to you?" Mademoiselle Popelin was asked. "In England, it is rather sad to see how considerable a number of women object to employ a woman doctor." "It is the same with us," she answered, "but despite that, there are a large number of women who prefer to entrust their affairs to women." Both women agreed—there was no reason why men alone should represent clients in court, litigating in the interests of both sexes; however, the barrier against female lawyers would not be removed in England until 1922.

Feminists from around the world found a welcoming platform in the *Sunday Times*. A correspondent from the paper was always present at the Pioneer Club House at Bruton Street, a club that was created for the "New Woman," which hosted a variety of events including lectures. The *Sunday Times* was filled with lengthy reports of the animated debates that went on there, on controversial topics such as "What to do with our wife beaters" ("the cheapest of all the many domestic recreations with which the British workman may occupy his spare time or wet day or after bank-holiday carouse"). They questioned whether Eve was the first Pioneer or if that credit should go to the daughters of the biblical Zelophehad, the five sisters who claimed their father's inheritance since he had no sons and, gaining it, set a precedent for the rights of other women of Israel to inherit in the absence of a male heir. When the subject in question was New Journalism, Arnold White argued that the prophets Ezekiel and Jeremiah were already the New Journalists of their time, and the nineteenth-century equivalent of the biblical prophetess Deborah was "the editor of the *Sunday Times*."

Rachel also tried to give female journalists their first exposure as frequently as she could, finding them "quite the equal of men, in accuracy, punctuality and discretion." She thought it was fair to her journalists and the public to acknowledge the writers' identity, but her honesty caused her to lose some of her up-and-coming talents; their bylines caught the eyes of other editors. Rachel remained undaunted, revealing in an interview, "No, I am not sorry when they leave me, for it generally means that they are making progress; and all this is for the benefit of women. Further, I believe in not standing still."

Along with championing women's rights, Rachel did also cater to what were traditionally considered women's interests. Adding a feminine touch to the *Sunday Times,* her Paris correspondent brought the latest in hairdressing news: "No one ever saw a French woman, high or low, displaying that inartistic mound of lightly compressed frizzy hair, which in England is worn alike by Princesses and shop girls." The paper also ran a regular column called "In Fashion's Footsteps," which helped readers keep pace with the latest trends, reinforced by

Alexander Pope: "Very quickly, so swiftly does the vogue change nowadays, and so rapidly do we seem to pass 'from grave to gay, from lively to severe.'" Rachel also initiated a unique column, "First Night Dresses," for which she sent a correspondent to the theatre to report only on the actors' costumes—"In act II, evening dress is very much in evidence, both for men and women, the mess uniforms of the officers adding greatly to the bright sadness of the scene," was the report from Roger Marshall's comedy *The Second in Command*.

In one of her columns, Rachel openly sympathised with the ladies of the Salvation Army, who rebelled against their repulsive brown uniform—"Beautiful uniform adds to the power of persuasion," she wrote, and suggested that a new uniform be designed for "the fair crusaders."

Drawing on her background as a high-society lady of fashion, she suggested outfits with balloon sleeves or "blouses with the fashionable ripple basque or Louis Quinze jackets, or new loose-backed coats, with skirts accordion-pleated, and veiled with chiffon."

From time to time, there were even notes on fashion for men. One issue reported on the new "stand-up collar with the corners turned sharply back so as to leave the throat free." Putting the garment in its wider context, the paper asserted that "this [was] evidently one result of the South African war," since men had become accustomed to the easy collar band of the khaki uniform. Upon Queen Victoria's death in 1901, male readers were advised that Bond Street shops offered many styles and patterns in gray and black trousers, to meet the mourning code.

She also had no reservations about including items that were far from headline material in her editorials, for the edification of her readers. "If it be possible for the readers of the *Sunday Times* to detach their minds from the maintenance of the Empire," she wrote, for example, they should open their hearts to the agony of the foodless and waterless cats left on their own in the summer holiday, "no better off than if they were in the Gobi desert, or marooned on a coral reef." She advised the holidaying owners further to leave a shilling a week in the hands of the milkman, butcher or caretaker "for puss's benefit."

What all this amounted to was that Rachel clearly had the woman reader in mind. She took the risk of printing articles that might be off-putting to male readers, who might skip them or even decide the newspaper was too feminine for their taste, canceling their subscriptions; for her, it was a risk well worth taking.

THOUGH RACHEL HAD been cut out of the Sassoons' family circle, she embraced her ancestry proudly. In the biographical note that she prepared for publications such as *Who's Who*, she always mentioned her origins and her parents' names, and in the interview that she gave to *Woman* magazine she did not hide the family rift—she was introduced as "one of the wealthy family of Sassoon, with whom, however, she had had but little intercourse since her marriage, which took place in a church." Though Rachel revealed in the interview that she had been baptised, this was apparently not widely known, and the *Jewish Year Book* continued to include a short biography of her in the section "Who's Who in British Jewry."

Rachel did not display any grudge toward her family, and when opportunity arose, she did not hesitate to send a *Sunday Times* cross-examiner to interview or write a profile on one of the Sassoons. Her aunt Flora, who still lived in Bombay—"in the land of the sun, in the land of the poppies, at the Gate of India"—ran the Sassoon firm there single-handedly, and Rachel admired her from afar as a role model of a supportive wife and a successful career woman:

The business capabilities of Mrs. Sassoon are the more remarkable since she was not brought up or trained for commercial work, but on the death of her husband in 1894 (to whom she always was a great help, accompanying him frequently to his office, and staying with him during his hours of work, so that he might have the advantage of her views), she studied the details for six months, and then took up the position that he had hitherto occupied. Mrs. Solomon Sassoon's career tends to prove that there is no post, however difficult, not even positions of the greatest financial importance, that cannot be taken up by a woman if she is in earnest and has the strength of mind and will to say, "I will succeed," and act with determination, so that success must follow.

Sketching the profile of her admired Indian relative in her newspaper, Rachel poked fun at the hypocrisy of the English Sassoons who had disowned her:

> Neither she herself nor her husband ever ventured to any part of the western world, where their co-religionists have in so large measure become free thinkers—agnostics with prejudice unsupported by practice, to whom pride and purity of race seem of greater moment than purity of faith and conduct. Mr. and Mrs. S.D. [Solomon David] Sassoon were not drawn by the high social and intellectual attractions which would have been open to them here; they had care to live in the beauties of their position, in the laws of their Jewish faith, in its ceremonial, in its severity, in its restriction.

One Sassoon with whom Rachel did maintain contact was her brother Alfred. A year after Alfred and Theresa Thornycroft married, they signed a postnuptial settlement, which was intended to help resolve some of their emerging differences. Though the promises they made each other in this document helped keep them together for a number of years, and the couple produced three sons, it failed to permanently sustain their relationship. "Her husband is behaving like a madman," wrote Rachel's old flame Hamo Thornycroft in his diary. "He is a caution to us westerns—don't be tempted to marry where there [is] Eastern blood and a Sematic [sic] nostril." Rachel invited her brother and his wife to a musical party she was hosting, but it was one of their last appearances together. Not long after, Alfred left Theresa for another woman. The Thornycrofts blamed the Sassoons for setting up a match between Alfred and a Jewish lady "to lure him back to the faith." Caught between her brother—the only Sassoon left for her—and his estranged wife—her close friend—Rachel continued to see them both.

Alfred moved to Eastbourne, hoping that the warmer climate and fresh air would ease the tuberculosis from which he, like his younger brother before him, was now suffering. He was too weak to travel to a sanatorium in Switzerland, and his doctors predicted that it was highly unlikely that he would recover. His mother and brother were quick to welcome the lost sheep back into the fold. It was a well-orchestrated reunion; Joseph came from Ashley Park, Flora from Brighton, and Alfred's three sons arrived with their nurse from their home in Weirleigh. Flora was delighted to see her grandchildren and was very warm and kind, bombarding them with questions without waiting for the answers. She told the boys that she had seen them once before, for although she had banished Alfred from her life, Flora had kept track of her favourite son and knew the names and birthdates of each of her baptised grandchildren. Unfolding a roll of paper, she pointed to the name at the top—David Sassoon. "Your great-grandfather," she said. Then, running her finger down to the bottom, "Yourselves." "Sure enough, there we were, at the foot of the tree, and it was the first time I had seen my own name in print," wrote Siegfried Sassoon in his memoirs.

After a rupture of eleven years, the reunion was exclusively a Sassoon event. Two were absent from the family gathering around Alfred's deathbed—his wife Theresa and his sister Rachel, who were not invited. They were also kept away from his funeral on April 22, 1895. It was Flora who dictated the closing chapter in her son's life, ordering his burial in the Sassoon family plot in London, against the will of his wife, who wanted him buried in their parish churchyard. "My father has become a Christian by religion after marrying my mother, but for some reason, the obsequies was Jewish," Siegfried wrote; the children found the ceremony eerie, and felt as if their father had been taken away from them by strangers.

CHAPTER NINETEEN

Rivals

Under Rachel's leadership, the *Sunday Times,* which once had a reputation for being Conservative, became Independent. "It is essentially a political, literary, musical, dramatic, fashionable and sporting paper . . . with more variety in its contents than class papers usually present," wrote the *Newspaper Press Directory and Advertisers' Guide.*

Fellow women journalists applauded Rachel. Her sisters at *The Humanitarian* praised the fresh features of interest she had added to the *Sunday Times,* and declared that under her "vigorous rule" it had improved "in tone and news," while those at *The Woman's Signal* congratulated her for increasing the circulation so much that "she was offered more than twice the sum she paid for the paper."

Her male colleagues, though, found it much harder to come to terms with Rachel. Her editorials were said to have "all the shrewdness and commonsense of her sex, but would have been better for a little manly punch," and she was teased that—typically for a woman—she summed up the most abstruse problems of foreign and domestic politics in "dogmatic assertion with which ninety nine of a hundred persons would not agree." Some of the men even joked that she had turned her broadsheet into the "she" to *The Observer's* "he," so when Rachel declared her wish to renew the *Sunday Times's* "sprightly girlhood like the eagle," her rivals were quick to pick up on the turn of phrase. An article published in *The Journalist and Newspaper Proprietor* taunted the thirty-five-year-old Rachel, asking whether she "intends to renew her youth through the medium of a paper?" Not content with that, they went on:

"If she does, she need not stop short at 'sprightly girlhood.' 'Cackling infancy' would have been quite appropriate."

Whether or not her views were indeed objectionable to that many people, Rachel was undeterred; she continued to write extensively about politics and foreign affairs. This was as much a reflection of her personal interests as it was her professional ones.

THE INTERIOR OF the Beers' home reflected their mutual admiration of French culture. The walls were bedecked with no less than sixteen paintings by Corot, the Poet of the Landscape, known for his mastery of light and shadow. The gem of the collection was *Paysage au Clair de Lune*, a landscape depicting a moonlit lake, with a shadowy figure in a boat and an enigmatic crouching woman among the trees. "These scented banks exude the sensuality of amorous nights. One boat on this lake, and we will start reciting in unison the most inspired lines of our poets," raved the critic Jules Castagnary when the painting was first exhibited at the Paris Salon of 1874. Rachel further pursued her interest in all things French by taking conversation and literary lessons from a French lady who came to her at Chesterfield Gardens.

Rachel certainly thought that France could teach Britain a lesson or two in international good manners. Always concentrating on the business at hand, Britain had gained a reputation as an impolite nation—"We English are racially impatient of emotion and sentiment," Rachel criticised her countrymen—while France's universal popularity "rises from their acquaintance with the art of making themselves pleasant."

Perhaps unsurprisingly, France was also Rachel's favourite holiday destination, and as a frequent traveller she marvelled at the new cross-channel ferry that allowed businesspeople to leave London in the afternoon and arrive in Paris by midnight. But in her estimation the cost of the journey was too high, and the ferry service itself was appalling. She wrote: "When the historian of the twenty-first century describes the relationship between the French and the English towards the close of the nineteenth, he will record with amazement the fact that direct intercourse between the nearest ports of England and France was principally maintained by tiny steamers between thirty and forty years old." Only half a dozen private cabins were available, and delicate ladies were forced to suffer their seasickness in public. She welcomed the introduction of modern cranes, to replace the endless strings of porters, like African coolies, slowly walking up and down the gangway with the passengers' luggage on their head.

Enjoying the benefits to be found elsewhere in their favoured country, the Beers followed William Gladstone and his family to Biarritz for a holiday. The mild climate and invigorating air had made it a haven for the international who's who, and the soirées and gay balls of the British winter colony were regularly detailed in the Court and Fashion columns of the London papers. In one issue of *The Observer*, the paper's gossip columnist, who was stationed there, reported that Mr. and Mrs. F. A. Beer were expected daily to return from an excursion into Spain and settle back at the Hotel d'Angleterre.

While Frederick and Rachel mingled socially with the powers that be, Rachel did not forget her duties as an editor, even at the risk of appearing hypocritical. When Prime Minister Salisbury took a month's holiday at his Chalet Cecil in Dieppe, Rachel chastised him that an escape "from his native land is not altogether flattering to the patriotism of his fellow subjects." Why is it, she wondered, that whenever British statesmen "stand in need of rest and a holiday, they repair to the coast of France to obtain what they need. The last places to which a French president or minister in high office would think of going on a holiday expedition, would be to Brighton or Scarborough." To remove any doubts that might be raised by her own choice of holiday destination, she quoted the eighteenth-century poet

William Cowper and pledged that she would never exchange the "sullen skies" of England and her "fields without a flower" for warmer France, with all her vines.

Although Rachel admired French culture, she was harsh in condemning the rapid changes in France's government, which seemed to "indicate moral as well as political defects in the French people." She also believed that France's colonial aspirations could be contrary to England's interests—"Friendship with such a power is impossible. Red and ruthless anarchy is waiting round the corner," she wrote. She reprimanded her colleagues who kept their heads thrust into the sand like ostriches to comply with their readers' wish to be let alone; they failed in their duty to alert the British public to France's restless colonial aspirations.

Rachel—who had taken the helm of the *Sunday Times* at a time when Britain seemed to be approaching involvement in an international conflict—constantly saw dark clouds of war gathering on the horizon. She believed the Great Powers were jealous of England for occupying "all the pleasant and temperate regions on the earth's surface," and she was anxious. Five million soldiers served in the Dual Alliance of France and Russia, and a further 5.7 million in the Triple Alliance of Germany, Austria and Italy. The splendidly isolated English, who had more to lose than their rivals, were obliged to join the armament race. "No one can tell when the thunderstorm will burst, but with limited number of men and a definite amount of wealth, the continual effort to increase armament beyond the available resources of the people can only end in war or exhaustion"—this was what Rachel feared.

With much alarm, and with her hospital background in mind, Rachel read Sir William McCormack's prediction that in future wars the number of severely wounded would be much greater than ever before. President of the Royal College of Surgeons and an expert on military medicine, McCormack concluded that with the penetration power of the new rifles, bullets could pass through the bodies of three men in line, shatter the bone and inflict serious or fatal wounds at a distance of more than two miles. "The moral of this," wrote Mrs. Beer, "is that as guns improve in penetration, so should our diplomacy. By this means only can the great war be averted, that will beat the record for slaughter, red ruin, and working-class disaster."

The Women's Suffrage Bill, coming before Parliament in May 1896, seemed to Rachel to be an antidote to the menace of war. "Most men seem to think themselves so much more attractive when quarrelling, that one is tempted to believe half the controversies in both international and domestic politics owe their origins to this masculine legend," was her cutting assessment; if women could get the vote she was certain their influence "could not fail to operate in favour of diplomacy and peace." But it took the Great War—and women's participation in it—for Parliament in 1918 to grant the vote to women over thirty years of age and, another ten years later, to approve the Equal Franchise Act.

One of Rachel's foremost concerns was how the home front would fare if there was a military confrontation. England was ill-prepared, since less than a fourth of the wheat it consumed was homegrown, and in Rachel's nightmarish scenario the country would fall prey to foreign speculators and the price of bread would soar beyond the reach of the working class and the unemployed. Dismissing the commander-in-chief's assurance that the navy was strong enough to ensure the supply of wheat, she called upon the government to increase wheat production and to store sufficient supplies of grain. Not just the prospect of hunger worried her: if prices rose to famine heights there might be "an insurrection in England against the existing structures of society, however successful the war may be."

In Rachel's mind, Germany loomed as the greatest threat for a potential conflict, an issue that she addressed frequently in the *Sunday Times*. She characterized Kaiser Wilhelm II as "impulsive and hysterical" and a "braggart disturber of the public peace," and though she complimented Germany's emphasis on technological education, which put it twenty years ahead of England, her compliment was double-edged. The progress of militarism, the vast amounts of money invested in the army, and the struggle between the reactionary forces "can only end in violent explosion," she predicted.

The United States was probably the only country that Rachel never saw as a potential threat, choosing instead to focus on the uniting power of a shared culture and history—"The memories of Westminster Abbey, the traditions of Parliament, Shakespeare's country and the lustre of English literature are theirs as much as ours," she wrote. Any future differences of opinion between the two branches of the Anglo-Saxon race could surely be settled by diplomatic means, since blood was thicker than water, "and the Americans are more to us than any nation of alien blood, as we shall see if ever England is forced to fight with her back to the wall." To Rachel, the marriage of the Duke of Marlborough and Miss Consuelo Vanderbilt from New York epitomised the benefit that could come from an Anglo-American alliance, "and if the Duke's taste and ambitions lie in the direction of a political career, the lady's millions will enable him to indulge them."

Americans' practicality was to be admired, as was their ability to spot the commercial value of ideas. Rachel also thought a great deal of American patriotism. The practice of flying a flag over every schoolhouse in the U.S.A. seemed exemplary to her; the Union Jack had always been raised proudly over her grandfather's schools and institutions in Bombay. "Nothing like the flag of England to focus the patriotism of English children, many of whom in these migratory days will pass their maturity under other skies," she mused.

Rachel was not blind to American faults, however; in fact, she was often highly critical of "Cousin Jonathan." After 120 years, American democracy was anything but a complete or conspicuous success; in many areas liberty was unknown and "Capitalist rule is supreme." The private enterprise of America had developed monsters capable of imperiling civilisation, she argued: "Instead of doing the honest business of the world, it steals the savings of the people by teaching them to speculate in myths." She also resented the corruption of the English language by American imports in words and spelling, and called for the establishment of a standard of purity of the English tongue.

Russia was a source of fascination and repulsion for Rachel. She remarked with great foresight, "Revolution seems to be the sole avenue to freedom open to the Russian people," and she hoped that Alexander III's death would liberate Russian Jews from persecution there. She criticised the Rothschilds of Paris and Frankfurt and other Jewish tycoons for having condoned this persecution by providing Russia with funds; in her estimation, they cared "for cash gains, more than for the agony of their co-religionists." Rachel expected that the British alliance with the new tsar would include greater freedoms for both Jews and Protestants. Paraphrasing Heinrich Heine, the German-Jewish poet who stated that every nation has the kind of Jew it deserves, and echoing the experience of her own family, she added:

> If they are welcomed, they become nationalised and are absorbed. When they are persecuted they wax mighty and multiply, but maintain a separate people. English insularity and French levity have gained enormously when blended with the persistent purpose and the cosmopolitan traditions of the people of the Dispersion.

Being "scrupulously fair in allowing all sides of any question to be fairly heard," the *Sunday Times* published an interview with political writer Madame Novikoff, who was generally seen as "MP for Russia" for her efforts to explain Russia to Englishmen, and England to the Russians. Novikoff, who often wrote for *The Observer,* was asked about the state of Russian Jewry. "We must try to make them happy," was her promising opening remark. However, she then continued, "But the matter is largely in the hands of the Jews themselves." They are aloof, she argued, and too many of them display hostility to Russian creeds and ideals, and exploit the people's passion and need. "As a rule, their ideal is a material one. The worship of the Golden Calf, which was ordered when Moses was on the Mount, continues to this day. They never believed in immortality in our sense of the word and therefore adored the good things of this life—the fleshy and material side of human existence."

Though the "Witness Box" interviewers professed to be "cross-examiners," and indeed they did usually confront their interviewees with probing questions, Madame Novikoff was not challenged. She was invited to go on and express her opinion on other matters like Home Rule in Ireland, Armenia and Cyprus. The interview appeared next to Rachel's editorial and she may have even conducted it herself. Whether she did or not, she chose not to censor its contents.

Rachel's concern for her ancestral brethren stemmed from her overall compassion for persecuted minorities. She was shaken by photographs of the mass murder of Armenian Christians at Erzeroum by the Turks, published in *The Graphic*. A story was circulated about a woman who spotted the photographer while she was standing weeping by two corpses. She stopped crying for long enough to curse him: "May your house fall on your head! You English have deceived us!" Rachel concurred. "The Armenian woman spoke justly," she commented on the government's failure to intervene. "England's shame will yet come home to her. We have never proved faithless without suffering in purse and reputation later on. We broke our word in the Transvaal and deservedly lost the richest goldfield in the world."

With the election of the first two Indian MPs, Rachel hoped to see someday in Parliament "eighty or a hundred gentlemen of colour from a great dependency." But when MP Dadabhai Naoroji declared that the British were not observing any of the Ten Commandments in India, she stood firmly by her adopted country. She said that giving India peace by ending the internecine strife that tore it apart "is one of the most signal and beneficent merits of our occupation." Rachel did agree with the MP, though, that the financial relationship between India and England should be on a more equal footing.

Ever sympathetic toward the oppressed, Rachel Beer was alone

among the press in protesting "the high hand seizure" of the unin-
habited rocky island of Trinidade, some 650 miles from Brazil, to
serve as an anchorage for Sir John Pender's Eastern Submarine Telegraph Cable. Though Pender was a friend and business associate of
her late father-in-law, Julius Beer, she had no reservations in criticising the government for caving in to his interests. "Pender's cables
have done more harm to British reputation for good feeling and fair
play than any advantage gained"; she argued that up to that point
England had expanded and colonised without wanting to fight the
whole world, so why do it now, she asked. To her satisfaction, Britain
was eventually forced to hand the island over to Brazil.

Rachel was passionate about inventions and, most of all, new
methods of transportation. Fast trains, light railways, flying machines, the digging of the Panama Canal—all received her enthusiastic approval. She even supported the idea of placing a fleet of saloon
passenger steamers on the Thames, so that travellers who made the
crossing by bus or underground could instead do so by water. But
above all, she was passionate about "the horseless carriage," which
was exactly suited to those "too plump and too poor" to keep horses
or carriages or ride bicycles. " 'Automotors' will give us cleaner streets
and fewer painful sights of suffering horses," expounded Rachel. She
saw no possible hitches—"It is said that an ordinary person accustomed to street traffic can learn to manipulate the new machine in a
very short time." But in fact, there were other obstacles to machine-
powered carriages—the law required that a man with a red flag
needed to walk at least twenty yards ahead of these vehicles, and that
their pace could not exceed four miles per hour. All of this was intended to prevent accidents caused by frightened horses. Calling for a
change in the law, with characteristic humour Rachel commented,
"The time has arrived when horses must overcome their neurotic tendencies. We hear a great deal of the New Woman. What we want now
is the New Horse."

She marvelled at the limitless ingenuity of mankind and watched
enthusiastically the developments in electricity, which promised to "be-

come an agent of social and economic progress." And indeed, her residence was one of the first to be lit by electricity—"which for us was something quite out of the ordinary," Siegfried Sassoon recalled. A practical woman, Rachel was not satisfied with just recording the news; she also looked for solutions to some of the issues she reported on, using the new technology. After reporting on fire victims at Edgware Road and several other locations in the same week, she challenged inventors to construct new inexpensive fire escapes, ones "which could be readily used even by inmates who are not skilled in athletics."

RACHEL HAD ENTERED a very productive and invigorating period in her life. Returning home from the office late on Saturday nights, she was much less tired than after a society function. "Besides, in journalism, there is a sense of achievement, which, I fear, I should not experience as a result of much social relaxation," she told Arnold Bennett. "The fact is, the work suits me, and I find in it all the compensation I need for whatever trouble it may be."

But though things were going smoothly with the editorship itself, Rachel continued to wage wars on the home front. For one, the hundred-year opposition to Sunday newspapers had not yet died out. She asked the legendary journalist William T. Stead for his firsthand account of the Chicago riots, which erupted when the Pullman Palace Car workers protested a wage cut of 25 percent. Stead declined, excusing himself by stating that he never wrote for Sunday papers since he tried never to do any work on the Lord's Day, not even so much as writing a letter. She challenged him: why did he employ his milkman on Sunday mornings, then? Stead replied that he drank milk on Sunday "for the benefit of the cows." They would feel uncomfortable on Sundays, he said, if no one milked them. Rachel Beer was quick to respond: he should feel uncomfortable if no one read her paper on Sundays. "What is the objection to Sunday papers—almost all the work of which is done before Saturday midnight—when, so far as we know, no objection is raised to Monday papers, the work of which must be done on Sunday?" she argued.

"There is no *Sunday Times* published in heaven," thundered the Hampstead preacher Dr. Horton, who made an attack on those "who bury themselves in the *Sunday Times,* and renounce the scriptures for the journal." Mrs. Beer replied tartly:

> But if there be no *Sunday Times* in heaven, surely the few fleeting moments our readers enjoy on earth, might be worse spent than in reading a journal that they will be deprived hereafter. . . . We can ourselves, at any rate, confidently assert that we will never undertake to edit this journal in those regions which form the alternative destination of mankind.

By 1901 the Sunday Observance Act was very loosely enforced, though Rachel was sorry to say that "occasionally, through an excess of zeal on the part of the police, an unfortunate barber, baker or tobacconist is brought before the magistrates and fined." To her mind, it was just one example of archaic statutes that should be revised or struck from the books entirely. She was particularly astounded by a case from America in which a Yale student was imprisoned for kissing a girl:

> It was not that the young lady objected, because they were an engaged couple, but because there is a law still remaining on the Statute Book of New Haven, that it is penal to kiss on Sunday. . . . Perhaps one of these days we shall have someone in London sent to prison for not attending church. Except for the innocent victim, it would be rather welcome than otherwise, because the community must be shocked into making a protest, or these old statutes will still continue to linger on.

It actually took until 1969 for the seventeenth-century Sunday Observance Act to be repealed.

Other threats loomed over the profession. Rachel was disturbed that editors were hedged round by libel laws, menaced by heavy liabilities, and consequently, editorial comment upon individual malpractice was "generally toned down to a point where it timidly verges on inanity." She recounted a recent instance of an editor who was so careful to avoid committing a libelous act, even toward the dead, that he referred to Cain as "the reputed murderer of Abel."

There was also the constant worry that another paper might steal one of the *Sunday Times*'s initiatives. On one occasion, the threat came from a most unsuspected source. Rachel was saddened that there was no ceremony on Nelson's Day in Trafalgar Square, so on October 21, 1894, flying the flag of patriotism, she called for the Admiralty to place a guard of honour around Nelson's Column, and for the next year's anniversary, she planned to propose a wreath of laurel to be henceforth placed on the plinth of the statue. She shared the idea with her husband, and, without her knowledge, *The Observer* approached the Office of Works. When the idea was approved, Frederick ordered a large wreath on behalf of his newspaper.

Rachel first realised that her idea had been stolen when she saw the draft of Frederick's editorial for October 20, 1895, announcing that "the Navy League, at the suggestion of *The Observer,* will lay a wreath of laurel." Furious, she tore up her own editorial, and wrote instead:

> It has been a matter of notoriety in journalistic circles for some times past, that *The Observer* has watched the progress and evolution of the *Sunday Times* with vigilance and suspicion bordering upon jealousy. . . . We congratulate *The Observer,* for it shall never be said that journalistic ambition blinds us to merit in the nearest and dearest of our contemporaries. But we did believe that the honest *Observer* would have acknowledged the source of his inspiration, but we were mistaken. *The Observer* is resolved to get on.

She remembered the insult and, in the following years, the *Sunday Times* refrained from sending a wreath on Nelson's Day, while *The*

Observer continued to do so. But when Rachel eventually took over her husband's newspaper, she continued his tradition for him.

This was not the only clash between the two papers. In June 1895, Frederick promised his readers that *The Observer* would continue its policy of never being "a bigoted partisan of either Whig or Tory, Liberal or Conservative." He believed that "Sunday was not the most appropriate day of the week for the display of party animosities or the discussion of embittered party controversies." And further, in a dramatic move, he reduced the price of his paper by half—to two pence—hoping it would bring the paper "within the reach of a wider public than was possible in the era of high-priced journalism."

Rachel, who in her editorials called *The Observer* "our closest and most dangerous rival," was quick to respond and make a very public fuss about it, attributing the price cut to competition with her paper. If it was a fight they wanted, it was a fight they would get, she promised: "*The Observer*'s steady walk is already stirred into an amble. We shall extend our portly contemporary into a gallop before we have finished with him." On another occasion she remarked, "We notice with many grave misgivings that a struggle for existence has driven our respectable brother to react to occult practices and black magic." In this case, she was paying a backhanded compliment to *The Observer* on a scoop about the appointment of Edward Tyas Cook as the new editor of *The Daily News*. The story was repudiated by all concerned, but it turned out to be correct. "The ambitious *Observer*, Macbeth-like, has taken to listening to wizard voices, and publishes prophecies 'that lie like truth.' Even now it may be haunted by spirits and utterances, condemning it to 'sleep no more.' Pondering on what the consequences of this may be, we cannot close our eyes," she scoffed.

Despite the war of words in print, a close bond endured between husband and wife that was free of personal and professional rivalry. Rachel was very attentive to Frederick, and he often consulted with his "brilliant and indefatigable wife." Her outrage was more calculated than deeply felt. She seemed intent on generating fake competition with what she called "our aged contemporary" and "our elderly rival," but her declarations of war were not made out of anger. They were meant to stir the water, attract attention and increase circulation for both papers.

RACHEL'S NEXT CRUSADE revolved around the increase in public statues erected around London, some of which were merely "abortive attempts to perpetuate honoured names by distorted representations of forms and features," she argued. Although she came from a dynasty that had raised statues in the past, and had married into the family who had built the largest and most elaborate mausoleum in Highgate, Rachel questioned the human urge to multiply effigies in hammered stone. She called for a periodic evaluation of the claims of past worthies for permanent occupation on pedestals as members of the nation's illustrious dead. Out of the fifty-nine notables to whom statues had been erected in London, she named seven that should be replaced. The Duke of York's column in Waterloo Place seemed like an obvious target for removal—the Victorians detested the 138-foot monument for its ugliness and imposing height. Even worse, "the jumping down from the top and being smashed on the broad stones at its base, was a fashionable mode of committing suicide," according to contemporary journalist Max Schlesinger; "it's a pity that none of the poor wretches ever thought of overthrowing and jumping down with the statue."

But it wasn't on aesthetic merit alone that Rachel wanted the statue to be eradicated. This son of George III had been forced to resign the post of commander-in-chief because of "shameful traffic in military appointments carried on by his mistress," and had also contracted a considerable amount of unpaid debts to the tradesmen of London. Always a vehement critic of any abuse of power and privilege, Rachel cynically remarked that "it is possible, therefore, that the citizens of the metropolis seventy years ago, resolved to erect a standing reminder against the practice of giving unlimited credit, which, in the absence of fog, should stand as a beacon and warning for future generations." Her crusade failed, however, and though the spiral staircase has been closed to the public, the Duke of York's statue is still planted firmly in place.

But there was one cause that she never abandoned. She frequently combined her charity work with her journalism, and the State Children's Aid Association was especially close to her heart. She rallied her newspaper for their cause and even put 7 Chesterfield Gardens at their service, holding fund-raising events to awaken the public to the "ill effects of the institutional system." As many as fifty thousand children were crammed into large barrack schools that resembled convents or prisons. The poor conditions resulted in nothing but harm for these children—they contracted a variety of diseases, their mental powers were diminished and their nervous systems weakened. As a result of the incarceration to which they were subjected, the children became "dull, sullen and mechanical, unfitted by experience to grapple with difficulties." Many of them were morally corrupted, for the absence of healthy interests "leaves empty minds in which evil hastily finds a home."

The association called for an end to all barrack schools, and for homes to be built in working-class neighbourhoods where fifteen to eighteen children would live under the care of a "motherly woman." The children would then be able to attend local schools. State-regulated emigration to Canada was also planned for orphaned and deserted children who were in good physical and mental health with no vicious or criminal tendencies. They were to be taught farming and domestic work, and the hope was that across the Atlantic "they may have scope and opportunity for a healthy environment."

In her work with the State Children's Aid Association, Rachel once again drew on her knowledge of and admiration for the French. She envied the French social system, in which all children had the chance of a career and illegitimate mothers were granted government assistance, and the French culture, which led parents to advise their son to learn a trade, and save franc by franc for their daughter "so that she shall not go helpless to her husband." In England, she felt, parents and the state treated children as if "they were simply a worthless product of which there is an indefinite supply." Rachel was certain that when women got the vote and could be elected to public office, they "would surely in the first place have the interest of children at heart."

CHAPTER TWENTY

Double Burden

In what little spare time she had, Rachel continued to play the piano, and she filled her house with a whole range of musical instruments—a Bechstein upright grand pianoforte as well as a concert grand pianoforte, a cottage pianoforte by Pleyel, and even a Preston violoncello. Her musical soirées were held for selected guests and for the benefit of charity. At times, she would join the visiting artist in a piano duet. One of the first concerts she organised was given by the French duo of piano prodigies "The Little Doustes"—Louise and Jeanne Douste—who in later years would return several times to play at the Beers' residence. It was described as a glittering event that "united the worlds of high finance and diamonds," and indeed all of Rachel's concerts were highly attended; they received news coverage in the society pages and were reviewed by the top music critics of the day. Some of Rachel's guests could not overlook her origins—"A very clever, dark woman, Jewish in appearance," commented Lady Glover, one of her esteemed guests—but most just enjoyed themselves.

There was much competition between society ladies to secure the stars of the day, and several of the most esteemed artists performed at Chesterfield Gardens, including the American soprano Lillian Nordica, one of the greatest prima donnas of her time. The "Yankee Diva" had just arrived in London after her debut at the Metropolitan Opera in New York, and her performance in Rachel's drawing room preceded her opening concert at the Royal Albert Hall. On another occasion, as soon as he finished his part at Covent Garden, the Polish tenor Jean De Reszke jumped into the brougham waiting for him at the stage door and was driven to the Beers'. He sang a few songs and, while other artists continued entertaining the guests, jumped into a carriage and was off to his next engagement in Berkley Square. A few arias there and he returned to wind up the evening at 7 Chesterfield Gardens. It was hard work, he admitted, but when it added a hundred pounds to a man's daily earnings, the temptation was irresistible.

Intrigued by recent innovations in music, Rachel surprised her guests one day with a rather unusual concert by the German pianist and composer Johann Heinrich Bonawitz. Her acquaintance with Bonawitz had begun a decade earlier, when he had played Rachel's own compositions in his concert tours. The servants at the Beer home led the guests to the grand salon, where the chairs were—unexpectedly—arranged in rows facing a black, draped curtain, in front of which stood vases filled with palm fronds and flowers.

The lights of the chandelier were dimmed "so that the optical might not interfere with the auditory sense," and the music issued forth from behind the curtain. Undistracted by the dress, form, fingering, facial expressions and mannerisms of the musicians, the audience preserved a churchlike silence. At the end, Bonawitz came through the black drapes and explained that as a young boy he was sent to sleep early in a dark bedroom, from which he could hear his parents and his elder brothers and sisters playing Schubert and Mendelssohn. The sensation stayed with him, he said, and following Goethe's dictum that "true music is intended for the ear alone," he had developed this novelty of Invisible Musical Performances.

The Invisible Concert was warmly applauded, wrote *The Observer*'s critic, though the journalist—who was, after all, the Beers' employee—should be commended for his bravery in remarking that "some improvement in the management might be introduced." The *Guardian*'s reviewer was less enthusiastic, writing that it was doubtful whether the experiment "has sufficient advantages to be worthy of imitation." Still, Rachel's Bonawitz concert was the talk of the town, and two weeks later the pianist returned to the Beers' residence to give a charity performance.

Encouraged by her triumph with the Invisible Concerts and the tableaux vivants, which had been so widely attended by royals, Rachel set out to put on an entire opera in her salon. In a race with Puccini for the title of "Verdi's heir," Pietro Mascagni was a composer who was hungry for success, a desire owing much to unfavourable reviews commenting on the "poverty of his later works." In March 1896, he conducted his new opera *Zanetto* in La Scala, but it failed to sweep the Milanese off their feet. He was looking forward to a change of fortune with the opera's British premiere, which was scheduled for June at Mrs. Beer's residence. Both *The Observer* and the *Sunday Times* were recruited to promote the event, and tickets, at the price of one guinea, were obtainable at 7 Chesterfield Gardens. Rachel invited all her friends, and promised actress Maud Tree an enjoyable afternoon with the short, simple but bound-to-be-popular opera.

The romantic story of *Zanetto* had irresistible elements. On the balcony of her villa outside Renaissance Florence, the famous courtesan Silvia laments her lost years and the love that has passed her by. The young minstrel Zanetto comes along and reveals that he is searching for the beautiful Silvia. For a moment she is tempted by this possible last chance at love, but she hides her identity so as not to shatter his idealized vision of her. She persuades the innocent, amorous youth to abandon his search, and as he leaves, she cries, "Blessed be love, I can cry again."

The sisters Ravogli, who had made a splash in the London opera scene when they made their debut in 1890, played both roles—Sofia was the courtesan, and her younger sister Giulia took the trousers role of Zanetto. A hidden chorus added their voices, and a piano and a harp served in lieu of a full orchestra, and the *Sunday Times*'s critic complimented the "tasteful grouping of palms at one end of the spacious drawing room, [that] lent the requisite simulation of stage

effect." The intimate one-act opera, which was lost in the grand au-
ditorium of La Scala, found its appropriate setting in Mrs. Beer's
Mayfair drawing room. "There are a continuity and real sincerity
that are not to be found in any of Mascagni's work, not even in that
which made his name," rejoiced *The Times*. For Rachel it was the
beginning of a long and close friendship with Giulia Ravogli, who
was nicknamed "*Il Tenore*" for the masculine timbre of her voice.

SOME OF THE artists who performed for Rachel had also done so at
her uncles' mansions, but that was the closest she ever came to her
own flesh and blood. Following Alfred's death, the only Sassoons she
could truly call family were her equally ostracised sister-in-law Theresa and her three sons, who adored their aunt. Rachel visited
Weirleigh alone for tête-à-têtes with Theresa, but she always found
time to let the children show her around the garden. Picking a rose
for her, Siegfried was bewildered to see that her hand "with its magnificent rings, was positively grimy." Given Rachel's penchant for
writing longhand, Siegfried was probably commenting upon the ink
stains. "When had she last taken off her rings," the little boy wondered.

The three boys and their mother had an open invitation to visit
Chesterfield Gardens, and Rachel would send her luxurious brougham
to wait for them in front of Charing Cross station. A plump footman
in a brown uniform and cockaded hat would meet them on the platform and escort them safely out of the station. The coachman, who
seemed to Siegfried to be the footman's twin brother, smiled kindly as
they climbed aboard. The children could not suppress their excitement at the prospect of their aunt's generous presents—she once
bought Siegfried a cricket bat and, on another occasion, a toy printing press. As they cozily clip-clopped along to Mayfair, their mother
would remind them not to pester Auntie Rachel with questions about
gifts.

Rachel appeared somewhat distracted on these visits, and it was
difficult for the boys to follow her hurried murmurs. "Her gaiety

seemed absentminded, and when she smiled, it was like an after-thought," Siegfried remembered. Considering how many tasks Rachel was tackling on a daily basis, it is little wonder that she may have seemed preoccupied. Lunch would bring a series of succulent surprises, and as Rachel spent more time with her young guests she would become less and less languid, and would laugh in her low-voiced expressive way, "as if remembering half-forgotten happiness."

Rachel adored the boys, and after lunch she would take them on shopping sprees, pulling five-pound notes out of her purse as though they were florins. Though she had no children of her own, Rachel seemed to understand the key to a good relationship with children was doing things they enjoyed. She led them from Regent Street to the circus, or a pantomime show, or to Maskelyne and Cooke's mystery entertainment at the Egyptian Hall in Piccadilly, where they would all watch young ladies vanish before their eyes. In between visits, she would send them packages of fairy stories and children's books that the *Sunday Times* received for review.

Though she wanted to share in their interests, Rachel also wanted to help educate the boys and enrich their lives. She was the one who gave them their first unforgettable taste of the theatre, taking them to a matinee at St. James of *As You Like It,* with Julia Neilson as Rosalind. On another occasion, the boys sat in her packed drawing room, watching an act of Gluck's *Orfeo* sung by the Ravogli sisters. Siegfried observed Rachel gliding between her guests, many of whom she scarcely knew, acting the perfect hostess. These duties didn't prevent her from enjoying one of her chief passions, though, and she "seemed to forget [the guests] entirely during the interludes of music."

AND WHERE WAS their uncle Frederick through all of this?

The children only got an occasional glimpse of his limp and aimless figure, drifting into the room clutching a cigar, "which seemed more an appurtenance than a cause of contentment to his gentle brown bearded face." The reason they so seldom saw him was that in the summer of 1896 Frederick Beer was diagnosed with the illness described by Charles Dickens as one that "medicine never cured, wealth warded off, or poverty could boast exemption from; which sometimes moves in giant strides, and sometimes at tardy pace; but, slow or quick, is ever sure and certain."

At that time, nearly every person in Britain's cities had been infected with tuberculosis, but only one percent had developed the dread disease. The prevailing belief at the time was that, like mental depression and insanity, tuberculosis resulted from moral deficiency. And if it wasn't a sinful nature, foul behaviour or a lack of self-control that caused it, the Victorians believed that heredity was to blame.

Theresa Sassoon thought her brother-in-law Frederick was a most sweet-natured and charitable man, until the doom of ill health descended upon him; "I'm afraid poor Mr. Beer has a bad heredity," she would say to her sons. With the fear of the Great White Plague, the tubercular were stigmatised and treated like lepers, pariahs and outcasts. Prominent physicians pointed out that the disease was not spread from person to person, and there was no need to aggravate suffering by socially isolating the sick and acting as though they were a public menace, but these assurances did nothing to allay the public phobia—the general belief was that it was highly contagious and that breathing the same air as a tuberculosis patient was dangerous. Still, Theresa continued visiting 7 Chesterfield Gardens with her boys. Frederick, though, was careful—he suppressed his affection and refrained from eating at the same table as the boys, or even from chatting in the drawing room, to eliminate any risk of infection.

Frederick was too weak to go to *The Observer*'s offices, or even to handle the newspaper's affairs from home. In late October 1896, he transferred *The Observer* to a joint stock company with a capital of fifty thousand pounds. He kept two-thirds of the shares and gave the rest to his wife. "The transfer has been made merely to suit the convenience of the proprietor and as a family arrangement," was his public announcement.

Gradually, out of necessity, Rachel began to assume her husband's

"His grave countenance, commanding figure, rich turban and flowing robes, made up a picture worth beholding." Sir Richard Temple, Governor of Bombay, on the patriarch, David Sassoon. *Courtesy of the Sassoon family*

Bombay, spring 1858, David Sassoon and his sons. S.D., all set up and ready to go to London, gazes dreamily toward the horizon. *Courtesy of the Sassoon family*

S.D. set out to be a Jew at home
and an Englishman in public.
Courtesy of the Sassoon family

Flora Sassoon, Rachel's mother, in Ashley
Park. *Courtesy of the Sassoon family*

Coat of Arms of S. D. Sassoon of Ashley Park.
Courtesy of the Sassoon family

"She always seemed to be absolutely the most shy and silent woman I had ever met," remembered Justin McCarthy. From left to right: Rachel (seated), her brother Joseph, Uncle Reuben, and on the far right, her brother Frederick. Seated, in the second row, grandmother Farha, and underneath, in the centre, Rachel's mother. *Courtesy of the Sassoon family*

In the summer of 1885, Baron Horace Gunzburg and his sons visited Ashley Park. Flora sits stiffly with a reserved smile, while Rachel, clothed in a light white dress, seems troubled and gloomy. Joseph Sassoon is seated, third from the left. *Courtesy of the Sassoon family*

Even the couple's French black poodle, Zulu, proudly displayed the family crest. *Collection of the authors*

John Oldrid Scott designed for Julius Beer a strikingly spectacular mausoleum. A sketch from *The Builder*, 1878.

The gem of Highgate Cemetery is the mausoleum of Julius Beer, which towers above all others.
Collection of the authors

Henry Hugh Armstead's "Memorial to an Only Daughter," depicting the eight-year-old Ada embraced by an angel. *Collection of the authors*

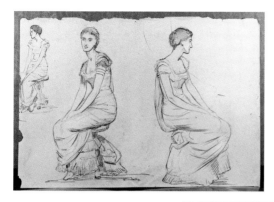

Hamo Thornycroft's sketches of Rachel, for his "A Sonata of Beethoven." *Courtesy of the Henry Moore Institute Archive, Leeds*

In her sittings for Henry Jones Thaddeus, Rachel wore a dress of deep golden silk with a low décolletage, *le dernier cri*. She chose to adorn herself with none of her exqusite jewels, and her only accessory was an ostrich feather fan on a tortoiseshell stick. *Courtesy of the Sassoon family*

Rachel never tried to conceal her Eastern ancestry. In costume balls she played up her exotic features by dressing as an oriental lady. *Courtesy of the Sassoon family*

Harry Bedford-Lemere's photograph of Rachel Beer's study in Chesterfield Gardens. Frederick's portrait is on the wall. August 1893. *Courtesy of English Heritage NMR*

"We always stopped to marvel at our multiplied reflections, which couldn't be counted." Siegfried Sassoon's recollection of the mirror room in his Aunt Rachel's Mayfair mansion. *Courtesy of English Heritage NMR*

The duo of publisher-editors: Rachel on the background of the *Sunday Times*, Frederick on that of *The Observer*, on the same day—Sunday, June 28, 1896.

Courtesy of Guardian News and Media Archive

For her editorials in the *Sunday Times*, Rachel Beer chose the heading "The World's Work," and the motto from Rudyard Kipling's "The English Flag."

Sicgfried Sassoon as the novelty of the Beers' presentation in the Press Bazaar of June 1898.

Courtesy of the Sassoon family

"I'm innocent! I swear it. Long live France!" cried Captain Alfred Dreyfus in 1895, before he was sent to serve a life sentence on Devil's Island. *Collection of the authors*

One of Rachel's letters to Esterhazy, 1899, written in French on her private stationery, bearing her home address and pelican coat of arms. *Collection of the authors*

Major Esterhazy was the "most marvelous, audacious and wonderful canaille that it was possible to imagine, either in fiction or history, and capable of every villainy, including murder." *Collection of the authors*

Chancellor House, Tunbridge Wells, Rachel Beer's shelter for the last twenty-four years of her life. *Collection of the authors*

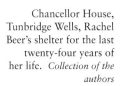

responsibilities at *The Observer.* "I do a great deal of work for Mr. Beer, and under his direction," she told Arnold Bennett:

> I have at times to take the whole responsibility of the two papers on my shoulders, but by this time I am so fully aware of his wishes, that I no longer feel the strain. Yet I recognise that though I am his wife, I do not own *The Observer,* and I am far more scrupulous concerning my work for it, than for my *Sunday Times,* which is quite my own property. Indeed, I have often tested in the columns of the *Sunday Times,* the public's view of things, which afterward I have, with full confidence, used in *The Observer,* and I have been able to avoid the sense of having injured my husband's property. With my own I can do as I please, but with that of other people, I feel it a duty to be more than usually careful.

The double burden began to take its toll on Rachel, however: "She always gave an impression of having slept badly the night before," remembered Siegfried Sassoon. Even before Frederick's illness, Rachel had passed many sleepless nights, and in one of her editorials she sympathised with Prime Minister Lord Rosebery, who confessed that he lay awake at night, thinking of the empire:

> Sleep is essential to all, for the repose and repair of the nervous centres which, during waking hours, are constantly engaged in fulfilment of certain important functions. Interference with repose is fearfully exhausting. . . . To men of active brain, the absolute rest of mind essential to repose is difficult. All mental devices for procuring sleep amount to this: that they concentrate the attention on something of absolutely no interest, and which is of a dull uniform nature.

Completing the questionnaire for the annual *Who's Who,* Rachel wrote under "Recreation," "varied work, and sleeping." Wondering whether the couches placed in her working room were for that purpose, Mr. Bennett gently asked her if the confession was meant to be taken seriously. She answered candidly—"Most certainly: in variety of work I find great relaxation, but for real recreation I rely on sleep. It is utterly harmless, quite impersonal, costs nothing, and does not entail competition. Yes, I do rely on sleep." Theresa Sassoon suspected that Rachel was taking too many of "those wretched sleeping draughts which Mr. Beer had got into the habit of, when his health began to fail."

ON MARCH 3, 1898, Frederick signed his will, in which he appointed "my dear wife" as the sole executor. He increased her yearly allowance of £1,100—which they had agreed upon in their marriage settlement eleven years earlier—to £2,000 for the remainder of her life, and left her "absolutely all my real and personal property." He was almost forty years old; Rachel was the same age. They were still childless, but Frederick's will proves that, in spite of his illness, the couple never lost hope—he ordered that a trust fund would be used "for the maintenance, education or benefit of any child or children of ours . . . and I appoint my said wife sole guardian of our child or children (if any) during minority."

It never crossed Rachel's mind to place her husband in a sanatorium, and on top of her double editorial responsibilities she also acted as Frederick's faithful nurse, making unexpected use of the two years she had spent at the Brompton Hospital for Consumption. When the Prince of Wales lost his footing and fell on the spiral staircase of Baron de Rothschild's country manor, injuring his kneecap, Rachel counted His Royal Highness's blessings in having "an accomplished and devoted nurse in the Princess, who has made herself proficient in the art of nursing, and holds a nursing diploma. She is constant and assiduous in her attendance on the Prince, bespeaking herself the loving and devoted wife." Rachel's description echoed her own role in her husband's sick chamber.

To mark the Diamond Jubilee of his mother's reign, the Prince of

Wales launched a Hospital Fund for London, the monies of which would be used for the maintenance of the hospitals and the upgrading of their services. Rachel suggested that it should also provide skilled nurses to attend to the sick in their own homes: "It is a humane and beneficial mission to send that true 'Sister of Mercy,' a gentle, well-trained competent nurse, into every poor home, where a patient is lying on a bed of suffering, whose recovery depends upon care and skill in attendance." Frederick Beer's donation of one thousand pounds was one of the largest.

Aware of the shortcomings of modern medicine, Rachel sought remedies everywhere. She was excited by new therapeutic methods that harnessed the hidden forces of the body and spirit. When she heard of Professor Edmond Savary d'Odiardi, a physician who conducted experiments testing the curative effect of electricity, she immediately set up an interview with him at his Notting Hill Gate Hospital. Word had it that the methods of the French prodigy had "given hope to the hopeless" and cured conditions thought to be chronic. The professor, who aimed to become the Pasteur of medical electricity and magnetism, boasted to the *Sunday Times* that since 1890, when he began working in London, not one of his patients had died. He claimed to have cured many cases of consumption, paralyses of the insane, gangrene and idiocy: "I employ the vapours of metals produced by electricity with a force of 70,000 volts. The vapour of gold, for instance, acts on nervous diseases and diseases of the mucous membranes, and also for consumption."

Frederick Beer was not to be one of d'Odiardi's successes. As her husband's condition deteriorated, Rachel scarcely went anywhere in the evenings and found it "much more entertaining to stay at home with Mr. Beer, than to spend half the nights at balls and parties." The artistic ventures at their home were scaled back but not completely halted. "Mrs. Beer's beautiful house with its marble hall and staircase is admirably suited for a concert of this sort," reported *The Country Gentleman* in late May 1898, of an event in aid of Catherine Gladstone's St. Mary's Training Home for Girls. Several of the students were present, dressed in neat uniforms. The performance was well attended, though owing to the recent death of Rachel's old friend, ex–prime minister William Gladstone, the planned program—the new and original comedy *Knicknacks*—was abandoned. In its place, Giulia Ravogli sang popular old Italian and Greek songs.

Preparations for the Press Bazaar at the Hotel Cecil in June 1898, during which the British press rallied to raise ten thousand pounds in aid of the London Hospital in Whitechapel, absorbed Rachel completely. "Cushions and Comforts" was the theme of the *Sunday Times* and *Observer* joint stall, and Rachel herself orchestrated the complex operation of obtaining tea cloths specially autographed by royalty, millionaires, artists and literary and dramatic stars. Dressed in white, she personally presided over the sale, assisted by ladies of the nobility and activists from the women's suffrage movement, the Women's Institute and the Institute of Women Journalists. Her special guest was Marguerite Durand, the directress of the recently established *La Fronde,* the Parisian feminist daily that was run entirely by women. Madame Durand brought for sale several autographed copies of the romantic novels of Émile Zola. For two days, the women sold Indian and Armenian embroidery, cushions and sachets, and Rachel's stall "seemed to make much money."

The novelty of the Beers' presentation was their trio of little sandwich-board men—Siegfried and his brothers, "in quaint yellow tunics, knickers and hats, paraded with yellow boards bearing the names of the two Sunday papers." The boys were taught to simultaneously bow and sweep their plumed hats as the Princess of Wales arrived. But at the crucial moment the daydreaming Siegfried froze in place and his brother Michael had to knock his hat off for him. The princess smiled reassuringly at the eleven-year-old, and Auntie Rachel curtsied, "though not deeply enough to cover up my confusion." To console the boy, Rachel gave him a copy of *The Time Machine,* autographed by H. G. Wells, but Siegfried did not feel that he deserved it.

All of Paris in a Fever

On Saturday, December 22, 1894, all seven judges of the military court in Paris found Captain Alfred Dreyfus guilty of treason. It was just two months after Rachel Beer started her editorship at the *Sunday Times,* and she stood out in her identification of the conviction as "one of the most remarkable incidents of the year." Forever concerned with the fragility of peace, for Rachel, Dreyfus's trial for espionage exposed "the volcanic forces that seethe and boil just below the thin crust of international convention and politeness."

Though she was in many ways a Francophile, Rachel was an ardent critic of the widespread corruption in France's political system. But since no details were leaked from the *in camera* trial, she had no reason initially to doubt the court's verdict. Her one worry at the time was that "the anti-Semitic rabble of Paris are already in full cry against his co-religionists, not because they are disloyal, but because they are Jews."

Rachel's involvement with the Dreyfus affair would require her to stand firm on many of the issues she cared about passionately, including justice, an end to persecution, and the fair treatment of minorities. And, perhaps more than anything, it underscored her view that an activist press was not only desirable, but necessary. A clearheaded editor, she would exercise caution and restraint, and it would take her nearly three years to begin her crusade against the perversion of justice.

THE FRENCH MAJOR Charles-Marie-Ferdinand Walsin-Esterhazy squandered his wife's dowry on frivolous living, stock market speculations and the maintenance of a prostitute known as "four-fingered Marguerite." Esterhazy was under financial strain, his military promotion had been halted, and he was filled with a counterintuitive loathing for all things French—"I would not harm a little dog, but I would have a hundred thousand Frenchmen killed with pleasure." He stepped into the office of Colonel von Schwartzkoppen, the military attaché at the German embassy in Paris, and demanded a monthly retainer for his services as a spy. But he was turned down—instead, he would be paid based on the quality of his information. On August 15, 1894, Esterhazy received one thousand francs in exchange for the mobilisation plan of the French artillery. A further memorandum (or *bordereau*) highlighting a list of several artillery secrets that he promised to divulge in the future was intercepted by the French Intelligence Service, who opened an inquiry into the matter.

Among the artillery officers on the General Staff there was only one Jew—Alfred Dreyfus. He was an assimilated Jew, who had been twelve years old when the Germans annexed his native Alsace. His parents, wealthy textile factory owners, had moved to Paris to maintain their French nationality, and Alfred had chosen a military career to revenge himself against Germany. There were no skeletons in his closet; his past record was impeccable and his career was on the rise. Dreyfus had no motive, financial or otherwise, for betraying his country. Two graphologists who compared his handwriting to the writing on the *bordereau* produced conflicting conclusions; nevertheless, a secret warrant was issued for his arrest.

Under the false pretense of a routine interview, Dreyfus, who was ordered to wear civilian clothes, arrived at the Ministry of War. As he was waiting, an officer wearing a black glove on the pretext that he had injured his right hand asked Dreyfus to write something for him. It was a trap. Three other officers were hidden behind a curtain, watching Dreyfus as he transcribed phrases from the *bordereau* and hoping to observe trembling in his hand. Suddenly, the officer stopped dictating, placed his hand on Dreyfus's shoulder and dramatically announced that he was under arrest for high treason. Though it was no longer a capital offense, Dreyfus was threatened with execution. Still reading the arrest warrant, the officer moved a folder, revealing a revolver that was hidden beneath. But the scapegoat refused to commit suicide as a way out. "I am innocent, kill me if you wish," Dreyfus protested, as he was dragged off to prison.

In further attempts to prove that Dreyfus was the culprit and had written the *bordereau,* the French ordered him to write while standing, sitting, lying down, with gloves and without them. Still, the graphologists could not produce a decisive report—Dreyfus's writing was not a clear match. The Minister of War hesitated to press charges, and to prevent Dreyfus's release members of the General Staff leaked news of the arrest to the anti-Semitic press. *La Libre Parole* announced that Dreyfus had already confessed to the deed; with this lie made public there was no stopping this snowball. Throughout the affair, which would last more than ten years, the press—both in France and outside of it—would be used by all sides to promote their interests.

On the third day of the trial, during one of the recesses and without Dreyfus's or his attorney's knowledge, the judges received a sealed envelope containing four secret documents, all of which were later discovered to be forgeries. Dreyfus's fate was sealed.

It was hardly a coincidence that the public degradation ceremony took place on the Jewish Sabbath, January 5, 1895. In the presence of four thousand army troops, Dreyfus cried out, "I am innocent! I swear it. Long live France!" Among the journalists who watched the meticulous theatrical performance was the Paris correspondent of the Viennese *Neue Freie Presse*: "The drum began to roll, and the military court clerk began to tear the buttons and stripes of his uniform, which had been partially unstitched beforehand," wrote Dr. Theodor

Herzl. Even his sword had been partly sawn off to ensure a swift break; the fragments were then thrown at the feet of the condemned man. As Dreyfus was marched off alone in front of his comrades-at-arms, the mob outside the courtyard, estimated at twenty thousand, shouted, "Death to Judas! Death to the Jews!" Dr. Herzl, who would go on to found modern Zionism, said years later that the anti-Semitic screams made him realise that his fellow Jews would never be integrated in their countries of residence and that only a Jewish state would solve the problem.

The world press either supported or passively accepted Dreyfus's conviction, but the humiliating scene and the anti-Semitic hysteria somehow escaped Rachel Beer's columns. Dreyfus's arrival at Devil's Island near Brazil on April 14, 1895, to serve a life sentence, was seen as a *fait accompli*, and not an undeserved one at that.

Meanwhile, Esterhazy sank deeper into debt and, having left his wife and daughters, settled into his mistress's apartment. He was openly passing more secrets to the Germans—his total contribution amounted to 170 documents—but Colonel von Schwartzkoppen, who thought that the French spy was the "most marvelous, audacious & wonderful canaille that it was possible to imagine, either in fiction or history, & capable of every villainy, including murder," soon realised that Esterhazy's information was useless. In early March 1896, Schwartzkoppen dictated to one of his mistresses, on thin blue paper, a note of dissatisfaction addressed to Esterhazy. He then changed his mind and tore up the *petit bleu*, throwing the fragments into his wastepaper basket. It was probably the same cleaning lady who had previously found the *bordereau* who brought this incriminating new material to the attention of French Intelligence.

The new head of the Intelligence Bureau, Colonel Picquart, at first thought that another traitor had been exposed, but further investigation convinced him that there was only one traitor—Esterhazy. To thwart Picquart's efforts to revive the case, the French military command sent him on a dangerous mission to the southern desert of Tunisia, and Major Henry, an acquaintance of Esterhazy, was promoted to fill Picquart's position. Before departing, Picquart shared his findings with friends, who passed them on to Auguste Scheurer-Kestner, the vice president of the Senate. But Scheurer-Kestner's public announcement of Dreyfus's innocence, pointing the finger at Esterhazy, failed to move a government unwilling to open Pandora's box.

SINCE RELATIONS BETWEEN Britain and France were already unsettled on account of colonial rivalry, it was strongly suspected that Dreyfus's salvation would come from England. French guards broke into his prison cell late at night on May 7, 1896, where they "cut up his mattress, laundry, shoes and books," according to researcher George Whyte. The order for the full-scale search came from Paris, following a rumour that the convict was studying English, using his dictionaries and exercise books to send coded messages to his family and to "foreign conspirators to plan his escape."

Six months later, another escape story was circulated. Desperate to inflame the waning public interest in his brother's fate, Mathieu Dreyfus approached Clifford Millage, the Paris correspondent of *The Daily Chronicle*. The British journalist, who believed that the Dreyfus case was trumped up, agreed to plant a false report in *The South Wales Argus* in Newport—a certain Captain Hunter of the ship *Nonpareil*, who brought phosphates from near Devil's Island, was alleged to have heard that Dreyfus had escaped on an American schooner.

The sensational story, published on November 2, 1896, was immediately picked up by newspapers in England and France. The nationalistic French press trumpeted the allegation that the so-called "Jewish Syndicate" was behind the efforts to rescue Dreyfus at all costs. In particular, the anti-Semitic *La Libre Parole* declared that its special correspondent in England had gone to Newport and interviewed the captain and the crew, who had confirmed the news. Only Captain Hunter and the *Nonpareil* had never existed—they were mere figments of Mathieu Dreyfus's imagination. However, the commotion resulting from the article failed to produce the desired response. Though it did get Dreyfus's name back in the headlines, the only real outcome was that the prisoner was subjected to harsher conditions. By a special order from Paris, he was shackled to his bed with two U-shaped iron joints.

A family tale recounted by Siegfried Sassoon has it that Rachel wrote a check for well over forty thousand pounds to charter a ship to rescue Dreyfus from Devil's Island. Allegedly, the person who talked her into the scheme turned out to be a crook, but she discovered it only after her bank had paid the money. Siegfried and his brothers thought that it was jolly fine of their aunt to try to help Dreyfus, but Hamo, the youngest, remarked that it would have been better still if she had sent some of the money to pay for their education. The story is not documented and, moreover, it is wholly uncharacteristic of the law-abiding and levelheaded Rachel. She showed great concern for the prisoner, but it would have been unlike her to have aided an illicit escape attempt. It seems that Siegfried's story is most probably another invention; it served Rachel's family to portray her as a woman who had more money than sense.

PARIS WAS ALL afever with whispers about a miscarriage of justice, but although every British newspaper had a correspondent in the capital, they adhered to a policy of noninterference. Rachel realised that "it is probably hard for anyone even in the midst of it to understand, and certainly for those outside who have to depend upon so-called 'information' served hot and hot for the baser newspaper purposes." She felt more than justified in her caution in reporting on the spy-mania in an atmosphere where "wild tales of every description are born and die a dozen by the hour." She refused to don the judge's robe, and was not impressed by reports of handwriting experts that were in Dreyfus's favour, since "such evidence is notoriously fallible."

The unrest in Paris worried her and she called upon the French authorities to settle the delirium of doubt. "This determination at all hazards to keep close shut the door at the Ile du Diable is, it is hardly

possible not to think, wrong. Not that we would boast ourselves better here in England. We also have our skeletons in the prisons. But
into our troubles has never entered the element of secrecy," she wrote
on November 14, 1897. From this point onward, Rachel fixed her
sights firmly on the case, desirous to see justice carried out without
identifying herself with either side. By refusing to hold a new, direct
and open inquiry, she warned, France ran "the risk of snapping forever and disastrously popular confidence in the soundness of State
management. Of such follies are revolutions made."

Esterhazy was overwrought. One moment he was planning to
flee, the next he was thinking of suicide. He chose neither option;
instead, he spent his time fabricating letters and telegrams and sending anonymous death threats to the Dreyfus family. The Minister of
War and the Chief of the General Staff, confident of Dreyfus's guilt
and wishing to put an end to his supporters' pressure, advised Esterhazy to write a letter asking to be brought to trial and then demonstrate his innocence. The recipient of that letter, General Pellieux,
drafted Esterhazy's declaration of innocence himself, citing him as the
victim of an "infamous plot hatched for [his] ruin." Esterhazy's line
of defense was that his acquaintance with the German military attaché was only social, that the *petit bleu* was a forgery, and that Dreyfus had imitated his handwriting in the *bordereau* to lift suspicion
from himself.

"Not for a moment do we say that Esterhazy is the criminal, but
it is obvious that his trial was a sham, such, in fact, as could not be
carried through in open daylight"—this was Rachel's verdict after
Esterhazy was acquitted unanimously. She rebuffed the French notion
that England's stance on the Dreyfus case stemmed from colonial rivalry: "Most emphatically we say that this is not so . . . it is the voice
of humanity at large, not nationality that protests." Gradually, the
British press began to leave the grandstands and descend onto the
pitch.

On January 13, 1898, *L'Aurore* published "J'Accuse," Émile Zola's famous open letter to the president, in which he accused the army

chiefs and the War Office of a "crime against humanity and justice, for political ends and to save the General Staff which was compromised." Zola detailed specific accusations and deliberately invited a slander suit, hoping to have a public hearing in a courtroom in which he could publicly challenge the case. Rachel admired Zola for his literary genius and for being "a devoted champion of truth," and was quick to crown his article as "one of the most outstanding documents in the history of the century." Still, she disapproved of his hysterical and dramatic language and his sweeping condemnation of the entire French army. (Yet more evidence against Siegfried's colorful tale about Rachel's private financial involvement in the scheme.) "For his boldness, M. Zola must necessarily stand his trial," she wrote, and her hope was that the proceedings would be open to the public: "If not, the last vestige of belief in the present regime in France must surely vanish. If so, there are some terrible revelations awaiting the world."

Flooded with statements from both sides, furnished with endless documents, some of them forged, British journalists continued to hunt for affirmative proof that would tip the scales one way or the other. French ministers and their staff, high-ranking as well as minor intelligence officers, and also German and Italian diplomats were all courted by the press. Scoops were sure to boost circulation: *L'Aurore* sold 300,000 copies of its special edition of Zola's "J'Accuse."

Robert Crawford was keen to be the one to get an exclusive: "It would make *The Daily News* famous in Europe—certainly in France—for the next ten years," he promised his editor in late March 1898. Acting as the Paris correspondent for *The Daily News* was a family tradition for the Crawfords. Emily had inherited the job from her husband, George Morland Crawford, and their son Robert later joined her in the role. Robert assured his editor that he did not need to worry about taking on Esterhazy. To sue for libel in England would be, for him, "the greatest blunder in the world, as the witnesses who were bullied into silence by the judge wd [*sic*] speak freely in England." However, the editor, Edward Cook, chose instead to follow Mrs. Crawford's advice, which was backed by her years of journalistic experience. She argued that caution was the wisest move, since the newspaper was owned by "big capitalists some of whom are also timid capitalists"; the reward for taking the courageous step, she warned, would be flowers of rhetoric from Dreyfus's supporters as well as a jail sentence for the editor.

The Paris correspondent for *The Observer* was Rowland Strong. He was a well-connected man who had started working for the paper before Rachel began assuming Frederick's editorial responsibilities. A fierce anti-Semite, he believed that the accusations against Esterhazy were based on "a slender thread." "A sort of cyclone of madness seems to have burst upon this unfortunate country," reported Strong, who also wrote for *The Pall Mall Gazette* and *The New York Times*. "Quarrels are breaking out among intimate friends; duels are in perspective; betting on the result will win not a few; family ties are being torn asunder." Determined to prove Dreyfus's guilt, he "carried on the campaign against him in the English press," according to his assistant and lover, the young Irish poet Chris Healy.

Strong was introduced to Esterhazy at the offices of *La Libre Parole*. His description of the fifty-one-year-old major, following that meeting, is far from complimentary, intentionally composed to evoke pity:

> He is a little, old man, sad-faced, and broken-down, badly dressed in thin, soiled clothes, with a wide waist coat . . . which was by no means fresh, and a battered silk hat, painfully over ironed.
>
> "What has Zola got against me?" he asked pathetically. "Why can't he leave a poor, broken-down man like me alone?"
>
> Certainly if Esterhazy has sold secrets to foreign governments . . . there is nothing in his dress and appearance to suggest it.

For his part, Esterhazy was not impressed by the thirty-three-year-old "little man with a red beard . . . whose cuffs were frayed and very dirty, [and] smelled of alcohol ten feet away; but he greeted me at once with a fervour which I found extraordinary in an Englishman."

Strong used sympathy to nourish his relationship with Esterhazy because he knew, in the words of researcher J. Robert Maguire, "that if he stuck to him closely enough and long enough he eventually would scoop the world press on the story." The pair frequently met at Strong's regular bar, where he often "tossed down fifteen or twenty whiskies with nonchalance." Esterhazy later complained that Strong wrote to him daily, bombarded him with telegrams and importuned his friends by telephone when he had not seen him for several hours, to inquire "what I had been doing, what I was going to do, why I didn't come to see him."

Esterhazy told Strong that if Zola were acquitted, 200,000 Parisians would pack the streets, ready to attack the government and pillage the houses of the Jews and massacre them. Though he himself was dying, he said, and though he had just one lung remaining, he declared that he would "shoot the wretches down like rabbits. If the crowd wants a competent soldier to lead them . . . I am here to lead them."

Rachel was utterly shocked when Zola was convicted and sentenced to a year's imprisonment and a fine of three thousand francs, "the victim of the French Army Moloch." Now, she felt, the affair had passed beyond "the mere horror of a possibly innocent man condemned; it had invaded the very holy of holies of French justice, and it now threatens the supremacy of the civil power in the nation." Of the Beers' two newspapers, the *Sunday Times* showed more interest in the unfolding French drama, but Zola's conviction made it into *The Observer* editorial, too: "It is plain that France would have another military dictatorship tomorrow, if there were any men popular enough for the job."

IN THOSE VERY same days, in February 1898, Oscar Wilde arrived in Paris from Naples after a bitterly futile attempt to reunite with his lover Lord Alfred Douglas. On the advice of Douglas, who was also an intimate friend of Strong's, the penniless Wilde had journeyed to France to ask the British journalist for financial help. Strong and Esterhazy were paying their devotion to Bacchus when Wilde entered the bar. Strong introduced them to each other. "We are the two greatest martyrs of humanity," said Esterhazy, "but I have suffered the most."

One of Wilde's close friends, a wealthy English intellectual who lived in Paris named Carlos Blacker, was a committed Dreyfusard. From his dear friend the Italian military attaché in Paris, Blacker had heard the full facts of Esterhazy's betrayal, and since it was clear that the French courts, government and the army would do anything to obstruct the retrial of Dreyfus, Blacker intended to publish the incriminating revelations in a London newspaper. In so doing, he hoped to create enough international pressure to leave French officials with no choice but to retry Esterhazy and acquit Dreyfus.

Out of friendship for Wilde, Blacker disclosed this secret information to him, hoping that the moral and intellectual stimuli of the case would intrigue Wilde enough that he would resume writing. However, Wilde felt that all of his friends, Blacker included, were avoiding him, and out of revenge, he revealed the plan to Esterhazy and Strong during dinner, adding, "The innocent always suffer, Monsieur le Commandant; it is their métier. Besides, we are all innocent until we are found out. It is a poor, common part to play, and within the compass of the meanest. The interesting thing, surely, is to be guilty and wear as a halo the seduction of sin." It may have been the alcohol or Oscar Wilde's flirtatious flattery that caused Esterhazy to let down his guard—"Why should I not make confession to you? I will. It is I, Esterhazy, who alone am guilty. I put Dreyfus in prison, and all France cannot get him out." Wilde and Strong both burst out laughing.

The following day, Strong cabled that he was told "on excellent authority" that Dreyfus's friends intended to publish in London new facts about Esterhazy. His news report sabotaged Blacker's plan. "Of course, Major Esterhazy whom I have questioned on this subject . . . declares that the documents, if they exist, are forgeries,"

Strong wrote; he did not divulge a word of Esterhazy's confession to him and Wilde. Instead, he portrayed him as an accomplished French secret agent: "If the French War Office had wished to set a watch upon the doings of the Triple Alliance, they could not have chosen an officer better-fitted for the task than Major Esterhazy, who spoke German and Italian like a native."

Meanwhile, Zola appealed against his conviction and was acquitted on a procedural error, but was then retried. On July 18, 1898, after being sentenced again to the maximum punishment, Zola fled to London to evade the guilty verdict and to continue his campaign to call attention to Dreyfus's wrongful conviction. He would remain there for almost a year.

By then, Esterhazy was facing an attack from another front: a cousin accused him of fraud and of stealing his inheritance of twenty thousand francs. Esterhazy had promised to invest the money with Baron Edmond de Rothschild—whom he claimed was an old school friend—but he took the money for himself instead. The cousin testified that Esterhazy and his mistress had confided in him that they had crafted false documents in the Dreyfus affair. The two were immediately arrested and were only released after a month of interrogation. Coming to Esterhazy's home to celebrate his release with two bottles of champagne, Strong found him in a highly flustered state—Esterhazy was sure that the inquiry would result in his arrest and the ceremonial breaking of his sword. To protect his future prospects, he met with publishers Fayard Frères and signed a contract to tell all in ten installments, for a total of ten thousand francs and a share in the profits.

Godefroy Cavaignac, France's new Minister of War, clung stubbornly to his "absolute conviction of the guilt of Dreyfus," but that wasn't enough to defuse the ticking bomb. A new examination of the entire corpus of documents was in full force. On August 24, 1898, Esterhazy appeared before the military board of inquiry, and that same evening he met up with Strong, livid with rage. If he was discharged from the army without income, he would be powerless against his cousin's civil lawsuit; he told Strong that nothing remained for him but to blow out his brains. He was in a state of great agitation, repeating again and again the threat that if he were abandoned to his fate by his military chiefs he would involve them, and indeed the whole of France, in his ruin. Strong coolly replied that suicide would be interpreted as an admission of guilt; Esterhazy groaned—he would have no way of making a living outside the army, he could not survive by picking up cigarette stubs on the streets. "I am the General Staff's right hand," Esterhazy cried. "No one knows the secrets of the Dreyfus affair as well as I." He challenged Strong: "Supposing, now, I were to go to a newspaper office and confess that I am the author of the *bordereau,* don't you think it will cause a great sensation?" The British journalist was cool-headed about the prospect: "Certainly, a great sensation, though perhaps not much astonishment."

Esterhazy asked for help in finding an English publisher for his book; Strong quickly advised him to allow an excerpt to be printed in a newspaper, to stir public interest and increase future book sales. He was leaving for London that night and he promised to have a word with the editors of *The Observer* and *The Pall Mall Gazette,* estimating that he could get "a round sum." Although he was under no obligation and could have published Esterhazy's confession himself on the following day, Strong was convinced of the major's sincere desire to give a signed statement, and was willing to wait. By Esterhazy's version, it was Strong who lured him to England, "promising to publish articles to clear him and said he would find him a respectable way of 'earning his living.' "

A chain reaction of events culminated in the discharge of Esterhazy from the army for "habitual misconduct." His main protector, Lieutenant Colonel Henry, head of the Intelligence Bureau, was arrested and confessed to forging documents. On August 31, 1898, Henry was found dead in his cell; he had slashed his throat with a razor. On that day, the Minister of War signed Esterhazy's dismissal without pension, and two generals also handed in their resignation.

Asked to comment on the recent dramatic events, Esterhazy, "retaining an amazingly cool attitude," stated that he would appeal his enforced retirement.

But on September 1, 1898, he instead set out on his escape route. Certain that he was being followed, he shaved his large grizzly moustache, transforming his appearance completely. He took no luggage, only his revolver, and bought some clothes en route.

An Encounter in London

On September 9, 1898, *The New York Times* broke the news: "There is ... considerable mystery about Esterhazy's movements. He is variously reported as at London, Ostend and other points. The net is closing around him." Other accounts claimed that he had hanged himself on the rue de la Rochefoucauld.

A few days earlier, Rowland Strong had received a cable from a "M. De Becourt," Hotel de Providence in Brussels. This communiqué was followed by a letter: "Find me the means of earning some guineas by articles and interviews without touching the big bomb, which I reserve for later. You will understand that it will only be the more interesting." Strong urged Esterhazy not to delay his arrival any longer. He knew that putting the fugitive up at a London hotel would be too conspicuous, so he invited him instead to the place where he himself was staying, the residence of his friend Thomas B. Fielders, a former *New York Times* reporter.

Esterhazy travelled at night and on Wednesday, September 7, he arrived at 6 St. James Street, opposite the Thatched House Club. Fielders's impression of the much-anticipated guest was not favourable—"to put it plainly, he has a villainous face ... in manner he was polite, like all Frenchmen who intend to benefit through you ... he made efforts to be pleasant and offhand, but they were not natural."

Strong wasted no time; he was eager to talk business. He needed some written proof of the former major's sincere intentions to present to his editor, Mrs. Beer. Determined not to limit herself to writing editorials and publishing Strong's reports, Rachel wished to play an active role in "one of the strangest and most deeply interesting dramas of human life ever acted upon the stage of Europe." Strong knew Esterhazy all too well, so he had not divulged to him his editor's sex and race.

Paris, September 9th 1898

Dear Sir,

I remember our meetings, and how much I held in high regard your proceedings. I also know what a loyal attitude *The Observer* always maintained in his numerous articles regarding the Dreyfus case, and how much it was always impartial. . . . Obedience to the orders of my chiefs has alone prevented me from speaking hitherto. I have been abandoned, and I have the right to defend myself. I am now only accountable to myself for what I should do. I believe that I should have been supported to the end. Nothing of the kind. It was thought cleverer to sacrifice me as one throws ballast overboard. Let me know if, in the case arising, I can rely on you and on *The Observer* whose independence I appreciate.

Esterhazy had chosen his words carefully, refraining from mentioning the *bordereau* or the nature of the confession that he was willing to make. Later, he would argue that this letter was dictated to him by Strong and that the journalist had also insisted that it should look as if it was written prior to his arrival in London. Rachel was pleased with the letter, but she waited to hear from Strong that the major was ready to talk.

On Sunday, after breakfast, lolling back in an armchair and puffing away at his English briar pipe, Esterhazy at last coolly recounted his version—the General Staff was certain of Captain Dreyfus's treachery but there was no material proof of his guilt, so he was ordered to forge the *bordereau*. "You thoroughly understood that on such evidence, Dreyfus would be dismissed from the army and that even a worse fate might befall on him?" Strong asked. "Yes, I understood that, and all I did was done through a sort of mediaeval loyalty to my chiefs," Esterhazy claimed.

It was time for him to meet Rachel Beer. The day was hot, so Esterhazy took off his jacket, then suddenly the door of the small living room was opened and Strong introduced him to the "directrice of *The Observer* and the *Sunday Times*." Esterhazy was embarrassed by his improper appearance, and doubly humiliated that he was to do business with a woman, and a Jewish one at that. "I had the perilous honour to start a relationship with this great Jewess, daughter of the Sassoons (from India) and a relative of the Rothschilds," he wrote in his memoir. Not bothering to hide his contempt for her, he described their first encounter:

A lady, still young, dressed with showy elegance, but of an incredible Semitic look. The elegance of this unexpected visitor could be credited to the art of the couturiere. As to the forms, they reminded me especially of the walking stick used by Picquart, assuming that this stick was flanked by two wooden arms with the gracefulness of two chopsticks ending with hands, hands with no gloves, stained with ink, with nails in mourning.

This stick was wrapped in an entirely white dress, decorated with evidently very expensive jewels, but in indisputable bad taste, and on top decked out with an enormous pink hat, the most incredible Jewish Judaic figure that one could see.

Imagine a blackish chicken neck, plucked of all its feathers, a yellowish oily head, but a special head: no face, two fixed eyes of a morphine-addict, a mouth with nice teeth, then a nose, only a nose, but what a nose.

The most fantastic Jewish nose that was ever produced by the twelve tribes; a nose with which it is impossible to turn when you enter an ordinary street; a nose which can only be driven in a cab, and even there, it will disturb the coachman;

and over this extraordinary monument, a ruffled mane, not curly but woolly—characteristic of this race, and badly dyed with piss-color henna.

Je l'ai fait, said Esterhazy as he put his arms on the table and began talking. "Without our asking any questions, he volunteered the statement at first that he himself was ordered to do the *bordereau* by or through a General Officer Sandherr," recalled Rachel, whose French was now impeccable. He remarked that such forgeries were made in every army; Rachel jumped to her feet, and Esterhazy retracted his statement immediately, saying that he did not suppose it was done in the English army. Rachel was well aware of the claims that Esterhazy was the traitor who passed the Germans secret documents—the *bordereau* being one of them—but she decided not to confront him about that at this stage.

Realising that the trumped-up charges and mock trial were caused by an "anti-Semitic craze and army Moloch worship," she aimed to secure a retrial for Dreyfus, and was deeply concerned that the prisoner on Devil's Island "may be liberated by death long before the slow-moving course of French justice arrives at its final decision." Rachel was content with Esterhazy's declaration that Dreyfus had not written the *bordereau;* however, she wished to publish his written confession, supported by other documents, so that the French political and legal systems would not be able to ignore it. An article based on an interview would not be legally binding and could be subject to libel. His confession, she assured him, would be published in five installments, at the price of one hundred pounds each. Strong was granted a generous reward as well, receiving five hundred pounds for his journalistic efforts.

At Rachel's request, Esterhazy agreed to write an introductory letter to his confession. He handed her copies of some letters and documents and promised to deposit more with a banker, to be published in *The Observer* at such periods as he thought fit. As soon as she left,

Esterhazy turned to Strong: "How come that a ferocious anti-Semite like you puts me in touch with Jews?"

With persistent rumours that the fugitive was in town, newspapers were sending reporters to hunt him down, and Rachel was worried that Esterhazy would sell his story to the highest bidder. Having been warned of his slippery nature, it is utterly puzzling that she did not insist on having him sign a detailed agreement and a statutory declaration. Apparently, she was so thrilled to have him in her grasp, and so afraid of alienating him, that she believed his rage against his superiors alone would ensure his confession. This lack of a signed contract worked well for Esterhazy, who had no intention of laying the golden egg just yet.

Wearing two different editorial hats throughout the negotiations with Esterhazy, Rachel was forced into a kind of professional schizophrenia. She did not divulge her activities for *The Observer* in the *Sunday Times*; indeed, in the weeks prior to his escape and during the haggling with him in London she refrained from mentioning the affair altogether in her *Sunday Times* editorials. However, in news articles within the body of paper, the *Sunday Times* published proofs of Dreyfus's innocence and pleaded for "even-handed justice."

Though Esterhazy spoke endlessly on the subject with Strong and Fielders, he delayed his promise to put words to paper, on the pretext that essential documents were due to arrive at any time from Paris. He bragged that his confession was worth a million and suggested that the Rothschilds should be approached, as they were certain to pay a fortune to secure the story that could release Dreyfus. He was sure that his bombshell would shatter France's political and economic stability, and that he would reap a great profit—a "*coup de Bourse*," in his own words. Fielders warned Strong that Esterhazy had no intention of committing himself to *The Observer* in writing; he would take the money and run.

The fugitive's hosts felt safe enough to take him out for dinner and lunch, though, and at his request they all attended a boxing match.

"Water closet," "whisky soda" and "steeplechase" were the only English words that Esterhazy knew, so Strong translated all of the newspapers for him. In the evenings, Esterhazy went out to buy a supply of the Paris papers; "he was greatly tickled at the notoriety he had achieved, and it was apparent that he was growing more important, in his own opinion, day by day," Fielders recalled. Esterhazy established contact with *La Libre Parole* and, at night, would go to the telephone office at Charing Cross, talking over the wire with the editor.

Esterhazy demanded an advance from *The Observer*, but Strong refused him—something more tangible was needed. This threw Esterhazy into a violent rage and he made an unexpected dash at Strong. Fielders was forced to get between them. Then, suddenly Esterhazy announced that he would be leaving for Brussels, as he had come to an agreement with a Belgian paper. Strong told him that he could do as he pleased and that he washed his hands entirely of the affair; having backed Esterhazy through thick and thin in the belief that he was innocent, Strong now changed sides—"I understood that it was no longer his intention to avow the authorship of the *bordereau*. At this point, our relations, amicable and otherwise, naturally came to an end." He told Mrs. Beer that she was at liberty to make what use she liked of the information that had been conveyed to her. Moreover, Esterhazy's statement had been overheard by several persons; its publication sooner or later was inevitable.

Since Esterhazy was reluctant to cooperate, Rachel contrived to draw him out of his lair. Esterhazy only learned that *The Observer* was planning to print a portion of his story just a day before they were due to go to press—and he was furious. Accompanied by his solicitor, Arthur Newton, he met with Mrs. Beer, but she admitted nothing, and to appease him she even signed a letter promising not to publish the letters he had given her without his authority.

Yet the very next day, September 18, *The Observer* published "Light upon the Dreyfus Case," a news flash announcing that Esterhazy had been in town for the past ten days. It was written by Rowland Strong. "For my own part," read Strong's report, "I am content, in a great measure, with the explanation which he has verbally given me himself—namely, that there is no longer any justice for him in his native country, and that the moment has come to make the necessary revelations." Again and again in their long conversations, Esterhazy had said that he acted in blind obedience to his military chiefs: "If I were ordered to take a gun and shoot my own brother, I should do so without the slightest hesitation," Strong wrote, quoting Esterhazy's adamant defense of his actions.

That news flash was a mere taster of the installment that was to be published the following Sunday. It established *The Observer*'s exclusiveness over the impending world scoop while keeping their cards close to their chest; the *bordereau* was not mentioned and Mrs. Beer kept her promise and did not allude to the letters Esterhazy had given her.

Full details of the hideaway were given by Strong: "a comfortably furnished flat, in a house rented by an American gentleman in St. James' Street, Pall Mall, opposite a fashionable club." A small army of journalists hurried to number six, but the woman who opened the door said that she "had not even heard either of Esterhazy or of Dreyfus." The journalists patrolled the neighbourhood, armed with a photograph of Esterhazy cut out of the *Petit Journal*, and scanned the faces of the passersby. The lucky ones who spotted the fugitive discovered that he was somewhat irascible toward his unwelcome callers. "The Major, when accidentally seen today . . . was pale, haggard and worn," reported *The Pall Mall Gazette*. "His cheeks were fallen. His chin was bristly . . . his small dark eyes were restless. His head, conspicuous for silver gray hair, hung forward. There was, in fact, a decided stoop about the tall, thin figure, which resembled that of a man of sixty." To discredit *The Observer* scoop, the French anti-Semitic press claimed that Esterhazy was in Paris, hiding with a sympathetic relative who was seeking to withdraw him as much as possible from those who meant him harm.

Esterhazy instructed his lawyer Newton to apply for an interim injunction against *The Observer*, and he issued a statement denying that he had made any revelations to them in connection with the Dreyfus case. He threatened Strong, telling him he would "burn [his] brain," and following the confrontation he left the flat and moved into Hotel Previtali, Covent Garden. On Monday afternoon, he met Mrs. Beer in the hotel's lobby. It was an emotionally charged encounter; he protested that the article was "highly imaginative" and complained that he "was misled by deceitful demonstrations of friendship, and was far from suspecting the outrageous manipulations engaged against me." For her part, Mrs. Beer insisted on adhering to the agreed-upon timetable and conditions—if he persisted in his refusal to write his confession she would publish articles attributing all of his statements to him. Alternating between threats and pleas, he appealed to her compassion: "I am alone in the country, where I know no one; I can hardly speak its language, penniless, without support." He made it clear, however, that he would fight her to the end, declaring, "I am counting on the English legal system for protection, and am committed to invoke it."

The pair met again and exchanged a few letters, but Rachel was resolved to carry out her threat. The following Sunday, September 25, *The Observer* used the conversations that Rachel and Rowland Strong had held with Esterhazy to compile a confession written in the first person:

> It is unfortunate that both Colonel Sandherr and Colonel Henry should be dead, for they both knew the facts; but it is quite possible to prove that I did write the *bordereau* in spite of the disappearance of those two witnesses.
> . . . I knew that I was committing a forgery, but I also knew that all intelligence departments in all countries in the world, are run on precisely the same lines as our own, and that it is impossible to achieve practical results in any other way.

The Observer article caused an immediate sensation and was telegraphed to *Le Temps* by its London correspondent. It appeared that same evening in Paris, becoming the talk of the town. The following morning, the cabinet finally accepted Lucie Dreyfus's appeal and transferred her husband's case to the Court of Cassation, the highest court in the French judicial system. This was the last step Dreyfus could take within the French legal system.

Esterhazy was enraged. So too were his friends and supporters, who dismissed the confession, claiming that the former major had probably been bribed by the Dreyfus Syndicate. In a short time, Esterhazy sold the "exclusive" rights to his story to several outlets, including a Parisian book publisher and both Belgian and French newspapers. When one New York publisher, the House of Appleton, refused to accept the story "even as a gift," the British publisher Grant Richards joined the band; he announced that he would publish Esterhazy's memoirs in England and in the United States by the end of the year. Richards, who paid Esterhazy one thousand pounds, stated on behalf of his client that the confession in *The Observer* was fictitious and that the whole truth would only be revealed in his coming book. In the months to come, Esterhazy would make quite a fortune from selling his memoirs many times over, while also touting his denials to the anti-Semitic French press.

Sales were booming and *The Observer*'s reputation was greatly enhanced by the two articles it ran on Esterhazy. Rachel's account was accepted as accurate by colleagues and rivals, politicians and the public, in England and elsewhere, but Esterhazy's denials injured her professional pride. Speaking with some signs of emotion, she told the correspondent of the *Westminster Gazette* that she was considering suing Esterhazy for libel: "For instance, I have never seen Baron Gustave de Rothschild, nor have I ever been in any of the Rothschild houses," she said. Having met Esterhazy three times, it was clear to her that their conversations were meant for publication: "For I have no other reason to be connected to the matter than for the sake of *The Observer,* and of helping the major to clear his name." Though the scoop swept the world press, Rachel kept it out of her *Sunday Times* editorials so as not to duplicate herself.

On October 20, Esterhazy issued a writ against *The Observer*, demanding damages for libel but not specifying on what grounds. He deliberately avoided mentioning that the *casus belli* was the authorship of the *bordereau*. Sir George Henry Lewis, the solicitor involved in most of the celebrated causes and press libel cases in the 1890s, represented Mrs. Beer. He challenged Esterhazy's lawyer, Arthur Newton, to submit the case to court, which would force Esterhazy to make a full public statement of his grievances. Mrs. Beer and Dreyfus's supporters were looking forward to the truth of the affair being revealed, and they were anxious to see the Frenchman called to the witness box of an English Court of Justice and cross-examined by a skillful counsel.

In mid-November, Fayard Frères published the first installment of *Les Dessus de l'Affaire Dreyfus* (*Undercurrents of the Dreyfus Affair*). Esterhazy was full of self-pity: "I must live and make a living for those who are near and dear to me . . . must my two little girls also be sacrificed to discipline and reasons of State?" He blamed his superiors for attempting to "break me, to fling me as a living prey to the pack; I have the right, I suppose, to cry 'Murder!'" But as to facts, the press agreed that his account was "the merest trash."

As Esterhazy burned the few remaining bridges that he had in London, a falling out with his British publisher Grant Richards was followed by an alarming letter from his French lawyer informing him that he would have to come to Paris to testify in the Court of Cassation. He had no intention of returning to France, fearing arrest, but England was unsafe for him too, since he could be extradited. In late November, with his libel suit against *The Observer* still pending, he fled to Rotterdam and made contact with a sympathetic *Daily News* correspondent there. Esterhazy portrayed the Dreyfus affair as a legitimate war of defense against the most terrible invasion that had ever menaced Europe—the Jews, whose single aim was "to conquer nations and become their mistress by the force of money, intellect, and revolution." "The Jews are the masters of France; one thing only stands aloof—the army, which detests them. . . . Not being able to master the army, the Jews have resolved to destroy it," he told the journalist.

Fearful that police detectives were on his tracks, Esterhazy moved from one cheap hotel to another. Whenever his new lodging was discovered, demonstrators would gather beneath his window. He shuttled between Rotterdam and The Hague, and his friends planted false news that he had boarded a ship to New York, his journey to exile financed by the French War Office to buy his silence.

Though Esterhazy categorically denied on every platform that he had ever confessed to *The Observer,* he was willing to settle his suit out of court. He probably feared, and for good reason, that he could all too easily go from being the accuser to the accused. For her part, though she had been determined to triumph, Rachel was aware of the high cost and uncertain outcome of libel suits; the English libel law was splendidly framed "to shelter the knaves," and it would be an impossible mission to drag French, German and Italian officials to testify in a London witness box. Esterhazy had not honoured his promise to provide a written statement to *The Observer,* but he had given a verbal one, and even for that he was entitled to compensation. So on her behalf, Lewis offered the agreed-upon fee of five hundred pounds, with fifty more for legal expenses. One of the clauses in the settlement was that Esterhazy give priority to *The Observer* for any future articles of his on the subject. He telegraphed his consent from Holland, and Newton withdrew the action. Each side presented the settlement as a victory.

In mid-January 1899, Esterhazy was summoned to testify in France in the Court of Cassation. There he was granted immunity. Under oath, he denied having confessed to Mrs. Beer and Mr. Strong that he was the author of the *bordereau,* and he refused to answer any potentially incriminating questions. After he declined to continue his testimony, the Procureur-General had a letter sent to him informing him that the civil investigation on the charges of fraud that had been raised against him by his cousin would be resumed within twenty-four hours. Esterhazy realised that if he delayed his departure he would risk arrest and a lengthy prison sentence; he left by the midnight train to Rotterdam, which saved him the great embarrassment of bumping into Rowland Strong, who had come to Paris to give his testimony in court of the conversations that he and Mrs. Beer had conducted with Esterhazy.

Meanwhile, in London, Rachel continued negotiations with Arthur Newton, who had offered her Esterhazy's signed confession for an additional one thousand pounds. She was interested in an interview and Newton gave her the fugitive's address in Rotterdam. "It's about time to keep your promise concerning the formal declaration and above all, documents," read her cable to Esterhazy, complete with prepayment for his answer. It seemed a rather incomprehensible move, taking into account Newton's shady character and Esterhazy's notorious lack of credibility, especially given that the second installment of his *Dessous de l'Affaire Dreyfus* had just been reviewed as "even more trashy and unconvincing than the first." But this move may have been less naïve on Rachel's part than it appeared—rather, it was a clever trick to extract a written statement from Esterhazy in order to restore *The Observer*'s reputation.

This was the second time that Rachel had made Esterhazy come to London. He arrived on February 20, under an assumed name, de Guillhem, which he used when he registered at the luxurious Charing Cross Hotel. Room 330, though, was in the modest quarters on the top floor (the sixth), which was occupied mainly by the hotel employees.

This time Rachel Beer was more cautious. She prepared an agreement for Esterhazy to sign and insisted on seeing his documents beforehand. She struggled to overcome the animosity between them, and the surviving correspondence from the affair, kept at the Bibliothèque nationale in Paris, shows that she went out of her way to win him over: "Are you willing to reconcile? I am not your enemy," she wrote to him.

All of her notes were written on her private stationery, bearing her home address and pelican coat of arms. The envelopes, though, were from the *Sunday Times* and not *The Observer,* an indication that she did not consider herself the formal, permanent editor of her husband's newspaper, but was merely waiting for his recovery.

The short missives she sent Esterhazy were written in French and in her nearly illegible handwriting, and demonstrate her efforts to mollify him and negotiate a cease-fire: "Please come tomorrow and have tea with me in the morning, if it's convenient. I shall be alone. We shall talk afterward. Your friend, Rachel Beer." But Esterhazy did all he could to avoid her. Twice she took the trouble to come to his hotel, waited for him in vain, and left a note—"Come to me in the evening." She phoned several times, and the hotel concierge left a message for Esterhazy informing him that "Madame Beer came with a cab and was looking for Monsieur. She waited three quarters of an hour at the entrance court. Will return tonight."

On one of those very days, Esterhazy published an open letter in a Brussels newspaper, declaring, "I am at this time at the end of my strength, and almost at the end of my courage." Rather than self-pity, his words hinted that he was contemplating a Samson-like act—he would place himself between the pillars and pull the house down.

In the end, Rachel's siege was fruitless. Though at her demand Esterhazy swore an affidavit before a solicitor to authenticate his statements, he did not submit it to her. He ignored her persistent pleas, while at the same time negotiating with *The Daily Chronicle,* which offered a hefty sum for his story. They were careful enough to sign him to a statutory declaration, rendering Esterhazy liable to prosecution for perjury and a possible imprisonment of seven years, but he blatantly defrauded them as well. The lengthy statement *The Daily Chronicle* published was identical to the third installment of the memoirs that he wrote for Fayard Frères, which appeared two days later. In both publications, he still refrained from confessing the authorship of the *bordereau.*

The Observer was furious and Strong did his best to smear Esterhazy's reputation: "His pockets are full of money. Barnum and Bailey have offered him prodigious sums to figure among their freaks. A theatrical manager would like him to act a role in a new military melodrama." The sarcastic barb was well placed—Esterhazy was, by now, pursued by autograph hunters as well as journalists—but despite his emerging sense of stardom, Esterhazy feared extradition and assassination. He threatened to use on himself his murderous-looking knife, the loaded revolver he concealed under his jacket, or the strychnine pills that he kept in his waistcoat pocket.

While pursuing Esterhazy, Rachel had also been striving for many months to meet Émile Zola. Aware that he had completed his new novel *Fecondite* and was writing the account of his flight from France and his adventures in England, she wished to secure its publication for *The Observer*. She sent messages to his English and French friends, who pointed out her merits to Zola: "She is Jewish, daughter of the Sassoons, financiers from London, completely devoted to the Dreyfus case." Zola and his solicitors feared extradition, and only a few confidants knew he was staying at the Queen's Hotel in Upper Norwood, London. It seemed as if Rachel was to be unsuccessful, however: "Whoever may call on you, under whatever pretext, show him the door and preserve the silence of the tomb," Zola wrote to his friend Ernest Alfred Vizetelly, son of his English publisher. "I will see neither the gentleman nor the lady. Tell them so distinctly, in order that they may worry you no more."

On May 29, 1899, based on new evidence, the Court of Cassation concluded that the *bordereau* had indeed been written by Esterhazy. In a preemptive move the day before, Esterhazy had summoned Serge Basset, the London correspondent of *Le Matin,* for an exclusive scoop. The French journalist insisted that his account of the interview had to be countersigned by Esterhazy in the presence of a witness. *Oui, c'est moi qui fait le bordereau* were the words that Rachel had longed to hear again, and at last, eight months after he confessed to her, Esterhazy repeated it publicly: " 'Yes, sir,' he said very deliberately, though a gleam of fire shone in his dark eyes. 'It is I who received an order from Colonel Sandherr to write the *bordereau*. That I admit.' " Still, to his last day, he never acknowledged that he had spied for the Germans. At *The Observer,* the staff raised a toast. "I have always felt confident that, in spite of his contradictions, Esterhazy would reiterate the confession which he first made to myself and Mrs. Beer," rejoiced Rowland Strong.

The court annulled the 1894 verdict and decided on a new trial in Rennes for Dreyfus. Though disappointed that the prisoner was not declared innocent, still Rachel was optimistic that the truth was powerful and would eventually prevail, and that "a dramatic triumph of poetic justice" would finally occur.

After four years on Devil's Island, Dreyfus was brought back to France. One hundred and fifty witnesses were summoned, among them Esterhazy, who was granted safe conduct and protection against his cousin's lawsuit. But he refused to come, fearing that if Dreyfus was acquitted and he was declared a traitor, public opinion would not allow the government to spare him. Lord Russell of Killowen, Lord Chief Justice of England, attended the trial, and Rowland Strong hoped that "the jingle of British handcuffs, distant, yet approaching, must already have sounded faintly in his [Esterhazy's] guilty ears." Strong was one of the witnesses, and again he recounted his and Mrs. Beer's meetings with Esterhazy.

On September 9, 1899, Strong cabled from Rennes: "The public filed off silently, tearfully, as from a graveyard. Men shook hands with one another without speaking, as if in memory of some departed friend. The sorrow and shame were too deep for words." "The Defeat of Justice" was *The Observer* headline, as by a vote of five to two Dreyfus was convicted yet again—"Ten years' imprisonment for the crime of being a Jew, for the crime of having survived five years of torture already." The *Sunday Times* sensed that "probably the whole court would have been glad to acquit Dreyfus, but they feared the result on the Army and to themselves. . . . The Court-martial has simply bowed its neck to the Army fetish." Optimistically, Rachel predicted that a way out would be found and the French Ministry "will endeavor to dispose of the case before the Exposition Universelle of next year comes on."

And so it was. Family and friends talked Dreyfus into ending his ordeal by accepting a presidential pardon on account of bad health. "To pardon a man for a crime of which he is innocent, is, of course, a logical absurdity," remarked Rachel. "But if the Dreyfus case should lead to a permanent and healthy revulsion of feeling against the curse of militarism, in its worst and most baneful form, this most deplorable event will not have lacked its beneficent and congratulatory side."

Seeking a full acquittal, Dreyfus appealed, but several years were to pass before the Court of Cassation finally annulled the second Rennes verdict on July 12, 1906, declaring that "it was wrongfully and by error that the conviction was pronounced." Yet the case was never brought before a military tribunal to officially pronounce Dreyfus innocent. The army allowed him to resume his service, and he retired after one year. Never knowing complete satisfaction at the resolution of the affair, he died on July 12, 1935. Almost a hundred years after the travesty of justice began, still the French army would not admit the disgrace, and in 1985 they refused to place a statue of Dreyfus at the École Militaire, in defiance of President Mitterrand, who had commissioned it.

Esterhazy, exiled in London, lost his source of income when Dreyfus was pardoned. He used the assumed name Fitzgerald, and then switched to Count Jean Marie de Voilement, making a living from expressing his indignation at English life in the French press. "The last time I saw him, he was fashionably attired and looking ten years younger," recalled MP and journalist Henry Norman. "He assured me he was overwhelmed with all sorts of offers for his future services and with letters from women admirers desirous of his acquaintance." Esterhazy died in 1923, and his tombstone in Harpenden carries a quote from Shelley: "He has outsoared the shadow of our night."

THE ANTI-SEMITISM that hung over "the Dreyfus affair" like a dark shadow would not be so easily laid to rest, but it did provide impetus for a new and groundbreaking chapter in Jewish history. In no other European country had Jews enjoyed *Liberté, Equalité, Fraternité* as early and widely as in the secular and republican France. If Jewish integration had failed there, what prospects did Jews have elsewhere? A year after Dreyfus's exile to Devil's Island, the Viennese journalist Theodor Herzl published *Der Judenstaat,* soon translated into English as *The Jewish State. The Observer* was among the first to acknowledge the significance of the idea of establishing "a Jewish Autonomous State in Syria." Herzl's plan was a despairing reaction to the spread of anti-Semitism, not stemming from religious and mystical motives but from a desire to found a political centre for the Jews.

At that time, Greater Syria was under the rule of the Ottoman Empire, and Dr. Herzl hoped to persuade the Sultan to lease Palestine to the Jews. Wearing her *Sunday Times* hat, however, Rachel feared that the Sultan's possible consent might be a publicity spin, so that the world would overlook the atrocities he and his people had committed. As she commented shrewdly, "It is to be hoped, at any rate, that the Jews in England are not so anti-Christian as to be bribed by any offers of land in Palestine for their convenience with the extermination that is taking place of the Christian Armenians."

The Fourth Zionist Congress, held in London in August 1900, was "a congress of publicity," designed to steer public opinion toward Zionism. "They seemed to be representative of all quarters of the globe come to a congress of nations. The confusion of tongues constituted a veritable Babel, but the good humour, the excitement and the cheers were unexceptionable," a *Sunday Times* correspondent reported from the gathering. In her editorial, Rachel was more reserved; no doubt the destitute Jews from underdeveloped countries would benefit from settling in farms in Palestine, "but how many Jews that are doing well here would admit that they are only temporarily sojourning in a strange land," she wondered, relying on the successful experience of her family as well as Frederick's.

The idea of a Jewish state might have a boomerang effect, Rachel

234 THE FIRST LADY OF FLEET STREET

feared; it would stir up anti-Semitism and disrupt integration, since Jews would be accused of double loyalty. She was somewhat relieved that at the closing ceremony of the Zionist Congress the delegates rose and sang "God Save the Queen." Nothing is more remarkable "than the attachment and loyalty shown by the Hebrew race to any country which treats it well," she wrote.

Hoisting the Flag at Pretoria

In the same week that Dreyfus was granted his pardon and the affair lost its journalistic appeal, another confrontation reached its peak: the South African Boer Republic's fight for independence. Three years earlier, in the spring of 1896, *The Observer* had warned for four successive weeks that the Boers were arming themselves to the teeth and that the British supremacy lay at their mercy. It criticised the government for not having established satisfactory footing in the region, and urged it to increase its military strength. The newspaper was denounced as alarmist and attacked as an enemy of peace, but the *Sunday Times* stood by its traditional rival: "the country must wake up if a great disaster is to be avoided," wrote Rachel Beer.

Rachel always preferred the negotiation table to the battlefield and kept suggesting that the government offer President Kruger an olive branch. Yet, she was worried that surrender to the annexed Dutch-speaking republic would cause the strongest disaffection among British colonists, and "imperil their position with the black races, who would set down the surrender as an abandonment of our Sovereignty, and be tempted to rise in rebellion." Her advice was to maintain steady pressure while making the necessary preparations for war: "It may be that Mr. Chamberlain [Secretary of State for the Colonies] has been barking rather too much, and has produced the impression on the Boers that he will not 'bite.' It may be necessary to show them that we are prepared to bite also if the duty be forced upon us, yet, a combination of firmness and tact, even at this eleventh hour, may effect wonders."

On September 17, 1899, when troops sailed from Southampton, *The Observer* seemed to be ahead of them on the warpath. The Boers had made up their minds to fight, with "the mad passion of self-aggression"; as a result, the British government had no other option but "to go through with this melancholy business firmly to the end." At first Rachel allowed *The Observer* to maintain its traditional stance, and took a milder tone in the *Sunday Times*—she prayed for peace and good will in her editorial: "though less hopeful, the prospect is not hopeless." The following week, *The Observer,* too, softened its tone: "It will not do for Great Britain to lose her head, for the matter is still one for negotiation."

As late as October 8, both newspapers believed that the possibilities for peace were not completely exhausted. With one voice, both of the Beers' newspapers condemned the British press for their convulsive impatience and excitement at the prospect of war (*The Observer*), and denounced the "Jingo claptrap and 'unwise writing in the newspapers' in favour of war" (the *Sunday Times*). Once diplomacy failed and fighting began on October 11, Rachel donned her khaki uniform and called for a swift resolution, with no stopping until the army hoisted the British flag at Pretoria. And when that happens, she recommended, "We ought to shame both our enemies and jealous rivals by showing ourselves magnanimous in the hour of victory."

This was the first war that the British Empire had waged against white people who were fighting for self-government since the American War of Independence. Lasting two and a half years, the Boer War was the empire's longest, and it was also the bloodiest of the nineteenth century. As many as three hundred journalists reported from the scene, and *The Times* alone had a staff of twenty in the field. Many newspapers hired the services of distinguished writers like Rudyard Kipling, Arthur Conan Doyle, Edgar Wallace and Winston Churchill to provide a personal angle from South Africa. By dispatching fifteen artists, correspondents and photographers, *The Black and White Weekly Illustrated* increased its circulation to over half a million. Newspaper magnate Alfred Harmsworth's newly established *Daily Mail* added illustrated supplements and reached a record million copies, maximizing profits by taking advantage of the wave of patriotism and the nation's collective concern for its 450,000 soldiers.

Though they could easily afford the expense, the Beers did not join the race to provide the most extensive and highly illustrated coverage of the war. They also declined to increase their staff or send men of letters on special assignments; Rachel made do, instead, with telegrams from news agencies. With the invention of the Folding Pocket Camera, the Boer War became the most widely photographed conflict, but the *Sunday Times* and *The Observer* refrained from printing any visuals, not even maps of the war zone. It was quite in character with Rachel's objection to the celebration of bloodshed. In her editorials, she did not romanticise the war or glorify it; she portrayed it as a painful means to establishing peace in the region.

In her husband's newspaper, she kept alive the tradition of launching special editions during wartime—this had also been done the year before for the Spanish-American war over Cuba—keeping *The Observer* up to date by publishing late editions "giving all war news received up to six o'clock." Although circulation and profits did not increase, Rachel continued the practice for ten months. She even offered an astounding Internet-like service: readers dwelling at a distance and unable to obtain copies of *The Observer*'s special war editions could "have important news that may come to hand telegraphed to them on depositing with the Publisher of the paper the necessary money to pay for the cost of transmission."

The financial interests of most newspaper proprietors in the South African gold mines explained the almost undivided advocacy of the Boer War, much to Rachel's dismay. Though she was now committed to the conflict herself, as early as five months before the war, in May 1899, she had warned that "the profit of the mine-owners is not a question over which there is any pressing necessity to risk a quarrel with the Transvaal government." The only major daily that actually opposed the war was the *Manchester Guardian,* and it paid for its opinions in diminished circulation. As the war lingered on, its South African correspondent John Atkinson Hobson complained that there no longer existed a free press in England, allowing adequate discussion of the vital issues of politics. Where Rachel differed from her colleagues was that she objected to silencing the pro-Boer Friends of Peace—in the name of free speech they too needed to be allowed a voice. That said, she did not agree with them; she felt that the duty of Christians in this emergency was not to turn "their country's left cheek to the enemy when it has been smitten on the right cheek."

The Boers proved skilled warriors, better organised and equipped than their British foes, and they soon gained the upper hand. Rachel did not hesitate to censure the British generals for showing plenty of dash and gallantry but no tactics: "We have not yet caught our bear (or Boer, which was it?), and so cannot dispose of his skin. For the sakes of both peoples, it may be hoped that he will not give us too long a run in catching him." Prime Minister Rosebery's statement that "as in former wars, the army would probably muddle through" seemed to her damaging, unpatriotic and very unheroic. She warned that muddling is fearfully costly, in terms of both life and money.

News from the front was heavily censored, but in letters home soldiers complained of being half starved en route and landing in South Africa thin as skeletons and weak as kittens. "What avails the sending out of more men if they are not handled properly? It only means the sacrifice of more lives to no purpose," Rachel protested. With so much money spent, the soldiers should not be sent into battle in such poor condition.

Rachel was also dismayed by the overenthusiastic send-off given to volunteers leaving for battle. She wrote, "The men, when at last they got off, felt that they had been through a scrimmage to which even a hand-to-hand fight with the Boers would be preferable." She opposed compulsory conscription, since the training of a larger number of youth to the use of the rifle "is more or less distasteful to all liberty-loving Englishmen," and when she heard news from the front that Boer women were fighting in the trenches, she expressed her hope that the British soldiers would not be forced to take up arms against a unit of "Boer Amazons."

Just over a year into the war, on December 23, 1900, in her editorial "Peace and the Closing Century," Rachel foresaw the conflict ending in a *Pax Britannica*—under British guidance, the Boers would learn to govern themselves properly. While some journalists, including J. L. Garvin, who would later replace her as editor of *The Observer*, considered the war a symptom of British decline and questioned whether the empire would survive the new century, Rachel envisioned a New Imperialism born of the war, a stronger empire built of federations, "the work we shall probably complete early in the twentieth century."

Despite her criticisms of how the war was being conducted, Rachel trusted the man at the helm. Also, like most of her editor colleagues, a sense of patriotism numbed her and enabled her to approve of acts she might otherwise have reviled—the army's policy of burning thousands of Boer farms in retribution for harbouring armed men, for example. The British soldiers were not alone in their ruthlessness, however; accusations of horrific conduct were levelled at both sides, and British patrols were treacherously fired on after being welcomed by Boer women acting as decoys.

The Observer saw social activist Emily Hobhouse's damning report on the concentration camps the British army had set up in South Africa as "a record of that dispassionate and human longing to do practical good to helpless sufferers, that is so eminently characteristic of our countrywomen." The newspaper rejected, though, her conclusion that the British were conducting the war by methods of barbarism. The high mortality rate in the concentration camps—here *The Observer* parroted the official line—was caused by Dutch mothers' incompetence: they "have no idea as to how a child ought to be fed, and none as to how it ought to be nursed when sick. They cook their own food very badly . . . and entertain a rooted objection to sending their children to hospital." The Dutch were averse to fresh air and habitually neglected sanitation, and even before the war, continued *The Observer,* the mortality rate there was appallingly high compared with more advanced countries. The British authorities had been a great help to these miserable people; "they would have died in far greater numbers if left to shift for themselves in devastated country." As it was, 27,000 white civilians died in the British concentration camps, 22,000 of them children, in addition to 20,000 "blacks and coloureds."

As the first troops returned home, Mrs. Beer joined the commander-in-chief's appeal to the public "not to treat the men to situations in public-houses or in the streets, and thus lead them into excesses which must tend to degrade those whom the nation delights to honour." Large crowds of rough elements, she feared, would seize on the opportunity "to assemble and indulge their savage propensities. What a pity it is all these ruffs can not be induced, or compelled, to join the army, and be subjected to its wholesome discipline!"

In spring 1901, a year before the peace treaty was finally signed, Rachel already sought a way for Britain to gain a better foothold in the region. She pointed to the lack of female society of a suitable kind as one reason why British men declined to settle in South Africa; to strengthen the outposts of the empire, she sided with the British Women's Emigration Association in encouraging middle-class women, or those who were independent, to sail to South Africa to secure a job and a husband. "Girls of the servant type" were not encouraged to go, since it was doubtful that they would be able to find any openings. Once they reached the Cape, Rachel hoped these eligible women would be placed in respectable situations, "so that they shall not fall into the hands of those diamond-ringed 'Continental friends' who are, so we are told, constantly on the lookout for fresh arrivals."

And the Tears in Her Eyes
Grew Large on Their Ledge

Like a juggler, Rachel was struggling to keep all her balls up in the air: the two newspapers, her social activities, philanthropic commitments and, above all, sustaining her husband through his painful and unstoppable decline.

She scaled back her appearances in the office. On Saturday afternoons, Gus Wingrove, the apprentice printer boy, was sent to bring the proofs of the next day's editorial page of the *Sunday Times* to 7 Chesterfield Gardens for Mrs. Beer's inspection. He was often kept waiting in the kitchen for the butler to bring the sheets back down from the third floor, and he would pass the time by nibbling from a plate of cakes. Young Gus got the impression that Mrs. Beer drank a little too much at lunch and was in the habit of falling asleep over the proofs—the butler would frequently have to rouse her and remind her that the messenger was still waiting below. Gus was usually sent back in the Beers' carriage, saving him the omnibus fare; he would arrive "in style in an open landau, with footman as well as coachman, and be greeted by ribald remarks from printers standing about outside St. Clement's Press."

A decidedly embarassing moment occurred in late 1899; the Beers' newspapers, as well as three others, were mentioned in the liquidation case of the Industrial Contract Corporation. It was alleged that the company had attempted to purchase the endorsement of those newspapers by gross bribery, sending them checks "for favourable notices." All of the newspapers emphatically denied the claim, and the Beers' solicitor said that the alleged recipient of the money, Mr. Hermann Schmidt, "has never been associated in any way with *The Observer*, and that his connection with the *Sunday Times* ceased many years ago." No member of the staff, he went on, had any personal acquaintance with Schmidt, or had received any payment of any kind from him. Fortunately, the court accepted the newspapers' statements and found no evidence of wrongdoing. The allegations were never discussed in the National Association of Journalists, and cleaning the stables was left to the newspapers themselves—"A dangerous malaria may be generated, unless we are careful to insist on sanitary precautions," wrote *The Times*.

The new year—1900—brought better fortune, with Rachel elected vice-president of the Society of Women Journalists; for Frederick's sake, however, she made a point of being publicly presented only as the "editress of the *Sunday Times*," even though she was actually controlling both papers. The annual meeting of the society took place at their home. As part of her philanthropic outreach, she created a holiday fund for female journalists "for the purpose of assisting members who need a holiday but feel unable to afford one," and was the main benefactor.

To her growing list of memberships Rachel added the Folk Song Society, whose object was to collect, preserve and publish folk songs and ballads. Most of the 110 members were musically interested, professional, middle-class men, and very few of the 37 female members had careers. A shining and startling exception, Mrs. Beer was offered a seat on the committee; it gave her an opportunity to display her patriotism and to continue her campaign for quality entertainment, and she promoted the society with lengthy articles and interviews in the *Sunday Times*.

The inaugural meeting of the Folk Song Society was held at Chesterfield Gardens on February 2, 1899. After a closed committee session in one of the drawing rooms, a *conversazione* in the salon was graced by the composer Edward Elgar, attracting a large attendance. In these days of commercialized, popular music, said the society's vice-president, Sir Hubert Parry, people "think that the common set rowdyism is the highest expression of human emotion"; it was the society's belief that, in actuality, folk music is among the purest products of the human mind. "It grew in the hearts of the people before they devoted themselves entirely to the making of quick returns," Parry added. Rachel also joined the rival Folk Lore Society, which collected legends and proverbs, myths, superstitions and old customs.

Another of Rachel's keen interests was mysticism, which was a perfect fit for her inquisitive nature. Like many in her day—including Prime Ministers Gladstone and Balfour, writers Lewis Carroll, Arthur Conan Doyle and Mark Twain, as well as biographer Leslie Stephen, Virginia Woolf's father—she was fascinated by mesmerism, thought transference, séances, clairvoyance, haunted houses and communicating with the dead. They were all members of the Society for Psychic Research, founded in 1882 by Cambridge philosopher Henry Sidgwick. Secularisation and the decline of religion had brought with it the spread of the occult and a new religion of spiritualism.

Science was hailed for its ability to explain the physical world, and though not only the clergy but some key members of the scientific community expressed hostility toward this new movement, the SPR set out to research uncanny phenomena and to test their validity using meticulous scientific methods. The attempt "to demonstrate the existence of the soul in a rationalistic culture" held particular appeal for Rachel, since matters of the spirit intrigued her greatly.

Rachel set up an interview with M. Jules Bois, the French writer and apostle of Satanism. "You think women are more physically and psychically spiritual than men?" he was asked. "Certainly," he answered. "Women, through their constant struggle against men's wills, have reached a purer mediumistic quality of mind than men, and it is through them that I believe humanity may in the near future develop new states and new powers, largely psychic but also correspondingly physical, which would today be called abnormal." The bond between feminism and spiritualism was no doubt music to the ears of the editress.

Despite Frederick's continued illness, Rachel remained adamant that she did not want to turn their home into a sanatorium. She made a point of maintaining the musical soirées, as well as afternoon "at home's" in aid of charities, so that past guests would not refrain from visiting again.

For two successive years, she hosted the annual exhibition of the Royal Amateur Art Society. "The beautiful rooms were filled by many well-known people, and the attention of many of the visitors strayed often from the pictures sent by the exhibitors, to the fine paintings which form the permanent decoration of the hall and staircase as well as the other rooms," flattered *The Observer* reporter on March 22, 1900. "The hall was reserved for the exhibition of photography and bookbinding—the sketches, watercolors, carvings, leatherwork and embroidery finding place in the reception rooms above." Six miniatures were loaned from Queen Victoria's collection, the Princess of Wales donated paintings, and the proceeds from the sale of over one hundred works of art were divided among three charities. The entertainment was provided by members of the Folk Song Society, who sang old ballads.

While the rooms downstairs were glittering and abuzz with guests, only a muffled hum of conversation, laughter, music and applause would creep upstairs to Frederick, alone in his darkened room.

WITH TWO NEWSPAPERS already in his small journalistic empire—*The Weekly Sun* and *The Sun*—T. P. O'Connor was interested in adding a third. Arriving at Chesterfield Gardens, he was ushered into a room where the Beers were seated. He noted their complexions—colorless, "with a suggestion of un-European darkness"—and recoiled at the sight of the "two poor little figures, small of stature, with thin and almost shrunken frames, with a look of pathetic shyness, crumpled up close to a fire. Their manner was that of two little affrighted mice."

They spoke in whispers and their apparent shyness actually embarrassed him. He concluded that a real business conversation would be quite impossible with the pair, and nothing came of the meeting.

For the Beers, accepting the meeting with O'Connor may have been their attempt to let one of the newspapers go—easing the burden on Rachel. The attempt failed, however, and she continued to work feverishly to keep her husband's enterprise thriving for him throughout his life.

Frederick's health had been fluctuating badly for the past four years. He was losing weight, there was swelling around his bones, and his abscesses were not healing. In the summer of 1900 it became apparent that the lesions in his lungs had spread to his bones and joints. His condition was so severe that two professional male nurses had to be hired, joined later by a full-time female nurse. While these appointments were an admission that she needed assistance, Rachel remained very much involved in caring for and even treating her husband.

For many years, it was believed that exposing consumptive patients to fresh air would help wash the impurities and germs from their lungs. In addition, sunshine, low atmospheric pressure, low humidity and the absence of winds were all thought to have beneficial effects. But, suffering as he was from tuberculosis of the bones, Frederick was far too weak to travel to a mountain sanatorium abroad. In place of that impossibility, Rachel came up with an extraordinary and quixotic idea: a tuberculosis patient could be placed in a hot-air balloon, which would lift them above the winds, fogs and rain clouds of London, to a height that could be regulated in accordance with the required density of atmosphere to aid their condition. She spotted a barely used balloon perfect for the purpose at Wembley Park, and proposed that another might possibly be found in the storehouse of the Crystal Palace. "A suitable balloon might be lent—or even given—whence the consumptive aeronauts might breathe a purer air, wafting on the gentle winds, and which in the hospital grounds would be firmly fastened to the outer shell of the revolving globe"; it seemed very simple to her. But her novel idea failed to gain support, and her fantasy never became reality.

Despite all of the bleak evidence before her, Rachel strove to nourish Frederick's hope. He had been a keen sportsman, and she bought a complete cricket outfit, practice net, stumps and all, and kept it ready for the moment when he would be strong enough to be driven in the family carriage to their Richmond house, which they had not used for a long time, and there the footmen could bowl to him. She kept Frederick's park hack at a fashionable livery stable, anticipating the day when he would mount his horse and ride in the nearby Rotten Row. "She must have loved him very much, for she never gave up hoping that he would get well again, showing a brave, proud face to the world, while she watched faithfully over him throughout his terrible lingering illness," remembered Siegfried Sassoon.

On the few occasions that Rachel referred to tuberculosis in her editorials, she sounded optimistic about recovery from the disease, which was the leading killer, after heart disease. In her view, since the disease was acquired, not inherited, it could also be prevented. "This is good news to the Englishman, whose climate has always produced the largest number of victims to this disease," she wrote in August 1898. The Congress on Tuberculosis, which was held in London in July 1901, was the first item in her editorial that week. She was happy to quote the legendary Dr. Koch, who praised England for having separate hospitals for the treatment and cure of the disease, resulting in the numbers of its sufferers falling at a greater rate than in any other European country.

The only breaks that she allowed herself from her various duties were the short visits she continued to make to her sister-in-law and nephews in Weirleigh. She undertook them on impulse, whenever she felt an urgent need to bare her soul. Once, when she missed her train, she hired a special one for the thirty-mile journey, a reasonable expense for her and an extravagant squandering of money in the eyes of her Sassoon nephews. Siegfried thought that she looked out of place in the country, "sallow and untidy and almost eccentric," as if she had dressed in a hurry. In London, he knew, she had autonomy and importance, was surrounded with luxuries, and exuded an "absent-minded graciousness and dignity which suggested a queen in exile." Though she remained amusing and charming with the boys, they felt that she was becoming more and more vague and peculiar.

Unable to leave her husband for more than a few hours at a time, she kept her visits short, spending most of her time with Theresa in the drawing room. Siegfried pitied her for having to return to her gloomy, opulent mansion. In better days, she had taken him to see *As You Like It,* and he often compared her life to the play's plot; he wished that she could be in the Forest of Arden, free of worry, able to "forget all about Mr. Beer's illness, and then go safely back to a palace, where he would be waiting for her, just as he was when she first knew him." Influenced by the tale of Orpheus and Eurydice—inspired by both the painting in Rachel's home and the opera version, which had been staged there—he cast his aunt in the role of the lover who was fighting to rescue from the jaws of death "the happiness which she had once known and which she refused to give up as lost beyond recovery."

If her nephew found her to be somewhat removed from reality, that trait may have helped her not to fully succumb to her despair. She continued to write learned editorials, pore over piles of research materials and read the books that were sent to her for review. The agonies of the present did not dim her passion for the future. She shared H. G. Wells's prophecy that the development of rapid transportation would put a stop to the mass migration from the countryside to the metropolis; by the year 2000, British citizens living in a radius of a hundred miles from London would be able to commute to the city for work on a daily basis. Herself a creative thinker, she marvelled at Wells's vision of the modern shopping mall, describing with wonder "a great gallery of shops and places of concourse and rendez-vous, a pedestrian place, its pathways reinforced by lifts and moving platforms and shielded from the weather."

She also continued to innovate as a publisher-editor, introducing new attractions to the *Sunday Times*. Prizes of two pounds, ten shillings; one pound, ten shillings; and one pound were awarded to the most successful solvers of six acrostics—"If side by side sit Jack and Jill, / In this they are—sit where they will"—while a junior competition for readers under fifteen years of age—"Find a number greater than twenty-eight which is equal to the sum of all the numbers that divide it exactly"—offered book prizes. To *The Observer* she introduced topics more suited to her own agenda, including articles about X-ray treatment for cancer, old age pensions, the changing family structure, women's holidays and philanthropy.

Rachel continued to acquire works of art, as well as champion artists' causes. In the spring of 1900, she purchased a painting by J. B. Roy, *The Choristers,* which portrayed five cherubic choirboys. She also obtained the right to make photographic reproductions of the painting, printed on a metal sheet, and announced that they could be bought for one pound at the *Sunday Times* offices, with part of the proceeds going to the Photographers' Benevolent Fund. She invited professional and amateur photographers "desirous of subscribing or assisting in any way with this Fund" to call at her home on Sunday at four o'clock.

NOW THAT THE abscesses along Frederick's spine and left shoulder blade had become gangrenous, he could no longer move and was lying speechless and inert. Still—even though improvement was not in sight—Rachel did not lose faith in the power of medicine. She praised the "secret order of workers," who were doing their best, and where they failed to cure at least offered cheer and comfort.

For the first seven months of 1901, she held all the strings together; but one by one she let them go. The musical soirées and her activities in various organisations were dropped first. The turmoil at her home took up more and more of Rachel's energies, and her preoccupation and ongoing distress were soon evident in her work. She stopped publishing the weekly interview column "In the Witness

Box," which had been dear to her heart, but her editorials remained to tell the tale, a deeply moving story of personal despair.

Until mid-July 1901, she kept up her pace of producing lengthy, well-informed editorials each week, dealing with at least four different issues from at home and abroad. But on Sunday, July 21, she supplied only one item for the *Sunday Times,* while she ended the editorial of *The Observer* with a poem, "The Garland: a Ballad of the Standard Rose." From that day onward, poems became an integral part of her editorials—and, as Frederick became ever more ill, they would eventually become their most prominent feature. The poems bear no credit, and having failed to identify them in the body of English poetry, and judging by their contents and tone, one can cautiously assume they were written by Rachel herself. She always considered the ability to recite poetry to be a lifelong asset, especially on occasions when "the memory may prove an invaluable companionship on the beds of sickness and in places where it is impossible to find reading material."

Some of the poems included in the *Sunday Times* and *The Observer* were composed in reaction to current events, while others may have been written in the past, but most of them reflected Rachel's current, sombre mood. It was not as if she stopped being able to write commentary on the major issues of the day—she continued to do so—nor did she need to fill up space. Her emotional state must have disrupted her professional judgment, causing her to place lyrical displays of sentiment in columns reserved for political and social issues. None of her staff dared to comment.

Several drawings of garden scenes by Edward Burne-Jones decorated the Beers' residence, and the first poem Rachel published described *The Garland,* a painting portraying a young woman in a red gown tending to a climbing rosebush: "Wet was her hair, and her eyes were wet, / And the tears in her eyes grew large on their ledge," went the verse. There was nothing in this painting, set in a fully lit, fortified garden, to indicate grief, yet Rachel viewed the scene through dark glasses. Taking poetic license with the picture, she went on to write, "She sank on the churchyard mound in a swoon, / The grave she had reached by the lamp of the moon." She called it "Picture Poem I," and the very same poem was recycled a week later in her *Sunday Times* editorial.

She also wrote verse about her precious Orpheus, painted by Watts: "He must ever gaze onward to guide / Her through dark of her doom, pour his breath / With the wail of his lyre to scare death." And *A Love Dream,* a lyrical statuette by Andrea Carlo Lucchesi, evoked wistful memories: "Love has come so long a way; / His dimpled feet have trodden o'er / The dusty rungs of learned lore." This latter poem was published first in *The Observer,* and then repeated in the *Sunday Times*. Two unfinished winter scenes painted by Rachel's sister-in-law Theresa Sassoon also inspired a poem, "Winter Away," with its evocative lines " . . . his warming glance / Melts the chilled earth from her frozen trance."

Rachel's political commentary on the lingering war in South Africa was also fortified by verse. She penned a mother's lament—"her world the Transvaal valley, crossed by birth / And death of her dear children and the pain / . . . Now in her place be laid / In love our Union flag—new Union made." In these lines, Rachel made poetic reference to the *Sunday Times*'s proposal of a new flag for the Transvaal, combining the British Jack and the Transvaal colors. She extended the idea of harmonious flags to other prolonged conflicts: on August 5, 1901, the eldest daughter of Queen Victoria, the Dowager German Empress, passed away, and Rachel opened her editorial with a poem that she dedicated to the late princess, suggesting that a united French and German flag for Alsace and Lorraine be created in her memory.

She wrote poems in the style of the metaphysical poets ("Thou art not fair, O Truth"), emulated Robert Burns ("Childie mi childie whan are ye camin"), and even tried some Irish influence ("And drink to the health / Of mi Kitty McGee"). Sometimes a poem just opened her editorial, and sometimes there would be as many as two or three. On July 28, she published in the *Sunday Times* the "Gregorian Chant," a reflection on her J. B. Roy painting *The Choristers*: " . . . With choral song the long-the last-cold home / Of heroes nigh forgotten in their case." The Italian translation of that poem—"*Il Canto Sacro*"—was published three weeks later in the *Sunday Times*, and again in *The Observer* on October 6. At the end of the month, the poem was presented for the fourth time, once again in English, in *The Observer*.

There were twelve instances in which the same poem was used in both newspapers, usually on different dates. There were also other occasions on which Rachel would publish a poem in a foreign language first (usually French) and then print its English translation a few weeks later, or vice versa. No doubt her subeditors were aware of the repetitions; however, they were careful not to upset the distraught editress. Both papers were at sea, but the *Sunday Times*, which had always been Rachel's own newspaper, was drifting far more than *The Observer*, like a rudderless ship.

For the column "A Book in Brief," in the *Sunday Times*, Rachel reviewed in extreme length *The Labyrinths of the World* by Johan Comenius, an unknown seventeenth-century Moravian educator and pastor whose work had only recently been translated into English. Rachel focused on the hope-inspiring story of a drowning sailor who stared death in the face and endured. Half of the review consisted of lengthy excerpts, and the first installment, on August 25, was abruptly cut off in the middle of a sentence with the promise "to be continued." It was a bizarre precedent for a book review to be carried over into the next week. In the second installment, the eclectic mixture of review and extensive copying also ended with "to be continued," but, alas, it never was.

From the beginning of September, Rachel's poems tell of a woman reduced to prayer:

> God saw His own created ones
> In sickness, sin, and pain,
> And sent Himself to doctor them,
> And make them whole again.

> And the Physician healing them
> And taking off their breath,
> Corrupted, died, for their disease,
> In awful earthly death;

At the end of the month, a poem chronicling endless hours of nightly torment—"But some unresting souls toss as the sea / In wakeful dreams. The chill hours take no heed, / Care not for all the raving sobs nor moan"—was included in both newspapers.

On November 3, it seemed as if she was already looking into the Beyond, trying to find some solace:

> Tell the songs of sympathy,
> Tales of how we may be free
> From happenings of mortality,
> From tears of toil and sleep's dull breath,
> The war of life and peace of death.

She stopped writing for *The Observer* altogether in mid-November. In the *Sunday Times,* she dedicated a poem to those who might find peace of mind in murmuring it to themselves in their spare moment or on carefully chosen occasions, "for, as Dante suggests, it may be as culpable to mourn when there should be rejoicing as to rejoice when there should be mourning":

> We have no God to give us grace,
> Nor any vale to hide our face,
> There is no lamp to light our road
> No path that leads to our abode.
>
> No melody for joy to ring,
> Nor any sorrows' songs to sing
> Nor mournful moan to give relief,
> And no salt tears to scour our grief.

The poem that she published on December 1—one of her last—speaks of the resurrection of the dead:

> When the dead waken from their sheltered sleep,
> And the eternal winds around them blow,
> Freeing the folds of their winding sheet,
> The deep-buried dust is summoned to grow.

Despite the solemn nature of so many of these poems, there were brief moments of light. Always drawn to technological inventions, the novelty of the Electrophone filled Rachel with hope. It provided a selection of live music, theatrical shows, public speeches and sermons, relayed to subscribers' homes through earphones and the telephone line. In her editorial from December 15, 1901, she imagined a large hall where orchestras, ensembles and soloists would perform continuously, day and night, and through the telephone line the life of "the lonely and the sick would thus be brightened, whilst those busy and in health may snatch some passing notes of melody during each day." Her editorial of that week ended with her poem "Tones Forlorn": "Bring love's dreamed bliss, / While moonbeams kiss / The dewy tears of eve."

After Christmas, the doctor diagnosed inflammation in Frederick's right lung. Frederick was slipping into a coma. For a brief moment, he regained consciousness and thanked all around him for their kindness. "At the end he was his old self again, gentle, charming and charitable to the world which had endowed him with great riches and the feeble constitution which had made his last years a living death," recalled his nephew Siegfried.

Frederick Arthur Beer died on December 30, 1901. He was forty-three years old. Like his parents and uncle before him, he died young.

The next day, the Beers' solicitor, George Malcolm Shaw Mackenzie, came to pay his condolences, and Rachel handed him her husband's will before he left. She seemed composed and in control.

Theresa and her three boys were enjoying the snow; the children were tobogganing on tea trays down the steep field outside the garden when the parlourmaid handed their mother a telegram. Frederick was dead, and Rachel wanted Theresa to come at once. She alerted the boys and hurried indoors to change. Siegfried and his brothers wondered if it would be appropriate to continue playing; for a long time they had been told that their uncle's death would be a happy release. Hamo suggested tossing a coin to make the decision, but since they had no coin they resumed sledding, "feeling sorry for Auntie Rachel and rather hoping we shouldn't have to attend the funeral."

They all arrived at Chesterfield Gardens, which was overflowing with white flowers Rachel had ordered. The house, which had always seemed funereal to them, looked as if it had been waiting all its life for this mournful event. For three days, Frederick's body had lain in his room. Theresa rushed upstairs. She later told her sons that Auntie Rachel refused to believe that Frederick was dead and that she did not want him to be buried at all. Rachel's mother, her brother Joseph and his family were notably absent, but a surprising visitor called on the day of the funeral. Frederick David Sassoon was the youngest of Rachel's uncles, just five years her senior, and the administrative head of David Sassoon & Co. in London. The Sassoons had severed all ties with Rachel fourteen years earlier, but though this uncle had never met Frederick he was registered as the relative who provided the information for the death certificate. As the family's representative, he came offering condolences, but not reconciliation.

TWENTY YEARS HAD passed since the iron gate to the catacomb in the lower part of the Beer mausoleum in Highgate was last opened to give entry to the coffin of Frederick's mother. On January 2, 1902, Frederick's body passed through it too, taking its place in that flamboyant testament to his father's grief.

Breakdown

The Observer carried a black-margined announcement of the death of Mr. F. A. Beer. The obituary maintained Frederick's official status as proprietor and editor, and referred to Rachel only as "a lady whose tastes have secured her keen interests in the conduct of her husband's journalistic property."

Throughout the turbulent years she spent tending to her increasingly ill husband, Rachel had never missed a column in the *Sunday Times*. Two days before Frederick's death, she wrote her editorial for that week, which dealt with a charity dinner for the Destitute Children's Society, the future of piano playing, and cruelty to dogs. On Saturday, two days after the funeral, Rachel sat down at her mahogany desk as usual, surrounded by the usual stacks of newspapers and magazines that were piled up on the floor. Just a day earlier, it had been leaked that Sir Ernest Cassel was the donor who had anonymously given £200,000 to build a sanatorium for consumptives on large and heavily wooded grounds, and Rachel now wrote in praise of the initiative as "an important step in the crusade against a national scourge." That week, and in those to follow, she dealt with issues that had always concerned her, such as trade unionism, education and safeguarding the might of the empire ("France and Russia have 300 torpedo boats, to which we should show 150 destroyers"). The scope, focus, fervor and flow of these writings revealed Rachel's old self.

On January 9, 1902, Shaw Mackenzie informed Mrs. Beer that he had examined her husband's will and found everything to be in order. At her request, the solicitor came to 7 Chesterfield Gardens to return the document. She did not consult with him, nor instruct him on what further actions to take. It was the last he ever saw of her. The gross value of Frederick's estate amounted to £460,000.

The aftershocks of all this upheaval would not strike her until the end of January—she became unable to write anything, and other members of the staff covered for her. Then, in the beginning of March, she collected herself briefly and wrote an editorial about the status of Prussian women as subordinate creatures. She was silent for the rest of the month, before returning in April to her favoured campaign for garden cities. After that, for over three months, the editorials were once again composed by various senior writers of the *Sunday Times*.

On numerous occasions, the manager of *The Observer* called at Rachel's residence to obtain her signature on documents, but he was not allowed to see her. He was told she had taken ill on the day of her husband's funeral and was unable to leave her room. The manager came to understand that Mrs. Beer was under the impression that upon the death of her husband the Observer Newspaper Company had been dissolved.

On August 3, 1902, Rachel made another attempt to pull herself out of her lethargy, producing an extremely lengthy, jumpy and incoherent editorial dealing with destitute children and how the clergy should help them. It was divided into three installments, but she never supplied the last one. Her subeditors at the paper bit their lips and kept silent. The disappearance of the motto "The World's Work," which always headed her editorials for the *Sunday Times,* marked the end of Mrs. Beer's active era in journalism. The date was September 14, 1902; she was forty-four years old. Officially she was still in charge, but only officially. The "Notice to Contributors" still read that the editor "does not in any case hold *herself* responsible for the return of rejected contributions," and letters published in the *Sunday Times* were still addressed to "Dear Madam," but she no longer responded to them.

ALL THE SIGNS indicated that Rachel was suffering from a case of pathological chronic grief that had resulted in a prolonged depression. Queen Victoria was a fellow sufferer. Over a period of just nine months, in 1861, the queen had lost her mother and husband. The death of her mother had already caused her a nervous breakdown, during which she locked herself in her chambers, and some rumours had it that the Prince Consort's death had turned her morbid melancholy into insanity. She was forty-two years old when Albert died of typhoid, and for the next forty years she waited for his return; clothes were laid out for him each evening with hot water and a towel. Her withdrawal from public life was interpreted as her fear "that the combined pressure of grief and royal business would drive her insane." The sovereign's behaviour was frowned upon by her subjects, who believed she was greatly overstretching the firmly established code of mourning.

There is no doubt that Rachel was completely numb with sorrow. The hectic world of journalism, which demands curiosity and an empathy for other people's miseries, became unsuitable for a woman who had lost all interest in life. Psychiatrists argue that children who suffer the loss of a parent during childhood are inclined to cling to a figure that represents security, and may suffer excessive grief if they lose that person later in life. Rachel's father died when she was nine years old, and, having married outside her faith, she had also lost her mother and brothers and the entire Sassoon clan. Frederick was her only family, her one dependable ally.

Rachel clearly needed a break; it was even expected of her to withdraw from her duties in her first year of mourning. Her livelihood did not depend on her work as an editor, and with the small circulation of both newspapers neither was profitable. With the advent of the sensational, commercially driven press, *The Observer* and the *Sunday Times* seemed almost obsolete.

Following Frederick's death, the only remaining support Rachel had was her sister-in-law. As a temporary relief, she moved to Tunbridge Wells, just six miles from Theresa Sassoon's home in Weirleigh. Tunbridge Wells was the nearest spa to London, a vibrant, fashionably modern holiday resort with long associations with royalty and a fast train service to the metropolis. Rachel took a short lease on a two-story stone mansion, which was soon to be enlarged and transformed into a palatial one-hundred-room hotel.

Upon leaving London, she gave a farewell gift of a poem to her readers, published just before Christmas 1902. It was inspired by her most valuable painting, Millais's *The Carpenter's Shop*: "The child speaks sorrowing: 'When again / My limbs shall pierced be in pain, / Without my mother, lamb and friend.'"

A YEAR HAD passed since Frederick's death. A study of London widows showed that a year after bereavement there was not one who had as yet recovered from her loss. Queen Victoria was still in a severe depression ten years after her husband's death, and her physician, Sir William Jenner, held that "these nerves are a form of madness, and against them it is hopeless to contend." But insanity as a result of bereavement was, and is, very rare, and however shattered the queen was, she was not mad, just highly strung—the victim of excessive grief.

Relocating to the serene countryside, far from the London mansion that was filled with grim memories of illness and death, did not alleviate Rachel's distress. Nor did the break from her hectic career and busy social life. On the contrary—she was out of her element and she felt exposed, unable to hide the symptoms of her lingering numbness. Theresa Sassoon saw it all, and was worried for her friend.

At first Rachel's behaviour was seen as no more than odd manifestations of grief, "but time showed that it had been the beginning of a mental decline," reconstructed Siegfried Sassoon. "Gradually, her natural shrewdness gave place to inattention, to irresponsibility, in managing her affairs." In her anxiety, Theresa overlooked family animosity and approached Rachel's brother Joseph. He consulted their mother and set about taking action. Their solution was extreme.

According to the Lunacy Act, a next of kin, heir or friend who suspected that his dear one might be insane had to approach two physicians to examine the person in question. Joseph Sassoon spared no expense and paid for the services of John Ebenezer Ranking, a prominent physician from Tunbridge Wells, and two former superintendents of the notorious Bethlem Hospital. George Henry Savage and his successor Robert Percy Smith were mental health experts who had prosperous private practices in London catering to the rich, and their signatures appeared on many certificates of lunacy.

In examining a patient, Dr. Savage set out to determine the soundness of mind of an individual who was no longer able to fulfill his or her duties. Yet he failed to offer a clear definition of either "insanity" or "duty." One is forcibly reminded of Rachel's conclusion following the hospitalisation of Edith Lanchester, the young lady who decided to live with her lover without marrying him; as Rachel had written seven years earlier, society must not allow respectable mad doctors "to imprison those from whom they differ in opinion."

Dr. Savage, who was seen as an authority on medical-psychological issues, linked eccentricity with madness: "Breaches of the conventional as well as the moral laws of society may be but symptoms of disorder or disease of the higher nervous system," he asserted in 1896. In his *Insanity and Allied Neurosis,* published earlier in 1884, he had argued that bereavement and abandonment to grief could lead to madness, and concluded that "widows are much more liable to break down than widowers." Dr. Savage had frequently witnessed the interplay between grief and "madness" in the wards of Bethlem. Women who had nursed a dear one for months, watching them slowly decline, would often sink into extreme weakness after the funeral.

In her letters, Virginia Woolf described Dr. Savage as tyrannical, shortsighted and "pigheaded," and she would use him as the model for Sir William Bradshaw in her novel *Mrs. Dalloway.* He was respected by his colleagues and feared by his subordinates, and the families of his patients were grateful to him for "straightening up" their relatives. In his thirty years of practice, the renowned psychiatrist secluded lunatics and penalized despair, making it "impossible for the unfit to propagate their views" until they shared his, if they were men, or his wife's, if they were women. She was a "proper lady" who spent her days embroidering and knitting.

In 1904, a year after he examined Rachel, Dr. Savage was summoned to see Virginia Woolf; she had suffered a nervous breakdown after losing her father, whom she'd been nursing for six months. Woolf began to hear voices "telling me to do all kinds of wild things." It was her second collapse—the first had followed the death of her mother in 1895. Dr. Savage, a longtime friend of the family, decided on a strict rest-cure treatment, which was often prescribed for educated, well-off women. It called for complete seclusion and no entertainment or stimulation whatsoever—no books, pictures, music, writing or sewing.

The principles of the rest cure were established by the American Silas Weir Mitchell, the leading neurologist of the time. He believed any brain work of more than two hours a day was harmful for women, causing nervous disorders that needed to be treated by an absolute rest of the intellect. The patient was sequestered away from her home, family and friends, and had to remain in bed, in a darkened room, for up to two months. The only action allowed was cleaning the teeth; even sitting was forbidden. The treatment included overfeeding, massage and electrical stimulation of the muscles. There was much similarity between the Victorian mourning ritual and the rest-cure treatment: both dictated isolation, reduced existence and a halting of all public activities. The method was adopted on both sides of the Atlantic by psychiatrists for the upper class and was endorsed by Sigmund Freud.

But the voices in Woolf's head did not quiet; birds still sang in Greek, and King Edward lurked in the azaleas, using the foulest possible language. For the first time in her life, Woolf tried to kill herself. Yet, her family did not ask for her to be certified as insane, dangerous to herself and unable to govern her own affairs. Nor did Dr. Savage declare her a person of unsound mind.

In comparison to Virginia Woolf and her auditory hallucinations, Rachel's "symptoms" seem relatively mild; however, other circumstances conspired against her. She was a nontraditional career woman doing a man's job, and she spent most of her time reading and writing. She was a childless wealthy widow, ostracised by a family who would not protect her, but on the contrary, considered her rebellious and eccentric.

Her contemporaries were repelled and fascinated by madness, and books on the subject were instant bestsellers. Insanity was also on the rise. In 1859 there was one diagnosed lunatic for every 536 sane Britons, while in 1901 this had increased to 1 in every 298—a 44 percent increase.

Rachel had covered the topic herself in happier times, informing her readers in September 1897 that the overthrow of the mind due to unrequited love or jealousy and "the high-pressure rate at which we live, worry, and overwork, the race for wealth, and the haste to be rich [accounts] for a comparatively small proportion of the madness of the nation." Fearlessly, Rachel was willing at that time to rationally discuss the proposal of a "lethal chamber for the unfit." She wrote that "in cases in which the patient saw no glimmer of hope, and there was nothing to look forward to but the peace and quiet of the grave, they should be allowed to die." But as alarming as the insanity figures were, Rachel thought that "they do not seem bad enough yet to warrant such drastic treatment."

Some family members tried to take advantage of the system and the times. Louisa Lowe was a mother of six and the wife of a vicar when she became a believer in spiritualism and chose to leave her husband and the church. He sent two doctors, friends of the family, to examine her under some pretext or other, and they both signed certificates of insanity. Mrs. Lowe was incarcerated in an asylum, while her husband took legal action to get hold of her money and inherited property. She finally rescued herself after a year of struggle, and, having witnessed the shortcomings of the lunacy laws, she campaigned for the need for reform. In her book, *The Bastilles of England*, published in 1883, she argued:

> The possibilities of abuse lying hid herein are infinite. Supposing that any unscrupulous person wishes to prevent a relative to whom he is heir-expectant from marrying, or from spending his money, or from altering his will, or performing any other legal act contrary to his interest, all he has to do is to find two out of the twenty thousand registered practitioners who will give certificates of insanity whereby he becomes entitled to imprison him, in his own house, or in a house hired by himself, anywhere, for the term of his natural life.

Eventually, all three doctors who examined Rachel concluded that she was of unsound mind. Dr. Savage's policy was to notify the person of his diagnosis, "much in the same way as smallpox or measles were notified." He maintained that there were many of unsound mind who should not be regarded as insane; his belief was that a person with unlimited wealth need scarcely ever be sent to an asylum. He prescribed home cure in cases in which there was hope for a speedy recovery, and advised that patients should live on the ground floor and must not be visited too frequently by near relations.

With the three depositions in their hands, the Sassoons could have had Rachel hospitalised. They had always regarded her as extravagant and temperamental, and now, with the loss of her husband, they feared that she could easily fall prey to fortune hunters, crooks or swindlers, or that she might squander her estate on charities. The family was aware that Rachel had kept Frederick's will to herself and had declined to submit it to court to be proved, registered and granted to her. There was a rising concern for the safety of her immense inheritance. Since they had severed all ties with her, it was supposed that she might have written them out of her will. Being childless, her natural beneficiaries if she had not yet written a will would be her mother Flora, her brother Joseph, his seven children, and Theresa's three sons. Siegfried and his brothers were the most in need, since Flora was well provided for by her late husband and Joseph had inherited the Ashley Park estate. No one knew whether any Beer relatives might suddenly appear out of the woodwork from Germany.

Although he had not seen his sister for the past fifteen years, Joseph signed a petition with Francis Hawksley, the family solicitor. He stated that since January 1903 his sister had been a person of unsound mind. The three physicians' reports in hand, Hawksley asked the court that "the Master in Lunacy might be directed to inquire concerning the alleged lunacy of the said Rachel Beer." The petition carried no examples or supportive information. Theresa, who knew Rachel better than any other member of the family, did not supply an affidavit. Did she object to the family's action to declare Rachel insane? Or did the Sassoons wish to keep the matter among themselves, without involving Alfred's Gentile wife?

Understandably, families were often reluctant to have one of their members certified, because of the shame and stigma that might rub off on the whole family. This was especially the case if there were marriageable children on the scene. Although none of his offspring had yet married, Joseph chose to proceed with his petition nonetheless. The fact that Rachel had been cut out of their lives after her marriage made it less of a disgrace.

A glimpse into the Sassoons' perception of Rachel's condition can be found in the manuscript of Siegfried Sassoon's second autobiography, *The Weald of Youth*. He sent the paragraphs about his aunt to his friend Dr. John Shaw Dunn for vetting. They had met during their military service, and Dunn, who was a pathologist, advised Siegfried to omit or alter any unpleasant allegations regarding his aunt having a mental disorder, including the phrase "decline into mental derangement."

The draft manuscript and other notes of Siegfried's are the only known description of Rachel's mental state at the time. "She had been incurably afflicted by an illness which tragically affected her brain," he wrote in his *Notes for Early Recollections* and in his draft for *The Weald of Youth*. The only evidence that he offered to support his claim was a visit of his aunt's to see his mother. At first Rachel appeared to be "more or less herself in a listless way." But when they were alone in the garden, she suddenly clutched Siegfried's arm and, "raving wildly in her rich voiced rapid undertones," broke out into "some confused and vehement dementia . . . I must take her to London—take her to London so that she could find some papers and burn them, she said, reiterated with vehemence." He felt helpless as he stared "from the daylight of sanity into the calamitous Hades of her delusions, knowing that I could never call her back to be as once she had been, so oddly affectionate and charming."

Dr. Dunn advised Siegfried to cross out the words "vehement dementia" as well as "raving wildly," suggesting "speaking excitedly" instead. Siegfried's implications that Rachel had always been a "degree removed from reality"—the example that he gave was the racehorse she kept for her invalid husband—were also crossed out by Dr. Dunn. After receiving Dunn's advice, and spending more time reflecting upon the matter, Siegfried decided to omit his reminiscences of his aunt Rachel from the book altogether.

JOSEPH SASSOON'S PETITION and affidavit, and the medical opinions of the three physicians hired by the family, were presented to the Royal Court of Justice. On May 19, 1903, it instructed barrister Thomas H. Fischer, the Master in Lunacy, to hold an inquiry.

Though Rachel had the right to file a response against this inquiry, which could end with the certification of her "insanity," she did not do so. She was too weary and downtrodden to act. Her own testimony would not be enough, and finding an expert who would dare to challenge the illustrious and authoritative Dr. Savage was almost impossible; she felt powerless. There was no one to support her through her breakdown, and she felt unable to face life's challenges alone.

Since Rachel did not present any arguments against her evaluation, the court did not hold an inquisition in front of a jury. The Master in Lunacy took the trouble to see Mrs. Beer at her home in Earl's Court, Tunbridge Wells. A week later, based on his conversation with her and the documents provided by the Sassoon doctors, he declared that "the said Rachel Beer is a person of unsound mind, and that she is not sufficient for the government of herself, her manors, messuages, lands, goods and chattels."

One would need to outstretch both one's arms fully in order to unroll the enormous official document, which was written in calligraphy on parchment and sealed with red wax. Rachel's certificate of insanity is just one in a huge box of them, all issued in the same year. They are standard in form; only the name, date and address of the examinee differ on each. No details are provided to explain why these momentous decisions were made.

Once Rachel had been officially declared insane, she was stripped of the right to manage her own property, and her brother Joseph was nominated as her administrator. Since Rachel refused to submit her husband's will to court, it was neither proven nor validated, so the inheritance was not passed on to her. For a time, no one could find it, and when it mysteriously resurfaced she had already been certified. On August 10, 1903, Sir Francis Henry Jeune, the president of the Royal Court of Justice on the Strand, heard the motion for "a grant of administration with the will of Mr. Frederick Arthur Beer, whose wife was found to be a person of unsound mind."

"Can this be so?" exclaimed the judge. "I thought she had been editing *The Observer.*"

"She was closely connected through her husband with *The Observer,*" said Mr. Priestley, K.C. "But not now. It is a very sad case. It is probably caused through the loss of her husband."

At the end of the short session, Joseph Sassoon was appointed the sole executor not only of his sister's property, but of Frederick Beer's as well, for the use and benefit of his sister until she became of sound mind.

"Tragedy of a Fortune" read the heading in *The Daily Express* on the following day. In the *Sunday Times,* the court decree was marked coolly, quietly and obliquely. The notice to the contributors no longer said that the editor does not in any case "hold *herself* responsible for the return of rejected contributions"—the one word that had embodied her leadership was omitted. Both newspapers were now part of the estate that Joseph controlled, and he wanted to get rid of them as quickly as possible.

The Master in Lunacy's verdict was not used to force Rachel into incarceration in an asylum or treatment in a private home; instead, her brother Joseph hired the services of three mental health nurses to live with her. The senior among the three, Miss Ethel Marguerite Ross, was in charge of the house affairs, and she also acted as Mrs. Beer's personal assistant. Given Rachel's status, she needed a person to fulfill this role, regardless of the declaration of her failed mental health. Experts from the Lunacy Commission were supposed to re-evaluate Rachel regularly, to give her the chance to change the decree, but this was not done.

The appointment of her brother as the administrator of her financial affairs did not bring Rachel back into the family fold, and she remained banished, as before. But it must be said of the Sassoons that they did not spare her any material comforts. For some years, a luxurious mansion on Mount Ephraim in Tunbridge Wells had stood vacant, and in late December 1903, Joseph took over the lease for the house and the five and a half acres surrounding it. Called Chancellor House, it was originally a twelfth-century manor home, and a fine old cedar tree near the entrance was said to have been brought from the forests of Lebanon by a Knight of the Crusades. It was rebuilt in the mid-seventeenth century by the notorious Judge Jeffreys, whose harsh meting out of justice earned him the nickname "the Hanging Judge." A hundred years later, Sir Richard Heron, Secretary for Ireland, expanded the house, and adorned some of the rooms with unique carved marble masterpieces. Queen Marie Amelie of France, who fled to England with her husband, King Louis Philippe, following the 1848 revolution, spent her years of widowhood in Chancellor House, where she hosted the Prince of Wales.

The vast building easily swallowed the contents of 7 Chesterfield Gardens, and the furniture and paintings were spread among the lounge, hall, four reception rooms and fourteen bedrooms. There were stables and garages, two guest cottages, old turf lawns for croquet and tennis, beautiful gardens and magnificent trees and shrubs. It was needlessly large for a reclusive widow, but with a staff of nine it kept Rachel in comfort and splendour, allowing her to enjoy her accustomed standard of living. The annual allowance of two thousand pounds from her husband's estate left her well provided for.

The younger Sassoons were less enthusiastic about the accommodation provided for their dear aunt, however. Certain that they were her favourite nephews, Siegfried and his two brothers had expected to inherit a considerable portion of her substantial fortune. The promised wealth shaped Siegfried's plans; he was reluctant to engage in "some unpoetical profession." His brother Hamo was more cynical—their aunt had probably already endowed all of her wealth to some "dotty institution"; in any case, "people with softening of the brain always go on forever." Hamo predicted their aunt would live to be a hundred, "and receive a telegraphic congratulation from her Sovereign."

ONE BY ONE, Joseph Sassoon resigned his sister from all the organisations to which she belonged. He did not transfer Frederick's cellar of choice wines to Rachel's new home, but sold it by auction instead, including the valuable vintage 1858 clarets. The sale yielded over three hundred pounds, which went toward the five-hundred-pound annual rent of Chancellor House.

As for Rachel's business ventures, the *Sunday Times* and *The Observer* had been captainless ships since January 1902, doing without both their proprietor and editor. The Sassoons were not interested in journalism, and the job of selling the papers was entrusted to Mr.

Hawksley, the family solicitor and one of London's foremost legal minds. *The Observer* was presented as having "a large circulation amongst the Titled and Wealthy Classes," and was offered to Ralph David Blumenfeld for five thousand pounds, lock, stock and barrel. "There was, of course, not much lock, very little stock and you could not see the barrel," Blumenfeld wrote in his memoirs. He was an American journalist, living in London, and the acting editor of *The Daily Express. The Observer* was a trifle heavy for his taste; so, knowing that the Beers' two newspapers were in deep financial distress, he offered five thousand pounds if the Sassoons "threw in the *Sunday Times* as well." Hawksley asked for time to consult with his clients and called Joseph. Quick as lightning, Hawksley came back with a positive answer, but even then Blumenfeld was ultimately not tempted enough to make the deal.

It was the *Sunday Times* that was sold first, in March 1905, for a mere £2,500, to the New Aurora Syndicate Limited, headed by Hermann Schmidt. The German-born financier had earned the nickname "Silver Schmidt" after moving to London, and he had a keen interest in investing in newspapers, using them to promote his various worldwide ventures: six years earlier he was suspected of accepting bribes in exchange for planting favourable notices in *The Observer* and the *Sunday Times*. In 1897 he launched the successful *Sunday Special*. Like previous proprietors of the *Sunday Times,* he valued the paper's esteemed history and decided to merge the highbrow acquisition with his own, much-younger publication. Schmidt gave priority to the older name, and the new publication was called *The Sunday Times and Sunday Special*. The offices in Fleet Street were moved to the *Sunday Special* headquarters at 186 Strand.

Schmidt took an active part in editing—the financial articles that he contributed to were "execrably written by his own hand," and had to be deciphered and decoded into English by his editor, Leonard Rees. Ten years later, Schmidt sold the paper to the Berry Brothers, owners of the popular *Boxing* magazine, for almost £100,000, "which, in view of subsequent developments, turned out to be a ridiculously low price." Only in 1931 did the paper become the *Sunday Times* again.

Alfred Harmsworth owned the *Daily Mail, The Daily News* and the *Weekly Dispatch,* which sold hundreds of thousands of copies a day. Though these were healthy figures, it was said that no intelligent man cared to read his newspapers, which were not taken seriously by the ruling classes, and this frustrated the press baron, since his main ambition was to become "an authority in the life of the nation." Harmsworth, who had ten years previously failed to be elected as a Conservative MP, hoped that owning a prestigious paper might help him politically. He was anxious to acquire a survivor of the old journalism, but, unable to realise his dream of owning *The Times,* he settled for *The Observer.* In May 1905, he paid the Sassoons £4,000 for a paper that, in his words, "lay derelict in the Fleet ditch." It had experienced an annual loss of £12,000 to £15,000, and its circulation was a mere 2,000 copies in winter and 4,000 in summer—the common fate of a quality press at the time.

To celebrate his acquisition, Harmsworth published a Centenary Commemoration issue, which sold out, with thousands of potential buyers left wanting. Reassured that he had made the right purchase, he offered the following week a facsimile reproduction of *The Observer* published for Nelson's state funeral—hoping to cash in on the public's sense of nostalgia. But he soon discovered that the losing newspaper would require heavy investment, and it was not until 1908 that he found the editor he was looking for in J. L. Garvin. A history of double ownership almost repeated itself when Harmsworth, now Lord Northcliffe, was offered the ownership of the *Sunday Times,* which he considered his main rival. Though it now showed a profit of £11,000 a year, he declined. Ten years after the Beers' era, *The Observer*'s circulation soared to 200,000, while the circulation for the *Sunday Times* peaked at around 30,000.

After the Storm

With time, Rachel began to improve and take some part in the life of Tunbridge Wells, albeit in a very sedate way. In the summer, everybody came out to see and be seen during cricket week, which took place not far from her home. In the autumn, they all drove for fox hunting to Eridge Park, the home of the Marquess of Abergavenny. Accompanied by Miss Ross, Rachel would come to meet the hounds in her smart, four-wheeled dogcart, with its pair of high-stepping horses. As Siegfried trotted past her she appeared uninterested—"her large dark eyes would stare at me, apathetic and unrecognising, from under a hat of the latest mode. Someone was sitting there, but it was only a brooding sallow stranger, cut off from the rest of the world." For some reason or another, this was a further passage he struck from the final version of *The Weald of Youth*.

To the three pianos that she had brought with her from the house in London, Rachel now added a new two-manned chamber organ, which had been especially built by Walker and Sons to suit the acoustics of her lounge. She herself played the grand instrument, and she would also invite the organist of St. Mark's Church, William Wooding Starmer, to entertain small groups of guests for the sake of charity. With her concern for the future of women still intact, she joined other ladies of the town in giving financial support to the Leisure Hours

Club, which offered young working-class girls a safe haven from pubs, alcohol and men.

Rachel's nephew, meanwhile, travelled occasionally to Brighton and there rediscovered his grandmother Flora, who now seemed to him good-hearted and generous. The passing years had mollified her sense of disgrace over her son's marriage; she was always glad to see her grandson, and Siegfried forgave her for their one-time estrangement. Flora Sassoon had not amended her will to include Siegfried and his brothers, but she was generous in her presents; once, as they drove along the front at Hove, she stopped and bought him a gold cigar case. Siegfried visited other members of the Sassoon family and would sometimes even spend weekends with them, but he never called on his aunt Rachel, even though he lived just a few miles away from her. His mother, Theresa, still visited her old friend.

THOUGH FAR FROM the front, Tunbridge Wells was made well aware of the ravages of World War I, and Rachel did all she could to help. In the autumn of 1915, a German zeppelin wandered off its route to London and dropped three bombs on the town, but thankfully there were no casualties. Its proximity to the southeastern coast made Tunbridge Wells a military centre, and in the course of the war many wounded soldiers were brought to be treated there, at the Rust Hall VAD hospital.

Rachel became a major benefactor of the hospital, and when it became too small to accommodate the huge numbers of wounded, she paid for the rent of additional grounds, as well as for two hostels for the nurses. A new ward, which she financed and equipped, was to be named after her. Rachel's assistant Miss Ross arranged concerts, entertainments and a fancy dress competition in the town's Opera House and its Parish Hall for the wounded soldiers. "An ample supply of cigarettes also added to the soldiers' enjoyment," commented the *Courier* of Tunbridge Wells. Mrs. Beer paid for it all, but whenever a speech and a handshake were called for it was left to Miss Ross to do the honours.

All of Rachel's nephews ended up in uniform. In October 1915, Hamo Sassoon, Siegfried's younger brother, was killed at Gallipoli. Siegfried himself suffered from shell shock, and two of his cousins were wounded. In the course of their service, Siegfried and his cousin Teddie managed to fulfill the Sassoon patriarch's desire and visited the Holy Land, while another cousin, Arthur, journeyed from Bombay to Basra and Baghdad, tracing backwards the patriarch's journey almost a century before.

Unable to maintain Ashley Park, Joseph and his wife rented it out and moved to a much smaller house in the vicinity. Joseph, who had suffered from asthma for many years, died in January 1918, and Rachel's affairs were thereafter administrated by the Sassoons' lawyer. A year later, Flora Sassoon passed away at her home in Brighton at the age of eighty-two. She did not leave her daughter even one memento. Mother and son were both buried in the family plot in London.

IN ORDER TO secure Rachel's cash flow, the administrator of her estate decided to realise a part of her property and sell her precious Millais, the painting that Frederick had inherited from his father. *The Carpenter's Shop* had been offered at auction once, in 1886, but it had failed to reach the reserve of £1,000, and so had remained with him. Frederick and Rachel had willingly lent the painting to various galleries, and in 1921, after it had been on loan to the Tate for nine years, an offer of £10,000 came in from the National Gallery of Victoria in Melbourne. The estate administrator was willing to leave the painting with the Tate for the slightly steeper price of £10,500; the Pre-Raphaelite section of the Tate lacked substantial works, and the Millais would fill the void.

Being Orthodox Jews, the Sassoons would never have bought a painting depicting Jesus; but Siegfried considered the painting an integral part of his family's history and the nation's heritage, and he publicly challenged his cousins to keep it in England. In an open letter in the *Nation and Athenaeum,* he showed no reservations in stating that the owner of the painting, his paternal aunt, was declared a lunatic and had no say in the matter. In a theatrical gesture, he placed a goldfish in the fountain of the entrance hall of the Tate Gallery— a public reminder that "may induce some Sassoon, more affluent than myself, to come forward with the money needed." The Sassoons were unmoved; however, the Tate managed to obtain the Millais for its permanent collection, regardless, through its own funds and the help of donors. The money from the sale paid for the full purchase of Chancellor House in 1923, after twenty years of renting. While Rachel maintained her comfortable lifestyle, the rest of her relatives were not faring quite as well. Joseph's sons were forced to sell Ashley Park to a property developer, below the asking price.

The attitude of Rachel's nephews toward her is both regrettable and puzzling, particularly in the case of Siegfried. During lunch with her son on May 15, 1924, Theresa divulged her dramatic news: "Poor Rachel hasn't long to live." Siegfried was hopeful that they would be inundated with his aunt's money within a year or two: "We have been waiting for it about twenty years!" he wrote in his diary. He was even blunter with his friend and fellow poet Robert Graves, with whom he shared the news in rhyme:

> When Auntie Rachel hops the twig
> My friends no more will call me Sig
> But pass me with a blank look.
> My income then will be immense;
> And I'll publish (at my own expense)
> Not poems—but my Bank Book.

But Siegfried's desire to dance on his aunt's grave was premature. Whatever the reports on Rachel's declining health, Chancellor House remained lively and grand. And it was keeping up with the times— a car had been bought and was driven by the indispensable Miss Ross. Not only that, but Rachel had a four-valve wireless set in her bedroom, with two loudspeakers. Ever a technophile, she must have been thrilled with these purchases.

Every summer the grounds of Chancellor House hosted the actor-director and impresario Ben Greet and his players, who arrived from London and performed Shakespearean plays, using the trees and bushes as part of the set. An orchestra and dancers entertained the audience of eight hundred, and the strains of the house's magnificent organ flowed through the open windows, producing a charming effect on the lawns below. Profits from the ticket sales were donated to the local General Hospital. When the matinee was over, guests were invited to stay for tea and refreshments, but Mrs. Beer no longer participated in these meet and greets.

ON APRIL 29, 1927, Siegfried Sassoon published a poem in the *New Leader*: "I accuse the Rich of what they've always done before / of lifting worldly faces to a diamond star." On that same day, Rachel Beer passed away in her home. For a year, she had suffered from stomach cancer, and in her last days she developed acute bronchitis, which—in turn—led to heart failure. No other ailments, physical or mental, were stated in her death certificate. She was sixty-nine years old.

Declared a person of unsound mind, Rachel was not permitted to write a will. Had she been able to, there is little doubt that she would have asked to be laid to rest beside her husband in the Beer family mausoleum in Highgate. Her nephews were well aware of her love for Frederick and her protracted period of mourning for him, but they did not take the trouble to honour what would surely have been her wish.

In the 1911 census, Miss Ross, who filled out the form for the entire household, wrote down "Jewess" for Mrs. Beer's nationality, but Rachel was a baptised Anglican and in her years at Chancellor House had infrequently attended the church of St. Paul's for spiritual support. And yet she was buried in unconsecrated ground at the Tunbridge Wells Borough Cemetery. Out of the eight relatives who inherited from Rachel's estate—Joseph's six children and Theresa's two surviving sons—only five made an appearance at the funeral. Siegfried used the pretext of a slightly painful rib injury resulting from a car accident to excuse his absence. However, Ben Greet and several of his players came all the way from London to pay their respects. The ceremony was conducted by the vicar of her parish church, and the grave was covered with a profusion of flowers, including a wreath of Rachel's favourite forget-me-nots and rosemary from her own garden.

The *Sunday Times* of May 1, 1927, was thirty-two pages long, but it included not one word on the passing of the woman who had for ten years been its proprietor and editor. Only two weeks later, in the weekly column of T. P. O'Connor, "Men, Women and Memories," was there a brief, somewhat patronising account of their meeting twenty-five years earlier, when he had attempted to buy their newspaper. Intending to compliment the present owner of the *Sunday Times*—his current employer—O'Connor belittled Mrs. Beer's journalistic achievement ("she made something of a hash of it"). His memory failed him on several facts, but he remembered her looks vividly—"she was a not unattractive figure; with very finely proportioned though slight limbs and lambent lights in the sombre shy dark eyes." *The Observer* mentioned her death laconically, minimizing her role in the newspaper by describing her as a "one-time proprietrix" who took a very active interest in public affairs and was "one of the most energetic friends in England of the movement for the vindication of Captain Dreyfus."

The gross value of Rachel Beer's estate was £318,283 at her death. In July 1927, her massive collection of paintings was carefully packed and transported to London, to be auctioned by Christie's. The highest price—£1,995—was paid for a Corot, and the total amounted to over £23,000. Her jewels fetched £4,000, and Chancellor House with its contents, close to £10,000. It was all divided between Rachel's Sassoon inheritors. It enabled Siegfried to buy Heytesbury, his dream manor house in Wiltshire, set in 220 acres of parks and forests.

The young Sassoons were not aware that the bulk of their aunt's jewelry had been missing for many years. What was found in her bedroom was just a fraction of her casket of jewels; the majority was in a bank vault in London, where it had been stored since Rachel's Mayfair days. Quite by chance, in 1949, the precious collection of diamonds and emeralds surfaced, including a magnificent tiara, a half-hooped bracelet, the Collet necklace of ninety-eight diamonds, as well as a great number of brooches, bangles and necklaces. This surprise second windfall delighted them.

All of the money the Sassoons inherited from their aunt had been made by Julius Beer in transportation and communications. When he died in 1880, Frederick had also inherited a bulk of shares of the Great Western Railway. He had never sold them, and after his death they were held by Joseph Sassoon, the executor of Rachel's estate. But now Rachel's nephews cashed in the stocks. "By Christmas, I shall be the proud possessor of £43,000 in 4.5% Railway Stock. And this, [the solicitor] says, is only ²/₃ of the full amount which I shall receive from the Beer estate," Siegfried wrote to a friend in October 1927. Julius Beer's ingenuity and diligence in the 1860s and 1870s was enough to sustain the Sassoons comfortably and free from money worries until a hundred years later.

Rachel's marriage had lasted fifteen years, and for the remaining twenty-five years of her life she had lamented the loss of her husband; but still, Frederick's name was absent from her tombstone. At her death, her nephews brought her back to her family origins, identifying her only as "Daughter of the late David Sassoon."

So much of her life had been reduced, so much had been displaced.

Afterword

More than one hundred years after the end of their era, we have dropped the Victorians' code of mourning, yet their obsession with death is still intriguing. Just like them, we visit the places where they laid their dead to rest, strolling through on our weekends and holidays. Their cemeteries, a capsule of frozen time, have once again become tourist attractions.

But wandering around can be precarious for the visitor and damaging to the graves, so all tours to Highgate West Cemetery are guided, on fixed hours. Unlike the Victorians, we pay an entrance fee. They wore their best Sunday clothes and hats for a visit to Highgate, but nowadays safari outfits and pith helmets might be more appropriate, given the overgrown vegetation and slippery lanes.

Broken pillars, shrouded urns, burnt-out torches, weeping angels, praying marble children and sunken mothers, sleeping lions, faithful dogs, and a pelican tearing its flesh to feed its young; the enigmatic images and inscriptions befit the spooky atmosphere of a cemetery long ago abandoned and only recently restored.

Then as now, the gem of the place is the mausoleum of Julius Beer, towering above all others. It carries no epitaph and no dates, no symbol that reveals his identity.

. . .

THE LEGALISATION OF cremation in 1888 and the end of the Victorian era with the death of Queen Victoria in 1901 brought with it a sharp decline in elaborate burials. The private cemeteries lost much of their appeal. The result was a drop in income for the owners, which made it impossible for them to keep their cemeteries open. After the deaths of Frederick and Rachel Beer, no surviving family member stepped forward to pay for the maintenance of the Beer mausoleum.

In its heyday, Highgate Cemetery employed twenty-eight gardeners: in 1950 the very last one was dismissed. The place was falling to pieces, and the graves were vandalised and robbed. From a fashionable, serene park, it became a Gothic mess. Perhaps not home to vampires, but certainly home to badgers, squirrels and foxes, its disheveled shrubs and fallen trees were turning it into a jungle.

Fallen into decay by neglect, the Beer mausoleum carried the signs of all the passing years, symbolic of the family's slide into oblivion. When the novelist Olivia Manning saw the mausoleum in the 1950s, she was told that Julius Beer had been "the diamond king." He had been mistaken for the South African De Beers. She found the building ugly; hosts of pigeons had made its pyramid roof their home. Several of the windows were broken, pigeons flew in and out of the vents, "and the tomb was murmurous with their calling. At least, I thought, someone had found a use for the funerary pomps of the past."

In the 1960s, the cemetery was a favourite spring outing for journalist and writer Alan Brien. He was appalled by the smell of corruption, and he crowned the mausoleum as the largest pigeon house in Europe. Peering in through the iron gate, he saw that the floor was knee-deep in bird droppings, "a lifetime's accumulation of guano, with half-sunken on the rotting surface the decaying corpses of dead birds killed in some incestuous war. . . . Julius Beer, whoever he was, has raised for himself a bird Belsen, a privy for pigeons, all his money has turned to a tower of excreta." The American novelist John Updike, who joined Brien on his visit, recalled that "the mosaic murals of pre-Raphaelite angels were clouded with lime."

"You ass, Julius, you absolutely silly puffed-up old capitalist ass, you were so full of yourself, we don't even know what you did!" hollered Brien, as if his words could burst open the iron gate.

The decaying pomposity of the Beer mausoleum became a representation of man's futile, infantile desire for immortality, and it inspired several poets. The Scottish poet laureate Edwin Morgan wrote in 1973 that "In the diamondman's invisible bones / nothing takes root but death." And Alan Jenkins, in his poem "Pornography," blamed Julius Beer for loathing the world so much as to deliberately build his monument to shut off the view of London. Beer's wife and womenfolk, wrote Jenkins, now consume him "in the public places of hell, / Brandish on a fork / his head, and a Bill / of Rights for cannibals."

Nowadays the guides tell of a penniless young immigrant from Frankfurt who hit it big in the London Stock Exchange and became a newspaper baron. The money, earned and not inherited, did not buy Julius Beer social recognition. In 1878, they say, he exacted his revenge by building the tallest monument on the highest spot of the necropolis. His goal was to block the view of London from the weekend strollers, to be a thorn in the flesh of those who snubbed him, and to erect a permanent reminder of his existence to future generations. The fertile, eerie soil of the cemetery breeds other myths: not only was Julius Beer a man of pride and vengeance, goes one, but he also murdered his family, who were all buried inside with him.

WHEN THE "Victorian Valhalla," as poet John Betjeman called it, became impossible to maintain, its owners, Raybourne Ltd., closed it to the public in 1975. However, the Victorians were back in fashion at that time, after decades of scorn, and the cemetery was purchased by a group of volunteers, who bought it for a token from Camden Council. The Friends of Highgate Cemetery started a clearing operation on Saturday afternoons.

The iron gates of the Beer mausoleum could not be opened—they were entirely blocked by mountains of pigeon waste. A window on the roof was removed, and the first cleaners were lowered down, wearing breathing masks. They shovelled out the pigeon droppings and tried to scrub the graffiti from the marble walls. The lower ground of the mausoleum had been used as a storeroom for wheelbarrows and tools. These supplies were lying next to the coffins of the Beer family, which were found broken open and empty.

While Julius Beer crowns the west side of Highgate Cemetery, Karl Marx heads the east side. These two German-born Jews, who found receptive ground in England for their opposing aspirations, still remained aliens in their adopted country. They were both buried in March, Beer in 1880, Marx in 1883. While Beer erected a marble mausoleum for his family, Marx was put to rest inside his wife's narrow and humble grave, to be joined by his four-year-old grandson, his daughter and his mistress. His comrades found the grave difficult to locate, and in 1956, after the remains were dug out and removed to a more open spot one hundred yards away, a grandiose bronze bust was placed on a gray granite plinth by the British Communist Party.

Of the many notables resting in Highgate, English Heritage chose the Beer mausoleum as the first private memorial to be restored, and picked up the bill of forty-two thousand pounds. In 1993 scaffolding was erected to wash and repair the outside walls and restore the marble interiors, with their deep red and blue decorations. The layer of gold, which was almost rubbed off the magnificent mosaic dome, was revived and coated.

Only the white marble, life-size sculpture of the winged angel and the child had escaped with minor stains, which were gently brushed off with a dental steam cleaner. Perhaps Julius had got his wish. His grief for his daughter Ada had stood the tests of time and Nature, and defied the efforts of others to desecrate it.

Acknowledgments

For their warm hospitality and generosity in sharing with us their family history as well as photo albums, our deepest thanks go to the Sassoon family: great-nephews of Rachel Beer, Mr. Joseph Sassoon, Scotland, and his brother Mr. Jacques Sassoon, London, and Mr. Hugh Sassoon, London; Mrs. Jean Sassoon, widow of Hamo Sassoon, Rachel Beer's great-nephew; Lord James Sassoon and his wife Sarah, London; Tania Gardner (Sassoon), Scotland.

Dr. Yaron Ben-Naeh of the Hebrew University, Jerusalem, kindly shared with us his knowledge and information about the history of the Sassoon family.

The diligent work of the following archivists made it possible to trace the roots of the Beer family: Dr. Michael Lenarz, Juedisches Museum, Frankfurt am Main; Dr. Michael Matthäus, Institut für Stadtgeschichte Frankfurt; Dr. Norbert Heyeckhaus, Jewish Cemetery Database Project, Germany, and Maike Strobel, Abteilung Judaica, Universitätsbibliothek Frankfurt am Main; Dr. Shlomo Meyer, Director of Leo Baeck Institute, Jerusalem, Israel, and Professor Robert Liberles, Ben Gurion University, Israel, enriched us with their immense knowledge of German Jewry.

Mr. Gavin McGuffie and Ms. Mariam Yamin from the *Guardian* and *Observer* newsroom and archive, Mr. Micholas R. Mays from the *Sunday Times* archives, and Ms. Wiebke Singer from Reuters were very helpful during different phases of our research.

Mr. Richard Quirk from the Friends of Highgate Cemetery guided us to the Beer mausoleum and provided us with intriguing details from the cemetery's archive. Mrs. Miriam Rodrigues-Pereira, honorary archivist of the Spanish-Portuguese Jewish Community in London, enlightened us regarding the cemetery where the Sassoons are buried.

For their contribution to the understanding of Julius Beer's involvement in the American Civil War and the Erlanger loan, we thank Dr. Richard I. Lester, Eaker College for Professional Development, Maxwell, Alabama; Marc D. Weidenmier, Associate Professor of Economics at Claremont McKenna College, California; John M. Coski, Historian and Director of Library and Research, the Museum of the Confederacy, Richmond, Virginia; Lia Apodaca, Manuscript Division, Library of Congress, Washington, D.C.; and Dr. Charles Hubbard, Professor of History at Lincoln Memorial University, Harrogate, Tennessee.

J. Robert Maguire from Vermont was a well of knowledge about the Dreyfus affair. Bill Burns of Long Island, New York, was an important source on the transatlantic cable.

Christopher Bearman allowed us to read his Ph.D. thesis about the English Folk Music Movement and supplied us with more information.

Max Egremont, Siegfried Sassoon's biographer, and Professor Peter Stanskey, the biographer of Philip and Sybil Sassoon, kindly answered our many queries.

In Tunbridge Wells, we found enthusiastic patriots of the town and its history, who taught us a great deal about the years that Rachel Beer lived there: Mr. Chris Jones and Mr. Geoffrey Copus of the Local History Group, Mr. Christopher E. Beach of the Tunbridge Wells Borough Cemetery, and Ms. Sue Brown of Tunbridge Wells Library.

WE SPENT NUMEROUS hours and long days at the National Archives, Kew, at the British Library at St. Pancras, and at the British Library

Newspaper Reading Room at Colindale. Plowing through mountains of material was made possible and pleasant thanks to the staff of these libraries. Special thanks go to Mr. Victor Bristoll of Colindale.

For their time and invaluable insight regarding 7 Chesterfield Gardens and Rachel Beer's art and jewelry collection, we are grateful to Mr. Martin Beisly, senior director, British and Irish Art, and Nineteenth-Century European Art; Mr. David Warren, director of jewelry; and Mr. Giles Forster, specialist in Nineteenth-Century Furniture, Sculpture and Decorative Art Department, Christie's, London. Special thanks to Ms. Lynda McLeod, the attentive librarian at Christie's archive, London.

Miss Edit Laczo was our industrious researcher at Tunbridge Wells, and Ms. Sally Roberts was our know-all expert on British genealogy. Ms. Victoria Worsley and Mr. Ian Kaye of the Henry Moore Institute Archive, Leeds Museums and Galleries, found for us valuable documents that helped us re-create the relationship between Hamo Thornycroft and Rachel Sassoon. Ms. Ruth Debel and Ms. Masha Baron translated for us from French, documents regarding the Dreyfus affair.

WE ARE IMMENSELY indebted to Jeremy and Carole Robson, Scott Mendel, Gary Brozek, Jessica Feehan and Ljiljana Baird for their ideas and contributions to the shaping up of this book. And last but not at all least, to our dedicated editor Angela Polidoro at Random House, the dream ally of any writer.

Notes

Frequently mentioned names, books and archive collections are abbreviated as follows:

Cambridge: Cambridge University Library, Department of Manuscript and University Archive
Columbia: Columbia University Libraries, Rare Book and Manuscript Library, Siegfried Sassoon Papers
SS: Siegfried Sassoon
ST: the *Sunday Times*
WW: Rachel Beer's column, "The World's Work"

Prologue

vii   of *"unsound mind"*: J 121/5374 & C 211/66, National Archives, Kew
ix   " ... *the nineteenth century is the woman's century"*: Rachel Beer, "The Woman's Century," WW, *ST*, June 25, 1899

Chapter One: Portraits and Personalities

3   *Harry Bedford-Lemere:* Twenty-one surviving images of the house are kept at the English Heritage National Monument Records Centre, Swindon
4   *The renowned C. J. Phipps:* Charlotte Gere, *Nineteenth-Century Decoration,* Weidenfeld and Nicolson, London, 1989
5   *"multiplied and diminishing reflections"*: SS, *The Old Century and Seven More Years,* Faber & Faber, London, 1938
6   *"drawn simply back, revealing the ears, into a French pleat"*: Myriam Maisel, *My Daughter Rachel, My Son Frederick* (unpublished manuscript)

6   *"It certainly shows a concern for veracity and 'likeness' "*: Email exchange with Dr. Brendan Rooney, April–December 2007

6   *racquets, golf and billiards: The Ludgate*, Vol. 5, November 1897–April 1898

7   *"instructing the people to become useful citizens"*: "Association of Women Pioneer Lecturers," *The Times*, September 21, 1893

7   *"the oriental aristocratic features and magnificent diamond tiara"*: The *Sporting Times*, May 24, 1890

7   *"pale, blue satin, trimmed with handsome embroidered gauze"*: John *Bull*, May 30, 1891

7   *Tableaux Vivants at Rachel Beer's home: The Nursing Record*, February 19, 1891; *The Nursing Record*, March 5, 1891; *John Bull*, March 7, 1891; Barry J. Faulk, *Music Hall and Modernity*, Ohio University Press, Athens, Ohio 2004

8   *"until the curtain went down after several encores"*: Lady Glover, *Memories of Four Continents*, Seeley, Service and Co., London, 1923

Chapter Two: Flight from Baghdad

9   *Jews in Baghdad:* Abraham Ben-Yaacob, *The Jews of Babylon, 1038–1960* (Hebrew), 1965; David Solomon Sassoon, *A History of the Jews in Baghdad*, S. D. Sassoon, Letchworth, 1949; Ferial J. Ghazoul, *Ard Al-Sawad—A Novel Formulation of People's History of Iraq*

9   *About the Sassoon family:* Abraham Ben-Yaacob, *Chapters in the History of Babylonian Jewry—The Sassoon Family from Baghdad* (Hebrew), 1989; Stanley Jackson, *The Sassoons*, Heinemann, London, 1968; Cecil Roth, *The Sassoon Dynasty*, Robert Hale Ltd., London, 1941; Peter Stansky, *Sassoon: The Worlds of Philip and Sybil*, Yale University Press, New Haven, 2003

10   *a descendant of King David:* David Solomon Sassoon, *A History of the Jews in Baghdad*, S. D. Sassoon, Letchworth, 1949

10   *"Give honour, ye nations, to the seed of David":* Rabbi David d'Beth Hillel, *Unknown Jews in Unknown Lands*, Ktav Publishing House, New York, 1973

10   *forced to flee the Holy Land:* Stanley Jackson, *The Sassoons*, Heinemann, London, 1968

11   *"The fine race of Jews":* Reverend Joseph Wolf, *The Jewish Expositor and Friends of Israel*, vol. X, 1825, James Duncan, London

12   *"a very rude appearance":* Rabbi David d'Beth Hillel, *Unknown Jews in Unknown Lands*, Ktav Publishing House, New York, 1973

14   *not to tarry in Basra:* David Solomon Sassoon, *A History of the Jews in Baghdad*, S. D. Sassoon, Letchworth, 1949

15   *the Sassoons hushed up: Illustrated London News*, December 5, 1863; *The Jewish Chronicle*, January 2, 1885; *The Jewish Chronicle*, October 30, 1896

16 *Only in 1942:* David Solomon Sassoon, *A History of the Jews in Bagh-dad*, S. D. Sassoon, Letchworth, 1949

17 *he was extremely cautious:* Rabbi Ya'aqob Menashe (a Sassoon descendant), *The Newsletter of Midrash Ben Ish Hai*

17 *"Whatever moves over sea":* Stanley Jackson, *The Sassoons,* Heinemann, London, 1968

Chapter Three: Opium and Further Expansion

20 *Opium trade with China:* Maisie J. Meyer, *From the Rivers of Babylon to the Whangpoo,* University Press of America, Maryland, 2003; Carl Trocki, *Opium, Empire and Global Political Economy,* Routledge, London, 1999; Hunt Janin, *The India-China Opium Trade in the Nineteenth Century,* McFarland & Company, Jefferson, NC, 1999; Siddiqi Asiya (ed.), *Trade and Finance in Colonial India,* Oxford University Press, 1995; Maggie Keswick & Clara Weatherall (eds.), *The Thistle & The Jade: A Celebration of 150 Years of Jardine, Matheson & Co.,* Frances Lincoln Ltd., 2008; Yangwen Zheng, *The Social Life of Opium in China 1483–1999,* Cambridge University Press, 2005; Gregory Blue, "Opium for China—the British Connection" in T. Brook and R. Wakabayashi (eds.), *Opium Regimes: Britain, China, Japan,* University of California Press, 2000; Madhavi Thampi (ed.), *India and China in the Colonial World,* Social Science Press, 2005

21 *he noted that his chief competitor:* Stella Dong, *Shanghai,* William Morrow and Co., New York, 2000

21 *"the injury to health and morals":* Hugh Hamilton Lindsay, *Report of Proceedings on a Voyage to China,* B. Fellowes, London, 1834

23 *carrying 1,075 chests:* The Times, August 28, 1851

23 *"A matter of race":* Hansard's Parliamentary Debates, House of Commons, Vol. 225, 1875

24 *"no different from exporting":* Rabbi Ya'aqob Menashe, *The Newsletter of Midrash Ben Ish Hai*

Chapter Four: Their Dual Identity

25 *Jews in India:* Shalva Weil (ed.), *India's Jewish Heritage,* Marg Publications, Mumbai, 2002; Abraham Ben-Yaacob, *The Jews of Babylon in the Diaspora* (Hebrew), 1985; Nissim Rejwan, *The Jews of Iraq,* Weidenfeld and Nicolson, 1985; Joan G. Roland, *Jews in British India: Identity in a Colonial Era,* Brandeis University Press, 1989; Prakash Narain Agarwala, *The History of Indian Business: A Complete Account of Trade Exchanges from 3000 B.C. to the Present Day,* Vikas, Delhi, 1985; Jacob Sapir Halevi, *Even Sapir Book* (Hebrew), Sifriyat Mekorot, Jerusalem, 1970; Shlomo Reinman, *Solomon's Travels* (Hebrew), Vienna, 1884; Asher Amschewitz, *Roses for David* (Hebrew), Warsaw,

1880; Thomas A. Timberg, "Baghdadi Jews in Indian Port Cities," in Thomas A. Timberg (ed.), *Jews in India*, Vikas, New Delhi, 1986

25 *Indian Jewry and Great Britain*: Maisie J. Meyer, "Spanning Oceans: Solid Links Between Baghdadi Jews in India and China" (presentation); Ruth Fredman Cernea, *Almost Englishmen: Baghdadi Jews in British Burma*, Lexington Books, Lanham, MD 2007; Chiara Betta, "From Orientals to Imagined Britons: Baghdadi Jews in Shanghai," *Modern Asian Studies*, 37, 4 (2003), Cambridge University Press

25 *They did not mingle with the other Jews*: Sifra Samuel Lentin, "The Jewish Presence in Bombay" in Shalva Weil (ed.), *India's Jewish Heritage*, Marg Publications, Mumbai, 2002

26 *"rich turban and flowing robes"*: Sir Richard Temple, *Men and Events of My Time in India*, John Murray, London, 1882

26 *"proselytised to Christianity"*: Rabbi David d'Beth Hillel, *Unknown Jews in Unknown Lands*, Ktav Publishing House, New York, 1973

26 *"imagined Britons"*: Chiara Betta, "From Orientals to Imagined Britons: Baghdadi Jews in Shanghai," in *Modern Asian Studies*, vol. 37, no. 4, Cambridge University Press, 2003

27 *"to inspire the pupils in the pious respect"*: Moritz Steinschneider, *Reshit Hallimud*, Berlin, 1860

28 *"some of the most noted ducal palaces in Italy"*: The Jewish Chronicle, October 30, 1896

28 *"It is strange to say"*: Sassoon Archive, Hebrew University, Jerusalem

29 *"The classes which he is to attend"*: Ibid.

29 *"to learn not only what English gentlemen know"*: Illustrated London News, December 5, 1863

29 *the bi-weekly paper* Doresh Tov Le'amo: David S. Sassoon, "A Unique Jewish Newspaper," *The Jewish Chronicle*, July 3, 1908

30 *"Two soldiers were blown"*: Ibid.

30 *"to be employed in any manner that your Lordship"*: Letter of June 20, 1857, published in *The Times*, August 3, 1857

30 *"You justly feel that any attack"*: Letter of June 25, 1857, published in *The Times*

Chapter Five: Gaining a Foothold

32 *Jews in Victorian England*: Todd M. Endelman, *The Jews of Britain 1656–2000*, University of California Press, Berkeley, Los Angeles, London, 2002; Todd M. Endelman, *Radical Assimilation in English Jewish History, 1656–1945*, Indiana University Press, Bloomington, 1990; Vivian D. Lipman, "The Anglo-Jewish Community in Victorian Society," *Studies in the Cultural Life of the Jews of England*, Dov Noy and Issachar Ben-Ami (eds.), Magnes Press, Jerusalem, 1975; Vivian D. Lipman, *A History of Jews in Britain since 1858*, Leicester University Press, Leicester, 1990; Stephen Aris, *The Jews in Business*, Jonathan Cape, London, 1970

32   *A convoy awaited:* Sassoon Archive, Hebrew University, Jerusalem
33   *"the happy free-born sons of commerce":* James Elmes, *Metropolitan Improvements,* Jones & Co., London, 1827
33   *"English Protestantism":* Todd M. Endelman, "The Englishness of Jewish Modernity in England," in Jacob Katz (ed.), *Toward Modernity,* Transaction Publishing, New Brunswick, NJ, 1987
34   *"xenophobic feelings":* Todd M. Endelman, "Communal Solidarity among the Jewish Elite of Victorian London," *Victorian Studies,* Indiana University Press, Spring 1985
34   *"an almost perverse attraction":* Vivian D. Lipman, "The Anglo-Jewish Community in Victorian Society," *Studies in the Cultural Life of the Jews of England,* Dov Noy and Issachar Ben-Ami (eds.), Magnes Press, Jerusalem, 1975
35   *From the foot of the North Cape:* Sassoon Archive, Hebrew University, Jerusalem
36   *"What the Jews were in Egypt, they are in England":* Israel Finestein, "Anglo-Jewish Opinion During the Struggle for Emancipation (1828–1858)," in *Transactions,* Vol. 20, Jewish Historical Society of England, 1964
37   *"to adhere faithfully to the holy religion of our forefathers":* Taken from the will of Sassoon David Sassoon, 1867, Principal Registry of the Family Division, London
37   *"extensive and most enjoyable pleasure grounds":* The Times, June 16, 1863
37   *Ashley Park:* James Thorne, *Handbook of the Environs of London*; Michael Dane, *The Sassoons of Ashley Park,* M. Dane, Walton on Thames, 1999; *The Jewish Chronicle,* November 27, 1863
38   *"painted white and gold":* Eliza Haweis, *Beautiful Houses,* Sampson Low and Co., London, 1882
39   *"possessed of a desire for information concerning animals and their ways":* Rachel Beer, "The Wonga Wonga Pigeon and the Intelligent Ass," WW, *ST,* June 30, 1901

Chapter Six: Candidly and Constantly

41   *The excessive fee:* Mary Ann Steggles, *Statues of the Raj,* BACSA, London, 2000
42   *coat of arms: Anglo-Jewish Notabilities: Their Arms and Testamentary Dispositions,* Jewish Historical Society of England, 1949
42   *a sculpture of his wife and himself:* Elfrida Manning, *Marble and Bronze* (unabridged draft), Henry Moore Institute Archives, Leeds Museum and Galleries
42   *"purchasing the crop before it was even planted":* Carl Trocki, *Opium, Empire and the Global Political Economy,* Routledge, London and New York, 1999

43 *"doing business largely in opium":* The Times, January 14, 1875

43 *"the Jewish rotting of China":* Arnold Leese, "An Occasional Report on the Jewish Question, etc.," *Gothic Ripples,* No. 49, Anti Jewish Information Bureau, Guildford, February 28, 1949

43 *"great injury was done in India by the appointment of the Commission":* Rachel Beer, "The Opium Commission Unveiled," WW, *ST,* January 29, 1895

43 *"jewelled merchant ancestors":* SS, "Ancestors," in *The Old Huntsman and Other Poems*

44 *"They made it in the East by dirty trading, millions and millions of coins":* Robert Graves Papers, Special Collections, Southern Illinois University, Carbondale

44 *rock-bottom prices:* Benjamin J. Israel, *The Bene-Israel of India,* Sangam, London, 1984

44 *He was also a council member of Jews College:* The Jewish Chronicle, July 19, 1867

45 *"he seemed to fall into gentle sleep":* The Jewish Chronicle, April 14, 1865

45 *"entertain brotherly affection for each other":* Taken from the will of David Sassoon, courtesy of the Sassoon family

46 *"slenderness that tells more of intellectual energy":* The Spectator, February 6, 1869

46 *"the arms are in particular ugly":* Illustrated London News, July 17, 1869

47 *to take him to Woolner's studio:* The Gentleman's Magazine, August 1867

Chapter Seven: Fatherless

48 *Spanish-Portuguese cemetery on Mile End Road:* Bevis Marks Records part IV, Spanish and Portuguese Jews' Congregation, 1977

49 *"must be closed and liquidated":* "Business and Finance," *The Times,* July 3, 1867

51 *"Grace was said by one of the pupils":* The Jewish Chronicle, January 15, 1869

51 *A tutor in residence, Arthur Read:* Michael Dane, *The Sassoons of Ashley Park,* M. Dane, Walton on Thames, 1999

52 *"passages here, closet there, steps up, steps down":* Eliza Haweis, *Beautiful Houses,* Sampson Low and Co., London, 1882

52 *"Your heritage in worldly goods may not be great":* David Sassoon, *The Ashlesian Republic: A Whimsical Memoir of a Childhood at Ashley Park* (unpublished), courtesy of Mr. Joseph Sassoon

53 *"Will dear Uncle Solomon accept a few kisses":* Sassoon Archive, Hebrew University, Jerusalem

53 *a most favourable review:* Neuen Zeitschrift für Musik, September 9, 1881

53 *Other reviews of Rachel's compositions: The Musical Standard,* June 3, June 19, June 24, December 30, 1882; *The Musical Standard,* March 3, 1883

54 *"Both of them had a passion for jewels":* SS, draft of *The Old Century,* mss 1110, Bound Volumes No. 13, Siegfried Sassoon Papers, Rare Book and Manuscript Library, Columbia University

55 *"the position of an unmarried daughter":* Beatrix Potter, "Testamentary Letter," January 1, 1886, *The Letters of Sidney and Beatrice Webb,* Norman MacKenzie (ed.), Cambridge University Press, Cambridge, 1978

55 *For ambitious English Jews of the time:* Todd M. Endelman, *The Jews of Britain 1656–2000,* University of California Press, Berkeley, Los Angeles, London, 2002

56 *Though women—Jewish or otherwise—could study:* Joan N. Burstyn, *Victorian Education and the Ideal of Womanhood,* Croom Helm, London, 1980

56 *"girl and boy students work shoulder to shoulder":* "Woman at the Arc, a talk with Mrs. Ayrton," *ST,* June 11, 1899

56 *"Years ago, it was conceded that women might reside":* Rachel Beer, "Women's Degrees," WW, *ST,* May 23, 1897

57 *"dunderhead male":* Rachel Beer, "Women and the 'Versity,'" WW, *ST,* February 9, 1896

57 *"the most shy and silent woman I had ever met":* Justin McCarthy, MP, "Notes from England," *The Independent,* October 20, 1898

Chapter Eight: A Court Jew

59 *History of Frankfurt Jewry:* Alexander Dietz, *The Jewish Community of Frankfurt: A Genealogical Study 1349–1849,* Isobel Mordy (ed.), Vanderher, Camelford, 1988; Robert Liberles, "Introduction: The World of Dietz Stammbuch," Alexander Dietz, *The Jewish Community of Frankfurt: A Genealogical Study 1349–1849,* Isobel Mordy (ed.), Vanderher, Camelford, 1988; Robert Liberles, "The Jews of Frankfurt 1750–1870," in *A Tale of Two Cities,* Vivian B. Mann (ed.), The Jewish Museum, New York, 1982; Amos Elon, *Founder: A Portrait of the First Rothschild and His Time,* Penguin, New York, 1996; Aron Freimann and Felix Kracauer, *Frankfurt,* Jewish Communities Series, Jewish Publication Society of America, Philadelphia, 1929

60 *"long dark prison":* Quoted in Niall Ferguson, *The House of Rothschild: Money's Prophets, 1798–1848,* Penguin Books, New York, 1998

62 *About Court Jews:* Selma Stern, *The Court Jew,* Transaction Books, New Brunswick, 1984; Leon Poliakov, *The History of Anti-Semitism,* Vanguard Press, New York, 1965; Alex Bein, *The Jewish Question: Biography of a World Problem,* Herzl Press, New York, 1990; Eoin Bourke, "The Frankfurt Judengasse in Eye-Witnesses Accounts," in Ann

Fuchs and Florian Krobb (eds.), *Ghetto Writing: Traditional and East-
ern Jewry in German Jewish Literature from Heine to Hilsenrath,* Cam-
den House, New York, 1999; Linda Schulte-Sasse, "Harlan's Jud Suss,"
The German Quarterly, vol. 61, no. 1, Winter 1998; Chase Jefferson,
"The Wandering Court Jew and the Hand of God, William Hauff's 'Jud
Suss' as Historical Fiction"; Walter P. Zenner, "Jewish Retainers as
Power Brokers," *The Jewish Quarterly Review,* Vol. 81, 1990; Marion
Kaplan (ed.), *Jewish Daily Life in Germany 1618–1945,* Oxford Uni-
versity Press, New York and Oxford, 2005

64 *Beer Löb Isaak zur Kanne made his fortune:* Alexander Dietz, *The Jewish Community of Frankfurt: A Genealogical Study 1349–1849,* Isobel
Mordy (ed.), Vanderher, Camelford, 1988

66 *when his mental health suffered a serious decline:* Correspondence with
Dr. Michael Matthäus, Institut für Stadtgeschichte Frankfurt, April
2007–September 2008

68 *The Philantropin School and Frankfurt Jewry in the nineteenth century:*
Jakob J. Petuchowski, "Frankfurt Jewry: a Model of Transition to Mo-
dernity," *Leo Baeck Institute Yearbook,* Secker & Warburg, 1984; Mi-
chael A. Meyer and Michael Brenner (eds.), *German-Jewish History in
Modern Times,* Columbia University Press, New York, 2000; Eugen
Mayer, *The Jews of Frankfurt,* Jewish National and University Library,
Jerusalem, 1965; Steven M. Lowenstein, "The German Jewish family,"
Leo Baeck Institute Yearbook, Secker & Warburg, 2006

68 *"for poor children of the Jewish nation":* Amos Elon, *Founder: A Portrait of the First Rothschild and His Time,* Penguin, New York, 1996

68 *"medieval and petrified":* Eugen Mayer, *The Jews of Frankfurt,* The
Jewish National and University Library, Jerusalem, 1965

69 *When Löb Joachim had finally passed:* Correspondence with Dr. Michael Matthäus, Institut für Stadtgeschichte Frankfurt

70 *Frankfurt banking scene:* Carl-Ludwig Holtferich, *Frankfurt as a Commercial Centre,* Verlag C. H. Beck, Munich, 1999

71 *"the Bank for the whole world":* Charles Knight, *Knight's Cyclopædia
of London,* 1851

Chapter Nine: A German in London

72 *German Jews in England:* Pauline Paucker, "The Image of the German
Jew in English Fiction," in *Second Chance: Two Centuries of
German-speaking Jews in the United Kingdom,* Werner E. Mosse and
Julius Carlebach (eds.), Mohr, Tübingen, 1991; Todd M. Endelman,
"German-Jewish Settlement in Victorian England," in *Second Chance:
Two Centuries of German-speaking Jews in the United Kingdom,* Wer-
ner E. Mosse and Julius Carlebach (eds.), Mohr, Tübingen, 1991; Todd
M. Endelman, "Leaving the Jewish Fold in Germany," *Leo Baeck Year-
book,* Secker & Warburg, London, 1995; C. C. Aronsfeld, "German

Jews in Victorian England," in *Leo Baeck Yearbook,* Secker & Warburg, London, 1962; Michael Ragussis, *Figures of Conversion,* Duke University Press, Durham, NC, 1995; Anne Aresty Naman, *The Jew in the Victorian Novel,* AMS Press Inc., New York, 1980

73 *he advertised: The Times,* March 13, 1855

75 *"thus the reigning family [was] more German than English":* Heinrich Dorgeel, *The German Colony in London* (German), 1881; *The Times,* November 29, 1881

76 *"None of us had any notion":* SS, *The Old Century and Seven More Years,* Faber & Faber, London, 1938

77 *The Civil War and the Erlanger loan:* Richard Lester, *Confederate Finance and Purchasing in Great Britain,* University Press of Virginia, Charlottesville, 1975; Ella Lonn, *Foreigners in the Confederacy,* University of North Carolina Press, Chapel Hill, 1940; John Christopher Schwab, *The Confederate States of America,* Burt Franklin, New York, 1901; Harry Simonhoff, *Jewish Participants in the Civil War,* Arco Publishing, New York, 1963; Frank Lawrence Ousley, *King Cotton Diplomacy,* University of Chicago Press, Chicago, 1966; Bertram Korn, *American Jewry and the Civil War,* The Jewish Publication Society of America, Philadelphia, 1951; Burton J. Hendrick, *Statesmen of the Lost Cause,* The Literary Guild of America, New York, 1939; Frank J. Merli, *Great Britain and the Confederate Navy,* Indiana University Press, Bloomington, 1970; Judith Fenner Gentry, "A Confederate Success in Europe: The Erlanger Loan," in *The Journal of Southern History,* 36, May 1970; Eli N. Evans, *Judah P. Benjamin,* Free Press, New York, 1988; Charles Carlenton Coffin, *Four Years in Fighting,* Ticknor and Fields, Boston, 1866; Douglas B. Ball, *Financial Failure and Confederate Defeat,* University of Illinois Press, Urbana, 1991; Lynn Marshall Case and Warren F. Spencer, *The United States and France: Civil War Diplomacy,* University of Pennsylvania Press, Philadelphia, 1970; Charles M. Hubbard, *The Burden of Confederate Diplomacy,* University of Tennessee Press, Knoxville, 1998

77 *a delegation to Richmond:* Laws and Joint Resolutions of the Last Session of the Confederate Congress (November 7, 1864–March 18, 1865), NY AMS Press, 1965; Lynn Marshall Case and Warren F. Spencer, *The United States and France: Civil War Diplomacy,* University of Pennsylvania Press, Philadelphia, 1970; Journal of the Congress of the Confederate States of America, 1905

77 *"They secured a pass to Richmond without difficulty":* Ella Lonn, *Foreigners in the Confederacy,* University of North Carolina Press, Chapel Hill, 1940

77 *"the terms were so onerous that we could not assent to them":* Official Records of the Union and Confederate Navies in the War of the Rebellion, United States Naval War Records Office, United States, 1922

77 *To help grease the deal:* Douglas B. Ball, *Financial Failure and Confederate Defeat,* University of Illinois Press, Urbana, 1991

78 *secretly signed the contract*: February 23, 1863, *Journal of the Congress of the Confederate States of America*, published by United States War Department, vol. 6, published 1904–5

78 *Erlanger and Beer travelled to London*: Charles Carlenton Coffin, *Four Years in Fighting*, Ticknor and Fields, Boston, 1866

78 *The deal gave the Rothschilds*: W. W. Murphy (American Consul-General at Frankfurt), *Harper's Weekly*, VII, 1863

Chapter Ten: A Girdle Round the Earth

80 *Telegraphy and submarine cables*: Daniel Headrick, *The Invisible Weapon*, Oxford University Press, New York, 1991; Daniel Headrick and Pascal Griset, "Submarine Telegraph Cables: Business and Politics, 1838–1939," in *Business History Review*, 75, Autumn 2001; Edward Brailsford, *The Life Story of Charles Tilston Bright*, Archibald Constable and Co., Westminster, 1899; K. R. Haigh, *Cableships and Submarine Cables*, Adlard Coles, London, 1968; Ken Beauchamp, *History of Telegraphy*, Institute of Electrical Engineers, London, 2001; Jorma Ahvenainen, *The Far Eastern Telegraphs*, Suomalainen Tiedeakatemia, Helsinki, 1981; Anton Huurdeman, *The Worldwide History of Telecommunications*, John Wiley, New Jersey, 2003; K. C. Baglehole, *A Century of Service—Cable and Wireless Ltd.*, Bournehall Press, Welwyn Garden City, Herts, 1969

80 *Birkenhead and Liverpool Railway*: *Liverpool Mercury*, January 18, 1866

80 *Hayling Railways*: *Hampshire Telegraph and Sussex Chronicle*, August 18, 1878

80 *tramway to be built in Madrid*: Albert Martinez Lopez, "Foreign Capital and Business Strategies: Comparative Analyses of Urban Transport in Madrid and Barcelona, 1871–1948," presented at the XIV World Economic History Congress, Helsinki, August 2006

80 *his own banking firm, Beer & Co*: *The Times*, February 20, 1868

80 *the Public Works Construction Company*: Memorandum of Association of the Public Works Construction Company (1871), The National Archives, Kew, BT 31/1597/5329

80 *Madeira and Mamore rivers*: Neville B. Craig, *Recollections of an Ill-Fated Expedition*, Lippincott and Co., Philadelphia and London, 1907

81 *"many gentlemen with names absolutely unknown"*: Algernon Mitford (Baron Redesdale), *Mitford's Japan*, Athlone, London, 1985

81 *"The Turkish Government have voted"*: Letter from Julius Beer to Sir Henry Lytton Bulwer (April 11, 1870), Norfolk Record Office, BUL 1/380/9

82 *"and were barely awake for their appointments"*: L. E. Leyendecker, *Pullman Car Prince*, University Press of Colorado, Niwot, CO, 1992

82 *Pullman sleeping cars: The Times,* April 24, 1874
82 *The association ended badly: The Solicitors' Journal,* February 15, 1936
82 *"Hebrew millionaires and plodding Germans":* "Morning on the Stock
Exchange," *Pearson's Magazine,* Vol. 1, January–June 1896; Stanley D.
Chapman, "Merchants and Bankers," in *Second Chance: Two Centuries
of German-speaking Jews in the United Kingdom,* Werner E. Mosse and
Julius Carlebach (eds.), Mohr, Tübingen, 1991
82 *"I wonder where he got it?":* John Pollock, *Time's Chariot,* J. Murray,
London, 1950
83 *"a patient waiter is no loser":* The Century Illustrated Monthly Magazine, Vol. 35, 1888
84 *Julius became a director:* Edward Brailsford, *The Life Story of Charles
Tilston Bright,* Archibald Constable and Co., Westminster, 1899;
George Bradshaw, *Bradshaw's Railway Manual: Shareholders and
Guide Directory, 1869;* J. Wagstaff Blundell, *Blundell's Manual of Submarine Telegraph Companies,1872; The London Stock Exchange Yearbook, 1872–1879*
84 *"prominent in the financing of these important schemes":* Charles Bright,
Submarine Telegraphs, Crosby Lockwood and Son, London, 1898
84 *"always ready to furnish means":* Cyrus Field, "Europe and America:
Report of the Proceeding at an Anniversary Banquet," London, 1873, in
Bill Burns, *History of the Atlantic Cable and Undersea Communications,* www.atlantic-cable.com
84 *to China and Japan:* Jorma Ahvenainen, *The Far Eastern Telegraphs,*
Suomalainen Tiedeakatemia, Helsinki, 1981
85 *seldom appeared outside the board room:* Willoughby Smith, *The Rise
and Extension of Submarine Telegraphy,* Arno Press, New York, 1974
85 *"How marvellous she is—this Electra!":* Souvenir of the Inaugural Fete
in Commemoration of the Opening of Direct Submarine Telegraph with
India, June 23, 1870
86 *disillusionment would creep in:* Daniel Headrick, *The Invisible Weapon,*
Oxford University Press, New York, 1991

Chapter Eleven: 170 Strand

88 *General information about Victorian newspapers:* Mason Jackson, *The
Pictorial Press: Its Origin and Progress,* Hurst and Blackett, London,
1885; George Boyce, (ed.), *Newspaper History from the Seventeenth
Century to the Present Day,* Constable for the Press Group of the Acton
Society, London, 1978 ; Lucy Brown, *Victorian News and Newspapers,*
Clarendon Press, Oxford, 1985; Thomas Hay Sweet Escott, *Masters of
English Journalism: A Study of Personal Forces,* T. F. Unwin, London,
1911; Mark Hampton, *Visions of the Press in Britain, 1850–1950,* Uni-
versity of Illinois Press, Champaign, 2005; Dennis Griffiths, *Fleet Street:
Five Hundred Years of the Press,* British Library, London, 2006; Cyril

Bainbridge, *One Hundred Years of Journalism,* Macmillan, London, 1984; A. P. Wadsworth, *Newspaper Circulations 1800–1954;* Transactions of the Manchester Statistical Society, Manchester, 1954–1955; Keith Williams, *The English Newspaper,* Springwood Books, London, 1977; Stephen Koss, *The Rise and Fall of the Political Press in Britain,* Vol. 1: The Nineteenth Century, Hamish Hamilton, London, 1981; Stanley Morison, *The English Newspaper,* Cambridge University Press, Cambridge, 1932; Arthur Aspinall, *Politics and the Press,* Harvester Press, Birmingham, 1973; Bob Clarke, *From Grub Street to Fleet Street,* Ashgate, Aldershot, 2004; Francis Williams, *Dangerous Estate,* Longmans, London, 1957; James Grant, *The Metropolitan Weekly and Provincial Press,* Vol. 3, Tinsley Brothers, London, 1872; Kennedy Jones, *Fleet Street and Downing Street,* Hutchinson, London, 1919

88 *General information about* The Observer: Marion Miliband (ed.), *The Observer of the Nineteenth Century, 1791–1901,* Longmans, London, 1966; Alfred M. Gollin, *The Observer and J.L. Garvin, 1908–1914,* Oxford University Press, London, 1960; Joanna Anstey and John Silverlight (eds.), *The Observer Observed,* Barrie & Jenkins, London, 1991; Donald Trelford, *The Observer at 200,* Quartet, London, 1992; James Louis Garvin, *The Observer, 1791–1921,* Observer House, London, 1922

88 *"group of gentlemen interested in finance":* "Birthday of *The Observer,*" *The Observer,* December 3, 1905

93 *offered the editorship to his friend Edward Dicey:* Brian Harrison and H. C. G. Matthew (eds.), *Oxford Dictionary of National Biography,* Oxford University Press, Oxford, 2004; Frederic William Maitland, *The Life and Letters of Leslie Stephen,* Duckworth, London, 1906

94 *He would constantly remind his staff:* John St. Loe Strachey, *The Adventure of Living,* Hodder and Stoughton, London, 1922

94 *"a man of much intellectual subtlety":* Thomas Hay Sweet Escott, *Masters of English Journalism: A Study of Personal Forces,* T. F. Unwin, London, 1911

94 *investors with Credit Foncier Egyptien:* Samir Saul, *La France et L'Egypte,* Comité Pour L'Histoire Economique et Financier de la France, Paris, 1997

94 *"The great Julius Beer":* Quoted in *The New York Times,* September 20, 1879

95 *"and thus the most stirring news of the gigantic conflict":* "The Story of *The Observer,*" *The Observer,* June 2, 1895

95 *"nothing could happen to mar":* G.W. Stanley, a speech at the anniversary banquet of the Globe Telegraph Company, Buckingham Palace Hotel, March 10, 1873, in *History of the Atlantic Cable and Undersea Communications,* Atlantic-Cable.com

95 *the librettist W. S. Gilbert, who left immediately for Paris:* Jane W. Stedman, *W. S. Gilbert: A Classic Victorian and His Theatre,* Oxford Univer-

sity Press, Oxford, 1996; Hesketh Pearson, *Gilbert: His Life and Strife,* Harper & Brothers, New York, 1957; Michael Ainger, *Gilbert and Sullivan: A Dual Biography,* Oxford University Press, New York, 2002

95   *"very noisy Frenchmen of the small bourgeois type":* W. S. Gilbert, *The Observer,* September 11, 1870

96   *"The French are crouching like criminals":* Ibid.

97   *"stood in sore need of reorganisation":* Edward Dicey, "Recollections of Arthur Sullivan," in *Fortnightly Review,* vol. 77, January 1905

97   *"The whole work sounds like caricature":* Arthur Sullivan, "Royal Italian Opera," *The Observer,* June 19, 1870

98   *"I had to consider other people's interests":* Edward Dicey, "Recollections of Arthur Sullivan"

98   *the incident did nothing to mar Dicey's lifelong friendship:* Arthur Jacobs, *Arthur Sullivan: A Victorian Musician,* Oxford University Press, Oxford, 1984

98   *drama critic Clement Scott:* Clement Scott, *Freeman's Journal,* December 26, 1898; Clement Scott, *The Drama of Yesterday and Today,* Vol. 1, Macmillan, London, 1899; Clement Scott, *In the Days of My Youth,* T. P. O'Connor (ed.), Pearson, London, 1901

99   *"threatening me with prosecution":* Letter of June 18, 1871, in Karl Marx, *Letters to Dr. Kugelmann,* Martin Lawrence, London, 1934

99   *"There was a sort of easy-going":* John St. Loe Strachey, *The Adventure of Living,* Hodder and Stoughton, London, 1922

99   *"If you are not sure, leave it out":* Ernest Bendall, Dicey's Obituary, *The Observer,* July 9, 1911

100 *"an admirably conducted newspaper of the highest character":* *Quarterly Review,* October 1880

101 *"The excitement of the city was the very breath of his nostrils":* "London and Paris Gossip," *Trewman's Exeter Flying Post,* March 19, 1880

101 *"all the genius of his race for finance":* Ibid.

Chapter Twelve: Five Funerals

103 *scarlet fever:* Anne Hardy, *The Epidemic Streets,* Claringdon Press, Oxford, 1993; Caspar Morris, *An Essay on the Pathology and Therapeutics of Scarlet Fever,* Lindsay and Blakingston, Philadelphia, 1858

103 *"so deadly, that medicine is unable to stay its course":* Dr. Charles West, *Lectures on the Diseases of Infancy and Childhood,* Seventh Edition, Revised and Enlarged, Longman's and Co., London, 1884

103 *put to rest in the Terrace Catacombs:* Highgate Cemetery Archive, 1876

103 *On Highgate Cemetery:* Felix Barker and John Gay, *Highgate Cemetery, Victorian Valhalla,* John Murray, London, 1984; Friends of Highgate Cemetery, *In Highgate Cemetery,* Revised edition, Highgate Cemetery Ltd., London, 2005; James Stevens Curl, *The Victorian Celebration of Death,* Sutton Publishing, Thrupp, Stroud, 2000; James Stevens Curl,

"The Architecture and Planning of the 19th Century Cemetery," *Garden History: The Journal of the Garden History Society*, Vol. 3, No. 3, Summer 1975; N. B. Penny, "The Commercial Garden Necropolis of the Early 19th Century and Its Critics," *Garden History: The Journal of the Garden History Society*, Vol. 2, No. 3, Summer 1974; Catharine Arnold, *Necropolis: London and its Dead*, Simon and Schuster, London, 2007; Hugh Meller, *London Cemeteries*, Scolar, Aldershot, 1994

104 *"the dead have slept in undisturbed and gloomy splendour"*: Felix Barker and John Gay, *Highgate Cemetery, Victorian Valhalla*, John Murray, London, 1984

105 *"the only strikingly spectacular monument"*: Nikolaus Pevsner, *The Buildings of England*, Penguin Books, Harmondsworth, 1951

105 *the leading architectural journal of Victorian England: The Builder*, May 18, 1878

105 *Armstead sketched several scenes of a woman and a little girl*: Royal Academy of Arts Picture Library, Item 04/2262, London; Arthur Fish, "Parables in Marble," *The Quiver*, February 1900; also, Arthur Fish, "Children's Memorials," *The Quiver*, Annual Volume, Cassell & Co, 1900

106 *"wherein a few hours may be profitably spent"*: Edward Slack, "A Spring Afternoon in a Cemetery," *Essays: Literary and Miscellaneous*, T. Eddington, London, 1893

107 *He bequeathed a lifetime annuity*: Will of Julius Beer, 1880, Principal Registry of the Family Division, London

107 *moved just around the corner, to Portland Place*: David King, *The Complete Works of Robert and James Adam*, Heinemann, Oxford, 1991; National Property Board Sweden, *The Swedish residence at 27 Portland Place, London W1*. Julius Beer's home is now the residence of the Swedish ambassador.

107 *Millais's* The Carpenter's Shop: John Guille Millais, *The Life and Letters of Sir John Everett Millais*, Methuen and Co., London, 1899

107 *"so horrible in her ugliness"*: Charles Dickens, *Household Words: A Weekly Journal*, June 15, 1850

107 *"great difficulty in believing"*: "The Pictures of the Season," *Blackwood's Magazine*, July 1850

108 *from the Frankfurt painter Leopold Bode*: Email exchange with Dr. Jürgen Eichenauer, City Archive, Offenbach am Main, 2009

108 *"We hope the London public may be permitted"*: *The Academy*, July 10, 1880

108 *The Electrician*: Alexander Trotter, *Autobiography*, SC MSS 066, The Institution of Engineering and Technology, London

108 *"never sought to influence the free opinion"*: Obituary, *The Electrician*, March 6, 1880

109 *Rigi Kulm Hotel: The Times*, September 3, 5, 12, 16, 18, 1879; *The Observer*, September 7, 1879; *The Saturday Review*, September 13,

1879; *The Pall Mall Gazette,* September 16, 1879; *The Penny Illustrated Paper and Illustrated Times,* September 20, 1879; *The New York Times,* September 20, 1879

110 *"the crusty portier and the crusty clerks":* Mark Twain, *A Tramp Abroad,* Chatto and Windus, London, 1880

110 *Dr. Arnold Beer, Julius's older brother:* Email exchange with Dr. Michael Matthäus, Institut für Stadtgeschichte, Frankfurt, April 2007

110 *"out of health for some months":* Obituary, *The Observer,* March 7, 1880

110 *he went for a drive with his London friends:* James Matthews's memoranda, www. manfamily.org

Chapter Thirteen: The Marriage Market

114 *"These nabobs, with their spicy flavour of the orient":* Anthony Allfrey, *Edward VII and His Jewish Court,* Weidenfeld and Nicolson, London, 1991

115 *"Privy Purse for Turf purposes":* Cecil Roth, *The Sassoon Dynasty,* Robert Hale Ltd., London, 1941

115 *one possible vocation—marriage:* Patricia Jalland, *Women, Marriage and Politics, 1860–1914,* Oxford University Press, New York and Oxford, 1988

116 *"the bride-cake weighed 180 lbs":* "The Rothschilds," *The Illustrated London News,* January 29, 1881

116 *She identified deeply with Dr. Sophia Kovaleskaya:* ST, April 19, 1896

116 *"herd of geese":* Laura Marholm Hansson, *Modern Women* (translated from German), John Lane, London, 1896

117 *"Few among women can be lover, mother, gourmet, saint":* Rachel Beer, "Wives," WW, ST, October 20, 1895

117 *One of Rachel's male readers:* "Anti-Pioneerdom," in "Letters to the Editor," ST, February 17, 1895

117 *The Edith Lanchester affair:* Karen Hunt, *Equivocal Feminists: The Social Democratic Federation and the Woman Question, 1884–1911,* Cambridge University Press, 1996

118 *Upon Miss Lanchester's release:* Rachel Beer, "Grant Allenism," WW, ST, November 3, 1895

119 *"sweet oriental eyes and oriental skin":* The Observer, April 30, 1882

119 *"like a bottle of Batty's Nabob Pickles":* Letter from Alyce Thornycroft to her brother Hamo, 1882, Papers of Hamo Thornycroft, 4/86, Henry Moore Institute Archive, Leeds Museums and Galleries

119 *In November 1882, he began working:* Papers of Hamo Thornycroft, Henry Moore Institute Archive, Leeds Museums and Galleries

120 *Hamo began to feel that Rachel:* Elfrida Manning, *Marble and Bronze,* Treford Books, London, 1982

120 *"lost [his] heart to her entirely":* Ibid.

120 *"on whom I thought when I wrote* Tess*"*: Scott McEathron, *Thomas Hardy's Tess of the d'Urbervilles: A Sourcebook,* Routledge, London and New York, 2005

120 *the Thornycrofts tried to distract their son's*: Elfrida Manning, *Marble and Bronze,* Treford Books, London, 1982

120 *Agatha was not unaware of Rachel's presence*: Elfrida Manning, *Marble and Bronze* (unabridged manuscript), Papers of Hamo Thornycroft, 4/86, Henry Moore Institute Archive, Leeds Museums and Galleries

120 *She began the day with Mary Gladstone*: Mary Gladstone, *Mary Gladstone (Mrs. Drew), Her Diaries and Letters,* Lucy Masterman (ed.), Methuen, London, 1930

121 *he later reported to Agatha Cox*: Letter from Hamo Thonrnycroft to Agatha Cox, April 10, 1883, Papers of Hamo Thornycroft, Henry Moore Institute Archive, Leeds Museums and Galleries

121 A Sonata of Beethoven: *The Times,* May 5, 1883

121 *"He proves in his graceful statuette of Miss Sassoon"*: *The Observer,* May 7, 1883

121 *The Athenaeum was more contentious: Athenaeum,* June 19, 1883

122 *nevertheless, Hannah's mother*: Richard Davies, *The English Rothschilds,* Collins, London, 1983

122 *"If the flame seized on the cedars"*: *The Jewish Chronicle,* October 5, 1877

123 *Apostasy had been quite common*: Todd M. Endelman, *Radical Assimilation in English Jewish History,* Indiana University Press, Bloomington, 1990

123 *While the Thornycrofts*: Letter from Hamo Thornycroft to Agatha Cox, January 13, 1884, Papers of Hamo Thornycroft, Henry Moore Institute Archive, Leeds Museums and Galleries

123 *Flora perceived Alfred's act*: Michael Dane, *The Sassoons of Ashley Park,* M. Dane, Walton on Thames, 1999

124 *"there are few better ways of spending three hours"*: New Shakespeare Society, 1875

124 *he failed to arrive at the Gunzburgs' home*: Interviews with Jacques Sassoon and Joseph Sassoon (Joseph Sassoon's grandsons) (2007–9)

126 *"Before the days of Florence Nightingale"*: Rachel Beer, "The Queen's Nurses," WW, *ST,* July 7, 1901

126 *Many ladies of wealth and culture answered Nightingale's call*: Lee Holcombe, *Victorian Ladies at Work,* David and Charles, 1973; Jane Lewis, *Women in England, 1870–1950,* Wheatsheaf, Brighton, 1984

126 *"and all the gradations of rank between these two"*: Lee Holcombe, *Victorian Ladies at Work,* David and Charles, Newton Abbott, 1973

127 *"In the treatment of the sick, as much depends upon the nurse as on the doctor"*: Rachel Beer, "The Prince and the Hospitals," WW, *ST,* February 2, 1897

127 *"sputum, instead of being burnt"*: Rachel Beer, "Consumptive Aeronauts," WW, *ST,* July 8, 1901

127 *"no better than white slavery"*: Rachel Beer, "How Women can Cooperate," WW, *ST,* September 22, 1895

128 *a family plot*: Albert Montefiore Hyamson, *The Sephardim of England,* Methuen and Co., London, 1951; Bevis-Marks Cemetery Records

Chapter Fourteen: A Newspaper Heir

129 *he gave up his studies at Cambridge*: Information supplied by Phillipa Grimstone, Magdalene College Library, Cambridge, 2008

130 *Dicey encouraged him*: A. Wallis Myers, "The Sunday Newspaper World," *The Ludgate Monthly,* Vol. V, November 1897–April 1898, White and Co., London, 1898

130 *"full freedom of judgment"*: Henry Lucy, *Sixty Years in the Wilderness,* Smith, Elder, London, 1909

131 *"had never sent empty away the printer's boy"*: Ibid.

131 *Kate Webster was a domestic servant*: Shani D'Cruze, *Murder: Social And Historical Approaches to Understanding Murder and Murderers,* Willan Publications, Devon, 2006

131 *"All sensational reports of executions"*: Edward Dicey, "The First Topics of the Day," *The Observer,* August 3, 1879; *The Observer,* March 7, 1880

132 *"politely bowed out of the world"*: Edward Dicey, "The First Topics of the Day," *The Observer,* September 9, 1883

132 *"Who can tell how much the strain on the nerves"*: Edward Dicey, *The Observer,* December 15, 1872

132 *"On examination, it was found that Mr. Burke"*: *The Observer,* May 7, 1882

132 *he sent messengers*: Edward Dicey, *The Observer,* October 11, 1896

134 *"The speeches were brief and to the point"*: *The Observer,* July 31, 1887

Chapter Fifteen: *Rien sans Peine*

137 *she publicly denounced the Christian passion*: Rachel Beer, "A Costly Pursuit," WW, *ST,* September 8, 1895

138 *Siegfried Sassoon was told*: SS, *The Weald of Youth*

138 *"A Modern Royal Love Story"*: *ST,* December 26, 1897

139 *Martin Beisly*: Interview with Martin Beisly, London, October 2007

140 *Orpheus and Eurydice by G. F. Watts*: Email exchange with Mark Bills, Curator of the Watts Gallery, Compton, Surrey, April 2007

140 *pelican in an act of self-sacrifice*: E. P. Evans, *Animal Symbolism in Ecclesiastical Architecture,* Heinemann, London, 1896

141 *the premier London dog clipper*: The Strand Magazine, Vol. 11, 1896

142 *at the Gladstone estate at Hawarden:* Edward Russell, *That Reminds Me,* Fisher Unwin, London, 1899

143 *"It is doubly delightful to think of you taking my place":* "In The Witness Box," *ST,* March 6, 1898

143 *"a lady who is to blossom as a political hostess":* The Country Gentleman, May 5, 1888

143 *She suggested to Edward Dicey an article:* Rachel Beer, "Garden Cities," WW, *ST,* September 22, 1901

144 *connection with the paper was now at an end:* The Observer, March 31, 1889

144 *"could edit and laugh at the same time":* Francis Henry Gribble, *Seen in Passing,* Ernst Benn, London, 1929

144 *Mrs. Beer sailed into Traill's office:* Ibid.

145 *"They tell us that some changes are in store":* Fun, April 22, 1891

145 *"a boisterous bull calf in a crockery shop":* Francis Henry Gribble, *Seen in Passing,* Ernst Benn, London, 1929

145 *The playwright had been commissioned:* The Observer, May 3, 1891

145 *"Cooke is such an unspeakable greenhorn":* Letter from George Bernard Shaw to Emery Walker, May 7, 1891, in Bernard Shaw, *Collected Letters 1874–1897,* Dan H. Laurence (ed.), Dodd, Mead and Co., New York, 1965

146 *"I burned my boats and left the galleries forever":* Stanley Weintraub (ed.), *Bernard Shaw on the London Art Scene, 1885–1950,* Pennsylvania State University Press, University Park, 1989

146 *"a Jewish lady who had an interest in the paper":* Bernard Shaw, *Collected Letters 1898–1910,* Dan H. Laurence (ed.), Max Reinhardt, London, 1972

146 *"descended on* The Observer*":* Bernard Falk, *Bouquets for Fleet Street: Memories and Musings over Fifty Years,* Hutchinson and Co., London, 1951

147 *"a trifle ponderous":* Rachel Beer, "The Sunday Press," WW, *ST,* June 2, 1895

Chapter Sixteen: A Newspaper of Her Own

148 *History of the* Sunday Times*:* Harold Hobson, Phillip Knightly, and Leonard Russell, *The Pearl of Days: An Intimate Memoir of the* Sunday Times, Hamish Hamilton, London, 1972; "Our Seventy-Five Years," *ST,* June 20, 1897; "6000th number Today," *ST,* April 10, 1938

148 *"changed its owners almost as often as King Solomon":* Bernard Falk, *Five Years Dead: A Postscript to "He Laughed in Fleet Street,"* Hutchinson & Co., London, 1937

148 *Beckett turned to the occult:* Arthur à Beckett, *Recollections of a Humorist,* Pitman and Sons, London, 1907

150   *Alice Cornwell:* Brian Harrison and H.C.G. Matthew (eds.), *Oxford Dictionary of National Biography,* Oxford University Press, Oxford, 2004; Dennis Griffiths, *Fleet Street: Five Hundred Years of the Press,* British Library, London, 2006

151   *Hermann Klein, the then music critic:* Hermann Klein, *Musicians and Mummers,* Cassell and Co., London, 1925; Hermann Klein, *Thirty Years of Musical Life in London 1870–1900,* William Heinemann, London, 1903

151   *"could not write anything":* James Glover, *Jimmy Glover: His Book,* Methuen and Co., London, 1911

152   *Women in journalism:* Barbara Onslow, *Women of the Press in the Nineteenth Century,* Macmillan, Basingstoke, 2000; Marysa Demoor, *Their Fair Share: Women, Power and Criticism in the Athenaeum, from Millicent Garrett Fawcett to Katherine Mansfield,* Ashgate, Aldershot, 2000; Seth Koven, *Slumming: Sexual and Social Politics in Victorian London,* Princeton University Press, 2004

152   *"sections and regular columns written by and for women":* Seth Koven, *Slumming: Sexual and Social Politics in Victorian London,* Princeton University Press, 2004

152   *"a woman moderately intelligent":* Frances S. Low, *Press Work for Women,* Upcott Gill, London, 1904

153   *out of bounds for women:* Mary Billington, "Leading Lady Journalists," *Pearson's Magazine,* Vol. II, July–December 1896

154   *"that's what we women want so much":* Elizabeth Lynn Lynton, *Sowing the Wind,* New Edition, Chatto & Windus, London, 1890

154   *she intended to return to the first tradition:* "Our Seventy-Five Years," *ST,* June 20, 1897

155   *"the eye and the ear and the tongue":* W. T. Stead, "Government by Journalism," *Contemporary Review,* Vol. 49, May 1886

155   *"by the light of the Ten Commandments":* Rachel Beer, "The Approaching Corrections," WW, *ST,* September 13, 1896

155   *"I am an Imperialist":* Arnold Bennett, "The Lady Editors of London," No. VIII, "Mrs. Beer of the Sunday Times," *Woman,* August 10, 1898

156   *"corpulent and middle-aged":* Rachel Beer, "England's Destiny," WW, *ST,* November 3, 1895

156   *"to make the English public interested":* interview with Arnold Bennett, "The Lady Editors of London"

156   *"Profess to know more":* Rachel Beer, "Garden Cities," WW, *ST,* September 22, 1901

Chapter Seventeen: 46 Fleet Street

158   *she installed a telephone connection:* Freeman's Journal and Daily Commercial Advertiser, October 10, 1894; Women's World, August 14, 1897

158   *"As the bright sun streams in":* Arnold Bennett, "The Lady Editors of London," No. VIII, "Mrs. Beer of the Sunday Times," *Woman,* August 10, 1898

158   *"a paradise of equanimity":* Rachel Beer, "Handwriting and Happiness," WW, *ST,* March 3, 1895

159   *"we used to have a family council":* SS, *The Old Century and Seven More Years,* Faber & Faber, London, 1938

159   *"On Tuesday a shiver was sent through the nerves":* Rachel Beer, "Russia," WW, *ST,* September 30, 1894

159   *"they are incompatible with appetite":* Rachel Beer, "Deathbed Up-to-date," WW, *ST,* November 11, 1894

160   *"marvellous capacity in this respect":* Rachel Beer, "Home Politics," WW, *ST,* September 30, 1894; Rachel Beer, "Mr. Gladstone's Goodbye," WW, *ST,* July 7, 1895

160   *"were languishing for want of a job":* Rachel Beer, "Labour," WW, *ST,* September 30, 1894

161   *In the last round of the boxing match:* Rachel Beer, "Accidental Death," WW, *ST,* December 12, 1897; Rachel Beer, "Knock Down or Knock Out," WW, *ST,* December 19, 1897

161   *"My dear child," Mr. Stead said:* Rachel Beer, "Garden Cities," WW, *ST,* September 22, 1901

162   *"comfortable and harmless position of the fly on the wheel":* Ibid.

162   *"as an entomologist":* Rachel Beer, "The Ins and the Outs," WW, *ST,* June 30, 1895

163   *habitual drunkards, heartless libertines:* Rachel Beer, "Codlin and Short," WW, *ST,* June 30, 1895

163   *"Sodom and Gomorrah would have contained a virtuous population . . . ":* Rachel Beer, "Electioneering Libels," WW, *ST,* May 5, 1895

163   *"whose exhausted systems require":* Rachel Beer, "A Parliamentary Fiction," WW, *ST,* August 2, 1896

163   *Wealthy peers may have all the virtues of saints:* Rachel Beer, "The Peers Cabinet," WW, *ST,* June 30, 1895

163   *taxes on many of the luxury items:* Rachel Beer, "How to Raise Revenues," WW, *ST,* May 26, 1901

163   *"developed a secret power":* Rachel Beer, "The Stock Exchange," WW, *ST,* May 31, 1896

164   *"women accept the same class of work":* Rachel Beer, "Combination Among Women Workers," WW, *ST,* October 13, 1895

164   *advocating pensions for workers:* Rachel Beer, "Old Age Pensions," WW, *ST,* December 13, 1896

164   *cheap but respectable eating houses:* Rachel Beer, "Restaurants for Clerks," WW, *ST,* March 22, 1896

164   *leading London firm of drapers:* Rachel Beer, "Tall hat," WW, *ST,* March 24, 1895

164   *"the wastrels which the potter throws out"*: Rachel Beer, "The Unemployable," WW, *ST,* November 29, 1896

164   *"not as interesting as a blood curdler"*: Rachel Beer, "War Office accounts," WW, *ST,* August 8, 1895

165   *Duke of Cambridge should retire*: Rachel Beer, WW, *ST,* March 17,
April 28, June 23, August 18, September 29, 1895

165   *ranger of Hyde Park*: Rachel Beer, "Hyde Park," WW, *ST,* October 27,
1895

165   *the obesity of the majors and colonels*: Rachel Beer, "Inefficient Volunteer Colonels," WW, *ST,* December 1, 1895

166   *the Public Amusements Bill*: *ST,* February 3, 1895; March 17, 1895

167   *to live in one confined room*: Rachel Beer, "One Room Folk," WW,
ST, February 3, 1895; "The People at Play," WW, *ST,* November 25,
1894

167   *"when are you going to give another party"*: Rachel Beer, "Garden Cities," WW, *ST,* September 22, 1901

168   *"there are many people who don't use theatres"*: George Bernard Shaw,
"Concerning State-Aided Amusements," *ST,* September 9, 1894

168   *"there are other windows to the soul"*: Rachel Beer, "At Last," WW, *ST,*
March 15, 1896

168   *"the butcher boy will just yet desert his beloved comic songs"*: Rachel
Beer, "Municipal Music," WW, *ST,* December 6, 1896; Rachel Beer,
"The Promise of May," WW, *ST,* December 16, 1894

169   *"the jaded inhabitants of towns"*: Rachel Beer, "Wandering Congrega-
tions and Travelling Preachers," WW, *ST,* August 4, 1901

169   *"for Sunday, the one day out of seven"*: "Private Views: Mostly Unpopular," No. IV, *Punch,* June 7, 1899

169   *"one of the causes of the predominance of the Anglo-Saxon"*: Rachel
Beer, "Our Sunday," WW, *ST,* June 11, 1899

Chapter Eighteen: A New Woman

170   *Miss March Phillipps was to discuss*: "Women in Journalism," *ST,*
March 31, 1895

170   *"Whether a corps of Amazons will speedily be formed"*: Rachel Beer,
"Californian Amazons," WW, *ST,* May 9, 1897

170   *America was a laboratory for producing precedents*: Susan B. Anthony,
"In the Witness Box," *ST,* July 16, 1899

171   *Mademoiselle Marie Popelin*: "In the Witness Box," *ST,* August 29,
1897; Rachel Beer, "Women as Barristers," WW, *ST,* October 17, 1897

172   *"What to do with our wife beaters"*: "Pioneers on Wife Beating," *ST,*
October 2, 1894

172   *whether Eve was the first Pioneer*: Rachel Beer, "Ideal Women Pioneers," WW, *ST,* December 9, 1894

172 *Deborah was "the editor of the* Sunday Times*":* "The New Journalism before a Pioneer Jury," *ST,* March 3, 1895

172 *Rachel also tried to give female journalists:* Arnold Bennett, "The Lady Editors of London," No. VIII, "Mrs. Beer of the *Sunday Times,*" *Woman,* August 10, 1898

172 *"No one ever saw a French woman":* "Parisian Hairdressing," *ST,* October 25, 1896

173 *"Very quickly, so swiftly does the vogue change nowadays":* "In Fashion's Footsteps," *ST,* December 9, 1900

173 *"In act II, evening dress is very much in":* "First Night Dresses," *ST,* December 2, 1900

173 *"Beautiful uniform":* Rachel Beer, "A Revolt of Fair Crusaders," WW, *ST,* March 22, 1896

173 *fashion for men: ST,* March 3, 1901

173 *foodless and waterless cats:* Rachel Beer, "The Holiday Cat," WW, *ST,* October 6, 1895

174 *a role model of a supportive wife:* "What Women Can Do," *ST,* August 7, 1898

175 *"Her husband is behaving like a madman":* Journal of Hamo Thornycroft, March 11, 1890, Papers of Hamo Thornycroft, Henry Moore Institute Archive, Leeds Museums and Galleries

176 *"to lure him back to the faith":* Jean Moorcroft Wilson, *Siegfried Sassoon: The Journey from the Trenches,* Duckworth, London, 2003

176 *"Sure enough, there we were":* SS, *The Old Century and Seven More Years,* Faber & Faber, London, 1938

Chapter Nineteen: Rivals

177 *"in tone and news":* "Another Woman Editor," *The Humanitarian* (Monthly Review of Sociological Science), London, November 1894

177 *"she was offered more than twice the sum": The Woman's Signal,* September 26, 1895

177 *"all the shrewdness and commonsense of her sex":* Cecil Roth, *The Sassoon Dynasty,* Robert Hale Ltd., London, 1941

177 *"dogmatic assertion": The Journalist and Newspaper Proprietor,* June 8, 1895

177 *turned her broadsheet into the "she":* Ibid.

177 *"sprightly girlhood like the eagle":* Rachel Beer, "The Sunday Press," WW, *ST,* June 2, 1895

177 *her rivals were quick to pick up on: The Journalist and Newspaper Proprietor,* June 8, 1895

178 *sixteen paintings by Corot:* Catalogue of Collection of Modern Pictures and Drawings—The Property of the Late Mrs. Rachel Beer, Christie's, London, 1927

178 *literary lessons from a French lady: ST,* March 29, 1896

178   *leave London in the afternoon and arrive in Paris by midnight:* Rachel Beer, "Express Line to Paris," WW, *ST,* March 29, 1896

179   *"When the historian of the twenty-first century":* Rachel Beer, "Channel fares," WW, *ST,* May 19, 1895; *ST,* November 25, 1894; December 30, 1894; October 13, 1895; December 1, 1895

179   *Mr. and Mrs. F. A. Beer were expected daily:* "Court and Fashion," *The Observer,* February 7, 1892

179   *Rachel chastised him:* Rachel Beer, "Lord Salisbury in France," WW, *ST,* September 8, 1895

180   *she would never exchange the "sullen skies" of England:* Rachel Beer, "The English Speaking People," WW, *ST,* November 3, 1895

180   *"Friendship with such a power is impossible":* Rachel Beer, "France and England," WW, *ST,* January 20, 1895

180   *"all the pleasant and temperate regions":* Rachel Beer, "Britannia contra Mundum," WW, *ST,* January 12, 1896

180   *"No one can tell when the thunderstorm will burst":* Rachel Beer, "The European Outlook," WW, *ST,* September 22, 1895

181   *"as guns improve in penetration":* Rachel Beer, "Gunshot Wounds," WW, *ST,* August 4, 1895

181   *"more attractive when quarrelling":* Rachel Beer, "Woman Suffrage and Foreign Affairs," WW, *ST,* May 10, 1896

181   *"in favour of diplomacy and peace":* Ibid.

181   *Wartime and the consumption of wheat:* Rachel Beer, "The Price of Food in Wartime," WW, *ST,* October 27, 1895; Rachel Beer, "The Food Question," WW, *ST,* January 12, 1896; Rachel Beer, "The Navy and the Food Supply," WW, *ST,* March 1, 1896

181   *Germany loomed as the greatest threat:* Rachel Beer, "School Board Education," WW, *ST,* December 8, 1895

181   *Kaiser Wilhelm II as "impulsive and hysterical":* Rachel Beer, "Britannia contra Mundum," WW, *ST,* January 12, 1896; *ST,* February 9, 1896

182   *"The memories of Westminster Abbey":* Rachel Beer, "The English-Speaking People," WW, *ST,* November 3, 1895; Rachel Beer, "The English-Speaking Race," WW, *ST,* November 24, 1895

182   *"and the Americans are more to us":* Ibid.

182   *the marriage of the Duke of Marlborough and Miss Consuelo Vander-bilt:* "Marlbraux s'en va't en Guerre," WW, *ST,* September 22, 1895

182   *a flag over every schoolhouse:* Rachel Beer, "The British Flag over Board-School," WW, *ST,* July 19, 1896

182   *"Capitalist rule is supreme":* Rachel Beer, "Britannia contra Mundum," WW, *ST,* January 12, 1896; "Mr. Bryan," WW, *ST,* November 1, 1896

182   *the corruption of the English language:* Rachel Beer, "Diamond Jubilee British Academy," WW, *ST,* April 18, 1897

183   *She criticised the Rothschilds:* Rachel Beer, "Cash or Conscience," WW, *ST,* December 9, 1894; "The Russian Loan," WW, *ST,* December 23, 1894

183   *"If they are welcomed, they become nationalised"*: Rachel Beer, "Hep Hep," WW, *ST,* October 14, 1894

183   *"scrupulously fair"*: "In the Witness Box: Madame de Novikoff," *ST,* April 21, 1895

184   *mass murder of Armenian Christians:* Rachel Beer, "Frozen Music," WW, *ST,* December 8, 1895; "Egin Massacre," WW, *ST,* October 18, 1896

184   *the first two Indian MPs:* Rachel Beer, "The Three Indias," WW, *ST,* November 17, 1895

185   *"the high hand seizure"*: Rachel Beer, "Our Latest Acquisition," WW, *ST,* July 28, 1895; "Trinidad, Brazil, and M. de Soveral," WW, *ST,* August 9, 1896

185   *"Pender's cables have done more harm"*: Rachel Beer, "Britannia contra Mundum," WW, *ST,* January 12, 1896

185   *a fleet of saloon passenger steamers:* Rachel Beer, "Shall We Shut Up the Thames," WW, *ST,* November 24, 1895

185   *"the horseless carriage"*: Rachel Beer, "Automotors," WW, *ST,* December 15, 1895; Rachel Beer, "The Capsized Omnibus," WW, *ST,* March 31, 1895; Rachel Beer, "Seeing is believing," WW, *ST,* August 22, 1897; "Motor-car Restrictions," WW, *ST,* November 1, 1896

185   *"the New Horse"*: "The New Horse," WW, *ST,* June 16, 1895

186   *"which for us was something quite out of the ordinary"*: SS, *The Old Century and Seven More Years,* Faber & Faber, London, 1938

186   *new inexpensive fire escapes:* Rachel Beer, "The Fire Fiend," WW, *ST,* January 13, 1895

186   *"in journalism, there is a sense of achievement"*: Arnold Bennett, "The Lady Editors of London," No. VIII, "Mrs. Beer of the *Sunday Times,*" *Woman,* August 10, 1898

186   *why did he employ his milkman on Sunday mornings:* "Letters to the Editor," *ST,* January 27, 1895

187   *"But if there be no Sunday Times in heaven"*: Rachel Beer, "Dr. Horton, Heaven and the *Sunday Times,*" WW, *ST,* May 17, 1896

187   *"it is penal to kiss on Sunday"*: Rachel Beer, "No Kissing on Sunday," WW, *ST,* March 24, 1901

187   *Editors and the laws of libel:* Rachel Beer, "The Duties of Directors," WW, *ST,* March 1, 1896

188   *Nelson's Day in Trafalgar Square: The Observer,* October 20, 1895; *The Times,* October 22, 1895 and October 22, 1901

188   *"It has been a matter of notoriety in journalistic circles"*: Rachel Beer, *"The Observer* and Ourselves," WW, *ST,* October 20, 1895

189   *Frederick promised his readers:* "The Story of *The Observer,*" *The Observer,* June 2, 1895

189   *"our closest and most dangerous rival"*: Rachel Beer, "A Score for *The Observer,*" WW, *ST,* April 19, 1896

189   "The *Observer's* steady walk": Rachel Beer, "The Sunday Press," WW, *ST,* June 2, 1895

189 *"occult practices and black magic"*: Rachel Beer, "No More Sleep," WW, ST, January 6, 1896

190 *public statues erected around London*: Rachel Beer, "The Sunday Times as an Iconoclast" and "The Duke of York's Statue," WW, ST, November 8, 1896; Rachel Beer, "Our Statues" and "Lord Strathnairn and Co.," WW, ST, November 15, 1896

190 *Max Schlesinger*: Max Schlesinger, *Saunterings in and about London*, Nathaniel Cooke, London, 1853

191 *State Children's Aid Association*: Rachel Beer, "Unhappy Children of the State," WW, ST, May 5, 1896; Rachel Beer, "State Children," WW, ST, March 6, 1898; ST, April 24, 1898; ST, July 10, 1898; ST, July 2, 1899; ST, July 30, 1899

192 *"they were simply a worthless product"*: Rachel Beer, "Children and the Married Women's Vote," WW, ST, June 14, 1896

192 *when women got the vote*: Ibid.; Rachel Beer, "Woman Suffrage and Foreign Affairs," WW, ST, May 10, 1896; Rachel Beer, "Leisurely Mr. Labouchere," WW, ST, June 21, 1896

Chapter Twenty: Double Burden

193 *"A very clever, dark woman, Jewish in appearance"*: Lady Glover, *Memories of Four Continents*, Seeley, Service and Co., London, 1923

194 *Invisible Musical Performances*: Nursing Record and Hospital World, April 14, 1894; The Musical Standard, April 14, 1894; The Musical Times, June 1, 1894; The Musical Times, June 1 and November 1, 1894; Percy A. Scholes, *The Mirror of Music 1884–1944*, Oxford University Press, London, 1947

194 *The Invisible Concert was warmly applauded*: The Observer, April 1, 1894; The Observer, April 8, 1894

194 *The* Guardian's *reviewer was less enthusiastic*: Guardian, April 9, 1894

195 *new opera* Zanetto: The Observer, June 7 and June 21, 1896; The Sunday Times, June 28, 1896; The Times, June 24, 1896; Hermann Klein, *Thirty Years of Musical Life in London 1870–1900*, William Heinemann, London, 1903; Hermann Klein, *Great Women Singers of My Time*, Routledge, London, 1931; Alan Mallach, *Pietro Mascagni and His Operas*, Northeastern University Press, Boston, 2002; William Irvine, "G. B. Shaw's Musical Criticism," *The Music Quarterly*, Vol. XXXII, No. 3, July 1946; George Bernard Shaw, *Music in London*, Vol. 3, Constable, London, 1932

196 *"with its magnificent rings"*: SS, *The Old Century and Seven More Years*, Faber & Faber, London, 1938

196 *"Her gaiety seemed absent-minded"*: Ibid.

197 *as though they were florins*: SS, *The Weald of Youth* (manuscript), Siegfried Sassoon Papers, Columbia

197 *"seemed to forget"*: Ibid.

197 *"which seemed more an appurtenance"*: SS, *The Old Century and Seven More Years,* Faber & Faber, London, 1938

198 *"medicine never cured"*: Charles Dickens, *The Life and Adventures of Nicholas Nickleby,* Chapman and Hall, London, 1865

198 *On Tuberculosis:* Linda Bryder, *Below the Magic Mountain,* Clarendon Press, Oxford, 1988; Henry Hyslop Thomson, *Tuberculosis: Its Prevention and Home Treatment,* Oxford Medical Publications, London, 1921; S. Adolphus Knopf, *Tuberculosis as a Disease of the Masses and How to Combat It,* The Survey, New York, 1911; Dr. Edward J. Bermingham, "Progress of the Treatment of Consumption," *The New York Times,* February 27, 1898; Thomas Dormandy, *The White Death: A History of Tuberculosis,* Hambledon Press, London and Rio Grande, Ohio, 1999; Barbara Bates, *Bargaining for Life,* University of Pennsylvania Press, Philadelphia, 1992

198 *"I'm afraid poor Mr. Beer has a bad heredity"*: SS, *The Old Century and Seven More Years,* Faber & Faber, London, 1938

198 *transferred* The Observer *to a joint stock company: The Observer,* October 25, 1896

199 *"I have at times to take the whole responsibility of the two papers"*: Arnold Bennett, "The Lady Editors of London," No. VIII, "Mrs. Beer of the *Sunday Times,*" *Woman,* August 10, 1898

199 *"having slept badly the night before"*: SS, *The Old Century and Seven More Years,* Faber & Faber, London, 1938

199 *Sleep is essential to all:* Rachel Beer, "A Sleepless Premier," WW, *ST,* March 24, 1895

200 *"an accomplished and devoted nurse in the Princess"*: Rachel Beer, "The Mishap of the Prince," WW, *ST,* July 24, 1898

201 *"It is a humane and beneficial mission"*: Rachel Beer, "The Prince and the Hospitals," WW, *ST,* February 7, 1897

201 *Professor Edmond Savary d'Odiardi:* "Many Medical Inventions," "In the Witness Box," *ST,* February 21, 1897

202 *The Press Bazaar: The Observer,* June 19 and June 26, 1898; *The Times,* June 29, 1898; *The Sunday Times,* June 26, 1898; *The Jewish Chronicle,* July 1, 1898; SS, *The Old Century*

Chapter Twenty-One: All of Paris in a Fever

203 *General information about the Dreyfus affair:* Marie Charles Ferdinand Walsin-Esterhazy, *Les Dessous de l'Affaire Dreyfus,* Fayard Frères, Paris, 1898; Alfred Dreyfus, *The Dreyfus Case,* Yale University Press, New Haven, 1937; T. Marcel Thomas, *Esterhazy—ou L'envers de l'Affaire Dreyfus,* Vernal, Paris, 1989; Guy Chapman, *The Dreyfus Case: A Reassessment,* Hart-Davis, London, 1955; Louis Begley, *Why the Dreyfus Affair Matters,* Yale University Press, New Haven, 2009; Henry M. Mobley, "English Reaction to the Dreyfus Affair," Ph.D. the-

sis, Middle Tennessee State University, Ann Arbor, Michigan, 1993; Ricky Lee Sherrod, *Images and Reflections: Response of the British Press to the Dreyfus Affaire*, Ph.D. thesis, Michigan State University, East Lansing, MI, 1980; James Brennan, *The Reflection of the Dreyfus Affair in the European Press*, Peter Lang, New York, 1998; Jean Denis Bredin, *The Affair: The Case of Alfred Dreyfus*, translated by Jeffrey Mehlman, Braziller, New York, 1986

203   *"one of the most remarkable incidents of the year"*: Rachel Beer, "Treachery in the Camp," WW, *ST*, December 30, 1894

208   *a check for well over forty thousand pounds*: SS, *The Weald of Youth* (manuscript), Siegfried Sassoon Papers, Columbia

208   *"it is probably hard for anyone"*: Rachel Beer, "Encore Dreyfus," WW, *ST*, November 28, 1897

209   *"Of such follies are revolutions made"*: Ibid.

209   *"Not for a moment do we say that Esterhazy is the criminal"*: Rachel Beer, "Le Debacle," WW, *ST*, January 16, 1898

209   *"Most emphatically we say that this is not so"*: Rachel Beer, "Dreyfus," WW, *ST*, January 30, 1898

210   *"one of the most outstanding documents"*: Rachel Beer, "L'Attaque du Governement," WW, *ST*, January 16, 1898

210   *"the greatest blunder in the world"*: Letter from Robert Crawford to Edward Cook, March 21, 1898, in Joseph O. Baylen, "Dreyfusards and the Foreign Press: the Syndicate and the Daily News, February–March 1898," *French Historical Studies*, Vol. VII, No. 3, Spring 1972

211   *"A sort of cyclone of madness"*: Rowland Strong, *The New York Times*, January 23, 1898

211   *"Quarrels are breaking out"*: Rowland Strong, *The New York Times*, December 12, 1897

211   *"carried on the campaign against him in the English press"*: Chris Healy, *Confessions of a Journalist*, Chatto & Windus, London, 1904

211   *"He is a little, old man, sad-faced"*: Rowland Strong, *The New York Times*, February 20, 1898

211   *"little man with a red beard"*: J. Robert Maguire, "Oscar Wilde and the Dreyfus Affair," *Victorian Studies*, Vol. 41, No. 1, Autumn 1997

212   *"if he stuck to him closely enough"*: Ibid.

212   *"tossed down fifteen or twenty whiskies"*: Ibid.

212   *"what I had been doing, what I was going to do"*: Ibid.

212   *"shoot the wretches down like rabbits"*: Rowland Strong, *The New York Times*, February 27, 1898

212   *"the victim of the French Army Moloch"*: Rachel Beer, "Zola's Triumph," WW, *ST*, April 3, 1898

212   *"It is plain that France"*: *The Observer*, February 29, 1898

212   *On Strong, Esterhazy and Wilde*: Robert Harborough Sherard, *Twenty Years in Paris*, Hutchison, London, 1905; Francis Charles Philips, *My Varied Life*, Eveleigh Nash, London, 1914; Oscar Wilde, *The Complete*

Letters of Oscar Wilde, Merlin Holland and Rupert Hart-Davis (eds.), Henry Holt, New York, 2000; Mark Hichens, *Oscar Wilde's Last Chance: The Dreyfus Connection*, Pentland Press, Bishop Auckland, 1999; Richard Ellmann, *Oscar Wilde*, Knopf, New York, 1988; George R. Whyte, *The Dreyfus Affair: A Chronological History*, Palgrave Mac-Millan, London and New York, 2005

213 *"We are the two greatest martyrs of humanity"*: Richard Ellmann, *Oscar Wilde*, Knopf, New York, 1988

213 *Blacker disclosed this secret information*: J. Robert Maguire, "Oscar Wilde and the Dreyfus Affair," *Victorian Studies*, Vol. 41, No. 1, Autumn 1997

213 *"The innocent always suffer"*: Frank Harris, *Oscar Wilde: His Life and Confessions*, Vol. 2, Bretano's, New York, 1916

213 *"Why should I not make confession to you?"*: Ibid.

213 *The following day, Strong cabled*: Rowland Strong, *The New York Times*, April 10, 1898

215 *nothing remained for him but to blow out his brains*: Rowland Strong, *The Observer*, October 9, 1898

215 *"I am the General Staff's right hand"*: Rowland Strong, Interview for *le Matin*, published in *The Guardian*, October 4, 1898

215 *"Supposing, now, I were to go to a newspaper office"*: Rowland Strong, *The Observer*, October 9, 1898

216 *Asked to comment*: *The New York Times*, September 2, 1898

Chapter Twenty-Two: An Encounter in London

217 *"Find me the means of earning some guineas"*: "Major Esterhazy Self-Revealed," *Pall Mall Gazette*, October 1, 1898

217 *"he has a villainous face"*: Thomas B. Fielders, *The New York Times*, June 11, 1899

218 *"most deeply interesting dramas"*: Rachel Beer, "The Fourth Act of Dreyfus," WW, *ST*, December 4, 1898

218 *"I remember our meetings"*: Letter from Major Esterhazy to Rowland Strong, September 9, 1898, in Marie Charles Ferdinand Walsin-Esterhazy, *Les Dessous de l'Affaire Dreyfus*, Fayard Frères, Paris, 1898

218 *"You thoroughly understood that on such evidence"*: Thomas B. Fielders, *The New York Times*, June 11, 1899

219 *"A lady, still young, dressed with showy elegance"*: Marie Charles Ferdinand Walsin-Esterhazy, *Les Dessous de l'Affaire Dreyfus*, Fayard Frères, Paris, 1898

220 *"Without our asking any questions"*: "The Bordereau," *The Observer*, April 9, 1899

220 *"anti-Semitic craze and army Moloch worship"*: Rachel Beer, "Fair Play in France," WW, *ST*, February 19, 1899

220 *"may be liberated by death"*: Rachel Beer, "The Fate of Dreyfus," WW, *ST*, November 13, 1898

221 *"How come that a ferocious anti-Semite"*: Marie Charles Ferdinand Walsin-Esterhazy, *Les Dessous de l'Affaire Dreyfus*, Fayard Frères, Paris, 1898

222 *"it was no longer his intention"*: "More on the Dreyfus Case," *The Observer*, October 9, 1898

223 *A small army of journalists*: "Esterhazy Found," *The Daily News*, September 19, 22, and 26, 1898; *Pall Mall Gazette*, September 19 and 20, 1898

224 *"highly imaginative"*: Letter in French from Esterhazy to Mrs. Beer, September 19, 1898, Henry Leyret, *Lettres d'un Coupable*, P.-V. Stock, Paris, 1898

225 *Speaking with some signs of emotion*: "Mrs. Beer Explains the Situation," *Westminster Gazette*, September 26, 1898

226 *Esterhazy issued a writ against* The Observer: *ST*, December 18, 1898; *The Times*, September 27 and October 21, 1898; *The Observer*, October 23 and December 18, 1898; *The Jewish Chronicle*, October 28, 1898; *Westminster Gazette*, September 20, 1898; *The Daily Telegraph*, September 21, 1898

226 *a legitimate war of defense*: "Esterhazy in Holland, An Interview," *The Daily News*, January 7, 1899

228 *"It's about time to keep your promise"*: Telegram in French from Mrs. Beer to Esterhazy in Rotterdam, January 9, 1899, Marie Charles Ferdinand Walsin-Esterhazy, *Les Dessous de l'Affaire Dreyfus*, Fayard Frères, Paris, 1898

228 *"even more trashy and unconvincing"*: *The Observer*, January 15, 1899; *the surviving correspondence from the affair*: Bibliothèque Nationale, Paris, NAF 16447, ff 199–218

229 *open letter in a Brussels newspaper*: Reprint in *The Times*, February 27, 1899

229 *negotiating with* The Daily Chronicle: *Daily Chronicle*, March 4 and 6, 1899

229 *"His pockets are full of money"*: Rowland Strong, *The New York Times*, March 19, 1899

230 *his murderous-looking knife*: *Manchester Times*, September 15, 1899

230 *"She is Jewish, daughter of the Sassoons"*: Letter in French from Ernest A. Vizetelly to Émile Zola, February 15, 1899, in Ernest Alfred Vizetelly, *Mon Cher Maître: Lettres d' Ernest Vizetelly à Émile Zola*, Yannick Portebois and Dorothy E. Speirs (eds.), Les Presses de l'Université de Montréal, Montréal, 2002

230 *"Whoever may call on you"*: Letter from Émile Zola to Ernest A. Vizetelly, February 16, 1899, in Ernest Alfred Vizetelly, *Émile Zola, Novelist and Reformer*, John Lane, London, 1904

230 *"Oui, c'est moi qui fait le bordereau"*: "Esterhazy's Repeated Confession," *The Observer*, June 4, 1899

231 *"I have always felt confident"*: Deposition of Rowland Strong, in P.-V. Stock, *La Revision du Process Dreyfus*, Paris, 1899

231 *"a dramatic triumph of poetic justice"*: Rachel Beer, "Justice at Last," WW, *ST*, June 4, 1899

231 *"the jingle of British handcuffs"*: Rowland Strong, *The New York Times*, August 6, 1899

231 *"bowed its neck to the Army fetish"*: Rachel Beer, "The Verdict—and After," WW, *ST*, September 10, 1899

232 *"The last time I saw him"*: Henry Norman, *The New York Times*, March 12, 1909; *The New York Times*, August 17, 1923

233 *"a Jewish Autonomous State in Syria"*: "The Projected Jewish State," *The Observer*, June 28, 1896; "The Proposed Jewish State and Armenia" (a letter to the Editor), *The Observer*, July 5, 1896; Benjamin Jaffe, *The British Press and Zionism in Herzl's Time (1894–1904)*; Josef Frenkel, *Lucian Wolf and Theodore Herzl*, in *Transactions*, published by the Jewish Historical Society of England, vol. 20, 1964

233 *"that the Jews in England are not so anti-Christian"*: "Maccabeans Unmasked," "In the Witness Box," *ST*, July 5, 1896

233 *"They seemed to be representative"*: "The Zionist Congress in London," *ST*, August 12, 1900

233 *"but how many Jews that are doing well"*: Rachel Beer, "Zionists in Conference," WW, *ST*, August 19, 1900

Chapter Twenty-Three: Hoisting the Flag at Pretoria

235 *About the Boer War*: Kenneth O. Morgan, "The Boer War and the Media, 1899–1902," *Twentieth Century British History*, Vol. 13, No. 1, 2002; Mark Hampton, *Visions of the Press in Britain, 1850–1950*, University of Illinois Press, Champaign, 2005; Denis Judd and Keith Surridge, *The Boer War*, John Murray, London, 2002

235 The Observer *had warned*: "A Question of Imperial Policy," *The Observer*, April 12, 1896

235 *"the country must wake up"*: Rachel Beer, "A Score for *The Observer*," WW, *ST*, April 19, 1896

235 *"imperil their position with the black races"*: Rachel Beer, "The South African Outlook," WW, *ST*, August 13, 1899

235 *Her advice was to maintain steady pressure*: Rachel Beer, "Peace or War in South Africa," WW, *ST*, July 9, 1899; Rachel Beer, "A Serious Situation," WW, *ST*, July 16, 1899; "Waiting for the Verdict," WW, *ST*, September 17, 1899; Rachel Beer, "Another Week's Grace," WW, *ST*, September 24, 1899; "The Fading Chances of Peace," WW, *ST*, October 1, 1899

236 *"Jingo claptrap"*: Rachel Beer, "The Possibilities of Peace," WW, *ST*, October 8, 1899; "The Transvaal—Is It Really War?," *The Observer*, October 1, 1899

236 *"We ought to shame both our enemies"*: Rachel Beer, "The Plunge into War," WW, *ST*, October 15, 1899; Rachel Beer, "War in Earnest," WW, *ST*, October 22, 1899

237 *Internet-like service:* The Observer, August 5, 1900
237 *"the profit of the mine-owners":* Rachel Beer, "Imperial Africa," WW, ST, May 7, 1899
238 *no longer existed a free press in England:* John Atkinson Hobson, The Psychology of Jingoism, Richards, London, 1901
238 *"their country's left cheek":* Rachel Beer, "The Friends of Peace," WW, ST, January 14, 1900
238 *"We have not yet caught our bear":* Rachel Beer, "War Oratory of the Past Week," WW, ST, December 3, 1899
238 *"if they are not handled properly?":* Rachel Beer, "Some Reserves, and a Moral," WW, ST, December 17, 1899
238 *She opposed compulsory conscription:* Rachel Beer, "No Conscription!," WW, ST, February 25, 1900
239 *"Boer Amazons":* Rachel Beer, "Some Undesirable Developments of the War," WW, ST, May 13, 1900
239 *a symptom of British decline:* James Louis Garvin, "The Maintenance of the Empire," in The Empire and the Century; A Series of Essays on Imperial Problems and Possibilities, Charles Sidney Goldmann (ed.), John Murray, 1905
239 *New Imperialism born of the war:* Rachel Beer, "Peace and the Closing Century," WW, ST, December 23, 1900
239 *"a record of that dispassionate":* The Observer, June 23, 1901
239 *"have no idea as to how a child":* "The Concentration Camps Blue Book," The Observer, December 15, 1901
240 *"not to treat the men to situations in public-houses":* Rachel Beer, "An Appeal and a Testimony," WW, ST, November 4, 1900
240 *lack of female society:* Rachel Beer, "Female Colonialism in South Africa," WW, ST, March 17, 1901; Rachel Beer, "Women for South Africa," WW, ST, April 7, 1901

Chapter Twenty-Four: And the Tears in Her Eyes Grew Large on Their Ledge

241 *Gus Wingrove, the apprentice printer boy:* Harold Hobson, Phillip Knightly and Leonard Russell, The Pearl of Days: An Intimate Memoir of the Sunday Times, 1822–1972, Hamish Hamilton, London, 1972
242 *Mr. Hermann Schmidt:* The Observer, December 10, 1899; The Times, December 2 and 5, 1899
242 *holiday fund for female journalists:* "Eighth Annual Report of the Society of Women Journalists, 1901–1902"
242 *Folk Song Society: Journal of the English Folk Dance and Song Society,* Vol. 5, No. 3, Cecil Sharp House, December 1948; Edward Elgar, Letters to Nimrod: Edward Elgar to August Jaeger 1897–1908, Percy M. Young (ed.), Dobson, London, 1965; Christopher Bearman, The English Folk Music Movement 1898–1914 (Ph.D. Thesis), University of Hull,

2001; "In the Witness Box: Mrs. Kate Lee on the Collecting of Folk Songs," *ST*, January 29, 1899; "The Folk Song Society, First General Meeting," *ST*, February 5, 1899; "A Folk-Song Function," *The Musical Times*, March 1, 1899

243   *General information on mysticism and the SPR: Proceedings of the Society for Psychical Research*, Vol. 1, London, Trubner, 1883; Renee Haynes, *Society for Psychical Research, 1882–1982, A History*, Macdonald, London, 1982; John J. Cerullo, *The Secularization of the Soul: Psychical Research in Modern Britain*, Institute for the Study of Human Issues, Philadelphia, 1982; Roger Luckhurst, "Knowledge, Belief and the Supernatural at the Imperial Margin," in Nicola Bown, Carolyn Burdett and Pamela Thurschwell (eds.), *The Victorian Supernatural*, Cambridge University Press, Cambridge, 2004; Alex Owen, *The Darkened Room: Women, Power and Spiritualism in Late Nineteenth Century England*, Virago, London, 1989

243   *an interview with M. Jules Bois:* "In the Witness Box," *ST*, June 6, 1897

244   *Royal Amateur Art Society:* Catalogue of the Art Loan Collection: at 7, Chesterfield Gardens, By Kind Permission of Mr. and Mrs. Beer—March 20–23, 1900, and March 26–29, 1901; *ST*, March 11 and 18, 1900

244   *"two poor little figures":* T. P. O'Connor, "Men, Women and Memories," *ST*, May 15, 1927

245   *spread to his bones and joints:* Michel Martini, *Tuberculosis of the Bones and Joints*, Springer Verlag, Berlin, 1988

245   *placed in a hot-air balloon:* Rachel Beer, "Consumptive Aeronauts," WW, *ST*, July 28, 1901

246   *"She must have loved him very much":* SS, *The Old Century and Seven More Years*, Faber & Faber, London, 1938

246   *the leading killer, after heart disease:* Anne Hardy, *The Epidemic Streets*, Claringdon Press, Oxford, 1993

246   *"sallow and untidy and almost eccentric":* SS, *The Old Century and Seven More Years*, Faber & Faber, London, 1938

247   *"forget all about Mr. Beer's illness":* Ibid.

247   *"a great gallery of shops":* Rachel Beer, "Are Great Cities Doomed?," WW, *ST*, July 28, 1901

247   *introducing new attractions: ST*, January 13, 1901

248   *She invited professional and amateur photographers:* Rachel Beer, "*Sunday Times*' Gregorian Chant," WW, *ST*, July 28, 1901

248   *where they failed to cure:* Rachel Beer, "Possible Remedies," WW, *ST*, October 20, 1901

249   *the ability to recite poetry:* Rachel Beer, "Literature and Children," WW, *ST*, December 8, 1901

249   *"Wet was her hair, and her eyes were wet":* Rachel Beer, "The Garland: a Ballad of the Standard Rose," WW, *ST*, July 28, 1901

250   *"He must ever gaze onwards to guide":* Rachel Beer, "Orpheus and Eurydice," WW, *ST*, October 20, 1901

250 *"Love has come so long a way"*: Rachel Beer, "A Love Dream," WW, *ST,* September 22, 1901

250 *"Winter Away"*: Rachel Beer, WW, *ST,* August 18, 1901

250 *"her world the Transvaal valley"*: Rachel Beer, "Left in Charge," WW, *ST,* July 28, 1901

251 *The Labyrinths of the World:* "A Book in Brief," *ST,* August 25 and September 1, 1901; "Book Received" (a poem), WW, *ST,* August 11, 1901

251 *"God saw His own created ones"*: Rachel Beer, WW, *ST,* September 1, 1901

252 *"But some unresting souls toss"*: Rachel Beer, "The Unfeeling Hours," WW, *ST,* September 29, 1901

252 *"for, as Dante suggests"*: Rachel Beer, "Notes for the Humble-Minded," WW, *ST,* November 17, 1901

253 *"At the end he was his old self again"*: SS, *The Old Century and Seven More Years,* Faber & Faber, London, 1938

254 *Hamo suggested tossing a coin:* Ibid.

Chapter Twenty-Five: Breakdown

255 *announcement of the death of Mr. F. A. Beer:* The Observer, January 5, 1902

255 *sanatorium for consumptives:* Rachel Beer, "The Crusade Against Consumption," WW, *ST,* January 5, 1902

255 *"France and Russia have 300 torpedo boats"*: Rachel Beer, "Naval Needs," WW, *ST,* January 12, 1902

256 *the manager of* The Observer *called at Rachel's residence:* The Times, December 2, 1902

257 *Queen Victoria's nervous breakdown:* Elizabeth Longford, *Victoria R.I.,* Weidenfeld & Nicolson, London, 1964; Peter C. Jupp and Clare Gittings (eds.), *Death in England,* Manchester University Press, Manchester, 1999

258 *A study of London widows:* Colin Murray Parkes, *Bereavement: Studies of Grief in Adult Life,* Penguin, Hammondsworth, 1975

258 *"these nerves are a form of madness"*: Patricia Jalland, *Death in the Victorian Family,* Oxford University Press, New York and Oxford, 1996

258 *On madness, women and the Victorians:* Elaine Showalter, *The Female Malady,* Virago, London, 1987; Charlotte Mackenzie, *Psychiatry for the Rich,* Routledge, London, 1992; Roy Porter, Helen Nicholson and Bridget Bennett (eds.), *Women, Madness and Spiritualism,* Vol. 1, Routledge, London and New York, 2003; Phil Fennell, *Treatment without Consent,* Routledge, London, 1996; Peter McCandless, "Liberty and Lunacy: The Victorians and Wrongful Confinement," in Andrew Scull, *Madhouses, Mad Doctors and Madmen,* University of Pennsylvania Press, Philadelphia, 1981; Elaine Showalter, "Victorian Women and Insanity," in Andrew Scull, *Madhouses, Mad Doctors and Madmen*

259 *certificates of lunacy:* Charles Mercier, *A Textbook of Insanity,* Swan Sonnenschein, London, 1902; Gerald Mills, A. H. Ronald and W. Poyser, *Management and Administration of Estate in Lunacy,* Butterworth & Co., 1927

259 *Dr. Savage:* George Henry Savage, *The Increase of Insanity,* Cassell & Co., London, 1907; George Henry Savage, *Insanity and Allied Neuroses,* Cassell & Co., London, 1884; "Lunacy and Law" (Dr. Savage's letter to the Editor of *The Times*), November 24, 1902

259 *Virginia Woolf and Dr. Savage:* Roy Porter, "Reading Is Bad for Your Health: European Notions through the Nineteenth Century," *History Today,* March 1, 1998; Joanne Trautmann Banks, "Mrs. Woolf in Harley Street," *The Lancet,* Vol. 35, April 11, 1998; Jeffrey Berman, *Surviving Literary Suicide,* University of Massachusetts Press, Amherst, 1999; Virginia Woolf, *The Flight of the Mind,* Nigel Nicolson (ed.), Letters, Vol. 1, Hogarth Press, London, 1975; Virginia Woolf, *Mrs. Dalloway,* Hogarth Press, London, 1925; Roger Poole, *The Unknown Virginia Woolf,* Cambridge University Press, Cambridge, 1978; Susan Bennett Smith, "Reinventing Grief-work: Virginia Woolf's Feminist Representations of Mourning in *Mrs. Dalloway* and *To the Lighthouse*" in *Twentieth Century Literature* 41 (1995), Hofstra University Press, Hempstead, New York; Stephen Trombley, *All That Summer She Was Mad: Virginia Woolf and Her Doctors,* Junction Books, London, 1981

260 *The principles of the rest cure:* Joyce W. Warren, *Women, Money and the Law,* University of Iowa Press, Iowa City, 2005; Charlotte Perkins Gilman, "The Yellow Wallpaper," in *The New England Magazine,* J. N. McClinctock and Company, Boston, 1892; Patricia Vertinsky, "Feminist Charlotte Perkins Gilman's Pursuit of Health and Physical Fitness as a Strategy for Emancipation," *Journal of Sports History,* Vol. 18, No. 1, March 2001

261 *"lethal chamber for the unfit":* Rachel Beer, "The Disposal of the Unfit," WW, *ST,* February 2, 1896

262 *Dr. Savage's policy was to notify the person:* "Dr. Savage's Speech at the General Meeting of the Medico-Psychological Association of Great Britain," *The Times,* November 21, 1902

263 *"decline into mental derangement":* Letter from Dr. John Shaw Dunn to SS, corrections to the manuscript of *The Weald of Youth,* July 21, 1940, Columbia

263 *"She had been incurably afflicted by an illness":* SS, *Notes for Early Recollections,* Hart-Davies Papers, Cambridge

264 *"raving wildly in her rich voiced rapid undertones":* Letter from Dr. John Shaw Dunn to SS, corrections to the manuscript of *The Weald of Youth,* July 21, 1940, Columbia

264 *Rachel Beer's certification:* J 121/5374 & C 211/66, National Archives, Kew

265 *"I thought she had been editing* The Observer*":* *The Times,* August 11,

1903; *The Daily Chronicle*, August 11, 1903; *The Daily News*, August 11, 1903; *The Daily Telegraph*, August 11, 1903

266   *luxurious mansion on Mount Ephraim*: Lady Hope, *English Homes and Villas (Kent and Sussex)*, J. Salmon, Sevenoaks, 1909; *St. John Cokbrans's Guide and Visitors Handbook to Tunbridge Wells and Neighbourhood*, 1884; Charles Hilbert Strange, "The History of Tunbridge Wells," *Royal Tunbridge Wells—Past and Present—July 1946* on www.tunbridgewellscitizens.org.uk; Alan Savidge, *Royal Tunbridge Wells: A History of a Spa Town*, Revised edition, Oast Books, Tunbridge Wells, 1995; Email exchange with Chris Jones (Secretary of the Local History of the Royal Tunbridge Wells Civic Society), July 2007–June 2009; Interview with Chris Jones, September 2008; Interview with Geoffrey Copus, September 2008

267   *"some unpoetical profession"*: SS, *The Weald of Youth* (manuscript), Columbia

267   *Hamo predicted their aunt would live to be a hundred*: Ibid.

268   *offered to Ralph David Blumenfeld*: Ralph David Blumenfeld, *The Press in My Time*, Rich & Cowan, London, 1932

268   *"execrably written by his own hand"*: Frank Rutter, *Since I Was Twenty-Five*, Constable and Co., London, 1927

269   *"an authority in the life of the nation"*: Alfred M. Gollin, *The Observer and J. L. Garvin, 1908–1914*, Oxford University Press, London, 1960

269   *"lay derelict in the Fleet ditch"*: Lord Northcliffe, *Daily Mail*, January 29, 1912; J. Lee Thompson, *Northcliffe: Press Baron in Politics 1922–1965*, John Murray, London, 2000

Chapter Twenty-Six: After the Storm

271   *Rachel became a major benefactor*: The Courier, November 12, 1915; July 14, 1916; April 13, 1917; February 1 and May 3, December 13, 1918; February 7, July 11, and September 5, 1919; December 9, 1921

272   *Unable to maintain Ashley Park*: Michael Dane, *The Sassoons of Ashley Park*, M. Dane, Walton on Thames, 1999

272   *sell her precious Millais*: Peter Stansky, *Sassoon: The Worlds of Philip and Sybil*, Yale University Press, New Haven, 2003

273   *a goldfish in the fountain*: SS, *Diaries, 1920–1922*, entry of September 5, 1922, Rupert Hart-Davis (ed.), Faber & Faber, London, 1981

273   *"Poor Rachel hasn't long to live"*: SS, *Diaries, 1923–1925*, entry of May 15, 1924, Rupert Hart-Davis (ed.), Faber & Faber, London, 1985

273   *"When Auntie Rachel hops the twig"*: Letter from SS to Robert Graves, December 12 (n.d.), Collection number 68, Box 28, Folder 9, Robert Graves Papers, Special Collections/Morris Library, Southern Illinois University

274   *Ben Greet and his players*: The Courier, June 9 and 23, 1922; June 22, 1923; July 4, 1924; January 9, 1925; July 2, 1926

274   *buried in unconsecrated ground*: The Courier, May 6, 1927; *The Tun-*

bridge Wells Advertiser, May 6, 1927; Email exchange with Michael Illston, Kent and Sussex Crematorium, July 2007

275 *to excuse his absence:* SS, *Notes for Early Recollections*, Cambridge

275 *The auctioning of Rachel Beer's property:* The Courier, July 15, 22, and 29, 1927

276 *"which I shall receive from the Beer estate":* Letter from SS to Glen Byam Shaw, October 13, 1927, Siegfried Sassoon Papers, Cambridge

Afterword

278 *"the diamond king":* Olivia Manning, in Ian Norrie (ed.), *The Hearthside Book of Hampstead and Highgate*, High Hill Books, 1962

278 *"a lifetime's accumulation of guano":* Alan Brien, "Intimations of Mortality," *The Spectator*, May 6, 1966

278 *"the mosaic murals":* John Updike, "Cemeteries," in *Transatlantic Review*, 32, London, Summer 1969

279 *"You ass, Julius":* Ibid.

279 *"In the diamondman's invisible bones":* Edwin Morgan, "London January 1973," *Selected Poems*, Carcanet, Manchester, 1985

279 *"in the public places of hell":* Alan Jenkins, "Pornography," *A Short History of Snakes*, Grove Press, New York, 2001

280 *Marx was put to rest:* Yvonne Karp, *Eleanor Marx*, Vol. 1, Lawrence and Wishart, London, 1972; John Mahon, *Harry Pollitt*, Lawrence and Wishart, London, 1976

280 *In 1993 scaffolding was erected:* Keith Taylor, "Conservation Report on the Julius Beer Mausoleum," Taylor, Pearce Restoration Services Ltd., September 1991; "Specifications of Work for the Conservation of the Julius Beer Mausoleum," Caroe and Partners Architects, February 1993

Sources

Archives

Leo Baeck Institute, Jerusalem
Bibliothèque Nationale de France, Paris
John Hay Library, Brown University, Providence, Rhode Island
Department of Manuscripts and University Archives, University Library, Cambridge
Christie's Archive, London
Rare Book and Manuscript Library, Columbia University Libraries, New York
The Museum of the Confederacy, Richmond, Virginia
Conway Library, Courtauld Institute, London
English Folk Dance and Song Society
English Heritage, City, Westminster and North London Team
National Monuments Record, English Heritage, Swindon
Germania Judaica, Köln
Newsroom, Guardian and Observer Archive
Guildhall Library, Archives and Manuscripts, London
Loeb Music Library, Harvard University
Highgate Cemetery Archives
Institut für Stadtgeschichte, Frankfurt
Archives of the Institution of Engineering and Technology, London
The Jewish Museum, London
Jüdische Museum, Frankfurt
Judaica Abteilung, Universitätsbibliothek, Frankfurt
Kent and Sussex Crematorium
London Metropolitan Archives
The National Archives, Kew
National Art Library at the Victoria and Albert Museum, London

National Portrait Gallery, Heinz Archive and Library, London
Bulwer of Heydon family papers, Norfolk Record Office, Norwich
Parliamentary Archives, House of Parliament, London
Principal Registry of the Family Division, London
Royal Academy Library, London
Special Collection Research Center, Southern Illinois University, Carbondale, USA
The Spanish-Portuguese Community Archive, London
Research Centre, Tate Gallery
The Times and the Sunday Times archives
Tunbridge Wells Museum and Art Gallery
City of Westminster Archives Centre, London

Books

Agarwala, Prakash Narain, *The History of Indian Business,* Vikas Publishing House, Delhi, 1985

Ahvenainen, Jorma, *The Far Eastern Telegraphs,* Suomalainen Tiedeakatemia, Helsinki, 1981

Ainger, Michael, *Gilbert and Sullivan: A Dual Biography,* Oxford University Press, New York, 2002

Allfrey, Anthony, *Edward VII and His Jewish Court,* Weidenfeld and Nicolson, London, 1991

Amschewitz, Asher, *Roses for David* (Hebrew), Kelter Press, Warsaw, 1880

Anstey, Joanna, and John Silverlight (eds.), *The Observer Observed,* Barrie & Jenkins, London, 1991

Aris, Stephen, *The Jews in Business,* Jonathan Cape, London, 1970

Arnold, Catharine, *Necropolis: London and Its Dead,* Simon and Schuster, London, 2007

Aronsfeld, C. C., "German Jews in Victorian England," in *Leo Baeck Yearbook,* Secker & Warburg, London, 1962

Aspinall, Arthur, *Politics and the Press,* Harvester Press, Birmingham, 1973

Baglehole, K. C., *A Century of Service—Cable and Wireless Ltd.,* Bournehall Press, Welwyn Garden City, Herts, 1969

Bainbridge, Cyril, *One Hundred Years of Journalism,* Macmillan, London, 1984

Ball, Douglas B., *Financial Failure and Confederate Defeat,* University of Illinois Press, Urbana, 1991

Barker, Felix, and John Gay, *Highgate Cemetery, Victorian Valhalla,* John Murray, London, 1984

Bates, Barbara, *Bargaining for Life,* University of Pennsylvania Press, Philadelphia, 1992

Bearman, Christopher, Ph.D. Thesis: The English Folk Music Movement 1898–1914, University of Hull, 2001

Beauchamp, Ken, *History of Telegraphy,* Institute of Electrical Engineers, London, 2001

Beckett, Arthur, *Recollections of a Humorist,* Pitman and Sons, London, 1907

Begley, Louis, *Why the Dreyfus Affair Matters,* Yale University Press, New Haven, 2009

Bein, Alex, *The Jewish Question: Biography of a World Problem,* Herzl Press, New York, 1990

Ben-Yaacob, Abraham, *Chapters in the History of Babylonian Jewry—The Sassoon Family from Baghdad* (Hebrew), Olam Hasefer Hatorani, Jerusalem, 1989

Ben-Yaacob, Abraham, *The Jews of Babylon, 1038–1960* (Hebrew), Kiryat Sefer, Jerusalem, 1965

Ben-Yaacob, Abraham, *The Jews of Babylon in the Diaspora* (Hebrew), Reuven Mas, Jerusalem, 1985

Berman, Jeffrey, *Surviving Literary Suicide,* University of Massachusetts Press, Amherst, 1999

d'Beth Hillel, Rabbi David, *Unknown Jews in Unknown Lands,* Ktav Publishing House, New York, 1973

Blue, Gregory, "Opium for China—The British Connection," in *Opium Regimes—China, Britain and Japan 1839–1952,* Timothy Brook and Bob Tadashi Wakabayashi (eds.), University of California Press, Berkeley, 2000

Blumenfeld, Ralph David, *The Press in My Time,* Rich & Cowan, London, 1932

Bourke, Eoin, "The Frankfurt Judengasse in Eye-Witnesses Accounts," in *Ghetto Writing: Traditional and Eastern Jewry in German Jewish Literature from Heine to Hilsenrath,* Ann Fuchs and Florian Krobb (eds.), Camden House, New York, 1999

Boyce, George (ed.), *Newspaper History from the Seventeenth Century to the Present Day,* Constable for the Press Group of the Acton Society, London, 1978

Brailsford, Edward, *The Life Story of Charles Tilston Bright,* Archibald Constable and Co., Westminster, 1899

Bredin, Jean Denis, *The Affair: The Case of Alfred Dreyfus,* translated by Jeffrey Mehlman, Braziller, New York, 1986

Brennan, James, *The Reflection of the Dreyfus Affair in the European Press,* Peter Lang, New York, 1998

Bright, Charles, *Submarine Telegraphs,* Crosby Lockwood and Son, London, 1898

Brown, Lucy, *Victorian News and Newspapers,* Clarendon Press, Oxford, 1985

Bryder, Linda, *Below the Magic Mountain,* Clarendon Press, Oxford, 1988

Burstyn, Joan N., *Victorian Education and the Ideal of Womanhood,* Croom Helm, London, 1980

The Cambridge Bibliography of English Literature (vol. 3), F. W. Bateson (ed.), Cambridge University Press, 1966

Case, Lynn Marshall, and Warren F. Spencer, *The United States and France: Civil War Diplomacy,* University of Pennsylvania Press, Philadelphia, 1970

Catalogue of the art loan collection: at 7, Chesterfield Gardens, W. By kind permission of Mr. and Mrs. Beer. 20–23 March 1900 and 26–29 March 1901, Royal Amateur Art Society

Cernea, Ruth Fredman, *Almost Englishmen: Baghdadi Jews in British Burma,* Lexington Books, Lanham, MD, 2007

Cerullo, John J., *The Secularization of the Soul: Psychical Research in Modern Britain,* Institute for the Study of Human Issues, Philadelphia, 1982

Chapman, Guy, *The Dreyfus Case: A Reassessment,* Hart-Davis, London, 1955

Chapman, Stanley D., "Merchants and Bankers," *Second Chance: Two Centuries of German-Speaking Jews in the United Kingdom,* Werner E. Mosse and Julius Carlebach (eds.), Mohr, Tübingen, 1991

Clarke, Bob, *From Grub Street to Fleet Street,* Ashgate, Aldershot, 2004

Coffin, Charles Carlenton, *Four Years in Fighting,* Ticknor and Fields, Boston, 1866

Cooper, Nicholas, *The Opulent Eye,* Whitney Library of Design, New York, 1977

Corrigan, D. Felicitas, *Siegfried Sassoon: Poet's Pilgrimage,* Victor Gollancz, London, 1973

Craig, Neville B., *Recollections of an Ill-Fated Expedition,* Lippincott and Co., Philadelphia and London, 1907

Curl, James Stevens, *The Victorian Celebration of Death,* Sutton Publishing, Thrupp, Stroud, 2000

Dane, Michael, *The Sassoons of Ashley Park,* M. Dane, Walton on Thames, 1999

Davies, Richard, *The English Rothschilds,* Collins, London, 1983

D'Cruze, Shani, *Murder: Social and Historical Approaches to Understanding Murder and Murderers,* Willan Publications, Devon, 2006

Demoor, Marysa, *Their Fair Share: Women, Power and Criticism in the Athenaeum, from Millicent Garrett Fawcett to Katherine Mansfield,* Ashgate, Aldershot, 2000

Dickens, Charles, *The Life and Adventures of Nicholas Nickleby,* Chapman and Hall, London, 1865

Dietz, Alexander, *The Jewish Community of Frankfurt: A Genealogical Study 1349–1849,* Isobel Mordy (ed.), Vanderher, Camelford, 1988

Dong, Stella, *Shanghai,* William Morrow and Co., New York, 2000

Dorgeel, Heinrich, *The German Colony in London* (German), A. Siegle, Leipzig and London, 1881

Dormandy, Thomas, *The White Death: A History of Tuberculosis,* Hambledon Press, London and Rio Grande, Ohio, 1999

Dreyfus, Alfred, *The Dreyfus Case,* Yale University Press, New Haven, 1937

Egremont, Max, *Siegfried Sassoon: A Biography,* Picador, London, 2005

Eighth annual report of the Society of Women Journalists, 1901–2

Elgar, Edward, *Letters to Nimrod: Edward Elgar to August Jaeger 1897–1908,* Percy M. Young (ed.), Dobson, London, 1965

Ellmann, Richard, *Oscar Wilde,* Knopf, New York, 1988

Elmes, James, *Metropolitan Improvements,* London, Jones & Co., 1827

Elon, Amos, *Founder: A Portrait of the First Rothschild and His Time,* Penguin, New York, 1996

Elon, Amos, *The Pity of It All: A Portrait of the German-Jewish Epoch, 1743–1933,* Picador, New York, 2002

Endelman, Todd M., "German-Jewish Settlement in Victorian England," *Second Chance: Two Centuries of German-Speaking Jews in the United Kingdom,* Werner E. Mosse and Julius Carlebach (eds.), Mohr, Tübingen, 1991

Endelman, Todd M., "Leaving the Jewish Fold in Germany," *Leo Baeck Yearbook,* Secker & Warburg, London, 1995

Endelman, Todd M., *The Jews of Britain 1656–2000,* University of California Press, Berkeley, Los Angeles, London, 2002

Endelman, Todd M., *Radical Assimilation in English Jewish History, 1656–1945,* Indiana University Press, Bloomington, 1990

Escott, Thomas Hay Sweet, *Masters of English Journalism: A Study of Personal Forces,* T. F. Unwin, London, 1911

Esterhazy-Walsin, Marie Charles Ferdinand, *Les Dessous de l'Affaire Dreyfus,* Fayard Frères, Paris, 1898

Evans, Eli N., *Judah P. Benjamin,* Free Press, New York, 1988

Evans, E. P., *Animal Symbolism in Ecclesiastical Architecture,* Heinemann, London, 1896

Falk, Bernard, *Bouquets for Fleet Street: Memories and Musings over Fifty Years,* Hutchinson and Co., London, 1951

Falk, Bernard, *Five Years Dead: A Postscript to "He Laughed in Fleet Street,"* Hutchinson & Co., London, 1937

Faulk, Barry J., *Music Hall and Modernity,* Ohio University Press, Athens, Ohio, 2004

Fennell, Phil, *Treatment without Consent,* Routledge, London, 1996

Ferguson, Niall, *The House of Rothschild: Money's Prophets, 1798–1848,* Penguin Books, New York, 1998

Fredman Cernea, Ruth, *Almost Englishmen,* Lexington Books, Lanham, MD, 2007

Freimann, Aron, and Felix Kracauer, *Frankfurt,* Jewish Communities Series, Jewish Publication Society of America, Philadelphia, 1929

Friends of Highgate Cemetery, *In Highgate Cemetery,* Revised edition, Highgate Cemetery Ltd., London, 2005

Galliner, Arthur, "The Philantropin in Frankfurt," *Leo Baeck Yearbook,* Secker & Warburg, London, 1958

Garceau, Édouard, *The Little Doustes,* Frederick Muller, London, 1935

Garvin, James Louis, *The Observer, 1791–1921,* Observer House, London, 1922

Gay, Ruth, *The Jews of Germany: A Historical Portrait,* Yale University Press, New Haven, 1994

Gilman, Charlotte, "The Yellow Wallpaper," in *The New England Magazine*, J. N. McClinctock and Co., Boston, 1892

Gladstone, Mary, *Mary Gladstone (Mrs. Drew), Her Diaries and Letters*, Lucy Masterman (ed.), Methuen, London, 1930

Glover, James, *Jimmy Glover: His Book*, Methuen and Co., London, 1911

Glover, Lady, *Memories of Four Continents*, Seeley, Service and Co., London, 1923

Gollin, Alfred M., *The Observer and J. L. Garvin, 1908–1914*, Oxford University Press, London, 1960

Grant, James, *The Metropolitan Weekly and Provincial Press*, vol. 3, Tinsley Brothers, London, 1872

Gribble, Francis, *Seen in Passing*, Ernst Benn, London, 1929

Griffiths, Dennis, *Fleet Street: Five Hundred Years of the Press*, British Library, London, 2006

Haigh, K. R., *Cableships and Submarine Cables*, Adlard Coles, London, 1968

Hampton, Mark, *Visions of the Press in Britain, 1850–1950*, University of Illinois Press, Champaign, 2005

Hansson, Laura Marholm, *Modern Women*, John Lane, London, 1896

Hardy, Anne, *The Epidemic Streets*, Claringdon Press, Oxford, 1993

Harris, Frank, *Oscar Wilde: His Life and Confessions*, vol. 2, Brentano's, New York, 1916

Harrison, Brian, and Matthew, H. C. G. (eds.), *Oxford Dictionary of National Biography*, Oxford University Press, Oxford, 2004

Haweis, Eliza, *Beautiful Houses*, Sampson Low and Co., London, 1882

Haynes, Renee, *Society for Psychical Research, 1882–1982, A History*, Macdonald, London, 1982

Headrick, Daniel, *The Invisible Weapon*, Oxford University Press, New York, 1991

Healy, Chris, *Confessions of a Journalist*, Chatto & Windus, London, 1904

Hendrick, Burton J., *Statesmen of the Lost Cause*, Literary Guild of America, New York, 1939

Hichens, Mark, *Oscar Wilde's Last Chance: The Dreyfus Connection*, Pentland Press, Bishop Auckland, 1999

Highgate Cemetery, a foreword by Sir John Betjeman, Friends of Highgate Cemetery, London, 1978

Hill, W. Henry, Arthur F. Hill and Alfred E. Hill, *Antonio Stradivari's Life and Work*, William E. Hill and Sons, London, 1902

Hobson, Harold, Phillip Knightly and Leonard Russell, *The Pearl of Days: An Intimate Memoir of the Sunday Times*, Hamish Hamilton, London, 1972

Hobson, John Atkinson, *The Psychology of Jingoism*, Richards, London, 1901

Holcombe, Lee, *Victorian Ladies at Work*, David and Charles, Newton Abbott, 1973

Holtferich, Carl-Ludwig, *Frankfurt as a Commercial Centre*, Verlag C. H. Beck, Munich, 1999

Hope, Lady, *English Homes and Villas (Kent and Sussex)*, J. Salmon, Sevenoaks, 1909

Hubbard, Charles M., *The Burden of Confederate Diplomacy*, University of Tennessee Press, Knoxville, 1998

Hunt, Janin, *The India-China Opium Trade in the Nineteenth Century*, McFarland & Company, Jefferson, NC, 1999

Hunt, Karen, *Equivocal Feminists: The Social Democratic Federation and the Woman Question, 1884–1911*, Cambridge University Press, 1996

Huurdeman, Anton, *The Worldwide History of Telecommunications*, John Wiley, New Jersey, 2003

Hyamson, Albert Montefiore, *The Sephardim of England*, Methuen and Co., London, 1951

Israel, Benjamin J., *The Bene-Israel of India*, Sangam, London, 1984

Jackson, Mason, *The Pictorial Press: Its Origin and Progress*, Hurst and Blackett, London, 1885

Jackson, Stanley, *The Sassoons*, Heinemann, London, 1968

Jacobs, Arthur, *Arthur Sullivan: A Victorian Musician*, Oxford University Press, Oxford, 1984

Jalland, Patricia, *Death in the Victorian Family*, Oxford University Press, New York and Oxford, 1996

Jalland, Patricia, *Women, Marriage and Politics, 1860–1914*, Oxford University Press, New York and Oxford, 1988

Jewish Historical Society of England, *Anglo-Jewish Notabilities, Their Arms and Testamentary Dispositions*, University College, London, 1949

Jones, Chris, *Tunbridge Wells in 1909*, Royal Tunbridge Wells Civic Society, Tunbridge Wells, 2008

Jones, Kennedy, *Fleet Street and Downing Street*, Hutchinson, London, 1919

Journal of the Congress of the Confederate States of America, pub. by United States War Department, vol. 6, 1904–1905

Judd, Denis, and Keith Surridge, *The Boer War*, John Murray, London, 2002

Jupp, Peter C., and Clare Gittings (eds.), *Death in England*, Manchester University Press, Manchester, 1999

Kaplan, Marion (ed.), *Jewish Daily Life in Germany 1618–1945*, Oxford University Press, New York and Oxford, 2005

Karp, Yvonne, *Eleanor Marx*, Vol. 1, Lawrence and Wishart, London, 1972

Keswick, Maggie, and Clara Weatherall, *The Thistle & The Jade: A Celebration of 150 Years of Jardine*, Matheson & Co., Octopus, London, 1982

King, David, *The Complete Works of Robert and James Adam*, Heinemann, Oxford, 1991

Klein, Hermann, *Great Women Singers of My Time*, Routledge, London, 1931

Klein, Hermann, *Musicians and Mummers*, Cassell and Co., London, 1925

Klein, Hermann, *Thirty Years of Musical Life in London 1870–1900*, William Heinemann, London, 1903

Knight, Charles, *Knight's Cyclopaedia of London,* Charles Knight, London, 1851

Knopf, S. Adolphus, *Tuberculosis as a Disease of the Masses and How to Combat It,* The Survey, New York, 1911

Korn, Bertram, *American Jewry and the Civil War,* Jewish Publication Society of America, Philadelphia, 1951

Koss, Stephen, *The Rise and Fall of the Political Press in Britain,* Vol. 1: *The Nineteenth Century,* Hamish Hamilton, London, 1981

Koven, Seth, *Slumming,* Princeton University Press, Princeton, 2004

Laws and Joint Resolutions of the last session of the Confederate Congress (November 7, 1864–March 18, 1865), NY AMS Press, 1965

Lentin, Sifra Samuel, "The Jewish Presence in Bombay," in *India's Jewish Heritage,* Marg Publications, Mumbai, 2002

Lester, Richard, *Confederate Finance and Purchasing in Great Britain,* University Press of Virginia, Charlottesville, 1975

Lewis, Jane, *Women in England, 1870–1950,* Wheatsheaf, Brighton, 1984

Leyendecker, L. E., *Pullman Car Prince,* University Press of Colorado, Niwot, CO, 1992

Leyret, Henry, *Lettres d'un Coupable,* P.-V. Stock, Paris, 1898

Liberles, Robert, "Introduction: The World of Dietz Stammbuch," in *The Jewish Community of Frankfurt: A Genealogical Study 1349–1849,* Alexander Dietz, Isobel Mordy (ed.), Vanderher, Camelford, 1988

Liberles, Robert, "The Jews of Frankfurt 1750–1870," in *A Tale of Two Cities,* Vivian B. Mann (ed.), The Jewish Museum, New York, 1982

Lindsay, Hugh Hamilton, *Report of Proceedings on a Voyage to China,* B. Fellowes, London, 1834

Linton, Elizabeth Lynn, *Sowing the Wind,* New edition, Chatto & Windus, London, 1890

Lipman, Vivian D., "The Anglo-Jewish Community in Victorian Society," in *Studies in the Cultural Life of the Jews of England,* Dov Noy and Issachar Ben-Ami (eds.), Magnes Press, Jerusalem, 1975

Lipman, Vivian D., *A History of Jews in Britain since 1858,* Leicester University Press, Leicester, 1990

Longford, Elizabeth, *Victoria R.I.,* Weidenfeld & Nicolson, London, 1964

Lonn, Ella, *Foreigners in the Confederacy,* University of North Carolina Press, Chapel Hill, 1940

Low, Frances S., *Press Work for Women,* Upcott Gill, London, 1904

Lowenstein, Steven M., "The German Jewish Family," in *Leo Baeck Yearbook,* Secker & Warburg, London, 2006

Luckhurst, Roger, "Knowledge, Belief and the Supernatural at the Imperial Margin," in *The Victorian Supernatural,* Nicola Bown, Carolyn Burdett and Pamela Thurschwell (eds.), Cambridge University Press, Cambridge, 2004

Lucy, Henry, *Sixty Years in the Wilderness,* Smith, Elder, London, 1909

Mackenzie, Charlotte, *Psychiatry for the Rich,* Routledge, London, 1992

Mahon, John, *Harry Pollitt,* Lawrence and Wishart, London, 1976

Maisel, Myriam, *My daughter Rachel, my son Frederick,* unpublished manuscript

Maitland, Frederic William, *The Life and Letters of Leslie Stephen,* Duckworth, London, 1906

Mallach, Alan, *Pietro Mascagni and His Operas,* Northeastern University Press, Boston, 2002

Manning, Elfrida, *Marble and Bronze,* Treford Books, London, 1982

Martini, Michel, *Tuberculosis of the Bones and Joints,* Springer Verlag, Berlin, 1988

Marx, Karl, *Letters to Dr. Kugelmann,* Martin Lawrence, London, 1934

Mayer, Eugen, *The Jews of Frankfurt,* Jewish National and University Library, Jerusalem, 1965

McCandless, Peter, "Liberty and Lunacy: the Victorians and Wrongful Confinement," in *Madhouses, Mad Doctors and Madmen,* Andrew Scull (ed.), University of Pennsylvania Press, Philadelphia, 1981

McEathron, Scott, *Thomas Hardy's Tess of the d'Urbervilles,* Routledge, London and New York, 2005

Meller, Hugh, *London Cemeteries,* Scolar, Aldershot, 1994

Mercier, Charles, *A Textbook of Insanity,* Swan Sonnenschein, London, 1902

Merli, Frank J., *Great Britain and the Confederate Navy,* Indiana University Press, Bloomington, 1970

Meyer, Maisie J., *From the River of Babylon to the Whangpoo,* University Press of America, Lanham, MD, 2003

Meyer, Maisie J., "Spanning Oceans: Solid Links between Baghdadi Jews in India and China," in *Jewish and Israeli Studies Series,* Center of Jewish Studies Shanghai (CJSS), Shanghai, 2007

Meyer, Michael A., and Michael Brenner (eds.), *German-Jewish History in Modern Times,* Columbia University Press, New York, 2000

Miliband, Marion (ed.), *The Observer of the Nineteenth Century, 1791–1901,* Longmans, London, 1966

Millais, John Guille, *The Life and Letters of Sir John Everett Millais,* Methuen and Co., London, 1899

Mills, Gerald, A. H. Ronald and W. Poyser, *Management and Administration of Estate in Lunacy,* Butterworth & Co., London, 1927

Mitford, Algernon (Baron Redesdale), *Mitford's Japan,* Athlone, London, 1985

Mobley, Henry M., "English Reaction to the Dreyfus Affair," Ph.D. thesis, Middle Tennessee State University, Ann Arbor, MI, 1993

Moeyes, Paul, *Siegfried Sassoon: Scorched Glory,* Macmillan Press, London, 1997

Morison, Stanley, *The English Newspaper,* Cambridge University Press, Cambridge, 1932

Morris, Caspar, *An Essay on the Pathology and Therapeutics of Scarlet Fever,* Lindsay and Blakingston, Philadelphia, 1858

Murray Parkes, Colin, *Bereavement: Studies of Grief in Adult Life,* Penguin, Hammondsworth, 1975

Naman, Anne Aresty, *The Jew in the Victorian Novel,* AMS Press Inc., New York, 1980

Newspaper Press Directory and Advertisers Guide, C. Mitchell, London, volumes of 1870, 1878, 1902

O'Connor, T. P. (ed.), *In the Days of My Youth,* Pearson, London, 1901

Onslow, Barbara, *Women of the Press in the Nineteenth Century,* Macmillan, Basingstoke, 2000

Ousley, Frank Lawrence, *King Cotton Diplomacy,* University of Chicago Press, Chicago, 1966

Owen, Alex, *The Darkened Room: Women, Power and Spiritualism in Late Nineteenth Century England,* Virago, London, 1989

Parliamentary debates, Hansard, House of Commons official report, vol. 225, 1875

Paucker, Pauline, "The Image of the German Jew in English Fiction," in *Second Chance: Two Centuries of German-Speaking Jews in the United Kingdom,* Werner E. Mosse and Julius Carlebach (eds.), Mohr, Tübingen, 1991

Pearson, Hesketh, *Gilbert: His Life and Strife,* Harper & Brothers, New York, 1957

Petuchowsky, Jakob J., "Frankfurt Jewry: A Model of Transition to Modernity," in *Leo Baeck Yearbook,* Secker & Warburg, London, 1984

Pevsner, Nikolaus, *The Buildings of England,* Penguin Books, Harmondsworth, 1951

Philips, Francis Charles, *My Varied Life,* Eveleigh Nash, London, 1914

Poliakov, Leon, *The History of Anti-Semitism,* Vanguard Press, New York, 1965

Pollock, John, *Time's Chariot,* J. Murray, London, 1950

Poole, Roger, *The Unknown Virginia Woolf,* Cambridge University Press, Cambridge, 1978

Porter, Roy, Helen Nicholson and Bridget Bennett (eds.), *Women, Madness and Spiritualism,* Vol. 1, Routledge, London and New York, 2003

Potter, Beatrice, *The Letters of Sidney and Beatrice Webb,* Norman MacKenzie (ed.), Cambridge University Press, Cambridge, 1978

Proceedings of the Society for Psychical Research, Vol. 1, Trubner, London, 1883

Ragussis, Michael, *Figures of Conversion,* Duke University Press, Durham, NC, 1995

Reinman, Shlomo, *Solomon's Travels* (Hebrew), George Bragg, Vienna, 1884

Rejwan, Nissim, *The Jews of Iraq,* Weidenfeld and Nicolson, London, 1985

Roberts, John Stuart, *Siegfried Sassoon,* Richard Cohen Books, London, 1999

Roland, Joan G., *Jews in British India: Identity in a Colonial Era,* Brandeis University, Hanover, NH, 1989

Roth, Cecil, *The Sassoon Dynasty,* Robert Hale Ltd., London, 1941

Russell, Edward, *That Reminds Me,* Fisher Unwin, London, 1899

Rutter, Frank, *Since I Was Twenty-Five,* Constable and Co., London, 1927

Sapir, Jacob, *Even Sapir Book* (Hebrew), Sifriyat Mekorot, Jerusalem, 1970

Sassoon, David Solomon, *A History of the Jews in Baghdad,* S. D. Sassoon, Letchworth, 1949

Sassoon, Siegfried, *Diaries, 1920–1922,* Rupert Hart-Davis (ed.), Faber & Faber, London, 1981

Sassoon, Siegfried, *Diaries, 1923–1925,* Rupert Hart-Davis (ed.), Faber & Faber, London, 1985

Sassoon, Siegfried, *Letters to Max Beerbohm,* Rupert Hart-Davis (ed.), Faber & Faber, London, 1986

Sassoon, Siegfried, *The Old Century and Seven More Years,* Faber & Faber, London, 1938

Sassoon, Siegfried, *The Old Huntsman and Other Poems,* Heinemann, London, 1917

Sassoon, Siegfried, *The Weald of Youth,* Faber & Faber, London, 1942

Saul, Samir, *La France et L'Egypte,* Comité Pour L'Histoire Economique et Financier de la France, Paris, 1997

Savage, George Henry, *The Increase of Insanity,* Cassell & Co., London, 1907

Savage, George Henry, *Insanity and Allied Neuroses,* Cassell & Co., London, 1884

Savidge, Alan, *Royal Tunbridge Wells: A History of a Spa Town,* Revised edition, Oast Books, Tunbridge Wells, 1995

Schlesinger, Max, *Saunterings in and about London,* Nathaniel Cooke, London, 1853

Scholes, Percy A., *The Mirror of Music 1884–1944,* Oxford University Press, London, 1947

Schwab, John Christopher, *The Confederate States of America,* Burt Franklin, New York, 1901

Scott, Clement, *The Drama of Yesterday and Today,* Vol. 1, Macmillan, London, 1899

Scott, Clement, *In the Days of My Youth,* T. P. O'Connor (ed.), Pearson, London 1901

Scull, Andrew, *Madhouses, Mad Doctors and Madmen,* University of Pennsylvania Press, Philadelphia, 1981

Sells' Directory of the World Press, H. Sell, London, 1897

Shaw, George Bernard, *Music in London,* Vol. 3, Constable, London, 1932

Shaw, George Bernard, *Collected Letters 1874–1897,* Dan H. Laurence (ed.), Dodd, Mead and Co., New York, 1965

Shaw, George Bernard, *Collected Letters 1898–1910,* Dan H. Laurence (ed.), Max Reinhardt, London, 1972

Sherard, Robert Harborough, *Twenty Years in Paris,* Hutchison, London, 1905

Sherrod, Ricky Lee, *Images and Reflections: Response of the British Press to the Dreyfus Affaire,* Ph.D. thesis, Michigan State University, East Lansing, MI, 1980

Showalter, Elaine, *The Female Malady*, Virago, London, 1987

Showalter, Elaine, "Victorian Women and Insanity," in *Madhouses, Mad Doctors and Madmen*, Andrew Scull (ed.), University of Pennsylvania Press, Philadelphia, 1981

Siddiqi, Asiya (ed.), *Trade and Finance in Colonial India*, Oxford University Press, USA, Delhi, 1995

Simonhoff, Harry, *Jewish Participants in the Civil War*, Arco Publishing, New York, 1963

Slack, Edward, "A Spring Afternoon in a Cemetery," in *Essays, Literary and Miscellaneous*, T. Eddington, London, 1893

Smith, Willoughby, *The Rise and Extension of Submarine Telegraphy*, Arno Press, New York, 1974

Souvenir of the Inaugural Fete in commemoration of the opening of direct submarine telegraph with India, 1870

Stansky, Peter, *Sassoon: The Worlds of Philip and Sybil*, Yale University Press, New Haven, 2003

Stedman, Jane W., *W. S. Gilbert: A Classic Victorian and His Theatre*, Oxford University Press, Oxford, 1996

Steggles, Mary Ann, *Statues of the Raj*, BACSA, London, 2000

Steinschneider, Moritz, *Reshit Hallimud* (First Reader), Friedlander Press, Berlin, 1860

Stern, Selma, *The Court Jew*, Transaction Books, New Brunswick, 1984

The Stock Exchange Yearbook, London, 1874–80

Strachey, John St. Loe, *The Adventure of Living*, Hodder and Stoughton, London, 1922

Strange, Charles Hilbert, "The History of Tunbridge Wells," in *Royal Tunbridge Wells, Past and Present*, J.C.M. Given (ed.), Courier Printing and Publishing Co. Ltd., Tunbridge Wells, 1946

Temple, Sir Richard, *Men and Events of My Time in India*, John Murray, London, 1882

Thampi, Madhavi (ed.), *India and China in the Colonial World*, Social Science Press, New Delhi, 2005

Thomas, Marcel, *Esterhazy—ou L'envers de l'Affaire Dreyfus*, Vernal, Paris, 1989

Thompson, J. Lee, *Northcliffe: Press Baron in Politics 1865–1922*, John Murray, London, 2000

Thomson, Henry Hyslop, *Tuberculosis: Its Prevention and Home Treatment*, Oxford Medical Publications, London, 1921

Thorne, James, *Handbook of the Environs of London*, Murray, London, 1876

Timberg, Thomas A., "Baghdadi Jews in Indian Port Cities," in *Jews in India*, Vikas, New Delhi, 1986

Trelford, Donald, *The Observer at 200*, Quartet, London, 1992

Trocki, Carl, *Opium, Empire and the Global Political Economy*, Routledge, London and New York, 1999

Trombley, Stephen, *All That Summer She Was Mad: Virginia Woolf and Her Doctors,* Junction Books, London, 1981

Twain, Mark, *A Tramp Abroad,* Chatto and Windus, London, 1880

Official Records of the Union and Confederate Navies in the War of the Rebellion by United States Naval War Records Office, United States, pub. 1922

Updike, John, "Cemeteries," in *Transatlantic Review,* 32, London, Summer 1969

Vizetelly, Ernest Alfred, *Émile Zola, Novelist and Reformer,* John Lane, London, 1904

Vizetelly, Ernest Alfred, *Mon Cher Maître: Lettres d' Ernest Vizetelly a Émile Zola,* Yannick Portebois and Dorothy E. Speirs (eds.), Les Presses de l'Université de Montréal, Montréal, 2002

Wadsworth, A. P., *Newspaper Circulations 1800–1954,* Transactions of the Manchester Statistical Society (Manchester), 1954–55

Warren, Joyce W., *Women, Money and the Law,* University of Iowa Press, Iowa City, 2005

Weil, Shalva (ed.), *India's Jewish Heritage,* Marg Publications, Mumbai, 2002

Weintraub, Stanley (ed.), *Bernard Shaw on the London Art Scene, 1885–1950,* Pennsylvania State University Press, University Park, 1989

West, Charles, *Lectures on the Diseases of Infancy and Childhood,* Seventh Edition, Revised and Enlarged, Longman's and Co., London, 1884

Whyte, George R., *The Dreyfus Affair: A Chronological History,* Palgrave MacMillan, London and New York, 2005

Wilde, Oscar, *The Complete Letters of Oscar Wilde,* Merlin Holland and Rupert Hart-Davis (eds.), Henry Holt, New York, 2000

Williams, Francis, *Dangerous Estate,* Longmans, London, 1957

Williams, Keith, *The English Newspaper,* Springwood Books, London, 1977

Wilson, Jean Moorcroft, *Siegfried Sassoon: The Making of a War Poet: A Biography, 1886–1918,* Duckworth, London, 1998

Wilson, Jean Moorcroft, *Siegfried Sassoon, The Journey from the Trenches,* Duckworth, London, 2003

Wolf, Reverend Joseph, *The Jewish Expositor and Friends of Israel,* Vol. X, 1825, James Duncan, London

Woolf, Virginia, *The Flight of the Mind,* Nigel Nicolson (ed.), Letters, Vol. 1, Hogarth Press, London, 1975

Woolf, Virginia, *Mrs. Dalloway,* Hogarth Press, London, 1925

Zheng, Yangwen, *The Social Life of Opium in China,* Cambridge University Press, Cambridge, 2005

Articles

Banks, Joanne Trautmann, "Mrs. Woolf in Harley Street," *Lancet,* April 11, 1998

Baylen, Joseph O., "Dreyfusards and the Foreign Press: the Syndicate and the

Daily News, February–March 1898," in *French Historical Studies,* VII, no. 3, Spring 1972

Bennett Smith, Susan, "Reinventing Grief-Work: Virginia Woolf's Feminist Representations of Mourning in *Mrs. Dalloway* and *To the Lighthouse,*" in *Twentieth Century Literature,* 41, 1995

Bermingham, Dr. Edward J., "Progress of the Treatment of Consumption," in *The New York Times,* February 27, 1898

Betta, Chiara, "From Orientalists to Imagined Britons," in *Modern Asian Studies,* vol. 37, no. 4, Cambridge University Press, 2003

Brien, Alan, "Intimations of Mortality," *Spectator,* May 6, 1966

Cordova, R., "The Woman Editors of London," *Cassell's Magazine,* May 1903

Curl, James Stevens, "The Architecture and Planning of the 19th Century Cemetery," in *Garden History,* vol. 3, no. 3, Summer 1975

Dicey, Edward, "Recollections of Arthur Sullivan," in *Fortnightly Review,* vol. 77, January 1905

Endelman, Todd M., "Communal Solidarity Among the Jewish Elite of Victorian London," in *Victorian Studies,* 28, no. 3, Spring 1985

Finestein, Israel, "Anglo-Jewish Opinion During the Struggle for Emancipation 1828–1858," in *Transactions,* published by the Jewish Historical Society of England, vol. 20, 1964

Frenkel, Josef, "Lucian Wolf and Theodore Herzl," in *Transactions,* vol. 20, 1964

Garvin, James Louis, "The Maintenance of the Empire," in *The Empire and the Century: A Series of Essays on Imperial Problems and Possibilities,* Charles Sidney Goldmann (ed.), John Murray, 1905

Gentry, Judith Fenner, "A Confederate Success in Europe: The Erlanger Loan," in *The Journal of Southern History* 36, May 1970

Ghazoul, Ferial J., "Ard Al-Sawad—A Novel Formulation of People's History of Iraq," *The MIT Journal of Middle East Studies,* vol. 7, Spring 2007

Headrick, Daniel, and Pascal Griset, "Submarine Telegraph Cables: Business and Politics, 1838–1939," in *Business History Review* 75, Autumn 2001

Irvine, William, "G. B. Shaw's Musical Criticism," in *The Music Quarterly,* vol. XXXII, no. 3, July 1946

Jaffe, Benjamin, "The British Press and Zionism in Herzl's Time (1894–1904)," in *Transactions,* vol. 23, University College, London, 1904

Jefferson, Chase, "The Wandering Court Jew and the Hand of God, William Hauff's 'Jud Suss' as Historical Fiction," in *The Modern Language Review,* vol. 93, no. 3, July 1998

Leese, Arnold, "Gothic Ripples: An Occasional Report on the Jewish Question," no. 49, February 28, 1949, Anti-Jewish Information Bureau, Guildford

Lopez, Albert Martinez, "Foreign Capital and Business Strategies: Comparative Analyses of Urban Transport in Madrid and Barcelona, 1871–1948," presented at the XIV World Economic History Congress, Helsinki, August 2006

Maguire, Robert J., "Oscar Wilde and the Dreyfus Affair," in *Victorian Studies,* vol. 41, no. 1, Autumn 1997

Morgan, Kenneth O., "The Boer War and the Media," in *Twentieth Century British History,* vol. 13, no. 1, 2002

Penny, N. B., "The Commercial Garden Necropolis of the Early 19th Century and Its Critics," in *Garden History,* vol. 2, no. 3, Summer 1974

Porter, Roy, *Reading Is Bad for Your Health: European Notions Through the 19th Century,* in *History Today,* vol. 48, no. 3, March 1998

Schulte-Sasse, Linda, "Harlan's Jud Suss: The Jews as Others under National Socialism," *The German Quarterly,* vol. 61, no. 1, Winter 1988

Stead, W. T., "Government by Journalism," in the *Contemporary Review,* vol. 49, May 1886

Updike, John, "Cemeteries," in *Transatlantic Review* 32, London, Summer 1969

Vertinsky, Patricia, "Feminist Charlotte Perkins Gillman's Pursuit of Health and Physical Fitness as a Strategy for Emancipation," *Journal of Sport History,* vol. 16, no. 1, Spring 1989

Wolf, Reverend Joseph, *The Jewish Expositor,* vol. 10, 1825

Zenner, Walter P., "Jewish Retainers as Power Brokers," in *The Jewish Quarterly Review,* vol. 81, no. 1–2, July–October 1990

Newspapers and Magazines

The Courier, Tunbridge Wells
The Daily Express
The Guardian
The Journal
The New York Times
The Observer
The Sunday Times
The Times
The Tunbridge Wells Advertiser

. . .

Aberdeen Weekly Journal
The Academy
The Art Journal
The Athenaeum
The Belfast News Letter
Blackwood's Magazine
Blundell's Manual of Submarine Telegraph Companies
Bradshaw's Railway Manual
The Builder
Cassell's Magazine
The Century Illustrated Monthly Magazine
The Contemporary Review
The Country Gentleman

The Daily Chronicle
The Daily News
The Daily Telegraph
The Electrician
The Era
The Fortnightly Review
Freeman's Journal
The Fun Magazine
The Gentleman's Magazine
Hampshire Telegraph and Sussex Chronicle
Harper's Weekly
Hearth and Home
The Hospital World
Household Words
The Humanitarian
The Illustrated London News
The Independent
The Jewish Chronicle
John Bull
Journal and Daily Commercial Advertiser
The Journalist and Newspaper Proprietor
Liverpool Mercury
The Ludgate
Manchester Times
The Music Quarterly
The Musical Standard
New Leader
Northern Echo
The Nursing Record
The Pall Mall Gazette
Pearson's Magazine
The Penny Illustrated Paper and Illustrated Times
The Punch
Quarterly Review
The Quiver
The Saturday Review
The Solicitor's Journal
Spectator
The Sporting Times
The Strand Magazine
Trewman's Exeter Flying Post
Westminster Gazette
Woman
The Woman's Signal
Woman's World

Index

mental decline, vii-viii, 258–259,
263–269
musical abilities and interests,
53–54, 193, 242–243, 270
nurses her husband, 200, 201,
245–246
nursing career, 126–127
on America, 182–183
on idea of Jewish state, 233–234
on international affairs, 180–185
on labour relations, 164
on need for quality entertainment
for the people, 166–167, 242
on opium trade, 43
on opposition to Sunday
newspapers, 186–187
on public spending, 164–165
on public statuary, 190–191
on Russia, 183–184
on womanhood and marriage,
116–117, 118, 126
on women's education, 56–57
on women's emancipation, ix,
144, 170–171, 172, 181, 192
ostracised by family, 136, 138,
174, 175, 176, 261, 263, 266
patriotism, 182, 188–189, 239,
242
philanthropy, ix, 7, 55, 126, 139,
142–143
refuses to ostracise brother, 124,
175–176
shyness, 57–58
social conscience and social reform
activities, 8, 43, 155–156,
164–165, 166–169, 191–192,
203–204
social eminence, 7
socialist views, 163, 164
society hostess, ix, 7–8, 193–195,
201–202, 244
Society of Women Journalists vice-
president, 242

technophile, 185–186, 248, 253,
273
Thornycroft sculpture of, 119–121
Who's Who entry, 174, 199
widowhood, 253–254
working practices, 158–159
see also The Observer; Sunday
Times
Beer, Sophia, 69, 70, 102–103, 112,
113
Beer, Thyrza, 76, 112, 113
Beer & Co. (banking firm), 80
Beer family vault and mausoleum,
104–106, 254, 277, 278–280
Beer Löb Isaak zur Kanne, 64–66
Beer zur Kanne family, 59, 62,
63–64, 64–67, 68
Belgrave, Lord, 90
Bendall, Ernest, 99
Benjamin, Judah P., 77, 78
Bennett, Arnold, 155, 158, 186, 200
Bernhardt, Sarah, 122, 168
Berry Brothers, 268
Bethlem Hospital, 259
Betjeman, John, 279
Bevis-Marks Synagogue, 34, 51
Biarritz, 179
Biggs, Charles, 108
Billington, Mary, 153, 155–156
Black and White Weekly Illustrated,
237
Blacker, Carlos, 213
Blandford, Dr. George Fielding,
118
Blumenfeld, Ralf David, 268
Bode, Leopold, 108
Boer War, 243–244
Bois, Jules, 243–244
Bombay, 16–18, 19, 25–26, 114
Bhau Daji Lad Museum, 42
David Sassoon Library, 27
Jewish synagogues, 34
Masina Hospital, 28

Thornycroft, Hamo, 119–121,
175–176
Thornycroft, Mary, 42, 119
Thornycroft, Theresa *see* Sassoon,
Theresa
The Times, 108, 109, 154, 196, 242
trade unions, 164
Traill, Henry Duff, 144–145
Treaty of Nanking, 22
Tree, Maud, 195
Trinidad, 185
Triple Alliance, 180
Trollope, Anthony, 75, 82–83
tuberculosis, 138, 176, 198, 245,
246
Tunbridge Wells, 258, 266, 270,
271
Twain, Mark, 110, 243

unemployment insurance, 164
Updike, John, 278

Valpy, A. J., 149
Victoria, Queen, 21, 42, 74–75, 107,
173, 244, 257, 258, 278
Virchow, Professor Rudolph, 70
Vizitelly, Ernest Alfred, 230

Wadsworth, Alfred P., 89
Wallace, Edgar, 236
Watts, George Frederic, 121, 140,
250
Webster, Kate, 131
Weekly Dispatch, 157, 269
The Weekly Sun, 244
Weirleigh, 176, 196, 246, 258
Wells, H. G., 202, 247

West, Dr. Charles, 103
West, Rebecca, 75
Westminster Gazette, 225
Whistler, J. A. M., 119
White, Arnold, 172
White, Henry, 148–149
Whittle Harvey, Daniel, 149
Wilde, Oscar, 212–213
Wilhelm II, Kaiser, 181
Willim, Dr. Melchior, 139
Wilson, Angus, 75
Windham, William, 90–91
Wingrove, Gus, 241
Wolf, Reverend Joseph, 11
Wolseley, Lord, 165–166
women
education, 56–57
emancipation, ix, 144, 170–171,
172, 181, 191–192
journalists, viii-ix, 152–154, 177,
242
lawyers, 171
"New Woman," 153, 170–171
Women's International Congress, ix
The Woman's Signal, 177
Woolf, Virginia, 243, 259, 260–261
Woolner, Thomas, 46
World, 151
Wortley, Archibald Stuart, 119

York, Frederick, Duke of, 190–191

Zanetto (Mascagni), 195
Zionism, 206, 233–234
Zola, Emile, 202, 209–210, 212,
214, 230
Zulu (RB's dog), 141

PARTNERS IN LIFE and work, Yehuda Koren and Eilat Negev are respected writers and journalists whose work has been widely published in Israel, Britain and Germany.

Their previous biographies are *In Our Hearts We Were Giants – A Dwarf Family's Survival of the Holocaust* (translated into ten languages) and *Lover of Unreason – The Life and Tragic Death of Assia Wevill, Ted Hughes' Doomed Love*, which received critical acclaim worldwide